# MEN AND HORSES

# MEN AND HORSES

*by*

## ROSS SANTEE

*with*
*more than one hundred orig-*
*inal drawings by the author*

*University of Nebraska Press*
*Lincoln                    London*

*Publishers on the Plains*

**UNP**

Copyright, 1921, 1922, 1923, 1924, 1925, 1926, by Ross Santee
Renewal copyright, 1954, by Ross Santee

First Bison Book printing: 1977

Most recent printing indicated by first digit below:
1    2    3    4    5    6    7    8    9    10

**Library of Congress Cataloging in Publication Data**

Santee, Ross, 1889–1965.
  Men and horses.

  Reprint of the ed. published by the Century Co.,
New York.
  1.  Cowboys—The West.  2.  Frontier and pioneer
life—The West.  3.  The West—History.  I.  Title.
F596.S23   1977     978      76–76–57158
ISBN 0–8032–5859–3 Pa
ISBN 0–8032–0919–3 Cl

Bison Book edition reproduced from the 1928 edition published
by The Century Co. by arrangement with The Ross Santee
Corral.

Manufactured in the United States of America

To
MY MOTHER

# CONTENTS

# THE PAYSON RODEO

# MEN AND HORSES

## THE PAYSON RODEO

A SORREL bronc was led into the middle of the street; a puncher chewed his ear while the saddle was eased on; the rider swung up and caught his stirrups.

"Turn him loose!" he yelled.

"Ain't much of a show this year," said a slit-eyed puncher standing beside me. A woman in an automobile shrieked. The sorrel bronc, his eyes bulging, was headed straight toward the car. Two punchers spurred their horses alongside and turned him down the street again.

"This country was about blowed up before the rain came," said the puncher. Still pitching and bawling, the sorrel bronc turned back again, while the rider raked him in the shoulders with the spurs and waved his hat at the crowd.

"Who 's the twister?" I asked.

"Wayne Honeycutt; works for the Bar T Bar's. Ya ought to have been here last year; they had some shore enough pitchin' horses. Ace Gardner's the next man up in the ropin'."

At the head of the street a corral had been built. As a calf was cut out of the corral, the two punchers charged him across the line. The starter dropped his flag. On came the roper on the dead run, his "piggin" string between his teeth, his rope swinging. The fourth puncher tied his calf in twenty-two seconds.

"Looks like the money," I said.

"George Cline ain't roped," said the puncher.

Two more calves were cut out of the corral, but the time was slow.

"George Cline 's up next," said my neighbor.

The calf came out of the corral on the run. As he crossed the line, the flag dropped. Down the middle of the street they came. Cline made his throw in front of the old saloon. He was off his horse before the rope tightened. As he raised his hands through the cloud of dust the crowd yelled.

# THE PAYSON RODEO

"Twenty-one," bawled a man through a mega-phone. The puncher beside me grinned.

A horse-race was starting at the head of the street when a man in a white apron came out of the eating-house. An iron bar, shaped like a triangle, hung on the porch. On this he pounded.

"Chuck," said the puncher, and we headed up-street with the crowd. On one side of the street was parked a long line of automobiles; on the opposite side, in front of the old saloon, stood some cow-ponies. Some Apache squaws were eating hamburger and ice-cream cones at a stand close by. The buck was drinking near. "Belly-wash," the puncher called it. The ice had been hauled from Globe, for Payson is a hundred miles from the railroad.

"We was n't goin' to have any rodeo this year on account of the drought; then the dance-hall burned down. But after the rains came and the country started greenin' up, we decided to have her, anyway. Of course the purses ain't much this year, but every one put up what they could. And 'most every man in town worked on the dance-hall, so it would be ready in time. There 's a pretty good crowd, though."

[5]

# THE PAYSON RODEO

As we walked up the street I counted the buildings: two general stores, two eating-houses, one garage, two dance-halls, the office of the justice of the peace, and the old saloon, which now does duty as a soft-drink place and pool-hall. At other times cows walk unmolested through the street, but to-day the place was alive with people.

The rodeo is an annual event, with three days of broncho-busting, bull-riding, calf-tying and horse-races down the middle of the street, and every night a dance that lasts until morning.

The eating-house was newly built and unpainted. Across the front in huge black letters was a sign, "Meals, fifty cents." On a bench at the end of the porch stood a wash-basin and a pail of water; on a nail above hung a towel.

"She's shore been popular," remarked the puncher as he wiped his face on a blue bandana; but later, while we sat comfortably on the porch and waited for the second table, others came who were not nearly so particular.

Flies were plentiful in the dining-room, but the meal was very good: fresh beef and cabbage, potatoes, string-beans, and hot biscuits and syrup, or "lick," as the punchers called it. A tourist asked

[7]

the puncher and me if we had ever been to Cheyenne or Pendleton, Oregon.   Neither of us had. He liked Payson, he said, as everything was real. He was driving through to the Grand Cañon, and had meant to stop only long enough to find out what the excitement was.   He had never heard of the place before, but now he was going to stay until the rodeo was over.

In the afternoon there were more horse-races down the street and more calf-tying.   One event was for men over fifty.   As Cline's father came down the street with his horse on the dead run, the puncher standing beside me said:

"Them Cline boys take to their ropin' honestly."

The bull-riding came next.   Down in the corral, by much prodding and pulling, a bull was dragged into the shute.   The surcingle was buckled on. The rider eased down off the corral fence and

# THE PAYSON RODEO

mounted. The shute opened, and out they came, the rider spurring his mount high in the neck, while the bull bellowed and bucked and tried to kick himself in the chin. As they headed straight into the line of cars, a puncher whirled his rope. His horse sat up, and the bull was caught. A rider on a buckskin horse roped him by the hind feet. As the rope tightened, the bull fell to the ground. The surcingle was unbuckled, and, still bellowing and hooking at the horses, he was led back to the corral.

One of the bulls was ridden with a saddle. The rider was thrown the third jump. Still pitching and bawling, the empty stirrups popping above his back, the frantic animal was finally caught. The rider limped back to the corral, holding his side. Two of his ribs were broken.

The event for boys under eighteen was won by a

gangling youth of about sixteen. He wore high-heeled boots, long-shanked spurs, and on his head a small, black derby hat. "Derby Jim," the puncher called him. While he waited for his turn to ride, he sat on the corral fence and munched an ice-cream cone. That evening I saw him walking with a girl. In front of an ice-cream stand they stopped. As the stage came in from Globe I saw him again. His long-shanked spurs trailed in the dust, and as he walked he munched another cone.

After supper a crowd gathered at the general store and waited for the mail.

"See you at the dance," said the slit-eyed puncher as he went to feed his horse. In front of the old saloon Ace Gardner and Jimmy Cline were roping three calves apiece for a side bet. It was sprinkling and nearly dark when the last calf was tied; the street was almost deserted.

The dance-hall was a huge, unpainted affair and, like the eating-house, was newly built. On a platform in the middle sat the orchestra. Built against the wall on each side was a long wooden bench. On the floor in one corner eight babies slept, wrapped in their various-colored quilts, while their fond parents danced. The tourist was there, and Derby Jim, and the bull-rider with the broken ribs. The slit-eyed puncher made me acquainted with his girl. Every one danced. Between dances the women sat on the narrow bench around the hall. A woman beside me held a baby in her arms. When the music started, she danced, while the baby slept peacefully on the narrow bench. At intervals the men walked outside on the porch and smoked. A few of the more fortunate walked deeper into the shadows, where some "white mule" was cached. At midnight the count of babies on the floor had reached fifteen. A tall puncher, after eyeing them gravely, finally selected a small bundle that was wrapped in a sky-blue quilt.

"Guess this one's mine," he said, with a grin.

He carefully stowed the bundle under the bench.

"Some of 'em's liable to get stepped on the way the crowd 's a-millin' here."

Every other dance was a tag. A man well over sixty, with snow-white hair, danced by, his boot-heels popping on the floor. He never missed a dance. At 2 A. M. I found the tourist and the slit-eyed puncher sitting on the porch. The tourist had been ready to go for an hour, he said, but could n't get his wife to leave. The slit-eyed puncher bewailed a blister on his heel and cursed the new boots he wore; but as the music started, he hobbled inside.

"I ain't missin' nothin'," he said, "even if my feet is afire."

At 4 A. M. the crowd still milled. Five babies still slept peacefully in their corner on the floor. On the porch the tourist dozed. The slit-eyed puncher had slowed up somewhat, but the rest of the dancers were going strong.

# The Bull-Fight

# THE BULL-FIGHT

THE program was an elaborate affair, pink in color and nearly a yard in length. In the upper right-hand corner, extending for a foot and a half down the page, was printed in box-car letters:

JUAREZ BULL RING
GRAND
PROFESSIONAL BULL FIGHT
3 MATADORS 3
IN COMPETITION
SUNDAY, July 30th, at 4:30 P.M.

In this great event will be introduced the renowned and well known Mexican matador José Sapien "Formalito," accompanied by the two brave matadors Joaquin Jiminez "Trianero," and Octaviano Acosta, which are well known to the bull-fighters' fans.

Also will appear the famous picador Lazaro Zavola "Pegote" and the great banderillero Evaristo Villavisencio "Sordo Chico."

[15]

# MEN AND HORSES

THE BULLS FOR THIS GREAT EVENT HAVE BEEN
WELL SELECTED AND ARE GUARANTEED FOR THEIR
FURIOUSNESS.

4  FEROCIOUS BULLS  4
OF CAMBRAY RANCH
DON'T MISS IT

The rest of the program was printed in Spanish, profusely illustrated with photographs of the bull-fighters in various poses.

"You won't like it," said my El Paso friend, "nor anybody else who likes horses. It's bad enough to watch 'em torture a bull before they kill him, but they blindfold the horses. I never saw a horse killed yet but what I did n't wish it was a Mexican instead."

Our seats were on the shady side of the bull-ring directly below the box of the president. Outside the entrance the band was playing. Except for a single Mexican, who sprinkled with a hose, the ring was empty. Half the crowd were Americans.

"Tourists," said my friend. "A fine place to bring a kid, ain't it?" said he, pointing to a woman with a baby in her arms. It seemed to me that every other Mexican present wore some sort of uniform. No two uniforms were alike, but nearly all carried the United States Army Colt 45 automatics. A Mexican with a battered felt hat and blue overalls sold bottled beer at sixty cents a bottle. As the band came in and took their places, a bullet-headed *hombre*, with a drooping black mustache, who sat beside me opened his fourth bottle.

"Let's go!" yelled an American.

"Play ball!" yelled another from across the ring. The bullet-headed *hombre* beside me muttered in Spanish. Down in the bull-ring the Mexican put away his tiny hose. There was a stir at the entrance, and about thirty soldiers marched in. The officer was in white, with black leather puttees. Around his neck he wore some brass arrangement that looked for all the world like a dog-collar. The rest of the outfit carried long rifles, and were clothed for the most part in cartridges. As they stood at attention and faced the entrance my El Paso friend spoke.

"If that bird in white would cut loose with a song now, I'd think I was watchin' a musical comedy."

It was sprinkling rain as the bugle sounded for the grand entrance, and a part of the crowd broke for shelter. First came the matadors, with their red capes, on foot. Directly behind them came the picadors, mounted on two of the poorest horses I have ever seen. One was a little brown, so poor he could hardly walk and so weak that he tottered under the weight of the bullet-headed rider. The picador Lazaro Zavola "Pegote" was mounted on a little gray cow-pony with the brand N E on his left hip. The little gray cow-pony was nothing but skin and bone, but he held his head high and marched to the music. Next came a team of horses, bells jingling as they walked, driven by a Mexican in a blue serge suit and high roller hat. The bugle sounded again, and as the team was driven out, the bull-fighters took their places about the ring.

A gate swung open, and the bull walked slowly down the narrow runway. At the entrance he stopped for a moment, snuffing. A Mexican partly hidden by the fence reached down and stuck two red rosettes in his shoulders. With a bellow, the bull came into the ring. For a moment he stood undecided, tossing his head at the crowd, then charged straight for the picador on the brown horse. Horse and rider went down together. The crowd cheered. Before the bull could charge again, a matador with a red cape darted between them, and the bull was drawn to the other side of the ring. The picador was unhurt, but the brown horse tottered to his feet,

bleeding in the neck and shoulder. With their red capes the matadors took turns in teasing the bull. Holding their capes in front of them, they stood quietly as the bull charged, stepping lightly to one side as the bull rushed by. After a certain amount of teasing, the picador Lazaro Zavola "Pegote" advanced to meet the bull. The little gray's right eye was blindfolded, but as the bull charged, the little gray turned his head and dodged as only a cow-pony can. The Mexicans hissed, while the picador reached down and readjusted the blind. As the bull charged the second time, the little gray stood helpless in the center of the ring. Horse and rider went high in the air and came down in a heap together. "The Brave Picador Lazaro Zavola Pegote" landed on all fours and took the fence at one jump. Blood pouring from his shoulder, the little gray struggled to regain his feet as the bull charged again. The Mexicans were on their feet, screaming. As the bull charged a third time, I turned my face away. My friend was cursing in a low voice, his face a chalky white. An American girl stumbled past me toward the entrance, tears streaming down her cheeks. When I looked at the bull-ring again, the little gray pony was gone. The band was playing, and the ring was full of hats. A Mexican with a rake covered with sand the black pool where the little gray had fallen. My friend blew his nose violently.

"They are nothing but a bunch of savages. I wish it had been a Mexican instead of that little gray horse," he said.

A dozen times the bull tried to jump out of the ring. On one attempt he became lodged across the fence. With ropes the Mexicans finally got him back.

# THE BULL-FIGHT

Next came the ban-
derillas. On foot and
hatless the banderillero
Evaristo Villavisencio
"Sordo Chico" ad-
vanced to the center of the ring. As the bull
charged, he stood motionless, the banderillas
poised above his head. The bull was almost
upon him when he leaped lightly to one side, at
the same time setting the banderillas in the bull's
shoulders. The banderillas were evidently well
placed, for the crowd cheered, and the bullet-
headed *hombre* with the drooping black mustache
threw his hat into the ring. Again the performance was repeated, the banderillas exploding with
a roar.

The bull was tiring now. He scarcely noticed
the red capes. With his neck and shoulders full
of the wicked banderillas, he stood panting in the
center of the ring, blood flowing from his mouth.

"Matador! Matador!" screamed the crowd.

With his sword hidden by the red cape, the
matador Jose Sapien "Formalito" advanced to
meet the bull. The bull was too weak to charge,
but the crowd cheered as the matador, kneeling

directly in front of the bull, touched him with his hand. The bull turned and walked slowly away. Again and again the matador faced him. As the bull lunged weakly toward him, the matador ran his sword full length into the bull's neck. With blood pouring from his mouth, the bull turned slowly away. Stumbling blindly to the edge of the ring, he sank slowly to his knees.

The Mexicans were on their feet, screaming. The bull-ring was full of hats. With bells jingling, the team was driven in, and the bull dragged from the ring. Bowing profusely, the matador threw the hats back to the crowd. The band played, while the Mexican with a rake covered with fresh sand the black pools in the center of the ring.

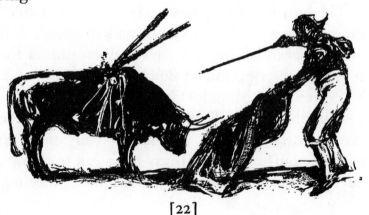

[22]

# Button—A Boy

## BUTTON—A BOY

THE two punchers crawled out of their blankets and built a fire. A third still slept.

"He shore hates to come out of it," said Shorty, pulling on his chaps by the fire. "But I don' blame him much at that. These mornings are pretty crimpy."

"All twelve-year-old kids are sleepy-headed," said Jimmy, who was starting breakfast. It was still dark in the cañon but at the first gray streaks in the east Shorty mounted his night horse. For some little time the sound of his pony's feet on the hard rock could be heard as they climbed the narrow trail to the mesa.

"Oh, bury me not," sang Jimmy as he mixed the bread. The crackling fire threw strange shadows amongst the trees. Button still slept.

[25]

# MEN AND HORSES

It was Button's first summer with a cow outfit. Ever since he could remember he had ridden a pony, and each summer he had spent a few weeks at the ranch. But this summer it was different. He had a mount of horses of his own, just like the rest of the punchers. It was the middle of August, yet he had only been to town once since school had closed. That was on the fourth of July, when he had ridden in with the outfit for the three-day rodeo. His high-heeled boots and long-shanked spurs had been the envy of every boy in town. He had yelled himself hoarse when Shorty won the bronco-riding, and how proud he had been when Jimmy won the roping contest! For wasn't he one of the outfit? If he could ever be as good a roper as Jimmy, or ride like Shorty, he'd be happy. He had a good mount of horses, Fingertail, Smoky, and Scout. But he wanted the Gila Monster, a little roan outlaw who pitched each time he was saddled.

"You're too little to ride pitchin' horses," said Shorty. Button sniffed.

"Ain't I a regular hand this summer? Ain't I one of the outfit?" Shorty had given him old

Rambler instead, a gentle old cow-horse, from his own mount of horses.   Each morning when the remuda came in Button always watched for the Gila Monster.

"Can't I ride him to-day?"   But to Button's disgust Jimmy would always rope Smoky, or Scout, or old Rambler.

It was broad daylight when Shorty reached camp with the ponies.

"Chuck!" yelled Jimmy as the horses were driven into the corral.

"That's an even dozen times I've called him this morning," said Jimmy.   Button still slept.

"Let him sleep," said Shorty.   "Maybe he'll be ready to get up to-morrow morning."

Breakfast was eaten in silence.   The dishes were washed and their horses caught up for the day's ride.   They were leaving camp when Button woke.

"Where's my horse?" he yelled.

"We can't wait all day on you," said Shorty. "And you have n't had any breakfast."

"I don't want any," said Button, pulling on his boots.

# MEN AND HORSES

"You can't ride all day on an empty stomach," said Jimmy. "Better put in a pot of frijoles; we'll be back this evening sometime."

"Don't let 'em burn, either!" yelled Shorty over his shoulder, as they started up the narrow trail.

Button was peeved. He kicked the Dutch oven and sniffed. The idea of a day in camp by himself was not to his liking. He wanted to go along. There was sure to be fun to-day, for the cattle were wild on Rock Creek. He wasn't getting a fair shake. The idea of leaving him in camp all day by himself just to cook a pot of beans! It wasn't his fault he hated to get up in the morning. If he only had a horse, he'd go to town. This was out of the question, however, for the horses had been turned loose. Even old Rambler, gentle as he was, refused to be caught afoot. After breakfast, Button sat for a while on the Dutch oven and whittled. Presently he grew tired of this, and for want of something better he put in a pot of beans. Again he sat on the Dutch oven and whittled.

His roving eye finally settled on the cliff across the cañon. He decided to climb it. It was a hard climb and took him all of an hour, but from the top he could see for miles. The two moving specks in the distance were Jimmy and Shorty. He watched them until they finally disappeared. The smoke was from the smelter in town. It was thirty miles, he knew. Just across the cañon, far below him, the remuda was grazing. He counted them. There was one horse gone. He counted them again, but this time the count was right. He tried to pick out his horses among the herd. There was Smoky, and Scout, and presently he saw old Rambler grazing at the edge of the bunch, and, a little below him, the Gila Monster.

Button climbed back down the cliff. He knew what he'd do. He'd catch a horse and go to town. As he passed the camp he gave the pot of beans a kick. Wrangling afoot was a tough job, but he finally managed to drive a dozen ponies down the narrow trail, and into the corral. Among the bunch was the Gila Monster. In a cloud of dust the ponies swirled and dodged. After a dozen throws he finally roped the Gila Monster around the neck. Tying him to a post, he drove the rest of the bunch out of the corral. After dragging in his saddle he put up the corral bars again.   He was sure he could ride him, but he was n't taking any chances of losing his saddle —at least not until he got the little roan uncocked.

It took him all of thirty minutes to get his jumper tied over the Gila Monster's head.   After the blind was on he had no trouble in putting on his saddle.   He wished Jimmy and Shorty would happen up as he stepped across the little roan; but, anyway, they 'd be surprised when they got to camp and found him and the Gila Monster gone to town.

The little roan stood quietly as Button eased into the saddle and caught his stirrups.   Button was pale, but with a deep breath he reached down and pulled off the blind—and then it happened. With a grunt the Gila Monster went into the air, and Button saw the ground slanting far below him. When they landed the second jump, Button had lost a stirrup and was holding to the horn with both hands.   The Gila Monster was bawling now, and the empty stirrup cut a deep gash over Button's eye, but he did not feel it.   Something was getting in his eyes.   He could n't see the ground any longer.   But he held on.   Everything was turning upside down.   The Gila Monster was still

[30]

bawling like a calf, but it sounded so far away now. He was getting sleepy, but he must hold on. Was n't he one of the outfit? Must hold on . . . must . . . hold . . .

When Jimmy and Shorty rode in that evening they found Button sitting on one of the Dutch ovens. He was very white, and above a blackened left eye that was tightly closed showed a long jagged cut. At his feet was a huge pile of shavings; on the fire, slightly burned, was a large pot of beans.

"What happened?" said Shorty.

"I got a fall," said Button, limping off toward the spring with a half-filled pail in his hands.

"Must have fell a long ways," said Shorty.

Jimmy said nothing, but after Button was out of sight he examined his saddle.

"Spur tracks," he said, "and right deep, I 'd say."

"Wonder what horse threw him?" said Shorty. "Sh! here he comes," said Jimmy.

Shorty was driving the ponies into the corral next morning when Jimmy called "Chuck!"

There was a whirl of blankets, and out came

# MEN AND HORSES

Button.    With his levis over his arm and his boots in his hand he limped over to the fire and started to dress.    Breakfast was eaten in silence.    After the dishes were washed, Jimmy picked up his rope and started for the corral.

"You can ride the Gila Monster if you want to to-day," said Jimmy.

Button grinned.

"Old Rambler 's a pretty good horse."

# A FOOL ABOUT A HORSE

# A FOOL ABOUT A HORSE

THERE'S no tellin' when you'll meet up with a cow-puncher. They're such a driftin' lot. You'll work with one for months sometimes, sleepin' in the same bed. Then some mornin' he'll pull out. Mebbe you'll see him again and mebbe you won't.

Steve always was a queer cuss, an' a fool about a horse. When I first met up with Steve he was breakin' horses for the Cross S outfit in Arizona. Most peelers is pretty rough on a horse, but Steve was different. He could teach a young horse most anything without half killin' him. Most of the horses in Steve's string was rank poison. But there was one little gray bronc in the bunch he called Three T.

Three T was gentle as a kitten, an' Steve taught him to do most everything 'cept talk. Three T would n't run with the rest of the horses. He hung around camp just like a dog. He nearly run Slim, the horse-wrangler, crazy at first tryin' to herd him. After the ponies quieted down in the mornin', Slim always went back to camp to auger the cook. But he would n't any more 'n get off his horse an' there 'd be Three T trailin' along after him. Slim would take him back out to the remuda, an' as long as he was in sight the little gray would graze quiet. But the minute Slim pulled out for camp there 'd be Three T right at his heels.

All this was n't settin' well with Slim, for he liked his coffee between meals. He 'decides to run the little gray off, but it 's no use. In an hour Three T 's back at camp hangin' around just like a dog. Slim quit botherin' him after that, and, since none of the rest of the horses was any trouble to speak of, Slim spends most of his time in camp augerin' old Sour Dough, the cook, and fillin' his paunch full of coffee and cold steak. An' when the outfit 's in camp, Steve 's always a-foolin' with that little gray bronc, teachin' him to shake hands an' other such foolishness, an' a-feedin' him biscuits and sich until the little gray got to be a plumb nuisance.

We were eatin' supper one night when the blow-off comes. The punchers is all settin' around on their heels stowin' away the grub. Three T's standin' just outside the circle waitin' for a biscuit, an' old Sour Dough's leanin' on the gonch hook airin' his paunch about the war. Nobody else is sayin' much, for it's a tender subject in this outfit. Most of the punchers is expectin' their call 'most any time, an' the idea of crossin' all that water ain't settin' well with none of them. Unless it's Steve, an' he's so quiet an' easy-goin' not even water makes much difference to him.

Old Sour Dough's right in the middle of tellin' what he'd do if he wasn't too old to be drafted, when the little gray bronc eases up behind him and takes a biscuit out of one of the Dutch ovens. Old Sour Dough's so interested in his own game he don't even know what's goin' on. Finally Dogie Si snickered and old Sour Dough turns round in time to see Three T standin' over the empty oven, with his nose out beggin' for more. Everybody laughed—everybody except the cook. He swings on the little gray with the gonch hook catchin' him just back of the ear. Three T's legs sort of buckled under him, an' down he goes to his knees.

I looked at Steve. His face had gone a chalky

white, an' he was makin' a queer noise in his throat. Old Sour Dough swung the gonch hook again— but it never landed. . . . It was n't much of a fight. Old Sour Dough 's unconscious an' Steve 's still makin' that queer noise in his throat when we finally pulled him off. Me an' the horse-wrangler washed the dishes an' sort of straightened up the camp. We 're just finishin' up when Dogie Si come back from the cook's bunk an' said old Sour Dough had finally come to. I looked around for Steve, figurin' maybe he 's dragged it. But there he was foolin' with that little bronc again, just as if nothin 'd ever happened. We 're eatin' supper not more 'n a week later when an Indian rides into camp. He 's come from headquarters with a note from the boss and Steve's notice to report in town.

It was sundown when Steve pulled out. At the top of the ridge he set the little gray up an' looked back for a minute. Then he waved his hand an' was gone.

The saloon is plumb full of people when I goes in. There 's a few Mexicans an' punchers scattered through the crowd, but most of the mob is tourists, an' they 're swarmin' around the bar like a

bunch of magpies.    Down near the end of the bar
I finally get close enough to get a foot on the rail.
I got a forty-dollar thirst, but when the Mexican
barkeep slides me a drink I sort of hesitate.    I'm
studyin' whether to take it out back some place an'
drink it, when somebody pokes me in the ribs.    I
never did feel comfortable in Juarez without a
gun, so I whirls around expectin' most anything.
An' if there ain't Steve!

"Bill Jones," says he, with a grin!

The first thing Steve asks about is that little
gray bronc.    I'd plumb forgot the little gray, for
the outfit shipped some horses to Texas not more 'n
a month after Steve left, Three T goin' along with
the bunch.    But when I tells Steve he don't say
nothin'.

"Here 's how!" says I when the Mexican barkeep fills 'em up again.

"How!" says Steve.


It 's awful good to see Steve.    I don't know
what makes it, but you get to know a man better in
a week out on the range than you will in a year's
time in town.

"Heard you was killed in France."

"No," says Steve, "it was in the laig."

"How 'd you like the army, anyway?"

Steve shakes his head.

"I done everything they told me, but I did n't do nothin' else. I finally got hit in the laig. I was in the hospital when the armistice was signed. Breakin' horses since I got out—New Mexico—come to Juarez to get drunk."

Coming from Steve, this is a heap of talk. Everybody 's leavin' the saloon, an' from a tourist I finally gathers there 's a bull-fight that afternoon; so me an' Steve has a few more drinks an' throws in with the crowd.

The place was pretty crowded, but we finally found a couple of seats on the shady side of the ring. Outside the entrance the band 's playin'. About half the crowd 's American tourists, I 'd say from the looks of their clothes. There 's one settin' 'longside of me an' Steve that said he was from New York. He wasn't a bad sort at that, in spite of the white suit he 's wearin'. Steve bought some bottled beer, an' the tourist give me a program. It 's printed in Spanish though, an' don't mean nothin' to me. We 're startin' on our second bottle when some *hombre* blew a bugle. There 's a hullabaloo at the entrance an' a bunch of soldiers marched in. I thought for a minute there's another revolution, for they're all carrying long rifles, and none of 'em's wearin' much except cartridges. The crowd don't pay 'em any mind though, so I eases back into my seat.

The *hombre* blew his bugle again, an' the bull-fighters entered the ring.

A bunch on foot come first, carryin' red capes. Just behin' 'em comes a bunch that's mounted. "Picadors," the tourist calls 'em. They're wearin' different clothes an' the horses they're ridin' look like they'd been dead for a week. Next comes a team of horses. The *hombre* cut down on his bugle again. The team was driven out, the bull-fighters took their places about the ring.

Another gate swung open an' the bull busts into the ring. He's pretty snuffy, an' the sight of them red capes soon gets him on the prod. They teased him around a while, when all of a sudden he sees one of the horses. I think it's queer the horse don't dodge, an' then I see he's blindfolded. I ain't finicky, but it makes me kind of sick when the horse goes down. The rider ain't hurt, but there's blood a-pourin' from the horse's neck an' shoulders.   The pony's tryin' to get his feet when the bull charges again.   The Mexicans is all on their feet, screaming.   Steve's a-makin' that queer noise in his throat, an' the tourist is cryin' like a baby.   An *hombre* just below me threw his hat in the ring.   I'm for kickin' him into the ring after it, when Steve an' the tourist pull me down.

They finally killed the bull.   The matador, Formalito they called him, did about as poor a piece of butcherin' as I've ever seen.   The bull don't even notice the red capes now.

He's standin' in the center of the ring, blood pouring from his mouth.   As the matador approached him the bull turned slowly away.   A dozen times the matador faced him, but the bull is too weak to charge.   Finally he runs his sword in the bull's neck.   Stumblin' blindly to the edge of the ring, the bull sank slowly to his knees, blood pourin' from his mouth.

Steve and the tourist is for leavin', but there's three bulls to be killed, an' I ain't given up hope of seein' a Mexican killed.   We finally compromise.   An' I promise to go with 'em after the next

# A FOOL ABOUT A HORSE

bull's killed if they don't kill a Mexican in the meantime.

We'd opened some more beer when the Mexicans took their places again. I ain't payin' much attention to anything except the beer, when I notice one of the horses.

He's nothin' but skin an' bones, but there's somethin' awful familiar to me in the way he moves around. I looked at Steve; his face had gone a chalky white, an' he's makin' that queer noise in his throat. Then I knew. I don't remember much that happened after that. Steve's down in the bull-ring an' has the picador by the

throat before any one knew what happened. Then all hell broke loose. There's a dozen Mexicans a-tryin' to drag Steve off that picador when I got to him. I broke a bottle over an *hombre's* head that had Steve by the hair, and then the whole remuda run over me an' I went to sleep. . . .

My head's a-splittin' when I woke up, but it don't take me long to figure out where I am. There's bars across the windows an' a bullet-headed *hombre* with a long rifle, standin' just outside the door. Steve ain't here. Must 'a' killed him, I figure, but my head's a-spinnin,' so I go to sleep again.

Sounds like the tourist's voice, but I'm afraid to look at first, for fear I'm hearin' things. But sure enough, it is.

"How's Steve?"

"All right," he says, an' sorta smiles an' introduces me to some lawyer friend of his.

We stopped an' had a drink, an' then he heads the car for home. I can't get no information out of either of 'em. They both looks wise an' sorta smiles at everything I says. It's an awful relief to me when we gets back across the bridge. El

# A FOOL ABOUT A HORSE

Paso never looked so good before. The lawyer finally stopped the car.

"My place," he says, an' asks me if I'll have a look around.

"What about Steve?"

"Oh, he's all right," he says, an' heads me for the barn.

Steve sorta grinned when we come in, an' then went on a-foolin' with the little gray.

He always was a queer cuss, an' a fool about a horse.

# QUITS

# QUITS

THEY never spoke, and all winter they had been range branding together. They slept in the same tepee. But Bill cooked his own meals and wrangled his own horses. Bob did the same. Occasionally they came to headquarters for chuck. Once they came together. Bill was out of flour, and Bob wanted some No. 2 shoes for old Blue Dog, his pet horse. They stayed all night at the ranch-house and pulled out together in the morning, each leading his own packmule.

Each kept his own calf tally. When Bill branded a calf he strung one of the calves' ears on a wire. Bob strung his on a separate wire, but both wires hung on the same tree. Their tally never varied much. They left camp about the same time in the morning. If Bill rode north, Bob went south, and they seldom met except at sundown. Bob was the best roper and usually got to camp first, but by riding late Bill brought in as many ears as Bob.

# MEN AND HORSES

Except for old Sooner, the dog, they were alone. He was a triflin' hound. He had come to their camp one night so poor and sore-footed he could hardly walk. He played no favorites at first. Both punchers fed him. One morning he followed Bob off. After that Bill never fed him again, or let him lie on his bed. And it was old Sooner who came near causing serious trouble. Bill came in late one evening with five ears in the pocket of his chaps. In the morning when he went to string them on his wire three of them were gone. He looked at Bob's tally, and then at Bob. Then he went inside for his gun. As he came out of the tepee he was just in time to see old Sooner swallow the two remaining ears he had thrown to the ground. Without speaking Bob took five ears from his tally and slowly tossed them to the dog. After old Sooner had swallowed the last one, he mounted and rode north with old Sooner at his heels. Bill shod a pony, and some time later he pulled out in the opposite direction.

It was dark when Bill got into camp that night. Bob was n't there. Bill tied up a night horse and cooked supper. A little later he hung up the beef and went to bed. But somehow he could n't sleep, and once he thought he heard a dog howling off toward the north. He pulled on his boots and saddled the night horse. Then he sat on his heels and waited, for the moon would be up in an hour. It was still black in the cañon when Bill started, but by the time he topped out on the mesa it was almost as light as day. The coyotes were yelping on all sides, but every little while Bill stopped and listened. Then away to the north he heard it again—the mournful howling of a lonely dog.

Old Sooner growled when Bill rode up. The horse was dead. Pinned under him with a busted leg was Bob all white and still. Bill cut away the boot and somehow carried him into camp that night. The next day he brought him on to the ranch. The rest of the outfit did what they could to make him easy. Bill waited on him like a woman, and it was Bill who carried him gently to the car when they finally started for town. But they did n't speak.

A year slipped by before I saw them again. We were gathering horses for the fall work. For a week the punchers had been stringing in from their line-camps. The night before we pulled out for Black River they rode in together with old Sooner at Bob's heels. The three of us were on wrangle together. They had plenty to say to me, but the way they ignored each other was something I could n't savvy. One morning while Bob and I were alone at the hold-up I could n't hold in any longer. "What's the matter with Bill?" I said.

"Nothin'," says Bob, "only I don't like him."

A few days later I spoke to Bill. "Ain't nothin' the matter," he says, "'cept we don't hitch." I could n't understand nor could the rest of the punchers. There had been no trouble between them. It had been funny to the outfit at first. But now we wondered why in the world Bob did n't quit, for Bill had acted white that night on the mesa.

Six weeks on the mountain. Moving camp every few days, which kept the pack-animals busy. We came down with the herd in October. Except for a few crippled horses, nothing much happened until we started to work the lower range. Then the bronco fighter quit. Every one was short on horses, so the foreman divided up his mount. Bill was n't much of a twister and uncocked his bronc in the corral. The bronc trotted around the corral a few times like an old horse. Then they opened

the gate. But as they came out, old Sooner jumped and barked. The old bronc downed his head and pitched straight for the fence, bawling like a steer. Four of them started to head him, but Bob was the first one there. The others went on the outside, but Bob took the fence. They went down in a heap together. Bill and the bronc was n't scratched. But Bob and old Blue Dog did n't get up. It was the old leg again.

They carried Bob into the ranch-house. The only time he flinched was when he heard a shot, and he knew they had finished old Blue Dog. We packed his leg in moss and made him as easy as we could for the long ride to town. A little later Bill came in. They did n't speak until they were alone. But as I passed the open window, on the way to the spring I heard Bob say: "This squares me for that night on the mesa. Now we 're quits again."

# THE RUMMY KID

# THE RUMMY KID

IT was still pouring rain when we woke the third morning.

"Might as well head for town," said the puncher, "unless ya want to turn this trip into a duck hunt."

"Don't you think there's any chance of it letting up?" I asked.

"Nobody but fools an' tenderfeet ever predict the weather in Arizona," said the puncher, and as he mixed the bread he cursed, softly, the weather, the leaky cabin, and finally the idea of ever coming to hunt on this particular mountain in the first place. As I went out to drive in the horses, I heard the puncher groan.

"Eight days huntin' an' not even one measly white-tailed deer."

We came off the mountain in a dense fog. The water that poured down the narrow trail ran halfway to the horses' knees. Occasionally the hazy outline of a pine-tree loomed suddenly beside the trail, only to be lost again in the mist and pouring

rain.  As the trail grew steeper, the occasional outline of the trees changed to scrub-oak and cedar.

"Helluva country," said the puncher as we
stopped to fix one of the packs.  "One day a man
can't get drinkin'-water, an' next day it's wet
enough to bog a snipe."

Below the timber-line the rain suddenly ceased,
but the fog was denser than ever.  At the foot of
the mountains another pack turned.

"Let's build a cigarette," said the puncher, and
from his hat he produced tobacco and brown papers.

"Wish this fog would let up until we strike the
main wash."  We had ridden for a couple of hours
before the puncher stopped again.

"We're off the trail," he said.  "We should
have passed an old wood camp a half-hour ago.
Wait here with the packs while I have a look
around."

The next moment he was lost in the fog.  I
waited; it seemed for an age before he returned.

"We're outa luck," he said briefly.  "I can't
make out nothin' in this fog."  As he rolled another cigarette he added, "Looks like we'd sleep
in a wet bed to-night."

# THE RUMMY KID

We smoked for a while in silence. Suddenly out of the fog I heard a voice, singing. I could hardly believe my ears. As the voice came nearer I looked at the puncher. He flashed a broad grin.

"It's the Rummy Kid," he said.

The song ceased abruptly as the Kid rode out of the fog.

"Hello, Rummy!" said the puncher.

The Kid smiled, and to me he gave a quick nod. He was just a boy, not over eighteen. His eyes were brown and wide apart; his face thin and drawn. A cigarette hung from his sensitive mouth, and the mop of hair that covered his low forehead was black and coarse as an Apache's.

"Horse-huntin'?" said the puncher. The Kid nodded. I wondered if he knew how to speak. Then I remembered the song.

"How far's the main wash?" asked the puncher.

"Quite a piece," said the Kid; "but I know a short cut."

The Kid wheeled his horse abruptly, and we followed him into the fog. There was no trail, and the going was rough and brushy. Presently the Kid stopped. We were at the edge of a broad wash. The Kid's face lighted up with another smile.

"Can't miss it now," he said, pointing.

I looked down the broad wash and turned to thank him. But the Kid was gone. It was raining again as the pack outfit strung slowly down the wash. Presently I heard the Kid's voice out of the fog, singing.

"Helluva country," said the puncher as he rolled another cigarette.

"Who was the Kid?" I asked.

"Oh, him?" said the puncher. "He ain't nothin' but a horse-wrangler. He landed in Globe with a circus. It was a sort of fly-by-night outfit, I guess. Anyway, it went broke while they was in town. The Kid hung around Globe for a while, sorta like a lost dog, until he met Slim. Slim was breakin' horses over on Cherry Creek an' took the Kid out to the ranch. That was four or five years ago. The Kid told Slim he was raised in Chicago and run away with a circus 'cause he liked horses. He never had much of a raisin', I guess. Anyway, he never went back. He don't belong in this coun-

# THE RUMMY KID

try, either. Everybody rides him unless Slim's around. Funny how them two took up with each other! Rummy's afraid of his own shadow, an' Slim would fight a buzz-saw.

"I never heard of Rummy ever fightin' but once. Him an' old Sour Dough was range brandin' one winter up the cedars. One night Shorty stayed all night at their camp. Old Sour Dough is pretty ornery, an' he had the Kid scared plumb to death. The way old Sour Dough kept ridin' the Kid finally got on Shorty's nerves. Finally he up an' tells the Kid that if he'll lick old Sour Dough he'd see that he got a fair shake. The Kid's plump desperate, an' he takes to old Sour Dough like a wildcat. He blacks both of the old boy's eyes, an' finally, when he's more dead than alive, old Sour Dough hollers enough. Next morning old Sour Dough can't see well enough to tell a horse from a steer yearlin'. But when Shorty starts for home the Kid goes with him. He's afraid to stay alone with old Sour Dough, even after he's licked him. The Kid savvies a horse, though. But he's chicken-hearted. Did ya notice his eyes? They're big and soft, like a woman's."

# MEN AND HORSES

As the Rummy Kid jogged slowly down the long ridge his eyes were on the ground. The trail that ran along the rocky backbone of the hill was well worn, and had been beaten down by countless unshod hoofs.

"It 's him, all right," said the Kid aloud, as he noted one unshod track much larger than the rest. "It 's the buckskin."

Near the end of the long ridge the trail turned off abruptly and disappeared into the brush. Here the Kid dismounted and dropped his bridle-reins. Slowly he worked his way to a large flat rock at the end of the ridge. Removing his battered felt hat, he crawled to the edge. The Kid caught his breath sharply. Far below the wild horses were grazing, and at the edge of the herd stood the buckskin stallion, tossing his head in the wind.

The buckskin stallion had been a yearling when the Kid first saw him. That was four years ago. But it seemed like yesterday to the Kid. Well he remembered the day. He had been horse-hunting on a long-legged bronc. As he rode out of the cedars he had come suddenly on a bunch of wild horses, grazing at the edge of the mesa. The Kid thrilled when he thought of the race that followed. Four miles across that open mesa, with the wind stinging his face. The thunder of flying hoofs on the hard ground. The big black that fell and never moved again. He could have roped any horse in the bunch that day—except the buckskin. As they came down off the rocky side of the mesa he could have touched a big bay maverick with his hand. The wild horses were all about him, yet the Kid had been unafraid. His eyes were on the flying buckskin up in front.

For some time now the Kid lay watching the buckskin stallion. Suddenly his pony nickered. As the Kid raised his head the wild bunch headed down the broad valley on the dead run, the buckskin far in the lead. A mile down the valley the big stallion stopped and turned. The Kid waved his hat. The buckskin wheeled and disappeared in a clump of cedars.

The Rummy Kid mounted his pony and trotted back up the ridge. The sun was not more than an hour high. At the edge of the mesa the remuda was grazing. The Kid counted them. There was one horse gone. Again the Kid counted the bunch, but one horse *was* missing. Slowly the Kid rode through the herd. Six X was gone. The Kid groaned, for old Six X was in the foreman's mount. "Another cussing," thought the Kid. As long as he'd lost a horse he wished it was one of old Sour Dough's mount. How he hated old Sour Dough. He hated them all—all but Slim. Slim never cussed him. Suddenly the Kid saw something move in a thicket, and the next moment old Six X came walking out of the bush.

At a gallop the Kid threw the horses together. It was sundown as they filed slowly down the rocky trail to the camp below. And above the clatter of the shod hoofs on the hard rock the Kid's voice could be heard singing.

The Rummy Kid lay in his blankets and stared

up at the stars. A dozen empty beds just like his own lay scattered about the little flat. The camp-fire at the foot of a large sycamore threw strange shadows among the trees. From his bed the Kid could hear the low voices of the punchers, who sat squatted on their heels about the fire.

The Kid could n't sleep, for he was leaving in the morning. It was only a week's trip, but the Kid was excited. In the morning he was going to take a mount of horses over on the Gila. Maybe he'd get to see Slim, for he was going to stop at headquarters on the way back. Suddenly the Kid sat up in his blankets. It was Ribs, the fore-man talking.

"It can't be done," said old Ribs, "unless we use a relay of horses. There's no one horse in this outfit can catch him. I jumped him out not over a week ago. I was ridin' old Hooker, and him grain-fed. I had the wind on the bunch and come bustin' right out of the cedars before they noticed me. I could have caught any horse in the herd except the buckskin. For three miles I cut the blood outa old Hooker with a double end of rope, but I never got close enough to the buckskin to get a smear. I was n't packin' a gun that day or I'd a' bored him through as he went down off the other end of the mesa."

The Kid lay in his blankets and thrilled, for old Hooker was the fastest horse in the outfit.

The sun was not more than an hour high as the Rummy Kid jogged slowly down the long ridge. Near the end of the ridge where the well worn trail turned off into the brush the Kid dismounted and dropped his bridle-reins. Slowly he worked his way to the large flat rock at the end of the ridge. Removing his battered felt hat he crawled to the edge. But the valley below him was empty. The buckskin stallion was gone. Slowly the Kid mounted his pony and trotted back up the long ridge. He had missed Slim, too. But across the edge of the mesa his pony struck a gallop and the Kid sang.

It was sundown as his pony started down the narrow trail to the camp below. Suddenly the Kid reined in his pony, and the song died on his lips. It could n't be him. It could n't be. Far below him he saw the punchers all gathered about the big corral at the edge of the camp, and securely tied to the snubbing-post in the center,

with a hackamore on his head, was the buckskin
stallion.

With a strange choking in his throat, the Kid
spurred his pony on down the rocky trail.
Through a mist the Kid saw the big stallion.  He
looked white now from the sweat and dust that
caked him.  It was old Sour Dough talking, but
the Kid heard him in a daze.

"Old Hooker was dead, and Ribs, the foreman
hurt.  We relayed on him," said old Sour Dough.
"It took nine of us mounted on grain-fed horses to
catch him, an' we 'll brand him in the morning."

The Kid choked back a sob as he stumbled out
of the corral.

"Come and get it, Rummy," said the cook.

"I ain't hungry," said the Kid, sniffing.

"Better eat somethin', Kid.  Slim's comin' tonight, an' he 's goin' to ride the buckskin in the
mornin'."  The Kid shook his head as he stumbled
toward the blankets.

"I 'll be damned," said the cook, "if the Rummy
Kid ain't cryin'."

As the Rummy Kid lay in his blankets he could

hear the low voices of the punchers about the fire.

Presently he heard Slim's voice.

"Where's the Kid?" said Slim. But when Slim came over to his bed the Kid pretended sleep. He hated Slim now. He knew the buckskin would fight. But Slim could ride. It would be the same old story again. They'd choke the big stallion down and blindfold him while they put the saddle on. Slim would swing up and catch his stirrups. Then they'd turn him loose. And finally the big stallion, with his head hanging and the blood streaming from his shoulders—broken.

The fire burned low before the punchers scattered to their blankets, but the Kid was wide awake when Slim came over to his bed. Sitting cross-legged on the foot of the Kid's bed Slim rolled a cigarette.

"Goin' to have some fun in the mornin', Kid," he said.

The Kid sobbed aloud.

"Why, what's the matter, Kid?" said Slim. "Who's been ridin' ya?"

"Nobody," sobbed the Kid. "You go to hell."

The punchers were all asleep in their blankets,

but the Rummy Kid lay staring up at the stars with round wide open eyes. Off toward the north a coyote howled. It was still dark in the little flat where the camp lay. But the moon was beginning to flood the edge of the mesa with its soft light. The Rummy Kid sat up quietly and pulled on his boots. Walking softly, he disappeared into the shadows. The buckskin snorted as the Kid took down the corral bars, and as the Kid approached the snubbing-post he struck out with both fore feet.

"It's all right," said the Kid in a low voice. "It's all right."

Again the wicked fore feet struck, but the Kid was quick. Slowly he approached. He could almost touch the hackamore with his hand. Then a knife flashed—

A thunder of hoofs on the hard ground. A sound like the wind through the pines. And the buckskin rushed on into the night.

# SAM

# SAM

WE could hear the Gila booming for some little time, but as we topped out, it suddenly turned to a roar.

"No use goin' any further. I would n't try to cross for all the horses this outfit owns. We 'd stand about as much chance as that snowball I hear you mention on occasions."

Shorty reined in his pony, and as he spoke we watched the river half a mile below us.

"There 's the Hook and Line ranch just across from where she spreads out a little.

"Now watch them logs go out of sight when they hit the box."

The logs drifted smoothly for a while, but as we watched they suddenly shot forward and disappeared in the wall of water that poured through the narrow gorge of solid rock.

"Anybody ever make it across?" I asked.

"I know a guy that did it, and he was n't drunk either," said Shorty.

Turning in his saddle, he pointed to a little spot

of green some twenty miles to the north on our side
of the river.

"There's where he lives.   Ever hear of Sam?"

"No."

"Well, the first time I ever saw Sam, he was
fightin' broncs for the old V.O. outfit.   I was
wrangling horses during the fall round-up—my
first job around a cow outfit.   I was just a button,
and you know how a kid looks up to a bronco-
twister.   This Sam was a slit-eyed devil, with a
face like flint; but, man, how he could ride!   He
never had anything to say and kept pretty much to
himself.   None of the outfit liked him.   Of
course there was n't anything said, for any one
with half an eye could look at Sam and see it
would n't be healthy.

"I did n't see much of him till we got to the old
headquarters ranch.   Then every morning, as soon
as the remuda quieted down, I'd beat it for the
bronc corral and watch Sam.   He never paid any
more attention to me than if I was n't there at all,
but I rather liked that, as the rest of the outfit kept
me on the prod most of the time anyway.

"One day he let me saddle a bronc!   I was that
swelled I forgot all about the remuda, and let six

head get away, with two of the boss's mount in the bunch. What he said was plenty, so after that I stayed with the ponies.

"About a week later I was holdin' the remuda on those open ridges when along come old Ben, the fence-rider. He got off his horse to auger me a while, so I up and asked him about Sam. Among other triflin' things, Sam had done six years for holdin' up a passenger-train out of Wilcox one night. He had been a member of Black Jack's old gang and was just naturally a bad *hombre*.

" 'And a good man to let alone,' says old Ben as he rode off down the ridge shakin' his head.

"The next day the foreman sent me along to help Sam back from Muskell with a new string of broncs. He never said a word all the way over, but when we got to the rim he pointed out that spot of green I just showed you. Then he told me about his kid, a little boy about eight months old. I dropped both bridle-reins, I was that surprised. To think of him carin' for anybody, least of all a kid!

"I thought maybe after that he 'd talk a little when I was around, but I never got more out of him than a nod.

# SAM

"When the fall work ended, I got a job drivin' team for old Barclay. Once in a while I'd see a V.O. puncher, but Sam had gone. They did n't know where, and, what's more, did n't care.

"Along in March I met Sam comin' down the street. We shook hands. Sam said he was workin' at the Hook and Line across there where I showed you.

" 'How's the little boy?' I says.

"He turned away for a minute, but when he looked at me again his face was harder than ever.

" 'He died last night.'

"Then he walked on down the street.

"I went back to V.O.'s in the spring and heard the rest of it from Slim, a puncher from Eagle Creek.

"It seems he and Dogie Si stopped at Sam's place one night when it was stormin' so they could n't make their camp. They found Sam's wife alone with the kid, and it was bad sick. And her a-cryin' for the doctor and wantin' Sam.

"So Si rode to Fort Thomas for the doctor, while Slim went to tell Sam across at the Hook and Line.

"The woman knew Sam could n't cross the river, but she was set on havin' him know about the kid.

# MEN AND HORSES

"It's pretty rough from Sam's place to the river, and Slim's horse fell twice. The last time he did n't get up, but Slim made the rest of the way on foot.

"He shot a couple of times before he could raise anybody. Then he yelled across that the boy was sick.

"That was all Sam heard.

"Slim wanted to tell him that they had sent for the doctor, and that he thought that everything would be all right.

"But by now Sam had his night horse saddled, and the next thing Slim heard was Sam cussin', tryin' to get his horse to take the water. Slim yelled at him to go back as they 'd sent for the doctor already, but Sam did n't pay no mind.

"It was so dark that after they hit the water Slim could n't see anything. He thought the drift had carried them down, but pretty soon here they comes right through the ice and logs that was streakin' by. They come out just above the box. Sam stopped long enough to bridle the horse, for when they hit the water he had slipped the bridle so the old pony could have his head.

"Then he was gone.

[78]

# SAM

"Now, you know Slim never had any more use for Sam than anybody else did, but he sat down and cried like a baby."

Shorty wheeled his horse, and we started back down the narrow trail. But I turned for one more look at the little patch of green off toward the north.

"Yeh," said Shorty, interpreting my glance. "A man's a queer animal, ain't he? About the time you think you've got one pegged he goes and upsets the dope.

"Let's be driftin'."

# THE HORSE-WRANGLER

# THE HORSE-WRANGLER

A TENDERFOOT looking for work around a cow outfit is apt to be disillusioned. If he gets a job of any sort he will be lucky if nothing worse happens. For the first few months he will be in his own way and every one else's. And there is no romance in shoeing horses and being pitched over a corral fence. But if a man will work and is willing to sweat until he is worth something to the outfit, he may eventually catch on. Around a cow outfit when a man sweats it means that he works for his chuck and gets no pay. Aside from tending the ranch and packing salt, wrangling horses is where most punchers start, and the horse-wrangler does n't stand very high in a cow camp. His relation to a top hand is much the same as a dish-washer's to the head cook in any first-class restaurant. The horse-wrangler has nothing to do with the cattle. He drags wood for the cook, and acts as sort of companion and head nurse to the herd of saddle-horses and pack stock that make up the remuda.

# MEN AND HORSES

The horses are brought in about sun-up. As soon as each puncher is mounted for the day the rest of the bunch are turned over to the horse-wrangler.

This was where my job began. I had nothing to do but take the horses out in the morning, water them at noon, and repeat the performance again in the evening. It sounds simple, but at times it's apt to be interesting.

If the feed is good a horse will fill up in a couple of hours. Then he lies down and sleeps for a while. If the ground is rough he sleeps standing. However, they don't all sleep at the same time, and a few that I've known did most of their grazing on a long trot.

On a mesa it's an easy thing to hold a hundred head of horses. But when the country is rough and broken a man can't see more than ten head at a time. He never knows what the other ninety are doing. In fact, I found on several occasions when throwing the bunch together that the other ninety had pulled out for parts unknown.

After the ponies quiet down in the morning the wrangler usually goes to camp for a while and augers the cook. If the cook happens to be feeling

# THE HORSE-WRANGLER

in good humor the wrangler may even be asked to help himself to the coffee and cold steak. However, this is the exception and never the rule.

Some days the wrangler can be gone for hours, and when he gets back he will find all the horses together, but again let him leave for twenty minutes and there won't be a horse in sight when he returns.

The herd of saddle-horses and pack stock are known as the remuda. Each puncher rides his own string of horses that are cut to him by the foreman. A puncher's mount usually consists of from eight to twelve head and a night horse. At night the horses are turned loose and each puncher wrangles in turn. Usually two or three men are on at a time. Their night horses are tied up the night before. The men leave camp before daylight. By the time it 's light enough to see a horse they start throwing the ponies together. The horses are counted and generally reach camp about sun-up.

If the outfit has a night-hawk he holds the horses together at night and drives the bunch in at daylight. A puncher's night horse carries his bed when the outfit moves camp. The average size of the remuda, depending on the number of men riding, is from one hundred to one hundred and twenty-five head.

The horse-wrangler must know each horse, but among the bunch, as in a crowd of human beings, there are always a few he comes to know best. For each horse has a personality decidedly his own. For instance, Rat was the cook's horse during the round-up. At other times he belonged to any one in the outfit that was short a horse. No matter how short the feed, Rat always had a crease down his back. But while most horses run in pairs he had no particular partner. His weakness was colts and strays. The sorrier the stray the closer Rat would stay with him.

One morning at Soda Cañon two little colts came in with the remuda. The range was full of mockeys (wild mares), and the colts had been left when the punchers ran the bunch out the day before. A mockey seldom goes back after her colt. So in the night the colts had found the remuda and had come in with the saddle-horses in the morning.

Rat immediately took charge. He fought every horse in the remuda that came near, until late in the afternoon old Slocum finally noticed them. Rat nickered and ran in a circle for a while, but decided he'd have to give them up. For old Slocum was boss of the remuda. In the way into camp at sundown Rat consoled himself by throwing in with a stray mule that belonged to a nester.

Shoestring, Bloucher, and Sailor all ran together. Any time a puncher found one he always knew the other two were not far away. Shoestring was a slim-bellied sorrel, an outlaw. Bloucher and Sailor were gentle as kittens.

Some days the punchers did n't change horses at noon. If they made camp by the middle of the evening, one of the punchers usually brought the horses they had ridden out to the remuda. In Shoestring's case that was n't necessary. The minute he was turned loose he left on a dead run, never stopping till he had found Bloucher and

Sailor, even if the remuda were four miles from camp.

In the foreman's mount was Three T, a little hook-nosed sorrel which always trailed the bunch. Any horse he could get to follow him off suited him. He disliked being herded. As long as I was in sight he would graze quietly, but the minute he found I'd gone to camp he'd pull out with as many horses as he could get to follow him. Going into camp at sundown he was always the last one down the trail. Any time he could get behind brush enough to hide himself he invariably stopped. If he was n't noticed he'd stand until he thought I was out of sight; then he'd quietly pull out in the opposite direction.

Burro was a flea-bitten gray that was seldom used except to pack or wrangle horses. One of the punchers said he'd been a good horse at one time. Still another 'lowed that if he was it must be just a late thing, as he had known him for twenty years.

Anyway, the night before the herd was moved to the shipping-pens old Burro was tied up to wrangle on. Next morning one of the packhorses did n't come in. So when the outfit pulled out, Burro went along packing a bed. There were

# THE HORSE-WRANGLER

some twenty-odd bulls in the herd to be shipped. Each one had to have his horns tipped before loading. A puncher generally rides his top horse to the shipping-pens. Stretching out an old bull is n't as much fun as it might be, and this trip, after the first half-dozen, the top horses began to quit cold. Finally a puncher led in old Burro.

It was nearly dark when the last bull was stretched, but Burro was still holding just as hard on his end and looking down the line like the old cow-horse he was.

Red was one of the pack-mules. His pet aversion was a rope. No one ever roped him in the corral; at least no one ever did it a second time, for it took the whole outfit to turn him loose. Any one could walk up to him, and if he just laid the rope over Red's shoulder, he would allow himself to be led out. He always carried the Dutch ovens when the outfit moved camp. As soon as he was loaded he backed up against the nearest tree, and leaned against it until the rest of the horses were packed. On any of the other horses the pack was always taken off before he was turned loose. Red had his own ideas about such things. If a puncher first slipped off the hackamore, Red would stand quietly while he was unpacked. But if he was unpacked first, it took the whole outfit and the dog to get the hackamore off.

Old Slocum was the leader of the remuda at the Bar F Bar, and acted accordingly. He was n't much to look at. He was hammer-headed, ewe-necked, with a huge body altogether out of proportion to his very short legs. His frayed tail made me think of a badly worn hobby-horse.

When the outfit worked from the big corral he was always the first horse up the narrow trail to the mesa. About half-way up he made his first stop to blow. Everything stopped when he did. No amount of cussing from below could make him move until he was ready.   The fighting and ruction among the horses below him he ignored completely unless they crowded him.   Then as he raised his head and flattened his ears they would fall away on all sides to give him room.   When camp was moved, old Slocum always carried part of the kitchen.   This was the only work he did. In his younger days he had been a cow-horse, a good one some of the punchers said.   I often wondered how he felt about being packed instead of ridden.   If he had any feeling about the matter he kept it to himself, for he was still the boss of the remuda and the leader.

One finds almost every kind of name in a remuda of horses.   Some of the horses are called after their brands, as Beer Keg, R Finger, Cross L, and Ten of Diamonds.   As a rule the first man who rides the horse names him.   A little gray bronc, for obvious reasons, was called Kettle Belly. The boss decided it did n't look as well in the horse book as it might, and renamed him Steve.   But the last time I saw the little gray saddled the twister was calling him Frijoles.

The horse-wrangler always rides the sorriest

horses in the outfit. If he happens to get one that looks particularly good, it's ten to one there's something decidedly wrong.

When the work started one fall on the mountain, the foreman was cutting each puncher his horses. Finally he roped a big black.

"Who gets him?" I asked.

"He's one of yours," says he.

It sounded too good to be true. As I was putting on the saddle, one of the punchers eased over and said: "Of course it ain't none of my business, but if I was you I wouldn't cinch him too tight. He falls over backwards."

At the shipping-pens one spring the punchers were all sitting along the top of the pen waiting to load. One of the old punchers was sitting on the opposite side, talking to an inspector. I never knew what the inspector asked, but as he nodded toward me, I heard the old puncher say: "Who? Him? Hell, no. He ain't nothin' but the horse-wrangler."

# A Cow-Puncher's
# Pinch of Snuff

# A COW-PUNCHER'S PINCH OF SNUFF

I ALWAYS wanted to be a cow-puncher. When I was a little kid on the farm in East Texas I could n't think of nothin' else. Most kids, I guess, is that-a-way, but they never could knock the idea out of me. That was all farmin' country, even then. But once in a while some one would drive a bunch of cattle by our place. I could n't have been more 'n eight years old when I followed one bunch off. It did n't make any difference to me that I was the only one afoot. I had a long stick, an' was busier than a bird-dog drivin' drags. I had an uncle livin' down the road about four miles. He happened to see me goin' by his place.

" 'Whatcha doin', kid?'

" 'A-working stock,' says I.

"He finally talked me into goin' on back home with him—

"I stuck it out until I got to be about fifteen. Then I pulled out for good. I've never been home since."

"You! Wagon!" yelled Shorty, as one of the packhorses stopped to graze. "Git up the country!"

The outfit was moving camp. A mile ahead we could see the dust from the herd as it moved slowly into Seven Mile. Shorty and I were trailing along with the remuda, far in the rear.

Of all the cow-punchers I have ever known Shorty was to me the most interesting. Shorty was thirty-four when I met him and foreman of the Cross S outfit in Arizona. We worked there

# A COW-PUNCHER'S PINCH OF SNUFF

through one round-up together, and in bad weather we slept in the same tepee. Aside from the fact that Shorty did everything a little better than any one else you would n't have guessed he was foreman. He was a little runt, with a pair of steel-blue eyes and a mop of hair as black and coarse as an Apache's. Of course his legs were bowed. Shorty was always the last cow-puncher to bed at night and usually the first one up in the morning. He talked incessantly. His stories, real or fancied, were told in a rambling, disconnected sort of way. To me they were always interesting. For I have never known a cow-puncher with a keener sense of humor or a point of view more decidedly his own.

"After I left home I got a job near Midland, greasin' windmills. But ridin' herd on a flock of them things did n't suit me no better than picking cotton. I wanted to be a cow-puncher, so I drifted into New Mexico. I did n't have no trouble findin' work, but it was n't what I wanted. It seemed that I could always land a job at anything 'cept punchin' cows. A fellow named McDougal finally put me on. The peelers all laughed when I hit the old man for a job. He did n't even smile.

" 'Button,' he says, 'they ride pitchin' horses at this outfit.   You 're just a kid.'

" 'I know,' I says, 'but I want to learn.'

"The old man knowed I meant it.   I stayed two years.   It was him that sold me my first horse.   A long-legged bay outlaw with a white snip on his nose.   The old man let me have him cheap.   And, man! how he could wipe things up.   At the end of two years I figured on goin' home to see the folks. I had a little money saved.   I 'd been all right I guess, if I 'd have kept away from town.   I lost the money playin' stud.   I would n't go home broke. I knew if I went back to the ranch that all the bunch would hurrah me.   I 'd planned a lot on that trip home—but I headed west again."

"Women beat me."

Shorty and I were on day herd together.   It was drizzling rain, and Shorty had just lighted a soto to warm his feet.

"I can get along with 'most any kind of man, but a woman is somethin' I don't savvy.   Yes ma'am and no ma'am is as far as I ever got with any of them.   It 's always been that way.

"When I was a kid there was a little girl that

lived a few miles west of us. She an' my sisters used to visit back an' forth. I had plenty to say around my sisters, but I could n't even talk to her. I was about fourteen, I guess, when we all went to a party together. They played kissin' games. I did n't have the nerve to take any part, but I wanted to bad enough. I finally did get up my nerve enough to ask her could I call next Sunday afternoon. I never will forget the thrill I got when she says, 'Yes.'

"Mother guessed what was up when she caught me combin' my hair, but she promised not to tell. If pa had found it out, I never would have heard the last of it from him.

"I rode an old pacin'-horse we owned called Dan. I did n't own a saddle, so I used a gunny-sack instead. The bridle was one of them old things with blinders on. But the pair of California spurs I wore made up for all the other things I lacked. I'd traded with a Mexican for them.

"It was one of them warm June Sunday after-noons. As I jogged old Dan along the road I fig-ured out a hundred different things to say to her. The gunny-sack was gettin' plenty warm by the time I got in sight of their house. But when I spied her standin' on the porch I shore did hang them California spurs in pore old Dan. I set him up, in front of her, just like a cuttin' horse. She smiled and spoke when I rode up.

" 'Where 's Buck?' I says.

" 'Oh, he 's gone fishin',' " she says, still a-smilin'. She knowed as well as I did that I never had nothin' to do with Buck, him bein' her young brother an' two years younger than me.

"She was pleasant enough an' asked me to get down. The gunny-sack was gettin' awful hot, but I kept a-settin' there on old Dan. I could n't say a word. Every little while, though, I 'd dig old Dan on the off side with the spur, hopin' she 'd think I was ridin' a bad horse. Finally I says:

" 'Well, I guess I 'll be goin' on.'

"She looked sorta surprised, but she smiled and says, 'Good-by.'

"I rode on past their place until I got outa sight of the house. Then I got down and let the gunny-sack cool off a while. I wondered if she 'd still be on the porch when I went back. Shore enough, she was. I hung the spurs in pore old Dan again and set him pacin' down the road towards home.

She waved her hand as I went by the house, an' I waved back."

Shorty laughed as he kicked the blackened soto.

"Just had a hell of a good time."

"From what I 've seen, a woman always gets the worst of the deal in this country, though," said Shorty.

"After I left McDougal's outfit I had an awful time gettin' a job. I was such a kid no one seemed to want to take a chance on me. At least not punchin' cows. I rode the chuck line clear across the State before I got another job. I stayed a year this time. The feller's name was Smith that finally put me on. He did n't have much of a spread, and I was the only hand he had. Smith had just been married, an' his wife was awful nice to me. Exceptin' for the fact that he treated me like a kid, I liked Smith, too. His place was ninety miles from town. Sometimes his wife would be alone for days when me and Smith was gone. Smith was good enough to her, and she seemed satisfied at that. There was n't no reason for it, but somehow I could n't help from feelin' sorry for her, just the same.

"I 'd been a-workin' there about a month, I

guess, when Smith sent me to town to get a load of chuck. Smith was ridin' the other way that day, and he pulled out before I got the team hitched up. I had a list of stuff to get that they 'd made out the night before. I was just ready to start when his wife came out. Her face was red as fire. I could n't think of what was up. An' then she asks me, will I get some snuff for her in town.

"I know there 's a lot of people use it in the South, but somehow the idea of a woman as nice as she was usin' snuff gives me an awful shock.

"We figured on a three days' trip each way from town. It was dark the night I got back to the ranch. Smith and his wife had just finished eatin' supper when I drove in.

" 'Go in an' eat,' says Smith, 'an' I 'll unhitch the team.'

"I 'd plumb forgot about the snuff until Smith brings it in the house. I never will forget the way he kidded me.

" 'Why don't you chew, instead?' says he. 'My God, use anything but snuff!'

"I was gettin' hot under the collar when I happened to notice his wife's face. She was standin' in the kitchen door. Her face was white as chalk;

with that I opens up a box and takes a dip myself. It made me awful sick. I finally had to
go outside an' get the air. But I never did let
on.

"From that night on Smith always called me
Swede. I always carried a box of snuff in the
pocket of my chaps. But I never could learn to
like the stuff.

"His wife never did mention that night to me.
I never did see her usin' any snuff, either. But
once a month, when I went to town for chuck, I
always brought back some snuff for her.

"I worked a year for Smith before I finally quit
and headed west again. They 'd both been awful
good to me. The mornin' that I left, Smith
hooked the wagon up to take me into town. I
had my old long-legged bronc tied on behind.
His wife was standing in the door.

" 'Is there anything you want from town?' says
Smith. Her face turned white as chalk. She
looked straight at him when she spoke. But I
could n't hardly hear her voice:

" 'Will—you—bring—me—back—some—snuff
—from—town?' she says.

"I looked for Smith to throw a fit. But he just

set there lookin' sort of queer and foolin' with the reins, and then finally he says: 'Sure!'

"Ever since I 've left McDougal's place I had it in my head that I 'd go home some day. There 's never been a Christmas since I left home but what I 've sorta planned on goin' back. A dozen times I 've had the money saved. But somehow the money always slips away. I would n't go home broke."

Shorty had been in Arizona ever since he left Smith's place. One rainy night in the tepee he showed me a picture of a sister he had never seen.

"She 's eighteen now," he said, "an' ever since she 's been a little girl, about once a year she writes to me. A fellow took some pictures of me once, when I was breaking horses for the Flyin' H. I sent 'em home to her. An' she writes back how interesting she thought they were. But mother wished that I 'd send home some pictures of myself.

"They did n't know me any more."

We were working down out of the pine and the juniper mesas, moving camp every few days. Headquarters was reached in November.

Headquarters was only thirty miles from

Globe, so the day before we went down to the pens some folks came out from town. Among 'em was the horse-wrangler's mother. Slim was out on the mesa with the ponies when she came. She looked a bit disappointed when she found he was n't there, till Shorty showed her the point where he 'd come off with the remuda. The drive had just come in, and the outfit was branding out. The other folks was right interested, but Slim's mother kept watchin' that spot.

It takes some little time to ease a hundred and fifty ponies off that point. But as soon as they hit the flat, they come on a run for the ranch. She did n't see Slim until he was most there. Then he come bustin' out of the dust to turn two broncs that was headin' down the wash. Slim let out a yell when he spied her. She just stood there and smiled.

Punchers as a rule don't have much to say when women-folks is around. But Slim's mother had white hair. The cook was poison on town folks and Indians, but I heard him tell her he 'd have made a tallow pudding if he 'd a knowed any one was coming.

That night Shorty did n't sit around the fire.

# A COW-PUNCHER'S PINCH OF SNUFF

He went off to bed without sayin' a word. I thought he was asleep when I turned in, but as I was fixin' the tarp he up and says: "Slim's mother did n't pay no one any mind but him. When he left, she watched him until he topped out on the mesa."

We went down to the pens in the morning and had just started to load when the passenger pulled up. Everybody hung out of the windows. Among them was Pecos, a kid that had ridden the Rough String the beginning of the work. He was so dolled up we did n't know him until he yelled.

"Where ya goin'?" says Shorty.

"Home," yells Pecos as the train pulls out.

It was sundown before we loaded out. The outfit piled into the two big cars and headed for town. Shorty and I were to take the horses back to the ranch. So we filled up on canned stuff and belly-washed at the little store. It was dark when we pulled out. But by the time we had hit seven mile, the moon had come up, and it was 'most as light as day. I started to auger a couple of times, but all I got was a "yes," or a "no." So we rode to the ranch without talkin'.

# MEN AND HORSES

I unsaddled and turned loose before I noticed Shorty. He was still standin', with his head down, leanin' against his pony. Figurin' his side was hurtin' him again, I went over to unsaddle his horse.

"The old side botherin' again?" I asked.

When he raised his head, I saw his face was wet.

"By God," he says, "every one sees his mother but me. I'm goin' home!"

# SHORTY BUYS A HAT

# SHORTY BUYS A HAT

"I'M headin' for the wagon-yard to feed my horse," began Shorty, "when this *hombre* speaks to me. He 's standin' in the doorway of a little store below the bank.

" 'Come in out of the rain,' he says, 'an' how 's things lookin' out your way?' "

"That 's Brown, I 'll bet a hoss," said Slim.

"Friend of yourn?" asked Shorty.

"Not exactly," said Slim, nearly putting the fire out. "But most every puncher trades with Brown at one time or other. He sold me a pair a boots onc't I could n't get into with a can-opener."

Shorty looked relieved.

"I 'm new in the country," said Shorty, "and since he 's sort of pleasant like, I stops to auger him a while.

" 'Where ya workin' now?' he says.

"When I tell him I 'm fightin' broncs for the Cross S outfit he opens up and names a lot of peelers that I knowed.

" 'They 're friends of mine,' says he, 'an' they

all trades with me. Come on inside and let me show ya what I got. Don't stand there in the rain.'

" 'I don't want to buy nothin',' I says.

" 'Of course, you don't,' says he. 'Come on in anyway and make yourself to home, for all the boys hangs out with me when they hit town.'

"He must have showed me several thousand dollars' worth of stuff. An' talkin' all the time about the boys I knowed who trades with him. A dozen times I start to leave, but he keeps draggin' down more stuff, and so I stick around. I'm easin' for the door when he tops me with a big black hat. It's miles too big. The rim's below my ears.

" 'The sheriff bought one yesterday,' he says. 'He's an old cow-man an' buys the best. He always trades with me.'

" 'I don't like a black hat,' says I, 'an' besides, this hat's too big.'

"With that he goes and puts five lamp-wicks in the lid and has his wife come in. She leads me over to a glass and then starts tellin' me how well I look.

"A man of my complexion shouldn't think of

wearin' anything but black. I did n't look so bad at that. Of course, I did n't want the hat, but since he 'd been so nice in showin' all the stuff, and his wife bein' sort of pleasant like, I finally buys the lid.

"It 's pourin' rain when I leaves town, and the old hat weighs a ton. I ain't any more than started when it 's down over both ears, an' by the time I hit seven mile it 's leakin' like a sieve. I 'm ridin' a bronc that 's pretty snuffy, an' every time I raises the lid enough to git a little light, I see him drop one ear. I finally decides to take the lamp-wicks out altogether. I 'm tryin' to raise the lid enough to see somethin' besides the saddle-horn when the old bronc bogs his head. I make a grab for leather when he leaves the ground, but I might as well have a gunny-sack tied over my head, for I can't see nothin'. When he comes down the second time I 'm way over on one side. When he hits the ground the third jump, I ain't with him. I 'm sittin' in the middle of the wash with both hands full of sand. I finally lifts the lid enough to see the old bronc headin' for the ranch. He 's wide open an' kickin' at his paunch.

"It 's gettin' dark, an' instead of a rain the whole

sky's leakin' now. I hangs my spurs and chaps upon a bush and hoofs it for the ranch. It's nine miles as near as I can figure out, an' the rain don't help my feelin's none. By the time I've gone a quarter the thought of that dry-goods pirate has me seein' red. I can't even manage to build a cigarette. My boots is full of water, an' when I hangs a foot in a cat-claw and falls for the third time killin's too good for that *hombre* in the store. I'm stumblin' along with that hat down over my eyes when I falls into Oak Creek. By the time I gits across I could have strangled his wife and child. I don't remember much about the last four miles, but when I gits to the ranch-house, I'm talkin' to myself.

"The old bronc's standin' in the middle of the corral as I come polin' in. He's a heap cooler than I am by now. But the sight of that black hat starts him snuffin' again. But I don't blame him much at that, until I takes the saddle off and finds the blankets gone. I builds me up a fire and stirs some chuck together. It helped a lot, but I ain't feelin' none too well, so finally I turns in.

"When I wakes up I'm feelin' fine, but the sight of that black hat soon gits me on the prod.

Wranglin' afoot don't help any, an' about the fourth time that hat slides down over my eyes I know I'm goin' to town. I slip old cedar in my shirt-front an' stuff a couple of papers in the hat alongside the lamp-wicks. I ain't takin' any chances, so I hangs old bonnet on a post while I let the hammer down on Mr. Bronc. He rags a little when I step across, but I ain't ridin' with my head in any sack this time, an' I gits the snake uncocked an' head for town.

"I'm almost peaceful when the sun comes out, but last night's sign there in the wash still keeps me geed up some. I'm gone about a mile when I finds my navaho a-hangin' in a bush, which helps my feelin's a heap. An' while I'm puttin' on my spurs an' chaps at seven mile, I almost laugh at the way that bronc unloaded me. The sun takes most of the killin' out of my mind, but anyway I head for town. I'll tell that dry-goods pirate what I think an' make him eat that hat, an' as I jog along I figure out my speech.

"He's in the store alone when I ride up.

" 'Hello,' says he, but I don't pay him any mind.

" 'There's your old black hat,' says I, a-throwin' the lid down on the counter.

# SHORTY BUYS A HAT

" 'What 's the matter with it?' says he.

" 'Ain't nothin' the matter, only you sold me a black hat I did n't want an' five lamp-wicks an'—"

Shorty raked a coal from the fire and lit his cigarette.

Slim loved a fight.

"What happened?" he said leaning forward.

"I 'll be doggoned if he did n't sell me a shirt an' six pairs of socks before I could get out of the place."

# A Night In Town

# A NIGHT IN TOWN

IT was Shorty's bald-faced horse all right. Slim was sure of that. But who could be riding him? The rider slumped in his saddle and wore no hat. Something white was tied about his head; must be an Indian. But as they came slowly up the wash, Slim saw that he held his hat in his hand. Slim spurred his horse across the wash, and where the trail heads into Bean Belly Flat he waited.

It was Shorty; both eyes were black, his nose was split, and the remnant of a silk shirt hung around his neck like a dicky. As he saw Slim his mouth cracked into a misshapen grin.

He hung his hat on the saddle-horn and rolled a cigarette.

"I've seen a few tenderfeet go bareheaded in the sun," said Slim.

"This hat's too small," says Shorty. "But it weighs a plenty."

A lump the size of a goose-egg extended from

one eye to the roots of his hair. He touched it gingerly.

"This one's the biggest. But the one over my ear's shore tender."

"'Things quiet in town, I s'pose," said Slim, "when a man ain't drinkin'."

"Nary a drop this trip," says Shorty. "I been on the police force."

"Must ha' been a race riot," said Slim. "But I ain't seen the papers lately."

"On the level, Slim, I never had a drink. Ya see there was a carnival in town. I had n't any more 'n landed when I met Bob. He's chief of police now, but we used to work together at the Diamond A's.

"I was huntin' a poker game, but stopped to auger him awhile. Finally he says they was puttin' on a few extra police durin' the carnival. He did n't expect any trouble, but would I help him out?

"Would I? I jumped at the chance. Pretty soft, I figured, seein' all the shows for nothin' and makin' wages besides!

"He goes up to his office and he pins on the

badge. I did n't want to take the handcuffs, but he says I might need 'em.

"Then he offers me a gun.

"I never savvied an automatic, and besides I was wearin' old cedar in my shirt-front, so I figures one gun enough.

"My Levis was brand-new, but I stopped at the brown front and bought some new pants. After I got into 'em the shirt I was wearin' looked pretty tough, so I slides that dry-goods pirate twelve more pesos for this piece of silk."

Shorty eyed it ruefully.

"He tried to sell me a new hat and a pair of boots. But I was rearin' to look the layout over, so I eased out on the street.

"I took in two movies without payin'. The guinea at the second shows calls me 'mister' plumb respectful, and leads me to a seat. That night at supper I met Dogie Si.

" 'Beats flankin' calves and fightin' broncs,' says I, 'and spoon vittles every meal.' Dogie was plumb jealous.

"The carnival was at the ball-park, half a mile from town. I 'd seen all the shows and was sittin' through that divin' act for the third time, when here comes a wild-eyed *hombre* yellin' for a cop. I was gonna help him hunt one when he spies my badge. I'd plumb forgot my dooty. But he reminds me in a hurry. A big Mexican was throwin' rocks at a stand full of glassware and crockery. The crowd was enjoyin' it, for that big Mex shore could throw. Every time he throwed somethin' smashed. At every smash that wild-eyed owner'd let out a squall, sort of like a dog a-howlin'.

" 'Look here, *hombre*,' I says, 'this ain't no baby-rack! Ya got to cut it out and come with me. Ya can't act that-a-way.'

" '*Si, señor*,' he says in a quiet voice, and come along plump peaceful like. He was n't a bit of trouble.

"We'd walked about a quarter when I rolled a cigarette. I was thinkin' how soft this job was 'longside of punchin' cows, when I struck a light. Then it happened—I was gettin' up on all fours and had old cedar out when it happened again. A mule must have kicked me. About the time my head would clear a little, I'd get it again. Finally the whole remuda run over me and I went to sleep.

# A NIGHT IN TOWN

When I woke up the Mexican was gone. I struck a few matches and found old cedar layin' in the dirt. Then I started figurin' it out. There was n't no horse-tracks in the dust. Must have been that *hombre's* hobnailed shoes. His tracks was everywhere. I struck more matches and cut his sign. He 'd gone back toward the park. I was 'most there when I met Bob.

" 'What 's the trouble?' he says.

" 'I 'm lookin' for a big Mexican with hobnailed shoes.'

" 'Well,' says Bob, lookin' me over. 'He ought to be easy to find—if you put up any kind of a fight a-tall.'

"I did n't look like much. I had old cedar in my hand and shore was on the prod.

" 'Why did n't ya handcuff the bird?' says Bob.

" 'Lucky I did n't. He might have killed me if we 'd been necked together.'

"The big Mex had gone straight back to the ball-park. The glassware was 'most gone when we found him, but he was throwin' rocks again. I itched to bore him through, but Bob says, 'No! Ya can't kill a man for throwin' rocks.'

" 'How come?' says I. 'Look what he done to me.'

"The big Mex acted plumb gentle when we gathered him again. *'Si señor,'* he says in that quiet voice, as we led him down the road.

"About half-way in we caught a ride. The *hombre* sat between us, and everything went fine until Bob struck a match. Then it happens again with Bob on the receivin' end.

"Do somethin'!" he sputters.

" 'Ya can't kill a man for throwin' rocks,' says I.

"Bob's breath was gettin' short. I was n't in shape for no more fightin.' So I lets the Mexican feel the butt of old cedar right where his hair was the thinnest. . . .

# A NIGHT IN TOWN

"When we got to town I quit."

Shorty rolled another cigarette.

"That divin' act shore was fine."

"What about the Mexican?" says Slim presently.

"Oh, him?" says Shorty. "He's still asleep, I reckon."

# THE LUNGER

# THE LUNGER

THERE'S no denying it. Old Buck Johnson certainly did have a way of his own around stock. Other people's calves was always a-follerin' old Buck home. Some folks went so far as to say that if a man got close enough he could see the rope between the calf's neck an' old Buck's saddle-horn. An' just after I went to work for him old Buck showed me a cow of his that had twin calves.

"Ever see that happen before, Shorty?" says Buck. I had to admit I never had, for one of them calves was at least a month older than the other. Naturally, there was some talk about old Buck through the country, but any stray puncher who happened by Buck's place was always sure of a meal for himself an' a feed of grain for his horse.

Buck's place was over on the river, just off the reservation line. As outfits go, he did n't have much of a spread. Sometimes old Buck put on a hand while he was brandin' up, but for the most part he lived alone. It was just a happen-so that I met up with Buck. I'd rode the chuck line clear across the State. It was my first summer in Arizona, an' I was such a kid that no one seemed to want to take a chance with me till I met Buck. My horse was plumb give out the night I happened by his place. I was headin' over towards the Flyin' V. I'd always worked on the flats in New Mexico, and this mountain country bothered me a heap. I was ridin' an' old long-legged bronc, an' he was just about to quit. I figured on easin' him up one more long ridge before I pulled the saddle off. It made me rub my eyes at first, for just as we topped out I saw a little cabin standin' in the clear. The chimney was a-smokin', an' the little patch of garden made me wonder if I was n't seein' things. Then Buck come out an' asked me to get down.

I worked for Buck for 'most two months until he got his calves all branded up. An' Buck was awful good to me. We usually rode together unless Buck's leg was hurtin' him, an' then I rode alone. For he was pretty badly crippled up. He was well over sixty, an' his hair was white as snow.

# THE LUNGER

It seems that Buck had done most everything from breakin' horses to dealin' cards. He'd been a ranger before the territory was a State, and then again I heard him mention somethin' that come up when he was tendin' bar. From his talk I gathered old Buck must be a Texan, but in any of his yarns he never did go back that far. The nearest he ever came to that was one night in the cabin, when I was readin' out loud to him. A nester kid had left a paper when he passed the ranch that day. The paper was all of two weeks old, but it was just before election, an' old Buck was all het up about the news. I was readin' a copy of the governor's

Ross Santee

[135]

speech. From the way old Buck kept sniffin' I 'lowed he was n't exactly in sympathy with the governor's politics. But he never did say nothin' until I got down to where the governor in the course of his remarks opined that he had landed in the State, afoot, some forty years ago.

"That 's nothin' to brag about," says Buck. "I was afoot myself when I first landed here." An' then old Buck told me that the sheriff had killed his horse just before he crossed the Arizona line.

Buck never did have much to say when we was ridin' together. He did most of his talkin' at night. Sometimes he 'd go for days an' never say a word, an' then again he 'd open up an' talk to me just like he 'd knowed me all his life. Buck always got breakfast while I was wranglin' horses in the mornin', as we usually left the ranch by sun-up. For old Buck liked to get back to camp by the middle of the evenin' an' work in his garden for a spell. He had a few head of broncs that I was breakin', an' every evenin' when we got back to camp I always fooled with one of them a while. There was n't none of them any trouble to speak of, except one bronc he called the Shinnery Boar. He had a way of fallin' over backwards, an' a dozen

different times he come within an ace of catchin'
me. Old Buck had told me several times he
thought I'd better turn the critter out, but I kept
thinkin' maybe the horse would give it up. On
this particular evenin' old Buck had dropped his
hoe an' come to watch the fun. The Shinnery
Boar was actin' worse than common, an' after he'd
buried the saddle-horn in the middle of the corral
for the third time old Buck told me to take my
saddle off.

"Did it ever occur to you," says Buck, "just
what might happen if you was in the saddle when
he hit the ground?"

I told old Buck I had a pretty good idea, but I
was n't figurin' none on gettin' caught. Old Buck
says somethin' about "lack of imagination" and
hobbles off towards the cabin to see how the frijoles
was a-cookin'. It made me hot under the collar,
but I did n't say nothin' until we'd got the dishes
washed that night. An' then I up an' told Old
Buck I'd never seen a horse that I was 'fraid of
yet—an' asked him what he meant by the imagination stuff.

"Nobody," says old Buck a-loadin' his pipe an'

hitchin' his bum leg over a pack-saddle, "admires
a game man more than I do. An' just why one
man will have more courage than another is somethin' I never could savvy. Of course, there's a
lot in gettin' used to anything. But I never did
know a bronco-fighter yet that ever had any imagination. If he had any he did n't break horses very
long. It's probably just as well they don't, for
most of us would have to work our stock afoot.
Sometimes a man will up and pull a thing that
he'd be scared to death to try a second time.
Maybe it's his liver that affects his nerve, but
mostly it's his imagination. An' then again it
may be somethin' else. I knowed a feller once
that sure did have me fooled. I thought he was
the gamest guy I'd ever seen. Ben Wilson was
his name, but everybody called him Kid, and he
come from some place back in Illinoy. The Kid
was a deputy sheriff when I met him, an' he'd been
in Arizona 'most a year. I'd been workin' for an
outfit up on Tonto, and we'd come to town to ship.
It was when they built the big smelter on the hill,
an' everything was wide open then. The night
our outfit got to town some Mexican killed a deputy named Hicks. We had n't any more than

landed when I met old Bob, the sheriff, comin'
down the street. Me and Bob had rode together
years ago, an' old Bob asked me if I would help
him out. They had the Mexican in jail, but the
whole town was in an uproar and the place was
full of punchers fillin' up, and they all was makin'
threats. Bob was afraid some fool would set the
fireworks off an' they'd try an' lynch the spick.
It seems the Kid had took him by himself an' then
stood off the crowd alone until he got the Mexican
behind the bars.

"None of us slept any to speak of that night,
but by mornin' the crowd had cooled off an' decided to let the law take its course. That was
when I fust noticed the Kid. He wasn't much to
look at. He was of medium height an' awful thin,
an' every little while he coughed. He wasn't the
sort of person you'd look at twice until you saw his
eyes. They wasn't any color to speak of, but they
bothered me a heap. Did ya ever see a dog when
it's been hurt? Well, that's the way the Kid af-
fected me. I got to know him awful well—at least,
I thought I did—for they put me on in Hicks's
place. There used to be a bench in front of the

sheriff's office, an' the Kid spent nearly all his time a-settin' in the sun. As the months went by he put on weight, an' I scarcely ever heard him cough. Whenever they sent us out to get a man the Kid was always first to leave, an' it used to make my blood run cold to see the chances that he took. I used to try to tell him not to risk his neck that way.

" 'Oh, that 's all right,' the Kid would say, and sort of smile, an' then I 'd get that look of his—just like a dog, when it 's been hurt.

"I 'd been a deputy for 'most a year, I guess, an' this night me an' Bob was just about to take a drink down at the old St. Elmo Bar, when all of a sudden we heard a shot—an' then two more. It seems a Mexican was runnin' wild in a pool-room further down the street. He had the place to himself when we got there, an' the biggest part of the street in front of the joint, for he was shootin' at everything that moved outside. A big crowd was a-gatherin', but they all kept 'way back in the clear. Me an' Bob was figurin' on how to gather the gentleman without committin' suicide, when here comes the Kid all out of breath. 'You all stay here,' the Kid says, 'an' I 'll take him in myself.'

# THE LUNGER

" 'Not on your life,' says Bob; 'he 'll kill ya before ya ever get ten feet.'

" 'Oh, that 's all right,' the Kid says.   An' then I got that look again.

"Before we got a chance to pull him back the Kid had slipped away.   The next thing I knowed he was standin' all alone out in the street, a-facin' towards the pool-room door.   The Kid was clear across the street from the pool-room, an' as he started walkin' towards the door the Mexican took a shot at him.   But it went wild.   The Kid was walkin' awful slow.   It seemed an age to me. You could have heard a pin drop in the crowd as the Kid walked towards that door.   He walked the distance clear across the street an' never made a move to pull his gun.   As he reached the door the Mexican shot again.   I thought the Kid was done.   But he kept walkin' straight ahead.   He walked so slow it did n't seem to me he hardly even moved.   Me and old Bob was up to the window by now, but before we got a chance to shoot I saw the Kid put out his hand.   An' in that quiet voice of his he asked the *hombre* for his gun.   I never saw the like before, for the Mexican hands it over to the Kid—and then collapsed.   I was weak as a kitten myself, but, man!—you should have heard that crowd.

"It's not more than a week after the Kid pulls that stunt that I'm settin' out on the bench in front of the office in the sun. I'd just filled my pipe when the Kid comes up the street.

"The Kid sets down on the bench without sayin' a word an' starts to roll a cigarette. His hands was shakin', so he finally give it up. I couldn't imagine what was wrong, he's so upset. An' then he asks me if I knowed the reason why he come out here. I said I'd knowed that all along his lungs was bad. The Kid nodded, an' then he says the doctor back in Illinoy had just give him a year to live when he left home.

"'What the hell does he know!' says I. 'Ain't ya been here nearly two years now?'

"'Well,' says the Kid, a-tryin' to roll another cigarette an' spillin' tobacco all over himself, 'I've been to see a doc just now. He looked me over awful close an' he tells me my lungs is all healed up an' I'm all right.' An' I'll be damned if the Kid don't break down an' cry.

"It's an hour later, an' the Kid an' me is still a-settin' on the bench. I had my arm around the

# THE LUNGER

Kid when Bob come out of the door. Bob says he wants some *hombre* that had just cut up a Chink down in the lower end of the town.

" 'There 's no use of both of you goin', for he 's not bad,' says Bob. An' then he tells the Kid that he can go. It sort of took my breath away, an' still I could n't help but laugh to see Bob's face, for the Kid he up and hands Bob back his badge an' says he 's through—that he 's not takin' chances any more."

# LION LORE

# LION LORE

GRANDMA HARROD always called them painters. I have always had a vivid recollection of the stories she told us when I was a small boy in Iowa. Grandma Harrod lived next door, and my youngest sister and I always stayed with her while the rest of the family were at church.

It was on these long winter evenings that she told us stories of her girlhood in Kentucky. Stories of bear fights and of painters that screamed like a woman in the woods at night. How the painter lay along the branch of a tree overhanging some lonely mountain trail and waited for the unsuspecting traveler to pass by. And how the painter sometimes followed the settlers to their very door.

She herself had once been followed by a painter. With her brother she had been working in a sugar-camp nearly a mile from the cabin where they lived. It was dark before they started home. They had only gone a little way through the woods when they heard the painter scream. Her brother had no weapon save the ax he carried, and the two had fled in terror. Once Grandma had fallen and as her brother helped her up they heard the painter scream again, this time much closer than before. Stumbling over fallen logs, they finally reached the cabin door just as the animal screamed again at the edge of the clearing where the little cabin stood.

This story always left me very weak, and although I heard it many times it was always a great relief to me when they reached the cabin door. For the story as Grandma told it lost nothing in the telling. Grandma Harrod was dramatic to say the least.

Having an illusion broken to me has always been very disconcerting. But years later when I was punching cows in Arizona I found that the painter is one of the most cowardly animals known.

There is probably no other animal that is known by as many different names. It is sometimes called the puma or cougar. The old-timer usually speaks of it as panther or painter.

But in Arizona it is simply called lion. I was always thankful the punchers did n't call them painters, for somehow the word "lion" has always sounded much safer to me. Even to this day the word "painter" always gives me a slight chill and sometimes causes weakness.

"To squall like a panther" is a common saying among cow-punchers in Arizona. And during one round-up I worked with a puncher who was known as Panther. He was one of the mildest-mannered men I have ever known, but whenever he yelled, when we were on the drive, he could easily be heard for half a mile.

The lion is found in the rough brushy country, and like all wild animals the lion has habits peculiar to itself. It is knowing these habits and understanding the nature of the animal that make the successful hunter. The lion hunts mostly at night. During the day he lays up, either on some ledge of rock or on some high brushy rim.

Unless he happens to be hunting, the lion, like the loafer wolf, always follows the same ridges and crosses through the same saddles when he travels through the country.

After one lion is killed the rest will often leave the country. They may be gone for months. But whenever they return they always follow the same old ridges and make their crossings through the same saddles.

The lion is particularly fond of horse and goat meat. He will seldom kill a calf if there is a colt or goat in the country. The loafer wolf always hamstrings his quarry and eats on the flank, but the lion breaks the animal's neck and cuts the jugular vein and usually makes his first meal from the brisket.

After the lion has made his kill and has eaten what he wants he always covers the carcass, usually with sticks and leaves. If the lion has a kill in the country he will usually be found hiding not far away. For unless he is frightened away the lion always stays near-by until the kill is eaten.

The lion will eat nothing that is spoiled or tainted. He will remove the entrails of a rabbit as cleanly as a butcher before he eats it.

The success of a lion-hunt depends upon the dogs, and of course this brings it back to the hunter who has trained them, for an untrained dog is useless on a lion-hunt. A good lion dog will never open on any other trail. But good lion dogs are very scarce, and it takes a hunter several years to train one.

Cleve Miller once told me that a man's lifetime was just long enough to break one mule and train one pack of lion dogs. Cleve has one of the finest packs of hounds in the Southwest, and during the month of February, 1923, he killed fifteen lions with his pack of dogs.

George England, another friend of mine, has hunted for years with two old spotted hounds he calls Old Rattler and Rusty.

Unlike most lion hunters, old George will let his dogs run anything. There is evidently some sort of understanding between old George and his dogs. For old George can always tell just what his dogs are trailing.

Old George has hunted on the Cross S range for years, and whenever he stays at the horse-camp his dogs often follow Bill Teal. One day when Bill was out hunting horses the dogs opened on a hot trail not over a mile from the camp, and the dogs were soon out of hearing. Bill cares nothing about hunting, and as soon as he found the horse he was looking for he went on back to the camp.

"Where are the dogs?" was the first thing old George asked when Bill rode up. Bill told him they were running something, but he did n't know what it was.

"How were they running?" asked old George.

"They was runnin' neck and neck when they passed me," said Bill.

"That 's a lion," said old George, and without another word he saddled up a horse and went to hunt his dogs. Bill said he figured that was taking quite a bit for granted, considering the country was full of different kinds of varmints. But in an hour old George came riding in with Old Rattler and Rusty at his heels, with a huge lion-skin tied behind him on the saddle.

The Cross S outfit always paid old George a bounty of fifty dollars for each lion and loafer that he caught. And the biggest year's catch George ever made while I was with the outfit was twelve lions and nine loafer wolves. Like most old lion hunters old George's dogs came first, and he was often more considerate of his dogs than of his friends.

The first time I ever saw old George the outfit was camped at Tanks Cañon on the upper Cross S

range. And it was just at sundown that old
George came into camp with Old Rattler and
Rusty at his heels.

The outfit had no night-hawk at the time, and
each puncher stood horse-guard for two hours during the night. My guard was from two until four
in the morning. Ordinarily I slept soundly until
the puncher I relieved came and woke me up. But
this night the dogs kept every one awake, for they
barked each time the guard came in. Occasionally they were quiet for a spell, but in a little
while they both broke out again.

Next morning I supposed of course that George
would make some sort of an apology for his dogs,
for they had kept the camp awake most of the
night. But instead of an apology old George
turned in and cussed us well for keeping Old
Rattler and Rusty awake.

When I asked old George if he had ever heard a
panther scream, George said he did n't know.
But George said he guessed they screamed all
right, for folks all said they did. Cleve Miller
said he never heard a panther squall, and Cleve has
been a cow-puncher and a lion-hunter all his life.

M. E. Musgrave, another friend of mine, said

yes.   Musgrave is in charge of all the government hunters in the State, and he has spent his lifetime in the hills.   And Musgrave says that once a person hears one scream he will not forget it till he dies.

The only incident I ever heard of any one ever being chased by a lion in Arizona was told me by Fritz Wolf, a rancher over on Stanley Butte. Wolf's outfit was working on the San Pedro at the time.

"It was nearly dark," said Fritz, "when the horse-wrangler went out to throw the horses together so they would n't scatter in the night.   The wrangler was nothing but a kid, and he came into camp a little later scared to death and pretty much skinned up.   The kid said he had been chased by a lion and his horse had bucked him off.   We all had a good laugh, for the kid was pretty spooky anyhow, and we knew that he was trying to alibi himself for gettin' throwed.

"The kid stayed with his story, and so next morning we went out to see if we could find any lion-tracks.   The kid had told the truth all right. We found the lion-tracks, and we could see where

# LION LORE

he'd run the horses for most a hundred yards. But whether the lion was chasin' the horses or the kid, was somethin' we could n't figure out."

Roping a lion is not a common thing, but it is sometimes done around a cow outfit.

A puncher over near Wilcox was range-branding when he happened into a lion that had just left its kill.

"I was n't packin' no gun," said the puncher. "But the country was pretty open, so I built me a loop and charged. The lion was too full to put on much speed so I did n't have no trouble gettin' a throw. But the lion run through my loop. An' instead of ketchin' her around the neck the loop drawed up around her belly. Everything begin to happen then, for the minute the loop drawed up my pony went to buckin'. I was in a helluva fix for a while, with a horse an' lion both buckin' on the ends of a thirty-five-foot rope.

"I finally managed to take up a little slack. An' when I did I pitched the rope up over the limb of a tree and drawed the lion up off the ground. I finally got my pony quiet enough to git off an' tie him, and as soon I got the pony anchored I killed the lion with rocks."

# LION LORE

Oscar Cline, a puncher I know from Tonto Basin, once roped and tied a lion.

"We was fixin' fence," said Oscar, "when we found a lion kill. The kill was only a few hours old, so I went back to the ranch an' got the dogs. An' it was n't no time at all until we jumped three lion kittens. The dogs killed one but we took the other two alive. We was just a-thinkin' we 'd lost the old one when she run out across a little flat.

"We had trouble in gettin' our horses close to her, but as I went by I managed to make a lucky throw and caught her round the neck. She choked right down, so I got off my horse and tied her with my piggin string.

"We figured we 'd take her in alive, so we left the old man to watch her while me an' my brother went back to the ranch to rig up some outfit. We never got to take her in alive, though, for we was n't any more than out of sight when she come alive an' started chewin' on the piggin string. This was too much for the old man. He did n't think much of the idea anyhow, so he knocked her in the head."

Bull Moore and another Double Circle puncher

once ran a lion into a cave. The cave was in a ledge of rock about six feet off the ground. The punchers finally decided to smoke the lion out, so Bull crawled back into the entrance and built a fire.

"The cave was pretty narrow," said the puncher, "and Bull had to crawl in on his belly. I was watchin' the entrance when I heard a riot inside.

"I thought for a minute Bull had gone crazy and had tried to ride the lion out, for they shot out of the cave together with Bull holdin' the lion round the belly with both arms.

"Bull lost his holt when they hit the ground together. But aside from bein' knocked out by the fall Bull was n't hurt. After Bull come to he said he did n't remember nothin' about takin' holt of no lion. But Bull said he was so scared when she run over him he guessed that 's what he 'd done."

The experience had evidently not cooled Bull's sporting blood, for Cleve Miller and I met him once when we were in a bear-hunt. Cleve and I had stopped to rest the dogs and let our horses blow, when Bull drove up in a flivver. Bull had evidently had several drinks, for he apologized for his empty bottle.

"Too bad I ain't got any more," said Bull.

# LION LORE

"With one more drink I'd like to get a-holt of some bear's tail an' whoop him right on down the road."

I have never forgotten my own misgivings when I went on my first lion-hunt. Aside from the stories Grandma had told me when I was a small boy, I knew nothing of the nature of a lion. I went prepared for the worst. Aside from the 30–40 rifle that I carried, I took a long-barrel six-shooter. The ammunition that I carried made it hard for me to mount a horse. I said nothing to Swede about my misgivings at the time, for Swede Larsen is a government hunter, and hunting lion to him is simply a part of the day's work.

Swede was camped on the upper Cross S range about sixty miles from Globe. The Government has many hunters in the State, and each has his own particular range. The hunters work on a straight salary furnished by the Government. And there is no bounty paid. Some hunters work on wolves and coyotes, using nothing but traps.

But Swede hunted with dogs. The bear are seldom molested unless they are found to be killing stock. But the lion and the loafer wolf have always been the foes of the cow-men, and of all the predatory animals that prey on live stock the lion and the loafer wolf are the most destructive.

Swede's dogs were all young, for his old lead dog had died shortly before he made the trip. There were three hounds and two wire-haired fox-terriers in the pack, and along with these we borrowed Old Rattler and Rusty from George England.

The wire-haired terriers, Stub and Sue, were only pups, but they ran with the other dogs and barked whenever the hounds opened. Of the other three hounds it was Jiggs who interested me most.

Swede never let his dogs run anything except lion and an occasional bear, and he always kept Jiggs at his heels, for Jiggs would run anything from a lizard to a cow. The lion is always found in country where deer are plentiful. And running deer was Jiggs's favorite pastime. Jiggs was whipped on an average of twice a day for running deer, but he never seemed to mind it.

One application of the rope was usually enough for the other hounds, but Jiggs seemed to feel the game was worth it, for the moment Swede finished with the rope and turned him loose Jiggs always barked and wagged his tail, just as if he'd enjoyed it. Jiggs was the fastest dog in the pack, but Swede never turned him loose unless the trail was hot. Then Jiggs would leave, as Swede said, "with a jar." On one lion that Jiggs treed he outran the other dogs so far that he was half-way up in the tree with the lion before the other dogs arrived.

Swede and I rode mules when we followed the dogs. We left camp long before daylight. During the dry season the dogs can work only for a few hours after the sun gets hot, but Swede and I were usually so far from camp by sun-up that it took us the rest of the day to get back.

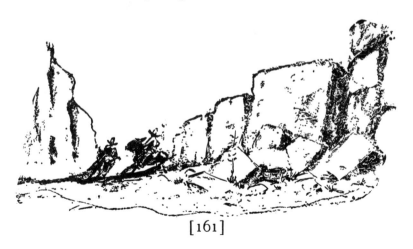

# MEN AND HORSES

The first morning we were out the dogs opened not over two hundreds yards from camp. It was too dark to see what they were trailing, but Swede thought it was a lion from the way they barked, until he finally dismounted and found a huge bear track.

It was too late to cut off the dogs, for the trail was hot, so we spurred our mules and tried to keep in hearing of the hounds. While we whipped and spurred, Swede cursed his dogs for running bear.

But visions of a bear-fight at early dawn were the things I thought about. Stories that Grandma told me years ago went flashing through my mind. My illusions were gradually dispelled, however, for we never could approach the bear. We whipped and spurred for all of fifteen miles, and never once did we catch sight of him.

One after another the young dogs gave out and quit, but Old Rattler and Rusty kept on. Twice Old Rattler barked treed, and Swede and I both cursed him well, for the moment we rode up he went bawling on down the cañon again. It was nearly noon before he finally quit.

Afterward old George told me that this was the

# LION LORE

way Old Rattler always did.  George often fol-
lowed his dogs afoot, and whenever he got behind,
Old Rattler barked treed and waited till old
George caught up.

The country was full of bear, and there was
scarcely a day but what we had a race.  Sometimes
Swede managed to cut off the dogs.  But more
often we ran the bear until the dogs gave out.
Swede and I hunted for a week before we found
any lion sign.

Then one morning as we were riding the rim of
Black River, Swede showed me a lion "scratch."
The scratch was in the pine-needles just underneath the rim.  And it was much the same as a dog
might make.  Swede said the lion's trail was hours

old, for it was only on the brushy side of the ridge that the dogs could take it at all.

For an hour we sat on our mules and listened to the dogs as they worked the trail slowly on down the rocky ridge.  Stub and Sue ran back and forth not quite knowing what it was all about.

Twice in his excitement, Stub tried to whip Old Rattler.  But Old Rattler simply shook him off and went on with his business of cold trailing. Swede had just dismounted, as he said, "to rest his saddle," when we noticed the new note in Old Rattler's voice.

The next moment the hounds all opened in chorus, and the whole pack left in full cry down the ridge. "He's jumped," said Swede as he swung up on his mule.  And we headed on the dead run down the ridge.  Swede lost his hat, and the biggest part of my flannel shirt was left hanging on the brush.  For a mile we followed.  Suddenly Swede pulled up his mule and listened. "He's treed," said Swede.  The bawling of the hounds had suddenly changed to a chorus of short sharp barks.

The lion was treed in a scrub-oak about half-way

down the side of the rocky ridge. The moment we came in sight of him he jumped out of the tree, with the pack in full cry at his heels again. But the lion only ran about two hundred yards before the dogs put him up another tree. This time the lion never moved when we rode up.

The actual killing of a lion is the poorest sport of all the hunt, for the lion never stands at bay and fights. And I have never heard of a lion charging a hunter. It is true the lion sometimes kills a dog or two if he happens only to be wounded, but the lion will not even face the dogs unless he is wounded or is in a corner. And the barking of the smallest dog is often enough to put an eight-foot lion up the nearest tree. Swede simply shot the lion through the neck, and it was quite dead by the time it fell among the dogs.

"Good lion dogs is mighty scarce," says Swede, "and I don't want my dogs tore up."

A month later, as we were coming in to mail Swede's reports, a party of tourists stopped us down by Cassadora Springs and asked the way to White River. When one of the women noticed the three lion-skins in the back of our flivver she grew very much excited. Nothing that Swede said could reassure her. She insisted that it was only modesty on Swede's part that made him talk the way he did; she was sure that hunting lion must be very dangerous.

As we drove on down the road Swede shook his head and laughed.

"It's no use," said Swede. "For you never can convince no one that the sport in lion hunting is all in listening to the dogs an' tryin' to keep in hearing when they run; they all insist it's dangerous."

# THE ROUGH STRING

# THE ROUGH STRING

"I LIKE 'em," said the Pecos Kid, "for an outlaw horse is usually gamer than a gentle one. I've rode the rough string an' been a-snappin' broncs since I was old enough to make a hand. An' a outlaw has always interested me a heap more than a gentle horse. For when you find a outlaw horse that's really game he's just about the gamest thing I know."

Every cow outfit of any size has its rough string. And to me the horses that make up the rough string and the peeler who rides them are one of the most interesting things about a cow outfit. For the rough string is made up of broncs and old outlaw horses that the average cow-puncher can't ride. The peeler who rides them usually draws a few dollars a month more than a regular puncher. Often for the trifling sum of ten dollars extra he rides these wild devils and does the work of a regular hand. It is more of a matter of pride than anything else with a peeler. The Pecos Kid rode the rough string at the Bar F Bar for years without any extra pay. For the wilder they came the more they interested Pecos. The best riders always draw the worst horses. And I never saw the Pecos Kid on a gentle horse in my life.

"Mebbe I've given the horse the worst of it," said Pecos. "But horses is a heap like humans anyway. For every one of them is different. But whenever you see an outlaw horse, nine cases out of ten you can trace it back to the ignorance or cruelty of some cow-puncher. Pebbles was that way. He's been in the rough string ever since, an' he's one of the best horses I ever rode.

"The boys tell me the peeler that broke him in was what you'd call a ridin' fool. Fact is, he rode too well. This peeler was sparkin' some nester gal that lived down the road a ways, an' every evenin' he'd ride down there an give his gal a show. They said that Pebbles never even humped his back until this peeler gigged him with the spurs and made him buck. But it was n't any time at all before he got so he could wipe things up.

"There's plenty of peelers who can ride the horse an' scratch him every jump he makes. An' Pebbles knows it, too. But he's throwed more men than any other horse this outfit ever had.

# THE ROUGH STRING

Most outlaw horses will break into when you first top 'em off. But Pebbles seldom does. For he knows as well as any one that the peeler settin' on his back can ride or he would n't be up there. But Pebbles is always watchin' for his chance to catch the peeler off his guard, or the first time any little thing goes wrong. Pebbles is almost sure to get his man.

"An' when the dust clears up, the peeler is usually sittin' on the ground with both hands full of dirt.

"A kid named Jones was ridin' Pebbles when I first went to workin' here. They had two rough strings out that fall. Jones rode the horse for 'most two weeks, an' Pebbles never did a thing. An' Jones began to think the boys was spoofin' him about the horse. But Pebbles was just waitin' for his chance, an' when he got this Jones he certainly got him right.

"Me an' Shorty was at the hold-up the morning it happened. Just sittin' on our horses a-augerin' about nothin' in particular while we waited for the drive to come in. The country was awful rough an' brushy up in there. An' from where we was in the cañon we could n't see a thing. But all at once we heard the rocks a-rollin'. I thought at first it was a steer or some one comin' off the hill.

" 'It's Pebbles,' says Shorty, 'a-buckin' with that Kid.' "An' as we listened we could hear old Pebbles hit. For each jump he took as he came off the hill, he started a different bunch of rocks to rollin'.

"We had started down the cañon to see if the Kid was hurt when Pebbles come a-bustin' out at us without any saddle or bridle on. But Shorty roped the horse as he went by.

"The Kid was unconscious when we found him. I thought at first he must be dead. But he was still sittin' in the saddle, upside down, and blamed if he did n't have his feet in both his stirrups.

"I filled my hat with water at a little spring not far away, an' it was n't but a little while until the Kid come to an' said he could ride in back to camp. We traded horses all around. For Shorty was the only one of us who was ridin' a gentle horse, an' he staked the Kid to it.

"The Kid was still wabbly on his pins, an' both his eyes had closed by the time I got him back to camp. Me an' the cook went all over him to see if anything was broke. For we was sixty miles from town. There was n't nothin' busted as far as we could see. But I held him while the cook painted his face an' arms with iodine. For they looked just like raw beef. That iodine sort of brought him out of it. For before I went back to the hold-up he set up an' talked a bit.

"The Kid said he had tried to head a steer. But as he went to dodge some brush his saddle turned a little bit. That was when Peb-bles saw his chance an' turned right off the hill with him.

"Not many horses could keep their feet a-buckin' off a place like that. Jones said he looked each jump that Pebbles made to see him fall. But Pebbles reached the bottom of the hill all right before he spilled the pack.

"Next day they gave the horse to me, an' the boss told me to set the hair on him. I rode him

four days straight. It
was enough to kill
'most any horse. But
the fourth evenin' as
we was comin' into
camp he broke
into with me,
an' it was only
by pullin' all
the leather I
could get, I
managed to
keep my seat. It
was a week before the
Kid could ride. But when
he did he asked for Pebbles
back again. The Kid shore
knowed a horse all right.

"They gave me Pebbles when Jones finally quit.
An I've had him in my string ever since. He's
never got me yet. An' what's more he never will
unless he catches me asleep. An' he's some horse.
For he can do more work than any other four I've
got.

[174]

# THE ROUGH STRING

"Bald Hornet was in the rough string when I first went to workin' here.  But I whipped it out of him.  For he's not game.  An' he always quits just like a dog with anybody that can ride.  For a horse always tells if a man has any fear of him.  You may fool the men you're workin' with.  But you'll never fool a horse.

"It was the way Bald Hornet had of pitchin' that got the boys afraid of him.  He'd make two or three jumps an' then he'd rear, just like he was goin' over backwards.  An' the minute the puncher loosened up his hold so he could get clear of him, bingo!  Bald Hornet would go right back to pitchin', an' throw his man while he was still loose on him.  He got me twice that way before I finally got it through my head that Bald Hornet never had no idea of goin' over backwards.

"Next time I stepped aboard him I took a heavy quirt.  He made about three jumps with me, an' then he reared, just like he was goin' over backwards.  But this time I did n't loosen up, an' when he hit the ground again I was all set for him.  An' it was n't long before he quit, for he did n't like that quirt.  Since then he's never even tried to pitch with me.  But every time they give the horse

[175]

some new man Bald Hornet always tries him out to see if he can ride. An' if he can Bald Hornet never bucks with him again.

"There never was no reason for Old Hooker bein' in the rough string, for he was just nervous an' high-strung. It was very seldom that he ever pitched. But any time he got excited he 'd rear an' throw himself right over backwards. He was one of them kind of horses that only one man should ride. For if you was quiet an' easy with him he 'd never do a thing. An', man! how he could run! You could ketch a cow on him 'most any place. I figured I 'd like to keep the horse myself. An' I never said a word. But when the boss saw how he 'd gentled down, he took the horse himself. An' Old Hooker is the top horse of this remuda now.

"Happy Jack is one of them horses there 's no accountin' for. For Happy was a gentle horse for years. The boys tell me he pitched a little when he was just a colt, but not enough to talk about. An' then he went along for several years an' never even humped his back. He was one of the gentlest horses this outfit ever owned. But one day for no apparent reason he bucked a puncher off.

Ross Santee

The boys all thought it was funny at the time, an' they give this guy the laugh. But from that day on he's always pitched, an' I'll say that he knows how. He's gentle an' kind to handle, an' a man can crawl all under him. But any time you get on his back you'd better be set for a ride. I've tried in every way I know to take it out of him. But it's no use. An' Happy Jack is game all right, for when you use the quirt on him it only makes him worse.

"There's lots of good horses that I know would be in the rough string if it was n't for the man who handled them. There's what you'd call a one-man horse. Take Asia, that Bill Griggs rides. He bucks with anybody that gits on his back 'cept Bill. An Asia has never even humped his back with him.

"An' then there's Shimmie that belongs to Swede. I think he's the worst I ever saw, for he won't let nobody even touch his nose 'cept Swede, an' Swede can do most anything with him.

"About the gamest horse I ever rode was one they gave me at the Diamond D's. An' he was about the sorriest one for looks I ever saw. I was just a button at the time, an' when I rode in there one

night an' hit 'em for a job a-peelin' broncs the boss
just laughed at me. It made me sore as hell. An'
I told him if he did n't think that I could ride, to
trot one of his rough ones out. An' if I could n't
ride him I 'd go on down the road that night. That
sort of interested him, an' he told me to come on
inside an' eat, an' if I thought I could handle the
rough string he 'd stake me to a job.

"Next morning they led old Sontag out. I had
some trouble a-gettin' my wood on him. For he
was the outfightin'est horse I 've ever seen. He
tried to use his teeth an' strike with those front feet
of his. But I finally got his foot tied up an' got
my tree laced on.

"When they turned him loose he broke into an'
went sky-high with me. I think he was the hardest
buckin' horse I ever rode. He had me pullin'
leather on the second jump. But by pullin' everything in sight I managed to keep my seat. And,
say! when that horse finally quit I was about the
worst done-up kid you ever saw, for I was limber as
a rag. But I 'd won myself a job. But if that
horse had taken one more jump I know they 'd have
had to pick me up.

"The rest of the rough string was made up of

broncs. The feed was short that spring, an' so old Sontag come in for most of the hard ridin'. An' what a horse he was! For he could do the work of any other six I had. But he never did quit pitching. It made no difference if I rode him two days straight. He always broke into with me when I topped him off next morning. An' like as not he'd kick at me when I got off that night. But the more I seen of him the more I liked the horse, an' I finally got so I could ride him when he bucked without a-pullin' leather.

"I worked there till the outfit shipped their second bunch of steers. That was along in June. An' then I quit. For I was quite a rambler in them days, an' I never stayed long in one place.

"The night before I left I made a trade, an' the boys all hurrahed me. But next mornin' when I pulled my freight I had old Sontag under me. An' a lucky thing I did. For that horse I traded for Sontag, for all his looks, was an awful yellow pup.

"I'd always worked in the mountains, an' desert country was all new to me, but it interested me a heap. I was n't goin' no place in particular, just driftin', but the third night out I camped on the edge of the desert with an old prospector. He knowed the desert like a book, an' he told me about this water-hole I'd strike about half-way across. He said it was a good place to camp, an' I would n't have no trouble a-makin' the rest of the way across the second day.

"I started next mornin' before daylight. I was packin' a canteen of water in the saddle-horn. But while old Sontag pitched with me that mornin' the canteen fell to the ground. The old desert rat handed it up to me after the horse had quit his buckin'. An' as he did, old Sontag just missed the old man, takin' a shot at him with one of them hind feet of his. An' as I rode out of hearing that old man was still a-cussin' me.

"It was cool when I started. But even then there was a feel about the place I did n't like. It was somethin' you can't explain. An' I wondered then about the horse. I'd used him pretty hard the last few weeks. An' I knowed if anything went wrong with him the game was up with me. I tried to think about somethin' else, but my mind was always comin' back to this. An' once I come near turnin' him around an' headin' back. But, hell! thinks I, it's just because the desert's new to me.

# MEN AND HORSES

"I was plenty thirsty when the sun came up. But I figured on nursin' that old canteen along. An' I rode for several hours before I went to take a drink.   I knowed it the minute that I touched the string.   An' it made me sick all over.   For the canteen was empty.   I could n't account for it at first, but finally I found a little hole.   It was where the canteen had struck a rock when it fell to the ground that mornin'.

"Oh, well, I thought, it won't be long till I strike that water-hole; then everything will be all right. But the place was like a furnace now.   An' the wind that seemed to come from everywhere felt, like a red-hot blast.

"I tried to talk to old Sontag to keep my nerve from quittin' me.   But my tongue was so swelled an' thick I could n't make it work.

"It 's funny what a man will think of when he gets in a place like that.   You 'd suppose he 'd think of all the water-holes he 'd ever known in all his life.   But, instead, the only thing I could think of was a little spring I used to drink at when I was just a kid.   I could even see the water-cress. An' them little bugs that skipped around on top. . . .

# THE ROUGH STRING

"I would n't admit it at first. But finally I knowed I'd missed the water-hole. The nearest water I knowed of was at the Colorada, and I knowed it was all of sixty miles. Could old Sontag make it? I shut my eyes and tried to keep from thinkin'. Old Sontag was still a-goin' strong. But I knowed no other horse I ever rode could make it there, an' I had my doubts of him.

"I guess I went batty as a loon, for I took to seein' things. The movin' shadow that we made looked like a brook to me, an' I could see green grass and shady trees.

"When I woke up I could n't imagine where I was. The moon was shinin' in my face, an' some woman was holdin' my head in her lap. I knew she was talkin' to me, but I could n't understand a word she said. Then all at once it come over me that the woman was a Mexican. She would n't give me anything to drink at first, but instead she made me suck a wet rag that she kept dipping in an olla at her side.

"It was n't but a little while before I could set up an' look around. An' the first thing I seen when I set up was old Sontag. But he looked more like a ghost than any other thing I know. He was caked with sweat an' so thin an' drawn that both cinches hung loose on him. But I don't guess I 've ever seen a horse, before or since, that looked so good to me.

"While I was watchin' him a Mexican went over to unsaddle him. But the minute he come near, old Sontag raised that hammer head of his an' let drive with one hind foot. Man! what a horse he was!

"You know when a man fools with bad horses all his life most people thinks there 's somethin' wrong with him. Mebbe there is. For a peeler seldom quits until he 's hurt or too broke up to ride no more. A man that fools with bad ones is bound to be gettin' throwed. An' any time you hear somebody say he 's never been bucked off, you can bet your life that he ain't done much ridin'. Mebbe I 've just been lucky, for I 've been throwed as much as any one who rides, but the only time I was ever hurt was once when I was ridin' an old gentle horse.

"The horse was just trottin' down the road when he stubbed his toe with me. But when the dust cleared up an' I got to my feet I found I 'd sprained both wrists an' broke my collar-bone."

# THE KETCH DOG

# THE KETCH DOG

YOU 'VE never seen one at a dog-show, and the chances are good you 'll never see one of them in town. For the only place you find them is where the country 's rough. For a ketch dog's job is to worry a steer till the puncher gets there with his rope. An' a ketch dog is liable to be any old breed. But he 's sure to have plenty of guts. And the chances are good he won't be old. For a ketch dog's life is short.

Keno was a ketch dog. The evening I rode into the horse-camp he was laying just outside the horse-camp porch, watching the trail that leads down to the lower ranch. As he heard my pony coming up the trail he made an effort to get up. But when I spoke to Keno he never even turned his head. And as I rode by the dog, he was looking past me down the trail.

It was good to see old Sour Dough again.

"You 're just in time," he said, "for I was just about to charge the food all by myself to-night. You 're all bleached out since you was workin'

here. An' you was black as an Apache then.
Let's see! How long's it been? Blamed if it
is n't goin' on three years this fall. This outfit's
all been shot to hell since then. First, there was
the drouth. An' then the boss went broke. She's
changed hands twice since then. There's only a
couple of the old hands left. They 've even got
me wet-nursin' the saddle-horses instead of out
ketchin' steers."

Supper over, I washed the dishes while old Sour
Dough went out to take the nose-bags off the horses
and milk his cow. He had finished the milking
and was helping Keno to his bed upon the porch as
I came outside the house. And then I noticed for
the first time that Keno could n't walk. He could
use his two front legs all right, but he was broken
down behind.

"He caught one too many of them big steers, an'
they finally broke him down. He got hurt just a
little while before Dave Morgan died.

"I s'posed you 'd heard about Morgan, though.
His horse turned over on him, down on Cedar Flat.
The punchers never found him till the second day.
And he never did come to until just before he died.
He knowed the game was up all right. But

# THE KETCH DOG

Morgan shore died hard. Some of the boys thought he did n't know what he was sayin', for when they asked him was there any folks or any one he 'd like to have them notify, he says that Keno was the only friend he had.

"You know the way that Morgan had of keepin' to himself. I knowed him a-goin' on four years, an' in all that time I never heard of him a-takin' up with any one. But at that there was never a better roper or rider ever lived.

"Me and him range-branded together all one winter up underneath the rim, an' I don't guess he spoke as many as a dozen words to me. I thought when I first met him he must be swelled about something that I 'd done. But later on I found he was that way with every one. He was n't quarrelsome or anything like that, an' he always tended strictly to his own affairs. But the way he had of lookin' at a man would make you tend to yours. Most any man will soften up a little if you only give him time. Specially if you 're alone with him. But Morgan never did.

"It was while me an' him was range-brandin' together that Keno come to our camp. I never could figure out where he came from. He crawled into our camp one stormy night after me an' Morgan had turned in. He was about the sorriest lookin' pup I ever saw. But he looked more like a wolf than a dog even then. It was me that got up an' fed him. For I took a fancy to him from the first. But he never did have no use for me. He was Morgan's dog from the start. That was the thing I never could understand. For I never saw Morgan ever pet the dog. I tried in every way I knowed to get the dog to make friends with me. He would let me feed him. That was all. A dozen different times after Morgan had told the dog to stay in camp I tried to coax him off with me. But he 'd just lay on Morgan's bed an' look at me with them wolf-eyes of his, as if who the hell are you. But the funny part about it was he 'd go with any one if Morgan told him to. I never knowed that Morgan had made a ketch dog out of him until one day along towards spring.

"When the weather cleared so we could ride, Keno was always there at Morgan's heels. We never rode together. If Morgan rode north, I went south, and we seldom met except at sundown. Each of us kept his own calf tally. The tally never varied much until along toward spring. We were just about branded up, except some wild stuff underneath the rim. The country was so rough and brushy up in there I was n't havin' any luck at all. Then Morgan started bringing in two ears for every one I caught. Morgan was a good roper, but there was n't that much difference between us two. It did n't set with me. About once a month one of us would go to headquarters and bring back a load of chuck. The last time Morgan went he left the dog with me.

"'Go on with him,' was all he said; I did n't think the dog would follow me, but, sure enough, he did.

"I 'd rode along about four miles, I 'd say, with Keno trailin' along at my heels, when I jumped a

little bunch of cattle underneath the rim. Six
head there was, with a spotted wine-glass steer up
in the lead and two long-eared maverick yearlings
in the bunch. I built a loop and opened up old
Drifter for the race. The country was awful
rough and brushy up in there. I did n't get a
throw until we 'd gone about a half-mile. There
was a little open flat I knew the bunch would have
to cross before they dropped off into Seven Mile.
It was here I made my bid. The spotted wine-
glass steer was still up in the lead as we crossed the
little flat. The two long-eared maverick yearlings were a-runnin' just behind. I roped one
yearling as the bunch turned off into Seven Mile.
I 'd plumb forgot about the dog. I had n't any
more than made my throw when Keno jumped and
caught the other one. He caught the yearling by
the nose and then set back. That long-eared
maverick yearling shore did get an awful fall.
An' Keno held him till I got the yearling tied. I
branded six all told that day. But four of them
I never would have caught if Keno had n't been
along with me."

Keno was as big as a "loafer" wolf when the fall
round-up began. He made friends with no one.

Old Sour Dough tried in every way he knew to get the dog to make up with him. He would let old Sour Dough feed him; that was all.

Most of the time he laid on Morgan's bed. For Morgan had told the dog to stay in camp. He would watch for Morgan from the time the outfit left till they got in at night. No one ever saw Morgan even pet the dog. No one ever thought he really cared about the dog, until the day the outfit moved to Cottonwood.

The day the outfit moved, the boss sent Morgan on ahead to see about the water over there. When Morgan left he told the dog to stay in camp.

When the outfit moved camp the kitchen was the first to leave. It took six mules to carry it. The horses with the beds came next. The remuda always trailed along behind. Old Sour Dough tried to get the dog to follow him, but Keno would n't move. He thought, of course, the dog would follow later on. The wrangler said he called to the dog. But Keno would n't come.

From Alkali to Cottonwood is fifteen miles. The outfit made it by the middle of the afternoon. The sun was shining when we broke camp, but by the time we got to Cottonwood it was storming hard back off toward Alkali. We only got a little of the storm at Cottonwood. But before we got the tepee up we were all soaking wet.

We were eating supper in the cook's tent when Morgan missed the dog. Without a word he caught a horse and started back toward Alkali. The outfit laughed—when Morgan had left.

"I never thought that slit-eyed devil cared for anything," said Slim.

"Two of a kind," said old Sour Dough, and the outfit all agreed.

But Morgan rode the thirty miles that night and brought the dog on back to camp with him.

A week before the outfit shipped, some folks came out from town. We were camped down at the lower ranch the night they came. Among them was the boss's wife and kid. The kid was only four years old, and he nearly ran his mother crazy riding herd on him. They had n't been there twenty minutes when the kid fell into the water-tank. It was old Sour Dough that fished him out. They put the kid to bed and hung his clothes out on the line to dry.

# MEN AND HORSES

Old Sour Dough was mixin' bread when he heard the kid's mother scream the second time. There was the kid, with nothin' on, half-way up the wind-mill tower. Old Sour Dough puffed and blowed a bit, but he finally got him down. The kid's mother could n't any more than turn around an' he 'd be into something else. Old Sour Dough said he finally had to turn his back, or he would have been a nervous wreck. He said the thing that scared him most was when he looked up and saw the kid on Morgan's bed.

Old Sour Dough could n't understand that part of it at all. For Keno did n't seem to mind. He even let the kid get on his back and pull his ears. No one but Morgan had ever dared to touch the dog before. And the kid took up with Morgan from the first. When the outfit got into camp the kid would always run to him. Morgan would swing the kid up beside him; sometimes he carried him around for hours on his horse.

It was the day before we moved the herd down to the shipping-pens. We were working the herd out in the flat below the ranch. A spotted wine-glass steer broke out a half a dozen times before we finished trimming up the bunch. We finally

[196]

# THE KETCH DOG

got the cattle worked, and started the herd to moving toward the big corral. The cattle had started stringing out. The dust was awful thick. We did n't see the kid until the spotted steer broke out and headed down his way. The kid was standing in the middle of the flat alone. The whole outfit started when the steer broke out. But Morgan was riding 'way up in the lead. I 'll always think that he 'd have caught the steer. He was cuttin' the blood from his horse at every jump. But he hit a hole an' fell.

The rest of us were 'way behind. The kid had turned and started back. The steer was almost there. Slim Higgins said he shut his eyes. He could n't bear to see the kid go down. Slim did n't even see the dog. But from somewhere Keno came.

# MEN AND HORSES

The outfit was eatin' supper that night when they missed the kid again. Morgan was on wrangle and old Sour Dough was still a-talkin' about how Keno threw that spotted steer. We hunted everywhere; we finally found the kid, asleep in Morgan's bed. His mother said she guessed we 'd have to let him stay till Morgan came. For when we threw the covers back to take him out Keno just looked at us—and growled. And then Sour Dough said:

"One day when Morgan left the dog in camp we was both late gettin' in. It was dark when I got back that night. But Morgan had n't come. I stirred me up some chuck, an' when I cut the beef of course I offered Keno some. But Keno would n't eat. He laid there on the foot of Morgan's bed, just lookin' down the trail, an' never even noticed me. Once after I hung up the beef an' hit the hay I heard him howl. I s'pose if it had been some other dog I 'd either have run him out of camp or took a shot at him. But there 's something about that howl of his that goes clear through a man. I got to thinkin' maybe Morgan was down some place with his horse on top of him. But just as I was pullin' on my boots to go an' have a look for him he came a-ridin' in. An' Morgan never even spoke to either one of us. But he did let Keno lick his hand.

"You know I never thought Morgan really cared about the dog till the day Keno got hurt. But Morgan rode in here that night about ten o'clock with Keno in his arms. He'd carried him that way from Alkali, and that's close on to twenty miles. I finally went to bed, for there was n't nothin' we could do. But when I got up in the mornin' he was still sittin' with his dog.

"The day they sent Morgan to the lower ranch I told him I'd look after Keno till he got back again. But you know this dog he bothers me a heap. For I have to help him in an' out each day. Most folks, I guess, would shoot him. But I ain't got the heart. The punchers always speaks of Keno as if he was my dog now. But he'll never belong to any one but him. Some folks that stays with me gets in the prod sometimes when Keno howls at night. One puncher said he'd shoot him if Keno howled again. But right here I told this button if there was any shootin' done round here I'd take a hand myself. Maybe I've just got used to it. But Keno never howls at night but

# MEN AND HORSES

what I wish there was somethin' that thought that
much of me.  An' there's times when I see him
layin' there I'd give 'most, 'most anything I know
if he'd only lick my hand.  For he always lays in
that same place each day, a-watchin' the trail that
leads down to the lower ranch.  Each time he
hears a puncher comin' up the trail he tries to raise
himself until he finds out who they are, then sinks
back again, still lookin' down the trail with them
wolf-eyes of his."

# THE SWEDE

# THE SWEDE

CARL was his name. He told the old man he 'd been to sea. That was all any of us knowed of him. He was n't a cow-puncher. The Swede's· job was tendin' the pump down at the lower ranch and sort of lookin' after things around the place. He could n't have been more than twenty. Them pump men is usually a sorry lot, an' he bein' a foreigner the punchers all let him pretty much alone. Of course it was funny to hear him talk. No one but the old man could understand him. But all the laughin' that I 've did was done behind his back. An' no one ever called him Swede. At least not to his face. He had an awful pleasant smile. But he was n't the sort a man would ever get familiar with unless you knowed him mighty well. Except for the long knife in his belt and some funny kind of sailor shirt, he dressed just like the rest of us. But somehow with them straight legs an' that blond hair he never did belong. The Swede never rode with the outfit. When he first came he did n't know how to saddle a horse. The old man give him an old pot-bellied gray to ride, when he was out workin' on the fence. And it was a sight to watch the Swede come trottin' up on that old gray. For he was plumb helpless on a horse.

Most of the time the Swede an' the old man was alone at the ranch. For the punchers seldom came to headquarters unless we wanted a fresh mount of horses or maybe a pack-load of grub. The Swede had been there 'most a month when the outfit came into the ranch to gather horses for the fall work.

I would n't have knowed the place. The ranch-house always looked like a boar's nest. But the Swede had mucked things out. An' any one would have thought a woman was waitin' on the place, it was that neat an' clean. He 'd built a sink in the kitchen an' had running water on the porch. An' he 'd even planted blue grass in the yard around the house. He was always busy at something. When he was n't nursin' that fool pump he was out somewhere a-fixin' fence. About the only time I ever saw him still was at night around the fire. Then he 'd just sit an' puff his pipe an' hold that little fuzzy dog. But he never said a word.

# THE SWEDE

It was while we were down at headquarters that they give Swede. this new horse. I figured it was a lousy trick. But Swede asked for him himself. "All right," the old man says, "if that's the thing you're lookin' for, it's just as well you get yours now as later on. You'll probably find him faster than that old pot-bellied gray."

He was a little bronc we called Shimmy. An' he was full of TNT. He'd stand an' shake all over when any one came near. Then he'd strike out with both fore feet an' try to use them teeth of his. Oh, he was a playful thing all right. Slim Higgins rode him once an' turned him in. Slim was a rider, too. But Slim said he hired out as a cow-puncher an' not to work with dynamite. Just why the Swede would pick out a horse like that was something we could n't figure out. It was n't as if Swede did n't know the horse. For he'd seen him fight too many times when any one came near. Of course we wanted to see the fun. For we thought the Swede would try an' ride him that afternoon. An' me and Slim offered to help Swede saddle him. But instead the Swede turned him into that little pasture down back of the house an' give him a big feed of grain.

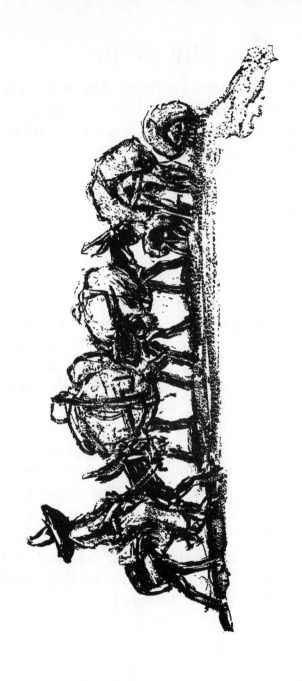

# THE SWEDE

The outfit pulled out for Black River next morning, an' we never came in again until the fall round-up was over. Once in a while a puncher would go in with the pack-mules after chuck. An' we heard there then that the Swede was still alive. Once when Bill Gilson went, Bill said the Swede was ridin' fence on Shimmy. But it was so seldom that Bill ever told the truth that none of us believed him. For none of us thought the Swede would ever get a saddle on him.

It was months before we saw the Swede again. An' it was awful good to see that smile of his the night that we rode in. For somehow a man gets awful tired of lookin' at them waddies that he's workin' with. The Swede came out and helped unpack. He'd ditched that funny sailor shirt. But he was still wearin' that long knife. An' I was surprised to hear him talk. For I could understand 'most all he said.

That night we all had quite a game around the fire. But it was the punchers that did most of the talkin'. For the Swede just sat an' puffed his pipe an' held that fuzzy dog. It was just before we all turned in that Shorty asked the Swede if he would n't like to ride with us to-morrow.

# MEN AND HORSES

"We're pretty short-handed," Shorty says, "an' it'll be a good chance to try out that new horse of yours." Most of us ducked our heads to keep from laughin'. But the Swede he flashed that smile of his and said he'd like to come.

Me and Slim Higgins was on wrangle next morning, an' we got into the ranch about daylight with the horses. Me and Slim had n't had no breakfast yet, but we waited to see the fun. For the Swede was standin' in the corral with a bridle on his arm when we rode in. I would n't have believed it if any one had told me. But the Swede walked up to that fool horse an' slipped the bridle on. He did n't even use a rope to catch him. An' Shimmy never even tried to buck when Swede got on him. The old man give us both the laugh when we came in to breakfast. An' then the old man said he could n't understand the thing himself. He said the Swede had fooled with that blamed horse for days before Shimmy let him touch him. Then one day he looked out an' saw the Swede up on his back. An' all the Swede ever had to do was whistle an' the horse would come trottin' up to him. But Shimmy would never let nobody but the Swede come near him.

# MEN AND HORSES

The outfit all went to town to let off steam after the round-up was over. An' the day me and Slim got back to the ranch we tried to steal a ride on Shimmy. Our horses was out in the pasture a mile or so from the house. An' we wanted to go in to camp that night. We 'd came as far as the ranch in the car. There was n't no horses up to wrangle in. But Shimmy was standin' in the corral, an' so we picked on him. Slim walked up with the bridle, but he never got to put it on him. For Shimmy struck with them fore feet the minute Slim came near. Slim was n't hurt to speak of, but it made Slim fightin' mad. I never saw a horse fight so. I went an' got a rope, an' we finally choked him down. Slim was puttin' the bridle on him when the old man came an' made us turn him loose. It was just as well we did, I guess, for just then the Swede came polin' in. An the old man give us both the laugh again. For the Swede he saddled Shimmy up an' went an' brought our horses in.

As the months went by I came to likin' this Swede awful well. An' I often wondered why he came to drift away out here. One night when we was alone at the ranch he told me why he came.

# THE SWEDE

"I was youst fourteen," he said, "when I leave home. Six year I bane on sea. But once when I was little boy I saw some pictures of the West. An' always I think sometime I like to go out there. So once when we landed in New York I youst quit ship an' come."

There was always something about this Swede that none of us could understand. He was hard as flint around the men. But when it came to animals he had the softest streak I 've ever seen. The rest of us despised that fuzzy dog, for he was always snappin' at your heels. But Swede would take this fool pup every place he went. An' if the dog got tired Swede would carry him. During the drouth the Swede brought in some eighty dogie calves, an' he carried most all of them in on that fool horse of his. For whenever Swede found a calf whose mammy had died, Swede would pick up the calf an' bring him in. It made a lot of extra work for him just feedin' them blame things. An' lots' of nights he was 'way after dark just gettin' through his chores. One day the old man spoke to him about how much he 'd saved the outfit by bringin' them calves in. It made Swede fightin' mad.

# MEN AND HORSES

"That was n't the reason I brought them in," says Swede. "I youst feel sorry for them calves."

It was the day the Swede was up on Slash cuttin' cedar posts that he came near losin' Shimmy. There's lots of wild horses up in there. But it never occurred to Swede that Shimmy might pull out and leave him. The feed was pretty good, so Swede pulled the saddle off and turned Shimmy loose to graze. Swede was busy with his posts, an' he never paid Shimmy any mind. For the horse always hung around him just like a dog. Swede had been workin' for an hour or so before he missed the horse. He hunted everywhere. He finally saw Shimmy on a ridge about three hundred yards away. A bunch of wild horses had come in while Swede was busy, an' Shimmy had pulled out an' gone to them. Anybody but the Swede would have kissed his horse good-by right then. For once a saddle-horse gets in with them wild horses it takes the whole outfit an' the dog to ever catch him. But the Swede slipped back to his saddle an' got his rifle. Then he started crawlin' on his belly toward the ridge.

Shimmy an' three of the wild ones was a-playin' together a little way from the main bunch. An'

Swede figured he might be able to cut them off when they started down the ridge. Swede had the wind on the bunch, an' he crawled within a hundred yards before they ever seen him. Then a sorrel stud threw up his head an' snorted, an' the wild bunch headed down the ridge a-runnin' like the wind. Shimmy an' the three that he 'd been playin' with was a-runnin' just behind. Swede made a run an' tried to cut them off. But it was n't any use. It was then Swede opened up with that old 30–40.

Afterwards when Swede was tellin' me about it he said he thought he 'd seen the last of Shimmy when they passed him on the ridge. It was then Swede started shootin'. But it was n't till he killed the horse ahead of him that Shimmy ever stopped. Swede says there was n't nothin' to it after Shimmy stopped an' saw him.

"For Shimmy he was pretty scared for all that shootin'. An' he youst stand an' shake all over till he hear me whistle. Then Shimmy he youst come to me."

# BUTTERMILK JONES

Ross Santee
Cross S Ranch
Arizona

# BUTTERMILK JONES

NAMES don't mean nothin' in this country, for no one ever asks any questions around a cow outfit, at least not personal questions. It's not considered polite, in the first place, and in most cases it's not apt to be healthy. Of course you don't expect a cow-puncher to carry visitin'-cards, and I've never met one yet who carried any letters of introduction. If a puncher says his name is Jones, Jones is what you call him, even if you happen to know that all his folks answer to the name of Smith back in Texas. If a puncher volunteers any information about himself, all well and good. If he don't, there's nothin' ever said; at least there's nothin' ever said when he's around.

Buttermilk Jones was n't even a cow-puncher. Jones was his real name, too, although I did n't think so at the time. He did n't come from Texas, either. We could tell that by his talk. Just

what Jones had done before he come to Arizona I
never did find out until a long while after he was
gone, for Jones did n't carry any credentials, and,
what 's more, he never volunteered any information about himself.   Naturally, I figured he was
on the dodge.

He walked into the ranch about sundown one
night and hit the old man for a job.   The outfit
had just finished supper when he came.   I cut
some steak and stirred him up some chuck.   And,
man, you should have seen that *hombre* eat.   I
thought he never would fill up.   It seems he 'd
hoofed it all the way from town, and that 's close
on to forty miles.   He 'd laid out in the brush the
night before.   This was the first he 'd had to eat
since he left town.   While he was eatin' supper I
looked him over awful close.   Any one with half
an eye could tell he was n't a cow-puncher.   He
was n't a prospector, either.   His shoes was worn
plumb through, but he was wearin' rubber heels.
What was left of the suit he was wearin' shore fit
him like the pictures of the clothes I 've seen in
magazines, like folks back East all wear.   He was
pleasant enough to talk to, and polite as sin when
he spoke, but any one could tell by lookin' at them

eyes of his he would n't do to trifle with. I figured he was wanted somewhere, and I wondered what he 'd done. He did n't belong in this country, that 's a cinch. He must have been all of six feet tall, and any one by lookin' at that chest of his could tell there was n't anything the matter with his lungs. "Jones," he said, was his name, "plain Jones," and he gave me that pleasant smile of his; but names don't mean nothin' in this country.

Just why the old man put him on was something I never could figure out, for a tenderfoot ain't no use around a cow outfit. The old man's awful queer about some things. He might have figured that Jones would drift as soon as he got a bellyful, for a tenderfoot sometimes gets it in his head, from readin' stories an' goin' to them picture-shows, that he wants to be a cow-puncher. But there ain't no romance in shoein' horses or fixin' fence, and when they find it out they don't stay long. And, still, the old man seemed to like this Jones. For the old man likes a man that 's hard. He never had a soft one in his spread. And whatever Jones was wanted for would n't bother the old man any, for he 'd heard the owls hoot himself.

He put Jones to fixin' fence at first. Then

later on he helped me pack out all the salt. Anything he put him at was all the same to Jones. Whatever he did Jones was willing enough. But he never made much of a hand. At first he hardly knew a steer from a cow, but the old man kept him on. Jones never took any pride in his outfit. At first he wore a pair of Bronc's old boots and overalls, but just as soon as he got paid he sent in town and bought him an outfit of his own, and a lot of shells for his gun. For Buttermilk was always shootin'. That gun of his was about the only thing he had any pride about, and he shore did keep it clean. His shirt was always comin' out behind, for he always cut pieces off the tail to clean that lousy gun of his. I've seen him hit jackrabbits on the run with that old 45. Of course he missed a lot of times. I thought it was an accident myself at first, for Bronc could n't shoot like that. And every night, no matter how late we got in, he'd sit and scribble in that little book of his.

Enough things happened to this Jones at first to make most anybody quit. He'd only been there about a month when he come by that name of Buttermilk. We were movin' a bunch of cattle

over on the river at the time. Old Ben was cookin'
on the trip, and Jones was wranglin' horses. He
got by doin' that all right, for Jones liked horses.
But when it come to doin' anything around the
herd, Jones was in his own way and everybody
else's.

The first night out we camped at Wilson's ranch.
After we got the cattle penned, we all eat supper
at that long table on the porch, for Mrs. Wilson
was at home, and she insisted that we eat inside.
It was easy enough to see a woman run the place,
for the porch was screened in with chicken-wire,
and the whole blame thing was covered up with
vines. Jones was wearin' a pair of the longest
shanked spurs I 've ever seen, and he was sittin'
on a bench with his back against the wire. He
had n't said a word all through the meal. The
punchers was all a-sayin', "Yes, ma'am," an' "No,
ma am," when Mrs. Wilson spoke, for punchers
don't have much to say when wimmen is around.
Bronc and me had just finished eatin' and was
goin' outside to smoke when it happened. Jones
started to git up at the same time. Then all at
once I saw him pitch across the table and knock

the whole thing over. Mrs. Wilson screamed, and Jones was still a-layin' on the floor when we got to him. I thought he 'd gone plumb loco till I found out what had happened. But it seems he 'd hung both spurs up in that chicken-wire.

Next mornin' we started the herd at daylight, and we 'd only gone about a mile when the old man sent me back to help Jones with the horses. I 'd gone about a half when I seen 'em stringin' down the wash. Old Pinto Pete, a horse of mine, was 'way up in the lead. The rest was all strung out in single file, and Jones was bringin' up the rear. He was ridin' an old hammer-headed dun we called Geronimo. The whole bunch moved along as if they all were half asleep, but when old Pinto passed a big flat rock, I saw him come alive. He pitched off down the trail just like a bronc. I spurred my horse off in the brush, or Pete would have run right over me, for it seems the cattle had stirred up a hornets' nest when they went by. Old Papago come next and then a mule named Mike. But when they passed that big flat rock, man! how they come alive. I supposed of course that Jones would ride around the hornets' nest, for he 'd watched the horses all go pitchin' down the wash.

# BUTTERMILK JONES

I guess Jones must have been asleep.   At any rate he kept a-comin' on.   Old Geronimo was just opposite the big flat rock when it happened.   Jones lost a stirrup and both bridle-reins the first jump. The second jump the old dun made, the stirrup opened up a cut right over Jones's eye.   When Geronimo hit the ground the third time he was alone with the hornets, for Jones was n't with him any more.   I was laughin' so I almost missed the horse when he come by.   In a little while Jones come a-limpin' up and got back on his horse. "Anyway, you never did get stung," says I.   But when I got a look at Jones's eyes I did n't say nothin' more.

That river is the hottest place in summer-time I ever saw.   The lard we had was even melted in the pail.   We camped at noon right in that little bunch of trees below old Simson's house, and old Ben put it in the shade to let it cool.   We all had finished dinner when Jones come in to eat, for he was holdin' the remuda, some little piece away. Jones filled his plate without sayin' anything, and then he spied that lard.

"How come the buttermilk?" says he, a-reachin' for a cup.

"The woman at the ranch-house brought it down," says old Ben, without battin' an eye. And Jones he filled his cup and took a slug of that blame stuff. I would n't have been in old Ben's boots for anything. We all were sittin' tight, and I was ready for 'most anything. Then finally Jones he laughed.

As the months went by I got to likin' Jones myself. For he always did the best he knew, and he never asked no odds of any one. He 'd talk about anything—'cept himself. At times he acted sort of queer. We sort of took him for granted now, but he never was really one of us. Sometimes he 'd sit out alone at night and look out across them hills. But whatever it was that bothered him, he always kept it to himself. And every night, no matter how late we got in, he 'd always scribble in that little book of his. He was quiet and easy-goin', too, until you got him riled, but the killers I 've known are all that way. I 've never met one yet who was really bad, who ever run off at the head.

Wranglin' horses to most cow-punchers is the lousiest thing that they can do. But Jones did n't

seem to mind. He knew every horse that the outfit owned and could tell just where they run. He
even made pets out of all of his. He had one
little sorrel bronc in his string that would follow
him round just like a dog. And Jones never
minded to stay alone. I 've come by the mesa lots
of times when he was out with the horses. Sometimes he 'd be a-scribblin' in that little book of his,
and then again I 'd find him shootin' jacks. But
mostly he run wild horses. The upper range was
full of them, and of all the fools I 've ever seen for
runnin' them blame things, Jones was the worst.

One night when we was camped down by the
big corral, the old man sent me to the ranch to get
a load of chuck. Jones started to come along with
me. He come part way, and then he made some
pore excuse and started back. I went on alone to
the ranch and got the mule packed up. A-comin'
back I took the upper trail. It was one of them
soft summer nights, and the moon was nearly full.
The mesa was 'most as light as day. It was one of
them kind of nights that makes you glad you 're
punchin' cows, instead of bein' cooped up in some
lousy town. I was half-way across the mesa when

# MEN AND HORSES

I heard 'em comin'.   There must have been all of
fifty in the bunch.   I took a turn or two around
the saddle-horn to keep from losin' Mike, for if
that blame mule had ever got with them wild
horses I shore would have had a race.   You could
almost feel the ground a-shakin' as they went flyin'
by.   A buckskin stud was in the lead, and they
were strung out for 'most two hundred yards.   I
wondered what had startled them, for horses don't
get out and run like that for fun.   I rode along
for 'most a mile, and then I met another one.   He
come near runnin' over me.   He was a big, black
maverick, and he passed so close I could see the
sweat glisten on his hide.   His breath was comin'

[226]

in great gasps.    But when he saw me he let 'er out another notch.    It was just a little further on that I found Jones.    He was the worst skinned-up cow-puncher I ever saw, and his horse was wringin' wet with sweat.    Jones was tryin' to roll a cigarette, but he was shakin' so he did n't make much of a job.    He sort of laughed when I rode up, and said he was n't hurt.    He 'd had his rope on that big black and got his horse jerked down.    It must have been some fight they had, judgin' from lookin' at the sign, for Jones had tied the big black down.    Just why a man would go through all of that, then up and turn a maverick loose, was something I could n't figure out.    It was the first I ever knowed that Jones was soft.    For when I asked Jones why he turned him loose, Jones said he felt sorry for the horse.

I never saw Jones riled but once, and that come up over a horse.    A puncher we called Cat Claw was ridin' through our work with us.    They sent him over from the Diamond D, and he was reppin' for that brand.    This Cat Claw was the meanest hand to fight a horse I ever saw, and he always packed a gun.    He never would have lasted one whole day in our outfit, for whippin' one of his horses over the head was somethin' the old man would n't stand. And there was n't a horse in Cat Claw''s mount that you could get close to on the ground.

Cat Claw was on wrangle the mornin' the blow-out happened. His wranglin' horse had got loose in the night. Without a word to Jones he caught up that little sorrel bronc of his, for he was always hangin' around the camp. I was watchin' Jones when Cat Claw caught the horse, and I saw Jones's eyes get hard. He offered to wrangle in Cat Claw's place, but Cat Claw missed his cue.

He swung up on the horse without sayin' a word. Just then the little bronc shied, and Cat Claw come down right over his eyes with that loaded quirt of his. He never got to hit him but once. For Jones was comin' now. Cat Claw tried to pull his gun, but it was n't any use. Hell, Jones did n't need a gun. Cat Claw was unconscious when the old man pulled Jones off. Without a word Jones got up on the little bronc and brought the ponies in. We all thought Jones had killed him at first, and me and Bronc was both a-hopin' that he had. But when Jones got in with the horses he was able to sit up. And then Jones

asked him how he felt, just as polite as sin. It sort of made my blood run cold to hear the way Jones spoke. When we got into camp that night, Cat Claw had pulled his freight, and I can't say I blamed him none.

This Jones was the politest man I ever saw. Not long before he left he went to town with me an' Bronc. Of course, we all got drunk. Me an' Bronc both talked a lot. And Bronc told Jones an' me about that night he held up No. 9. Bronc never would have mentioned it if he had n't been drunk. I talked a lot myself, but I ain't sayin' what I said. Whatever it was that bothered Jones was buried awful deep. For Jones he never said a word about anything he 'd done, and the more we drunk the politer this Jones got. He drunk as much as me an' Bronc, but he shore did keep his head, and finally he wound the whole thing up by puttin' me an' Bronc to bed.

I hated to see Jones leave myself. So did everybody else. And the old man had a talk with Jones the night before he left. I might have knowed there was somethin' up, for the old man sort of smiled when he waved this Jones good-by. I took Jones into town myself and brought his pony back.

# BUTTERMILK JONES

I'd come to likin' this Jones awful well, an' goin' into town I asked him why he did n't stay among his friends. I told him then we did n't care about anything he'd done, and whatever he was wanted for we did n't care a damn. Jones looked sort of foolish when I spoke, an' I was sorry I'd mentioned it, for he never said a word. But when Jones said good-by to me, he said he was sorry he had to leave. He hoped that sometime he could come back, and he shore did grip my hand.

The months went slippin' by, but we never had no word from Jones. I often wondered where he was, until one day a package came. The package was nothin' but a book. It did n't mean a thing to me until I looked inside. But on the fly-leaf in the front was a little note from Jones. He owed me an apology, he said, for he was n't nothin' but a writer, he hoped I'd like the book. And he hoped I'd always be a friend of his, even if he was n't wanted by the law. And then Jones said he was comin' back this fall and take a hunt. You could have knocked me off with a feather.

"The Diary of a Tenderfoot," was the name he called the thing, and he even told about the time he drunk the lard a-thinkin' it was buttermilk.

## MEN AND HORSES

The old man says that Jones has written books before, an' folks back East all knows him pretty well.  But, hell!  Names don't mean nothin' in this country!

# FLIVVER TRAMPS

# FLIVVER TRAMPS

"HE ain't a tourist," said the cow-puncher. "He's a flivver tramp. I'll bet that *hombre* hasn't bought a gallon of gasolene since he left Missouri. He ought to be good for thirty miles on what we staked him to. But he won't stop at the trading-post and fill his tank. He'll go a-foggin' right on past the place. When the gas we staked him to runs out he'll park himself along the road an' wave some other sucker down an' mooch enough to take him on a little further. You'd be surprised how many of 'em work that game in Arizona these days. But even at that it's hard to pass a man on the road when he's in trouble without givin' him a hand, specially when he's forty miles from nowhere.

"Since I've been haulin' salt to the horse-camp I don't guess I made a trip without meetin' up with one or two that wanted somethin'. Usually it's a little gas they want. An' then again it may be oil. It's these flivver tramps that make it hard on a regular tourist in Arizona if he happens to be in trouble. For lots of folks in this country are gettin' so they won't stop when they find a man in trouble on the road.

"Some of these flivver tramps will steal you blind if a man don't keep an eye on them. A car with three men in it stopped Swede Larsen once when he was goin' on a lion-hunt. Swede was movin' into the White River country an' had his outfit loaded on a truck. They told Swede they was broke an' asked him if he'd stake them to a little gas. It never occurred to Swede to keep an eye on them. But while he was fillin' up their tank, one of them stole his jack an' pump, six cans of corn, and two slabs of bacon along with half a sack of flour. No, there was n't no chance of it a-loosen' out, for Swede don't pack that way. He had this box of stuff all packed away down underneath the tarp, an' the hounds was layin' on it. Swede said he figured he was lucky that they did n't steal his lion dogs. But it happened they was tied. It made a Christian out of Swede, for now when anybody tries to wave him down, if Swede don't like their looks he goes a-foggin' right on down the road.

# FLIVVER TRAMPS

"I was with Swede on a hunt one day. We had stopped at Casadora Springs to let the car cool off and give the dogs a drink, when all at once the whole pack opened up at somethin' comin' off the hill. I thought at first it was the Indians a-workin' stock. But in a little while the thing showed up. It was a flivver runnin' on the rims. There was only one tire on the thing, an' it was crossways on the wheel. There was more strange noises comin' from that thing than I 've ever heard before or since. The *hombre* who was drivin' never made no move to stop. I guess he was afraid that if he did she 'd never start again. Some of the hounds was still a-barkin' twenty minutes after he went by. An' there was two of them we had to whip before we finally got 'em quiet.

"When Swede an I was comin' back we overtook a man on foot. He had the best graft for gettin' through the country that I 've ever seen. We carried him down to the trading-post, an' from there he caught a ride on into Globe. He carried his blankets in a little pack. An' on it he had painted a little sign that says, 'Coast to Coast on foot.'

"I cooked a month for Tiffany last fall down at

[237]

the trading-post, and half the folks that stopped in his camp-yard was broke. Some had their families with them an' everything they owned. The camp-yard was just back of the restaurant, an' when I was n't busy I used to watch the spread. One outfit drove into the yard one night with enough stuff in their flivver to fill a moving-van. They even had some stuff tied on the top. An' when the outfit started pilin' out, it made me think of a show I saw in Kansas City once when I was up there with a load of stock. For this *hombre* in the show took rabbits an' guinea-pigs an' things along with an awful pile of junk all out of one silk hat.

"In this flivver that I 'm speakin' of a man an' woman an' two kids was settin' up in front.

[238]

# FLIVVER TRAMPS

There was a crate of chickens fastened on behind with all the other junk they had that made a load for any ordinary car. But when the kids all started pilin' out behind I thought I must be seein' things. They come pilin' out so fast there may be some I overlooked, but I finally counted six, along with a pet rooster, two tom-cats, an' a goat.

"This *hombre* had a Missouri license on his car. Missouri and California had the most. But there were cars from everywhere, with stickers pasted on the wind-shields of places that they 'd been. Lots of them were regular tourists from the North a-goin' to California or comin' back. Most flivver tramps begin that way. Some stop an' work a while when they git broke, an' then they hit the road again until their stake runs out. Some get a taste for travelin' an' are never satisfied to stay long in one place again. A kid come into the restaurant one morning to buy a piece of beef. His family was camped out in the yard. While I was waitin' on the kid he told me about different places that he 'd been. I liked his looks, for he was a nice-appearin' kid. He told me he was ten years old. An' come to find out, he could n't read or write. The kid told me his family was always on the move, an' they had never stayed long enough in one place for him to go to school. I happened to mention it to Tiffany, who says there are hundreds of children like this kid who ought to be in school. And some who don't get half enough to eat.

"A man come into the restaurant one day and asked to buy ten cents' worth of stale bread. I s'posed he wanted it for chicken-feed, an' I give him all I had. But I happened to look out, an' they were eatin' it themselves. There was a woman an' two kids beside the man, an' they were washin' it down with water from the well. That was too much for me, so I called 'em all inside an staked 'em to a meal. Neither of the kids was over nine or ten, an' the way they tore into that beef would make you think they'd never tasted meat before. There was a California license on the car. The old man said he come originally from Illinois. But as near as I could get the truth, for the last four years he'd just been driftin' round, a-workin' for a little while when he got broke, then movin' on again. The whole family had been pickin' fruit out on the Coast. They'd been held up for a month down on the border because of the quarantine that Arizona had against the foot-an'-mouth disease. That used up most of their money. The old man had tried to get work in Globe, but there was nothin' doin' in the mines. So he was on his way back up to Illinois again. I fixed 'em up a basketful of chuck to carry next mornin' when they left, an' Tiffany staked 'em to some gasolene an' oil. I often wondered if they made it through, for Illinois is quite a jaunt from Arizona. But none of them seemed to be worried none.

"Some Gipsies stopped in the yard one night. They travel the best of any folks I've seen, for they all travel in high-powered cars. I never figured there was so much money in tellin' fortunes as there is—specially at four bits a throw. But during the quarantine on the foot-an'-mouth disease they fumigated every one before they let 'em into Arizona. An' on one old Gipsy woman who told fortunes on the street they found ten one-thousand-dollar bills.

"During the quarantine down on the border there were hundred of cars held up for weeks that was tryin' to go back North again. The guards would n't let 'em cross the bridge. But there was one religious outfit in the bunch who said that on a certain day an' time they 'd cross the river just below the bridge, an' cross on dry land, too. For the waters of the Colorado would part just like the Red Sea did when Moses led his children through.

"The whole camp turned out to watch 'em cross. An' there was considerable talk among the other tourists that might be called irrevent. Some offered to bet this Moses everything they had with any odds he chose that he would n't get across. But Moses would n't bet.

"He lined his cars all up in single file with him a-drivin' a flivver right up in the lead. There was considerable coachin' from that crowd. But Moses just looked straight ahead. When he hit the river the waters of the Colorado parted some. But it was n't for very long, for Moses killed his engine dead and never could get it started. He tinkered with his engine for a little while, but as the flivver settled in the sand the water kept a-gettin' higher. So Moses finally waded out an' come ashore an' left his flivver there. You can imagine what those tourists said. But at that they all turned in an' helped him pull his flivver out.

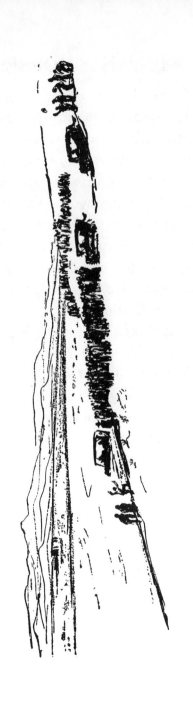

# MEN AND HORSES

"Some of the flivver tramps who stopped in Tiffany's camp-yard had different things to sell. One chap with a Mass. license on his car was takin' photographs. But the *hombre* who did the best of any that I seen was one who sold some kind of patent medicine. I got two bottles from that bird, an' when I went to get another one I found I was too late, for he 'd sold his stock all out. He never had a bit of trouble gettin' rid of everything he had, for that stuff sure had a kick to it.

"It was these flivver tramps who traveled on their nerve that interested me more than any of the rest. I was cookin' supper one evenin' when a young chap come to the kitchen door an' asked me if I 'd stake him to a postal card. I was pretty busy at the time. But there was something about the way this *hombre* wore his clothes that interested me. For the shirt he wore looked as if he 'd used the thing to clean his car. One pants leg on his trousers was pretty good, but the other had been tore off so short it was n't possible to tear it higher. I finally dug him up a postal card, but when he looked at it he shook his head an' says that it won't do him any good, for there was n't any stamp on it. I hunted up a stamp, and then he asked if he could borrow pen an' ink. I let him write the thing in there, an' when he asked me if I'd mail the card for him next mornin' on the train, instead of kickin' him out on his ear, I liked his nerve so well I told him shore I would. An' besides I was itchin' to know what kind of news this bird was writin' home.

"The card was written to his folks to some little town in Iowa. An' the only thing he says was that everything was going fine an' he was enjoyin' every minute of his trip to California.

"I told Tiffany I'd found a man that had more nerve than any one I'd ever seen before. But when I told the yarn to him, he says this *hombre* with the postal card was a piker for nerve 'longside the one he knew.

"This bird that Tiffany told me of come from either Nebraska or Kansas. Anyway it was some place up in there. He bought a pretty good-lookin' flivver an' got it for almost nothing, for the engine had been taken out of it. But otherwise the thing was good. Then he bought himself several tow-ropes an' had somebody push her down the road a ways and head the thing towards California. You know most any one will give a man

[245]

a tow.   At least they 'll tow him to the next garage.   Well, that 's the way this *hombre* worked
his way clear out to California.   He 'd get some
one to tow him up to some garage, an' of course
they 'd kick him out of there when they found out
what the trouble was.   An' then he 'd get his tow-
rope out and get some one to take him on a little
further.   None of the folks that towed him ever
found it out until he got to California.   An' the
bird that found it out an' told the yarn had towed
him almost forty miles.   He was towin' him down
across the Chuckawalla Desert, for he was goin' to
Los Angles.   There 's lots of sand down there,
and his own car was n't pullin' none too well.   He
did n't want to leave this bird out on the desert, so
he decided he might be able to fix the thing himself.   This bird from Kansas tried his best to talk
him out of it an' wanted him to tow him to the next
garage, which happened to be about thirty miles
further on.   But the *hombre* who was towin' insisted that he knowed considerable about cars.
An' if it was engine-trouble that ailed the car he
thought he could fix the thing.   But when he
raised the hood an' looked inside, there was n't any
engine there.

# FLIVVER TRAMPS

"I was curious to know what this *hombre* did to this bird from Kansas when he raised the hood an' found there was n't any engine there. Tiffany says he did n't know. But Tiffany says no matter what else ever happens to this bird from Kansas, one thing is sure: he 'll never starve to death."

# COME AN' GET IT

# COME AN' GET IT

MR. JONES was his name. An' Mr. Jones was what the punchers always called him. Mr. Jones was a good cook. The punchers all admitted that. An' what's more Mr. Jones admitted it himself. When it come to cookin' spoon vittles an' fancy things like that I've never seen his equal as a round-up cook before. For he cooked doughnuts as well as any woman. An' we never killed a beef but what he made a tallow pudding. But Mr. Jones wasn't what you'd call popular with the men. Slim Higgins said he didn't mind tippin' his hat to any one, but he did hate to just stand round and hold it in his hand.

The outfit was camped down by the big corral when Mr. Jones first came. A nester's hogs had been so bad at gettin' into the pots at night we had to swing the stuff all up on ropes to keep 'em from carryin' off the place. The first night Mr. Jones was there we hadn't any more 'n got to sleep when the hogs all come a-troopin' into camp. None of us paid 'em any mind exceptin' Mr. Jones. It was evident he did n't care for hogs. For when one of them started rootin' round his bed he started shootin'. Me an' Slim Higgins was sleepin' to-gether, an' our bed was closer to the cook's than any of the rest, an' mebbe you think we did n't flatten out. The first shot woke me up. An' I thought the second shot had hit me in the eye. But it was just a hog that stepped on me. Slim thought he was shot half a dozen times, but it was nothin' but the hogs a-passin' over us. I 've seen some cattle run at night, but that was nothin' to the way these hogs went through our camp. When the shootin' stopped, me an' Slim dragged our bed behind the biggest oak-tree we could find. The boys was all a-movin' round a bit. An' Shorty tried to talk us out of this oak-tree of ours. But we told him to find one for himself.

It was just before daylight when the hogs came back again. But me an' Slim was sittin' pretty good this time. For that oak was thick enough to stop a forty-five. An' nary a hog run over us. Slim said it was the first time in his life he was ever glad that he was thin. For when it come light enough for us to see, there was two dead hogs in camp.

I 'll admit we all slept better after Mr. Jones had left. For too much of this night shootin' is wearin' on the nerves. We only camped a week down by the big corral. But by the time we left, no puncher in the outfit could have approached within' shootin' distance of a hog on the fastest horse he had.

Mr. Jones cooked for the outfit just two months, an' he never did no shootin' after we left the big corral. But the boys all watched him mighty close a-figgerin' he might break out again. It was one rainy night, when we moved into Tin Cup Springs, that Mr. Jones blowed up an' quit. For Mr. Jones refused to cook with juniper. An' there was no other wood within fifteen miles.

The boys took turns a-cookin' after Mr. Jones had left. But that did n't set too well with none of us. An' Shorty finally went to town an' brought us out another cook.

George was the new cook's name. An' he was n't the kind of man who 'd ever get up an' go to shootin' in the night. For old George was the mildest-mannered round-up cook I 've ever seen.

# MEN AND HORSES

Slim said it was probably because he had n't been cookin' long enough to get hard-boiled. "Wait till he 's here a while," says Slim. For old George told us he had never cooked for a cow outfit before. "I punched cow some when I was a kid in Texas," old George says. "But this is my first job cookin' for a spread. I told Shorty when he hired me I could n't cook spoon vittles or fancy things like that. But Shorty says as long as I slung out the beef an' bread an' was able to cook frijole beans an' was n't too particular, he reckoned I 'd get by."

Now, I 'll admit old George was n't what you 'd call a particular man. For he was n't particular in sortin' the gravel from the frijoles. An' he was n't none too particular when he washed. Speakin' of a shot Shorty made one night when we killed a beef, Slim said the beef went down just like he 'd been hit in the head with one of old George's biscuits. But at that I 've seen a heap worse round-up cooks than old George. For if there 's anything a cow-puncher likes better than havin' a fiddler in camp it 's drinkin' coffee between meals. An' any time a round-up cook stands for that the punchers are usually for him. Even if they do crack a tooth occasionally on a gravel he 's cooked

[254]

in the beans. Old George was just that way, an' no matter how late a puncher got in he always found a pot of coffee, an' old George always stirred a little something up for him to eat. Dogie, the horse-wrangler, lost more horses while old George was with the outfit than he ever had before or since. For Dogie spent most all his time in camp a-augerin' old George an' playin' the coffee-pot. An' when old George left, Dogie was all upset. For Dogie says the chances are he 'll never find a round-up cook like George again.

But it was the manner of old George's leaving that interested me. For when he came George told me he had took the job to get away from his wife.

"You ain't married, are ya?" says old George. "Well, take my advice an' don't, for I ain't had no peace since then. Chances are I' d still be punchin' cows if it was n't for my ole woman. She made me give it up right after we got married. She made me quite playin' for dances, too. An' I was a pretty good fiddler, if I do say so myself. For I could play all night an' not play the same tune more 'n twice. This woman o' mine is always walkin' on my tail. She won't even let me play the fiddle in the house no more. Since we came to Arizona I've been workin' in the mine. It's goin' on fifteen years this fall since I started rootin' in the bottom of a shaft. An' except for an occasional shift the only time I've lost since then was durin' a strike in 1917. An' durin' the strike my ole woman like to run me wild. I tried to tell her I was just workin' there an' they'd probably settle things without consultin' me. But you can't reason with a woman. She's always sayin' what she'd do if she was just a man. It was just a happen-so that I met up with Shorty when he was in town lookin' for a cook. I never told the ole woman I was comin' either until just before I left. For I knowed she wouldn't let me come. Say, you don't have no idea how good it feels to be out in the hills with a cow outfit again. An' to be able to play the fiddle every night without some woman chargin' you."

Old George had been with the outfit just a week when the first letter come from his wife.

"She wants me to come on back home," says George. "She's writin' awful pitiful. But I ain't goin' back until this round-up's over.

Another week went by, an' old George got another one.

"But I ain't goin' back," says George.

Four letters came for George all told, at intervals of a week apart. The outfit was camped at the Spur Camp the night the last one came. Shorty an' I were the first two punchers in that night. We did n't see the Indian who brought the letter out. But when we got a look at George's face we knowed he 'd had another letter from his wife. When we asked him what the trouble was George never said a word when he handed me this note. I never saw the other ones. But this note was short an' what you 'd call right to the point. For all it says was:

"George come home at once or I'll sell the furniture."

We caught him up a horse, an' after old George left of course we laughed. But as we watched him ridin' down the trail towards town it was

# MEN AND HORSES

Shorty who spoke the thing we was all thinkin' of.

"Mebbe it ain't so funny after all," he says.

Just one month's freedom in twenty years.

A cook named Tommie Johnson finally finished out the work that fall. An' Tommie never quit until the day the outfit loaded out, down at the shipping-pens. Tommie could cook all right, but he was poison on Indians an' folks who came from town. As long as it was just the outfit he was cookin' for, a man could get along with him. But just let one outsider drop in for a meal an' Tommie was always on the prod.

There's a dish that's made in the cow-camp when the outfit kills a beef. It's made of the brains an' sweetbreads an' choice pieces of the steer. If there happens to be a woman around it's called a son-of-a-gun. But if there ain't no woman present the punchers calls it somethin' else that's always been a fightin' word.

Tommie was cookin' one night when a stranger who was driftin' through stopped off to get a meal. Tommie never said a word, but he started swellin' up. "Well, cook," says the stranger, a-tryin' to be sociable, "I see you goin' to have a son-of-a——for supper. "Yaas," drawls Tommie kind of slow. "If any more keeps droppin' in we're liable to have half a dozen."

When the outfit went down to the shipping-pens that fall Tommie had no more than seen the place than he started swellin' up. For when an outfit ships there's always lots of folks comes out from town to watch 'em load. An' every man an' his brother usually drops in for a meal. It was late when we got to the pens that night. For we'd had some trouble with the herd. An' Tommie was swelled up like a poisoned pup when we come in to eat. But he never said nothin' until next mornin' when we started loadin' out. Then Tommie said he'd quit if Shorty did n't put somebody helpin' him. The outfit was short-handed anyway, but Shorty finally wished the job on Slim. An' you can bet it did n't sit too well with him. Shorty said he figured the two of them would fight before the day was over, but it never occurred to him that they'd pull out together. But when the outfit come for dinner the two of them was gone. We did n't understand the thing at first, an' we figured of course they'd both be back. But a stranger who was there said he 'lowed they'd gone for good.

# MEN AND HORSES

"I just drove down from town to see the cattle loaded when I heard them two arguin', an' I stopped to watch the fun. Finally I heard the cook say, 'Tell Shorty I 've quit, an' he can send my check to town.' An' then I heard this skinny feller say, 'You can tell him yourself, for I 'm goin' with you.'"

About the cleanest round-up cook I ever saw was one we had one fall named Smith. Smith ain't his name, but it will do. I 've heard punchers kick about 'most everything. But this was the first time in my life I ever heard the punchers kick about a cook a-keepin' clean. But you can bet your life that any kickin' we did was done behind his back. For Bill Smith was a regular round-up cook. Just where Bill came from I never did find out. For in any of his talk he neved did go back that far. An' personal questions are never a healthy thing in any outfit. But from his talk I gathered that Bill had done most everything from pullin' teeth to tendin' bar. For one night in camp when Bill was cuttin' Slim Higgins's hair I heard Bill say that he could do 'most anything an' do it well.

"I never seen nothin' yet I couldn 't do," says Bill, "an' make a hand at it besides. I 've got some forceps in my war-bag there, an' I can pull a tooth as well as any doc." Slim offered to take Bill's word for this. For Slim was mighty quick in tellin' Bill that all his teeth was good.

"It was interestin' the way I picked it up," says Bill. "I had a toothache once that came near killin' me. I was on a round-up at the time an' could n't leave at first. But finally I could n't stand it any longer, an' I rode in town to see a doc. I had a few drinks in town before I went to see this bird. But I pointed him out the tooth that hurt. When he pulled the tooth I took a few more drinks an' went on back to camp. But when I woke up in the mornin' it was hurtin' worse than ever. For come to find out, this doc had pulled the wrong tooth on me. I saddled up an' rode on into town again. An' when I told him what the trouble was he sort of smiles an' says he 'll get the right one now. 'Mebbe you 'll look 'em over close next time,' says I. He put up quite a fight at that. But I finally got him down flat on the floor an' pulled out six of his."

It was while we was camped at Sycamore that the boys all took exception to Bill's cleanliness. There 's lots of deep water-holes in there, an' the boys all played 'em pretty strong whenever we was in camp. But the rest of us all put on our clothes when we come in to eat, 'cept Bill. An' the only clothes Bill wore while we was there was his hat an' a pair of boots. We finally did get used to it. But I 'll admit it did seem queer at first. For when we all come in to eat, there 'd be the cook a-shufflin' the skillet lids, not wearin' nothin' 'cept his hat an' boots.

One night when Slim an' Ben Hicks an' me was on wrangle we asked Bill if he would let us eat before we took the horses out, for we knowed it would be two hours anyway before we got back again an' supper was almost ready then. But old Bill would n't let us eat. "Yez 'll get no duff till you get back," he says.

The three of us was ridin' mules, an' they all was pretty salty. An' while we was augerin' the cook Ben Hicks reached down and hung a spur in the mule that Slim was ridin'. Ben jigged Slim's mule right in the flank, an' things began to happen then. For this mule of Slim's bogged down his head an' bucked right through the pots and pans. The coffee-pot was the first thing they upset, and the Dutch oven with the bread went next.

# COME AN' GET IT

But none of us waited to see no more. I never saw Slim make a better ride in all his life. But Slim said afterwards he was afraid the cook might kill him if the mule unloaded him in camp. An' you can bet the three of us did some tall explainin' to the cook when we got back to camp that night.

It was while we was camped at Sycamore that me an' Slim brought the bull in camp, an' Slim was to blame for this, for I'd of never thought of it.

The outfit was workin' up on the rim of Black River the day it come about. An' it was along the middle of the evenin' when Shorty told Slim an' me to go into camp an' get the night horses up. Slim an' me was n't long in pullin' out for camp. For we had n't none of us had anything to eat since mornin'.

We was just about a quarter from camp when we jumped this maverick bull. He was just about two years old, an' we did n't have no trouble ketchin' him. I started to build a fire, but Slim says: "No. There's no use waitin' here for the iron to heat. Let's take him into camp an' brand him there, for we can both be eatin' while the iron is gettin' hot."

# MEN AND HORSES

"What in the blankety blank do you mean by bringin' that thing in camp?" was the first thing the cook says. We told him we was only tryin' to save a little time, but we was n't gettin' anywhere until Ben Hicks spoke up.

Ben had crippled a horse that mornin', an' Ben had come on back afoot. "You all go in an' eat," says Ben, "an' let me brand the bull."

That sort of pacified the cook, an' me an' Slim was just about half finished with our meal when I saw Hicks turn the critter loose. An when Hicks tailed him up he pointed the bull t'wards camp. Of course you could n't blame the bull. For he was on the prod from bein' led, an' when Ben burned the Cross S in his hide it did n't help his feelings none.

My pony was the first thing the bull seen after Hicks had turned him loose. But that pony knowed considerable about bulls, an there was no chance of hookin' him. Just then the bull looked up an' spied the cook, an' right down through the camp he come a-knockin' the pots an' pans four ways at once. Slim got down behind some pack-saddles, an' I was hidin' behind a little cedar-brush. But it happened so quick the cook never

had no chance to hide. For the bull went right through camp an' right on out the other side with the cook in front of him. I've heard both plain an' fancy cussin' from round-up cooks before, but it all sounded like a talk in Sunday-school 'longside of this cook of ours. There was a cat-claw thicket at the edge of camp, but they went through it as if it was n't there at all. When they come out the cook was still up in the lead. The cat-claw thorns had scratched him some. For he was n't wearin' no clothes that cluttered up his speed. When they finally disappeared from view the cook had lost his hat. But he was still a-runnin' like a quarter horse with the bull right at his heels.

This was the last I seen. For me an' Slim decided we 'd both be better off if we was some place else.

It was late when we come back to camp that night, an' the cook had cooled off some by then. It seems the bull had finally put him up a tree, so Ben Hicks went an' drove the critter off. But before he did, Ben made the cook promise there would n't be no shootin' done when he got back to his gun.

# COME AN' GET IT

We was makin' a drive at the Seneca one mornin' when a puncher named Steve Johnson happened into us.  Steve had been reppin' for our outfit at the Terrapins, an' none of us had seen him in two months.

"As soon as I go to camp an' get a bite to eat I'll come on back and give you all a hand," says Steve.

"Not with that cook you won't," we says.

An' then we told him the only time a puncher dared to come within ten feet of the coffee-pot was when the cook yelled at us to come an' get it or he'd throw it out.

"Oh, that's all right," says Steve.  For Steve is kinda hard himself.

While we was augerin' with Steve, Ben Hicks rode back to camp an' told the cook that a puncher was comin' down the trail, an' this puncher said he was stoppin' for a meal, an' what's more he wanted it right now.

"Well," says the cook, a-strappin' on his forty-five, "just let him come an' see what kind of luck he has."

Steve had n't been gone long, at least not long enough for a healthy man to eat, when he come a-ridin' back again.

# MEN AND HORSES

"That cook is crazy as a hoot-owl," was the first thing that Steve says. "He was stirrin' the beans with a six-shooter when I rode into camp. I 've seen tough round-up cooks before, but the only thing this cook had on was his hat an' a pair of boots. It sort of took my breath away. Then all at once he bawls at me. 'Git down, you blankety blank,' he says; 'we 're goin' to eat here pretty soon.'"

Of course we laughed. But it did n't seem to bother Steve. For Steve says anybody 'cept a fool will change his mind occasionally.

w York in 1928. rt by illness, he Exit to Brooklyn. on, Requiem for rt stories, Song ars Publishers.

# THE WILLOW TREE

## Hubert Selby Jr.

**MARION BOYARS**
LONDON • NEW YORK

58 Beaumont Road, Kuring-gai, NSW 2080

Printed in 2007
10 9 8 7 6 5 4 3 2 1

A CIP catalogue record for this book is available from the British Library.
A CIP catalog record for this book is available from the Library of Congress.

ISBN 978-0-7145-3139-7

Set in Baskerville in 10½/13pt
Printed in England by Cox & Wyman

To honor one life is to Honor The Infinite Spirit of LIFE.

There are three men whose loving and generous support made it possible for me to write this book: Bernd Eichenger, Ritchie Price, and John Ritchey. Thank you my friends. I love you and am eternally grateful to you.

Ken Hollings may be the only true editor in the English-speaking world. His artistic vision and loving heart 'saw' this book and made it possible for me to 'see' it too. I love you and will always honor your courage.

This book is dedicated to all those who have not only survived, but have prevailed.

**Bobby** lay in bed listening to the rats scratching and squealing in the wall a few inches behind his head, the rats sounding as if they were ready to gnaw through his skull and chew on his eyeballs from the inside.

The first time Bobby heard the sound, when he was a little kid, he fell off the bed screaming and stumbled to his mother in the kitchen who continued wrapping a clean diaper around his baby brother and told Bobby to hush his mouth, Aint nothin but the rats an you bes be gettin used to them boy cause you goin to be livin withem your whole life an anyways theys in the wall an long as theys in the wall they dont be gettin toya so just be hushin an get out my way an shut up that yellin I got nough with this screamin baby – Bobby continuing to yell and scream, scrambling around the floor after his mother and when she picked up the baby to put him in his crib she almost tripped over Bobby, Damn, you bawlin little snake, you worsen the rats, now HUSH YOUR MOUTH FORE I BE FIXIN TO FEED YOU TO THOSE GAUDDAMN RATS – clutching the baby, shaking and trembling with rage, crying with frustration, trying to find some way to lash out at the forces that kept her locked, with 2 young kids, in a rat infested tenement filled with kids who were all the time yelling and screaming, it making no difference if it be day or night there just be screaming and yelling and banging up and down the stairs and no man, no mutha fuckin man to help raise those gauddamn kids, no man there more than a nights flop, and if they be there longer they be wantin to dig into her welfare check, but never no man to help her with these youngins, not so much to even look afterem while she be boilin water for coffee or maybe scramblin some eggs, an I just be a teenager my own self, O damn chile, get out my way, YUALL HEAR ME GAUDDAMN IT BE GETTIN OUT MY WAY BEFORE I be chewin on your neck – slowly folding onto the floor, sitting, squeezing the baby, rocking back and forth, Bobby crawling under the table watching his mother trembling and rocking, his face wet and sticky with tears, but silent, no sound, not even of crying, coming from him, just staring at his mother squeezing the crying baby, warding off all awareness of sound, noise, presence, surroundings with her rocking back and forth, back and forth, back and forth . . . time, space and everything within them disappearing for a brief moment as she went wherever she went at these times, Bobby knowing only when his moms stopped she wouldnt be yellin no more for a while an she be given him a hug an maybe some kool aid an it be alright. . . .

for a while. . . .

In time the terror tempered to fear and he lunged out of bed and ran to his mother . . . then, in time, he just ran out of the room and waited until he was awake, then went back to his room . . .

and now he just lay there thinking of the day, hearing the sounds and noises coming from the streets, and the wailing, crying and shouting in the building. But his hearing was fine tuned to the rats, the gnawing, scratching, squealing, scampering, frenzied rats covered with plaster and grit, mottled with balls of dust as they searched the darkness with fiery eyes and twitching noses on their way to and from the piles of garbage that nurtured them, fearless in their fear, ready to leap at anything threatening them and rip it to shreds with yellow teeth.

Bobby leisurely reached back over his head and tapped

the wall and smiled as he heard the sudden sounds of panicked scuttling and squealing, Nasty mutha fuckas. He banged harder on the wall, Run mutha fuckas. Some day Im gonna be gettin me a 5 gallon jug a rat poison an watch you fuckas squirm . . . yeah, you goin feel like you swallow fire. . . .

Bobby listened to them for another minute, then stretched with boredom and sat on the side of the bed.

He had 2 brothers in the small room with him, somewhere between ages 5 an 9, but their beds were empty. They always beat it out of the room when they heard the rats. Used to be he had to hug them quiet and tell them, aint nothin to be scared about. . . .

Yeah, aint nothin to be scared about, the rats out in them streets be bigger an meaner than the mutha fuckas in the wall – and he banged on the wall and laughed for a moment hearing only his laughter and the panic of the rats. . . .

He stretched and scratched then yanked his pants up, put on his shirt and sneakers then went into the living room and walked across the couple of feet to the chair by the window and looked out at the street, feeling the cool breeze on his face and thinking it was gonna be a nice day, not too hot an pretty soon school be closed for the summer, just a few more weeks, then maybe he be gettin hisself a job an make some bread so he an Maria can do a few things, like go somewhere, somewhere away from here, maybe catch a couple a movies downtown before they be so old even tv not be wantin em – then went to the kitchen and splashed some cold water on his face, shaking the excess off his hands into the sink, patting his face and rubbing it, feeling the water soft and cool on his skin, then brushing his hands through his hair and wrinkling his nose as he passed the dirty diapers on his way out of the house, down the 4 flights of dark, dingy stairs, to the street, the sudden brightness always causing him to blink and stand still for a moment. He used the toilet in the bar next door, then continued toward school.

His girl friend, Maria, was waiting for him on the stoop of

her building. She jumped up and they hugged and kissed and continued walking down the street with their arms around each others waists. Hows everything babe? you lookin good.

Im alright hon. Things are goin good. Alicia let me try her new lipstick, cool, eh? – tilting her head back and pushing her mouth toward Bobby.

Hey, that be cool. I gotta get me some a that – pulling her closer to him and kissing her, then licking his lips, Maria laughing. How I be lookin in my new lipstick – wiggling his hips and rotating his shoulders in an exaggerated feminine manner, Maria laughing louder and shoving him on the shoulder a couple of times until he bounced into a parked car, Hey, dontcha know you should be treatin womens with respect, dont they teach you that in school? – grabbing her arms and pushing her backwards down the street a few feet, both laughing, then putting his arm around her waist again, and she his, and continuing down the street and turning the corner into sudden shade. Four teenage Puerto Rican boys got up from a stoop, spread across the sidewalk and strolled toward them, glaring with hatred. Maria muttered, *madre Dio* and clutched Bobbys arm. Bobby narrowed his eyes as much as possible and stared into the face of the one boy who stepped forward, ignoring Bobby, and looking at Maria with hatred, You should be my girl, what you doin with this nigga punk? Bobby leaned forward and Maria clutched his arm tighter and pulled him back, continuing to look the other boy in the eye, You leave us alone Raul. We dont be hurtin you.

Hey, youre hurtin all a us goin out with this black piece a shit – Bobby lunged forward and hit Raul with his free hand as he yanked his other from Marias grip, Maria screaming and trying to protect Bobby as he and Raul grabbed each other and the 3 other boys rushed forward, one hitting Bobby on the shoulder with a chain, Bobby trying to spin Raul into the others as one of the boys separated himself from the pack and threw a liquid into Marias face and she screamed and started thrashing about, her screams unending and filled with pain and terror, each scream more terrified and terrifying as the 4 boys started beating Bobby, hitting him again with the chain, punching him, knocking him down, kicking his head and body and then people from the stoops and streets started coming at them, yelling, Maria still screeching, her hands covering her face being burned by the lye, squeezing her head, delirious with pain, spinning in erratic circles, staggering from parked cars to building walls, stumbling, falling on her knees, crawling, staggering to her feet, screaming, screaming, screaming and a couple of women held her and someone yelled to call an ambulance and a couple of men started dragging the boys off Bobby whose face was beaten and bloodied and Raul kicked him in the balls, Bobby yelling with pain but barely conscious, Raul breaking free and running as the sound of a siren became louder, the others following him, Bobby dragging himself up by leaning on a parked car and someone told him to lay still, he be needin a amblance and Bobby tried to say, No, but only an almost inaudible sound gurgled from his lips and he hung over the car looking for Maria but only able to see the blood filling his eyes and he started dragging himself down the street hearing his head calling for Maria, Maria, but only blood oozing out of his mouth, the siren getting louder and louder and someone brought a bottle of water and started pouring that over Marias face as the 2 other women continued to hold her, trying to comfort her and keep her from tearing the burned flesh from her face as Bobby continued to stagger off in the opposite direction, Maria, Maria, echoing in his head and then the police car turned the corner and everyone except the 3 women with Maria went back into darkened doorways or strolled away as Bobby staggered down the street, the parked cars hiding him from the cops in the prowl car, and soon he was totally hidden by people walking the street who glanced at him and the commotion down the street, the police, and just continued walking, and when Bobby banged into the wall of a building he groaned with pain and spun around the corner and ended up hanging over a short railing on the side of steps going down under a building, the area below his head soon splattered with blood, hanging there an eternity, gasping for air, trying to breathe through the pain while his head continued to call for Maria, Maria, MARIA, and another voice screamed at the punk muthafuckas and he unconsciously pushed himself off the railing and continued down the street determined to find Maria and kill those muthafuckin spic bastards, everything ceasing for Bobby except the pain and rage driving him forward through the crowded streets, people stepping aside as he approached, some asking, You alright boy? Yo needin help? but he said nothing hearing only MARIA, MARIA, MARIA over and over in his head and feeling the screaming rage driving him toward them spic muthafuckas so he could cut their fuckin throats but he couldnt see where he was going and he kept knocking into people and ricocheting off parked cars and walls, having the wind knocked out of him as he fell over a railing or the hood of a car, and from time to time he vaguely heard the gasp of a woman as he stumbled past her but could not see how she reached toward him to try and help him but even if he had he would have continued because he didnt want anyones help, he just wanted to get to Maria but he couldnt find her and as the shock from the beating and the sudden attack increased he became less and less aware of his surroundings, less and less aware of time and his face painfully wrinkled into a frown when he heard the name Maria in his mind and he was almost immobilized from confusion because he knew Maria but couldnt make a connection with her name or why he was moving, if he was moving, yet vaguely aware of her image in his mind, and it seemed like he was on a beach or some sandy place and there were buses all around him and he couldnt hardly move and he suddenly stopped and stood still, swaying back and forth, slowly leaning forward more and more, an inch at a time, and suddenly he was spinning around and felt himself slowly going over the edge of a subway platform and he knew there was a train coming but couldnt hear it and was almost crying trying to figure out how to not fall in front of the train and suddenly his breath was gone and he was hanging like a life sized rag doll between 2 subway cars as a guy staggered from a bar and bumped into Bobby then

reached out and held him so he wouldnt fall, while trying to
maintain his own balance and figure out what had happened and who this was in front of him and then became
aware that Bobby couldnt stand and he blinked his eyes
against the sun and the look on Bobbys face. . . . Damn boy,
what the fuck be happenin to yo face – Bobby hanging from
the mans arms, folded and bent trying to understand what a
face is – You bes be commin in here – holding Bobby under
his arms, the 2 of them staggering back into the bar and into
a dark corner, the bartender squinting at them, What the
fuck yo be bringin that in here fo Darryll? He be one fuckin
mess.

Where else I be bringinim. He needin a drink.

I dont want that mutha fucka dyin in here.

What the fuck you be talkin about. If he can swallow a
drink he be fine.

The bartender poured a couple of ounces of bar whiskey
into two glasses, I dont be wantin no trouble man.

The 2 other men at the bar strolled down and looked at
Bobby, Sheeit Marv, what trouble that dude gonna be givin
yo? He and the other man chuckled and shook their heads,
He sure did take a couple a bad licks.

If he be part of a gang could be some bad ass trouble.
Them kids be crazy the way they goes aroun doin people.

One of the men laughed louder, Dont you worry none
Marv, ol Darryll here be protectin yo.

Marv leaned his head back, O shit, oh deep purple shit –
and the three of them laughed as Darryll gulped his drink
then dipped his finger in the other glass and dropped
whiskey on Bobbys tongue after seating him and leaning
him against the wall, encouraging him to swallow, the other
three watching as Darryll continued dropping whiskey on
Bobbys tongue, suddenly seeming sober and having all his
body movements under absolute control and doctoring
Bobby with love and care and the skill of a brain surgeon.
Bobby coughed and gagged when the first of the whiskey hit
his throat, but kept it down, and Darryll soothed and
encouraged Bobby to keep swallowing and waited a few
minutes before allowing a few more drops to drip into

Bobbys mouth, That the way boy, you jus keep that down — few more drops — you be feelin jus fine shortly, and Darylls voice became rhythmic and hypnotic like a chant as he continued the procedure of putting the whisky into Bobbys mouth a few drops at a time and smooth talking Bobby to keep it down then waiting a few minutes before putting a few more drops in his battered mouth, the other 3 silent and mesmerized by the procedure, watching intently as they leaned against the bar, then looked at each other, still silent, when Bobby moved his head slightly and Darryll put a few more drops into his mouth and Bobby swallowed without coughing and now the drinking was going faster and Bobby actually moved his eyelids and 20 or so minutes later the glass was empty and Bobby was almost sitting up by himself, and they all stared at him for a minute, each other, then Darryll with amazement and approval, and smiled as a glimmer of life started to flicker in Bobbys eyes and Darryll started gently rubbing the back of Bobbys neck, then carefully opened his shirt and shaking his head as the others made various sounds when they saw the bruises and chain marks on his chest and shoulders, You be needin some doctorin boy. Gimme a clean rag an some water . . . an a couple more drinks. Marv continued looking at them as he got the water, rags, and poured more whiskey into the glasses. Darryll continued rubbing Bobbys neck and shoulders, squinting his eyes as he looked him over carefully, Well, yo be breathin so I guess you be alive. He leaned his head back and looked carefully at Bobby then gently dabbed at his face with a wet rag, Bobby wincing and moving his head, Thats okay boy. Here, have another drink — carefully holding the glass near his lips and allowing a slow trickle into Bobbys mouth. He swallowed and Darryll, again, waited before giving him more to drink, then once more started gently cleaning Bobbys face, backing off for a moment each time Bobby winced and moved his head, Dont be movin yo head too quick boy, it jus might be fallin off. The other 3 chuckled, then one of the men asked Marv if he had a firs aid box or somethin, and Marv said he thought there be somethin aroun somewhere, at leas some curachrome, and Darryll continued his process of alternating between dripping whiskey into Bobbys mouth and cleaning his face, gently rubbing his neck in-between and talking to him in a soothing voice; and Marv found a small battered cardboard box with a couple of bottles of peroxide, methiolate and bandaids and put them on the bar, then asked Darryll how the boy be doin as if Darryll were a surgeon, He be doin jus fine. He be a tough little sucker – and the process of whiskey, cleaning and waiting continued, and in time, painful time, Bobby was sitting more erect, leaning against the wall, his eyes opening in narrow slits from time to time, peering at the men staring at him, barely able to see their faces, all edges still fuzzy, but knowing they were faces he was seeing, but in seconds his lids would close and he would just lean against the wall, painfully conscious of breathing, surprised by the occasional low groan that forced itself from his mouth, a groan that forced his eyes open for a moment as he peered at the face near him, then allowed them to close as he fought the stinging pain of his face and the stabbing pains in his chest and stomach, his breathing too shallow to be visible, but the men could hear the air struggling its way noisily in and out of his battered nose and mouth, Darryll still rubbing Bobbys neck, Marv pouring whiskey into glasses for everyone, Sheeit, that little sucker be breathin like a champ. Yeah, after 25 rouns with Ali. They laughed and continued to look at Bobby with admiration and Darryll with adulation, Damn, yo alright Darryll. Yeah, can you dig that mutha fucka, he be staggerin his ass outta here so drunk he caint stand up his own self an now he aint hardly move couple inches this way an that. They all laughed, Aint seenim this sober since his momma giveim the titty. They laughed again and Darryll picked up his glass and emptied it, I damn sure aint be havin none a that. Everyone laughed and Darryll went back to doctoring Bobby with whiskey and the wet rag and soon Bobbys wincing was only slight and Darryll was able to start cleaning the cuts and scrapes with peroxide and then dab them with methiolate, the process taking more than an hour, Marv keeping their glasses filled, Darryll only giving Bobby an occasional drop after the second glass, This boy no drinker. Doan want him gettin drunk an fallen down. Now how the fuck you be knowin he no drinker??? sheeit, they be babies crawlin aroun on they knees be drunk. Might be, but not this boy. If theres one thing Im knowin its drinkin and he no drinker. Marv guffawed and laughed so loud tears came to his eyes, Ol Darryll could be layin in his natural grave an he be reachin for a drink. Sheeit, no way a little bruisin be stoppin him. They all laughed long and loud and Marv refilled their glasses and they toasted Darryll who smiled at them and drained his glass while still rubbing the back of Bobbys neck and making sure he didnt move too suddenly. Seems like some ice be a good thing about now. Marv wrapped some ice in a towel and Darryll put it on the back of Bobbys neck and head and in a few minutes Bobbys eyes started fluttering and staying open longer and he looked around, dazed, How yo feelin boy? Bobby squinted and started nodding his head, but stopped and groaned. Yeah, you be busted up some, better jus sit still. See can yo drink some more a this, Darryll holding the glass of whiskey to Bobbys lips, Marv, and the other 2 men, smiling and giggling, in spite of themselves, at the faces Bobby was making as he sipped the whiskey and gagged and coughed and swallowed, holding on to the bar and swallowing again and again as Darryll encouraged him to keep it down, An you be feelin fine. What the fuck you be talkin about Darryll? dont matter how much whiskey you be pourin down that boys throat it be one long ass time befo he be feelin fine. Yeah, aint no body can hold that much whisky . . . not even you Darryll – and they all laughed again, mostly with relief as they watched Bobby becoming more and more animated, wanting to pound their man Darryll on the back for fixin the boy. Darryll let a few more trickles of whiskey into Bobbys mouth then leaned back a bit and peered at Bobby for a moment, then put the glass on the bar, That be about all yo can take. Dont wantchyuall gettin drunk an fallin down an bussin yoself all up again. The others nodded with approval and joined Darryll in empty-ing their glasses and leaning against the bar for support, and watching Bobby move around on the stool. Darryll smiled at Marv, I think he be needin a coke cola about now, right boy? Bobby nodded his head, very slowly, and leaned against the wall. Marv put the coke on the bar and Bobby started reaching for it and groaned and stopped as the pain in his right shoulder shot through him, then slowly inched his left hand forward and picked up the glass very carefully and sipped a little, allowing the ice to rest against his lips as long as possible. From time to time Darryll pressed the ice pack against the back of Bobbys neck and head and soon he looked at them without blinking his eyes, able to see them clearly, and asked where he was? MARVS RESORT, the home of the righteous drink. They chuckled and laughed and Bobby looked at them dazed trying to figure out what in the hell they were talkin about and he shook his head puzzled and Darryll told him about bumping into him and what followed; and Bobby told them what had happened to him, very slowly, becoming increasingly alert and aware as he spoke, obviously in a lot of pain, but the whiskey having taken enough of the edge off so he could, at least, speak. The men nodded occasionally as they listened knowing there was nothing unusual in what had happened, and when he finally finished Darryll looked at him and told him he should be gettin to the mergency at the hospital. I jus call 911 an you be on yo way. Yo need some good doctorin boy. Bobby shook his head, No way. The men looked at each other and shrugged, not surprised at Bobbys reply, and Bobby went on to tell them he couldnt go there because theyd report it an then the fuckin poeleece be on his ass an he dont need those mutha fuckas on his case, an he sure as hell caint go home, the moms get all hysterical an those fuckin spics come he caint do shit. Well, what the fuck you goin to be doin, ride the muthafuckin subway for a month boy? Youre bad hurt. Bobby shook his head, bewildered, I be alright. I be holin up somewheres, plenty bandoned buildins – the men nodded – an get my strent back then I be gettin them muthafuckin spics. But somehow I got to be seein my girl . . . I dont know, I caint seem to think too clear right now . . . you know where Im comin from? The men nodded in agreement and sat with Bobby, sippin the whiskey Marv poured from time to time, watching Bobby make the inner adjustments needed for him to go where he had to go an do what he had to do . . . in time Bobby grabbed the edge of the bar and slowly slid off the stool, very tentatively putting one foot on the floor, then the other, the men simply watching, not helping, not interfering, allowing him to find the strength he had someplace within him. He stood for a moment, occasionally bending his knees, then stood straight, wincing the entire time, blinking his eyes as he attempted to focus his eyes, the men smiling as they saw him not only dealing with the results of the beating, but the whiskey he obviously had no experience with. He finally let go of the bar and faced them smiling, Hey, right the fuck on. That the way baby – and Marv refilled their glasses and Bobby tried to smile but it didnt get very far, but he continued to feel the strength in his legs and took another drink of his coke. He looked at them for a few minutes, shrugged his left shoulder slightly, then slowly started turning from the bar. He stopped and looked at them for a moment, silently, and Darryll put out his hand, palm up, and Bobby laid his left hand on it, and Darryll returned it, then the others gave Bobby five, and he started toward the door, the men leaning forward an inch at a time as Bobby had to spread his legs to keep from falling, but they stayed where they were and let him do it his way. He reached the door and leaned against it for a moment then grabbed the knob, feeling so many different kinds of pain he couldnt concentrate on one so was able to move . . . slowly, carefully, vaguely aware of something different, something new, impossible to define yet very real as something pushed him on. . . .

He started to turn to say something, but the pain stopped him so he nodded his head slightly and struggled first with the knob, then leaning his weight against the door slowly opened it, crack by crack, the brightness of the street slicing its way into the bar and his eyes, continuing to push the door even though blinking his eyes against the light was painful, then stopped momentarily when he heard Darryll say, You be cool, man, hear?

Yeah, you be one righteous dude – chuckling.

You need somethin you just give a holler, hear?

Bobby nodded slightly then eased his way out the door into the sudden brightness, noise and energy of the street.

The 4 men watched Bobbys exit, squinting against the light, their eyes opening as the door clicked shut returning the bar to its comfortable darkness. They stared at the door for a moment, then looked at each other and smiled, Sheeit, thas the most sober I ever see you be Darryll. Marv refilled their glasses and they continued to look at each other, smiling, grinning, heheheheing . . . Gauddamn. . . . Yeahhhh. . . .

Bobby lowered his head against the glare of the sun and the stares of the people, able to walk down the street very slowly, with just a little weaving, staying close to the buildings in case he might suddenly need support. Every step, every breath painful, not knowing if walking or breathing was more painful, but he continued moving, wanting to get to the abandoned buildings cross-town as soon as possible, not wanting any hassles with the cops, but unable to move faster than a goddamn kid stumbling after his mommy, yet his body was already covered with sweat and it burned like a muthafucka, every scrape and cut on fire. After just a couple of blocks he wanted desperately to stop and sit down on a stoop but knew he couldnt afford to, that hed freeze to the steps and never get his ass up and before you knew it somebody be callin the man an he get his ass in deep shit, so he forced himself to keep moving, to keep putting one foot in front of the other, one agonizing step at a time . . . .

eventually becoming aware of more garbage on the streets, of abandoned and stripped cars, boxes, crates and debris from all over the fuckin world, and he carefully picked his away around and over the accumulation of years of refuse and knocked into the railing on the side of the steps going down into the cellar of one of the many abandoned buildings, carefully clutching the railing as he slowly descended, easing his foot down gently on the next step, panting, sweat rolling like fire down his face and the rest of his body, all of his body so wet he looked for puddles of water on the ground. He reached the bottom and the sudden shade was so refreshing he had to lean against the wall catching his breath . . . then inched his way into the increasing darkness and coolness of the cellar . . .

in time reaching an area with broken cardboard cartons and old rags and leaned against a wall and slowly and carefully lowered himself to the floor, leaned against the wall, lifted his legs, rested his arms on his knees, then his head on his arms, and fell into sleep.


The paramedics tried to take Marias hands from her face and calm her and listen to the women holding her who were trying to tell them what had happened, twisting and spinning in erratic circles as Maria fought them, the women refusing to let her go, the paramedics continuing to reassure the women and Maria and eventually tugged Maria free of the women as she continued to scream and jerk around until one of the paramedics managed to hug her and force her hands down and the other one winced as he saw the burns on her face and quickly gave her an injection, telling her it was alright, theyd get her to the hospital in just a few minutes and everything would be alright, just take it easy, we/re here to help you, just let us take care of you . . . itll be alright . . . just hold on . . . Maria continuing to scream until the injection took effect and soon she was hanging from their arms and they carefully put her in the ambulance and laid her down on the stretcher and strapped her securely and started the weaving, wailing drive through traffic to the hospital where she was wheeled into the ER and started hours of waiting, strapped to a gurney in the hall, when the pain started pushing through as the painkiller started wearing off and Maria rolled her head back and forth, groaning, trying to free her hands and panicking when she was unable to move, her moaning growing louder and more desperate the more the pain increased and she started crying with pain and fear and in time a doctor looked at her, and the report, and told the attendants to wheel her into a treatment room, the nurses watching the gurney being placed under the light, barely hearing Marias moaning and crying above the noises that were a constant part of their working day, the screaming and yelling, the pleading, begging, demanding, the total terror in the faces of family members, and one nurse gently held Marias head while the other one assisted the doctor, Keep still honey so we can help you – but Maria was completely controlled by her agony and yelled and screamed and thrashed her head around, struggling against the straps, and the doctor yelled to keep her head still for krists sake, I cant do a fucking thing if you dont keep her from – you have to stay still or I cant help you – shit, look at this mess – wheres that fucking ointment for krists sake and give her 75 mg of Demerol . . . and soon they became aware that Maria was quieting and her head barely moved and only low moans were intermittently coming from her throat, Well, guess she aint no addict, 75 mg of Demerol never put a junkie out – and the nurse held Marias head as the doctor applied the ointment as rapidly as possible – jesus krist, just a fucking kid and some asshole throws lye in her face O shit, it looks like she may have gotten some in the eye – someone stuck their head in the doorway – Make it quick, we got a jumper whos breathin but just barely – Yeah, sure – and he finished medicating Maria and yelled for an orderly to get her to the burn ward, and filled in the forms and clipped them to her chart and Maria was wheeled out the door, still asleep, and started the journey to the 9th floor burn ward.

Maria was put into a bed and left in the merciful arms of sleep.

Neighbors told Marias family what had happened, and a friend watched the 2 younger children while Marias mother and grandmother rushed to the hospital, getting to her bed as Maria was in the process of regaining consciousness, almost collapsing when they saw her head completely covered with bandages, only tiny slits for her eyes and mouth, moving slightly and moaning from time to time, then going back into unconsciousness. A nurse was taking her blood pressure, Marias mother looking at her pleadingly, then at Maria, and asking in her limited English how she was. The nurse wasnt certain what the woman was saying but she understood the look of fear on her face and did the best she could to explain that she was very sick but would be alright, nodding her head and saying, *Bueno, bueno*, the mother nodding in return, *Si, si*, then turning to the grandmother and telling her in Spanish that Maria would be alright, both women crossing themselves and sitting next to the bed and keeping a silent vigil until Maria awakened. They could sense the pain of the other patients, hearing the moans and prayers, the anguish in many different languages, but their concern for Maria kept them focusing on her, and they watched her chest move slightly with each shallow breath, their hands folded on their laps. At first the women started to reach out to her whenever she moved, but soon stopped when they realized Maria was unaware of their presence so they sat silent, immobile, hands folded on their laps, the rhythm of their bodies and minds attuned with that of Marias breathing, less and less aware of their surroundings, seeing and hearing only the sobbing breath going into their little girls body, and as it left bringing the pain and terror that frail body and frightened mind was experiencing, the sense of that pain increasing with each breath as did the movement of her body, the increase imperceptible at first as they continued to hypnotically stare at her, but then the pained movements of Marias body became obvious and they simultaneously adjusted themselves on their chairs and the grandmother placed her hands on Marias legs, still praying, and her mother brushed the hair back from Marias face, trying to see her eyes, trying to take her childs pain away by gently rubbing her shoulders, holding her hands, softly talking to her, trying to soothe away the fear with gentle and loving words to her daughter, My little girl, it is alright, momma is here precious jewel of my heart – and she looked at Maria with a tenderness that somehow escaped the anguish that came from the marrow of her bones and felt like it would consume her in time, but now she would not allow that because her little princess needed the love from her mothers heart and so she would postpone her pain, for now, so she could soothe away her daughters pain and she gently rubbed Marias arm, and her heart with her words, feeling her words and her love being absorbed by Maria and believed in its power, yet Marias uneasiness increased and her body shook from time to time with sobs and pain and now the sobbing breath was leaving her body spastically, sometimes twisted with a whine and a choking moan and her mother told the grandmother she would go for a nurse and left the room, the old woman continuing to keep her hands on Marias legs and praying.

The sounds of Marias pain were still filling her mothers mind as she looked around desperately, not knowing what she was looking for, knowing only her baby was in pain and needed something and there must be someone here who could help her, a doctor, a nurse, someone, but her babys cries distorted her vision and she continued looking up and down the corridor, starting to move in one direction, then another, until finally she noticed the nurses station down the hall and she rushed in that direction and almost bumped into a nurse, instantly talking very rapidly in Spanish, the look of confusion on the nurses face increasing with each word, Do you speak English? Marias mother stared at her for a moment . . . *O si, si,* is Maria – twisting her hands in an attempt to find the right words in a language alien to her – my dau . . . girl – looking toward Marias room and gesturing, tears coming from her blinking eyes, trying to blink understanding to herself and the nurse, her desperation increasing with each breath, the nurse reassuring her that she would have the doctor see Maria just as soon as possible, and Marias mother rushed back to the room and continued soothing her daughter, telling her everything would be alright as the grandmother continued praying, her hands on Marias legs, Maria recognizing her mothers voice and trying to reach out to her but was unable to move her arms but the mother leaned close to her little ones face and continued to speak soothingly to her as Maria cried and wanted to hug and kiss her mother but the pain in her face made that impossible so the mother gently rubbed Marias shoulders and arms and kept her face just inches away from Marias and told her that momma was there and would take care of her little princess and Maria wept and simply said momma, momma, momma, the old woman holding tight to the legs of her granddaughter, silently praying, the words louder and louder in her head to disperse the confusion and pain of seeing this little girl in so much agony, her face all bandages, only tiny slits for eyes that were pouring tears and though the eyes were almost invisible the old woman could see the agony and fear in them and so she closed hers from time to time, trying to stop trying to understand how such a thing could happen to someone who every morning brought her grandmother a bowl of hot coffee and a piece of soft bread, what kind of world was this that threw fire into her little girls face, but she could not always keep her eyes from looking for Marias and feeling the pain fill her heart as the bandages became more and more damp from Marias weeping, and the mother told her little princess to give her the pain and she would wear it for her and give it to the Blessed Virgin who always looked over her and her precious baby, and the mothers soothing voice reassured and relaxed the girl lying on the bed and though she choked and jerked and shivered from time to time from crying, and moaned with pain and panic, she did become a little more relaxed and in time stopped tossing and twisting and moved only slightly as she continued weeping and calling to her mother as the women continued praying and soothing. . . .

Moishe looked down at Bobby, watching and listening to him breathe, studying his face, at first thinking he was just another drunk when he noticed the smell of liquor coming from Bobby, but he somehow didnt feel he was. His face, though badly beaten, didnt seem to be the face of a drunk. Moishe looked at his clothes, more than his face, to figure his age, and it seemed he was still in his early teens, and he wondered what a teenager was doing here. The kids were always beating each other up, but they never came here . . . actually just about no one ever came here, the entire area for miles around being deserted and, in some ways, resembling Europe right after the war but that was another time, another life . . . hopefully. But what was this boy doing here? Moishe looked up at the ceiling for a moment, then closed his eyes and sighed.

He shook his head and knelt beside Bobby, studying the bruises and cuts on his face, noticing the tremors in his body, some slight, almost imperceptible yet significant to Moishe, telling him there were many unseen bruises, but probably no broken bones . . . allowing all his senses to filter and assimilate the information before reaching out and gently touching Bobbys shoulders and holding them for a moment, then shaking Bobby slightly until he started moving his head.

Moishe continued studying Bobby, aware of how he was moving his head, the expression on his face, the evidence of pain even though Bobby was still not conscious, the only sound that of Bobbys shoulders rubbing against the flaking wall.

Bobbys movements started slowing so Moishe shook him gently, again, by the shoulders, this time a little longer, feeling Bobby resist him, knowing Bobby wanted to shake loose of Moishes hands, but was unable to do so. When Bobby started mumbling Moishe stopped shaking him and leaned back slightly and as soon as Bobby started moving or mumbling less he shook him again until he noticed Bobbys eyelids start to flutter then started talking to him, from time to time poking him gently on the leg when he seemed to be going back into unconsciousness, Bobby jerking his leg away, the movement lacking resolve and energy, scrutinizing him even more closely now that he was on the border of consciousness, continually in touch with his own inner response to Bobbys movements and what they said to him. He nudged his leg again and Bobby started to frown but stopped instantly as the pain registered. . . .

You should wake up already – his German accent strong yet his words clear. Bobby stirred, his movements and

expression reflecting his battle with the increasing awareness of pain as the numbing effects of the whiskey and sleep
were rapidly disappearing. Moishe continued watching and
was silent for a moment, then told Bobby he should talk to
him. Can you talk???? Say something. I need for you to talk.

Moishe continued to watch Bobby struggle against the
pain and consciousness, his body and face reflecting the
pain more and more. Youre hearing me???? Whats your
name? Tell me already your name.

Bobby started groaning and shifted his weight slightly,
Huh???? Wha???? Ohhhh. . . . Mutha fu. . . .

Tell me already your name.

Name???? Wha the. . . . Bobbys eyes started fluttering
open and he tried peering at Moishe, but pain closed them
almost instantly, but he continued forcing them open, Moishe
watching intently, letting his head hang forward for a moment then forcing it up, his eyes open in two swollen
slits . . . Who. . . . What you want???? Bobby struggling to
keep his balance and his eyes open, trying desperately to
remember where he was, remembering the beating, aware
of the pain and vaguely seeing this weird face of some old
honky in front of him, but there was nothing else, just an
increasing awareness of pain, everywhere pain, and it got
worse with every breath.

You know your name?

Huh???? — squinting, shaking his head, Wha the, course I
got a name yo — the effort of speaking sending shocks of
pain thru his body and igniting his face — Ooohhhh

Moishe reached out and steadied Bobby, Youre relaxing,
no talking for while — continuing to steady Bobby and
watching him deal with his pain, more and more certain
Bobby did not have a concussion. Bobby suddenly looked
at him, Yeah. . . . I remember. . . . This be a bandoned
building, Ohhh — he stopped talking and closed his eyes for
a moment, Moishe feeling the tremors going thru Bobbys
body, Youre hurting bad. Bobby took a slightly deeper
breath and raised his head for a moment, then lowered it
again, I be alright — his voice weak, thick.

Can you move . . . walk maybe?

Bobby wanted to say, How the fuck you think I got here yo crazy old man, but was able only to nod very gently for just a few inches.

You should go to the hospital.

Bobby shook his head and spoke through his pain, No – starting to push himself up, Moishe gently restraining him, Rest. Moishe watched the pain subside slightly, Theres somebody should know youre here? No . . . no – straining thru pain – no . . . raising his head again but this time keeping it up and looking Moishe in the face, Moishe easily understanding the pleading, 'please', in Bobbys look, Moishe continuing to look into Bobbys eyes then nodded his head and Bobby allowed his head to lower, his eyes to close. Moishe continued to support Bobby, thinking he could treat Bobby, feeling Bobby was safe and trusting his feelings. He continued kneeling beside Bobby until he raised his head slightly and looked at Moishe, then stood up, So . . . looking down at Bobby for a moment who had to be content with seeing only Moishes feet . . . wait. Moishe almost laughing out loud when thinking Bobby had a choice.

Bobby could hear Moishes footsteps slowly disappearing somewhere in the midst of the building, leaning slightly to the right as he strained to hear the inaudible sound of Moishes walking, suddenly more alert than he had been, wondering who this ol fool was, but more frightened he would not come back. Bobby was more and more over-whelmed with pain and knew there was no fucking way he could move, that he was stuck here no matter what hap-pened, even if them mutha fuckin rats come an start chewin up his ass there be no way he be movin so he continued to lean to his right and strain to hear somethin, anythin, that mean the old man be comin back but he be hearin nothin cept maybe there was some rat scratchin back there some-where but he be movin enough to keep them yella fuckers from eatin his ass, he aint about to lay still an let them nasty fuckers eat his ass O krist, where that ol man be, must be nough time fo him to go downtown an back by now, damn that ol fool, but I be gettin them mutha fuckin spics, I be killin they asses when I get – what the fuck that? leaning and straining more, the sound confusing yet somehow familiar as it echoed through the deserted cellar, becoming increasingly familiar, reminding him of something and as it became louder and closer he realized it was wheels of some kind and he started to frown but the pain quickly stopped that so he just kept his head raised and peered into the darkness until he saw the old man, pulling a large, red wagon behind him.

Moishe stopped in front of Bobby and smiled, So. . . . Bobby obviously puzzled and staring at the wagon for a moment, then slowly raised his head as far as possible to try and see the old mans face, but couldnt see above his chin. Moishe smiled, So . . . youre sitting, Im pulling – Moishe shrugging and kneeling and pushing the wagon against Bobby and holding it with a knee as he helped Bobby move and get in the wagon, the wagon tipping and starting to move as Bobby sat on the edge and almost fell down, Moishe holding the wagon and Bobby and suddenly Moishe started laughing as an old silent comedy flashed through his mind where a wagon kept tipping and rolling and Chaplin or Keaton, or someone slapsticked around with the wagon for 10 minutes and Bobby asked him what the fuck he be laughin at as he stretched across the wagon, the wagon tipping and Bobby slowly sliding down on the cement floor and Moishe shook his head and blinked away the tears of his laughter and put his foot against the wheel and helped Bobby roll over and eventually sit in the wagon. Moishe looked at him, fighting laughter, smiling, then lifted Bobbys legs and placed them in the wagon and Bobby sat there seeing himself sitting in a wagon like a kid, feeling like a fool, but hurting too bad to say anything. Moishe continued looking at Bobby for a moment, smiling, then picked up the handle, So . . . we go for a ride, ya? Bobby managed to raise his head, a faint smile in his eyes, Yo bes be drivin careful or I bus yo ass – and Moishe smiled and Bobby heard a giggle go through his head and maybe even it made a sound.


When the doctor finished examining Maria, medicating her

burns and replacing the bandages, he wrote several prescriptions, then took the 2 women to the hall to explain to them what would be done for Maria and the prognosis.

The grandmother clutched her daughters arm, watching her as she listened to the doctor. He told them that the burns were very serious, but he felt certain Marias eyes were alright, and when he said this both women blessed themselves and thanked the Blessed Virgin and Jesus, a few tears rolling down the cheeks of the old woman and the mother nodded, *Si, si, muchos gracias*; then the doctor hurriedly explained that he could not tell them exactly what would happen, at this time, that they would have to wait until her face was healed sufficiently before they could determine what additional treatment would be needed, trying not to show his impatience as Marias mother struggled to understand his words and what they meant, then translating for the grandmother, but he could not keep from looking at his watch from time to time, trying to remember to smile at the women who looked puzzled and frightened as they stared at him, then each other, and he tried to explain skin grafts but the more he did the more panicked the women looked, the more they clung to each other, expressions of terror passing through their eyes, sobs choking them, trying to reassure them with his smile and by patting their arms, wishing he did have the magic wand they wanted him to have that would instantly make everything better and thinking of the dozens of patients he still had to see that afternoon, almost all with families who were worried and concerned and wanted to know what was wrong and be reassured that everything would be alright, and as he started to leave the women thanked him and blessed him over and over, May all your children be strong and healthy – and he continued to back away, Thank you, thank you – nodding, walking backward down the hall until he could get free of their gratitude then turned and walked rapidly to the next patient.

Maria was sleeping, the bandages new, clean, antiseptic and promising relief and healing, hiding the visible evidence of Marias condition, the women mercifully having no idea how tortured and savagely burned her face was, not wanting to think of that but only that their little girl would live. Dazed and numb with panic and terror, they held each others hand, each in their own way praying to Jesus and the Blessed Virgin for release from pain for their child, and for her lifelong beauty to bless always the house in which she lives and suddenly the grandmothers head fell forward as tears wet her old skin and the daughter held her hand in both of hers, watching the tears fall from her cheeks to the linen on the bed . . . and in time she raised her head and looked at her daughter who dabbed at the tears with a tissue, and when she finished the old woman nodded, Thank you . . . but how can this be? Did I come to this strange land of ice and chills, and a strange language, so this little one can suffer? Did God put me here to die for her? Do I not know that to have children is pain, but is this the true pain of a mother, one who has given birth to 2 generations of children? If this is so why did I not then have this pain in the land of my birth . . . the land of your birth . . . and hers, our sweet little baby? Why am I here in such a madness of the world where people speak only to curse? O Mother of God what is it that I have done to bring such wrath upon this child???? What has . . . O God . . . God . . . God. . . .

and the old woman bent her shaking head, her tears falling on her daughters hands as they held hers, then raised them to her lips and kissed them, You have done no wrong mother, as Maria has done no wrong. Then who??? Who??? Why is Gods wrath upon my head and our babys face??? O dear sweet God, why????

I do not know. I know my little one is innocent and I know you did no wrong. What can we do but pray?

Pray? How can I pray . . . here? Do I pray in a strange language, one unknown to me? Do I pray to the God of this city??? this hospital where they wrap bandages around a little face and stick needles into arms? Is this where I pray? Can this God of cars and trucks and gangs hear the rattle of my beads? Can she????

they looked at the bandaged head

of Maria for a silent moment. . . .

Yes . . . her heart hears
our voices . . . and the beads. God will protect her . . . as
always. If she is not safe in the arms of God where can she
be???? Where can we be????

I do not know. I do not know the answer to that . . . or
anything else. I pray because I pray. . . . What else can I
do . . . even here????


Bobbys mother was climbing the stairs, with a large bag of
groceries and her youngest son and daughter trailing behind her, as two of her neighbors started telling her about
what happened to Bobby, and from time to time she would
stop and adjust the bag of groceries and tell her daughter
struggling up the steps along side her, Stop yankin on me,
you want me to be fallin down the stairs – an what this about
the poeleece, they be messin wit my boy? Uh uh, I hear he
be gone when they be comin aroun – O chile, be lettin me
go. . . . She stopped for a moment and sighed, I caint be
dealin with all this jus now – shaking her head and catching
her breath – damn, these kids like to be killin me with theys
draggin on me all the time, damn chile, let go a me –
shaking her head and lookin down at the steps for a moment
– I bes be gettin up these Gauddamn stairs – forcing herself
to move, the young children and the women following.
They say the girl got hurt bad, you know her? Her? Bobbys
gurl frien? How I be knowin his gurl frien? Damn.

They
reached her floor and she stood, catching her breath, in
front of the door for a moment before opening it, the young
children running in. She plunked the groceries on the
kitchen table and fell into a chair. Ah swear, them stairs be
doin me in someday. So what you be tellin me? Bobby got
his self beat up? He be goin out with a spic girl – an them
mutha fuckas whipim – seem like they dont like he be goin
out wit her. Whach yo mean? His gurl frien be a spic? Ah
hear she be real light skinned, you know. Hear they throw
lye in her face so – They do that? Thas right. Be a whole

bunchofem so – Thas right, Bobby never had no chance to – They sure enuff throw lye in her face? Thas what they say. Who all is, they? Helen be right there when it happen an she an Tom from cross the street, an who else? – Tina an – Yeah, thas right, Tina. . . .

Bobbys mother was nodding, hearing their voices more than the words, seeming to sit deeper and deeper in her chair as if she were somehow sinking into it and through it and disappearing into the floor. . . .

amblance come an take away the girl – Say she burned real bad an maybe bline – She be bline?!!!! Say could be. She be screamin somethin awful – Bobby get any lye? he not bline? Uh uh, no way he – But a buncha them gang up onim an – Hear tell they had chains an baseball bats – Bobbys mothers head jerked back and she stared at the women for a moment, the information forcing itself through her resistance, What they be doin to my boy? soun like they killinim. Not likely. Say he be gettin up an movin by the time the poeleece come an – Say he be leavin a trail a blood, he be bleedin somethin – Now what you be sayin that for? aint – Cause it be true. Yo can see for your ownself you be goin – Damn yo big mouth (Bobbys mother stared at them, blinking her eyes, shaking her head, slapping at the young hand yanking on her dress) Dont chyall be listen to her, she don know what she be talkin about no – Whach yo mean, I seed it with my own eyes bitch so you be – Who yo callin bitch, bitch, aint she be havin nough trouble without you be talkin about no trail o blood like it be some chicken bleedin all – Well they whoop his ass bad an he be bleedin – Sure he be (Bobbys mother continued to automatically slap at the hands tugging on her, not hearing the childs voice, hearing only the 2 women, but their voices were becoming fuzzy, hazy, and she was confused and started rocking back and forth, hearing a hum in her head, the sound becoming more and more gentle as she slipped inside herself to that place of refuge for a moment, a much needed moment, but very soon the hum became a whine and the womens voices intruded themselves upon her and she grabbed the hand tugging and allowed the child to crawl up on her lap). . . . Yo see someday that big mouth o yours be gettin you – You think he be daid?

The two women stopped talking and turned their heads simultaneously and looked at her, What that? You think he be daid . . . you think my Bobby be daid?

The women looked at each other for a moment, frowning . . . Uh uh, he be – No way that boy be dead. Dont you worry none, he be fine. Yeah, he be comin home soon enough. . . .

The women stared at her as she nodded her head, seeming to be looking at someplace in between them and above them, time suddenly heavy between words, the women suddenly aware of their own breathing, the child wiggling on her lap.

But he bad hurt???? The women continued staring at her as they eyed each other . . . then nodded their heads, Seems so.

The child on her lap stopped wiggling and stared up at her mother who was holding her gently with both hands, yet seemingly unaware of her presence. . . .

How I be knowin he alright? Might be I should be axin the poeleece.

You doan want to be doin nothin like that.

Why? Mah boy in trouble cept bein hurt?

Uh uh, he not be doin nothin, least ways we know – looking at each other and nodding their heads, But you dont want nothin to do with the poeleece – Yeah, no way. You know how they be doin peoples like us???? – she nodded her head, continuing to stare at the place between and above them – They not be doin shit for us. Mos likely they be tellin the welfare he not home and they be deductin that from yoall check, you know how they always be doin everythin they can to take our money. . . .

She blinked her eyes and looked at them, How I be knowin he alright?

He be lettin you know. Thas right, his friens know soon nough. Caint be doin him no good goin to the poeleece. Thas right, that be big trouble for everyone. . . .

nodded her head, almost absently, then her shoulders suddenly sagged and she pulled the child close to her, I surely got enough troubles now.

Now aint that the truth. . . .

No need you invitin more.


Moishe was very careful as he pulled the wagon, occasionally looking at Bobby, scrupulously avoiding, or kicking away, pieces of debris so Bobby would not be bumped out of the wagon, stopping before turning a corner, then very slowly turning the wagon and continuing on their journey through the darkness of the cellar, Bobby completely lost, not even knowing if he was still in the Bronx or if they had somehow crossed the river to whatever was on the other side, unable to see more than a few feet yet the old man never hesitated, always knowing exactly where to go, where to turn, like he could see in the dark like a cat, or a rat, or something. A couple of times the old man stopped and asked Bobby, How youre feeling, youre alright? Bobby barely nodding his head and the old man looking at him for a moment, nodding back. So . . . and continued pulling Bobby through the darkness, Bobby mostly aware of pain, but from time to time a fear would jolt him as he was suddenly assaulted with the simple truth he had no idea what might be hiding in the darkness just a few feet from him, an what kindda nut this ol man be . . . might be he some muthafuckin faggot what likes to chop up young boys, they be a whole shitload a them muthafuckas aroun . . . and Bobby would look into the darkness and think of trying to move his body, to get out of the wagon and outrun the ol fool and then the pain would grab his attention, but eventually the pain would step aside so the fear could take over again and it bounced back and forth like that until the final turn and Bobby could see a light in the distance and then, seemingly at once, they were in Moishes apartment and he stopped for a moment and gestured around him, So . . . this is where I live. What you think? smiling at Bobby.

Bobby blinked his eyes and shook his head, his amazement momentarily obliterating his fear and pain. . . . Damn. . . . I aint never seen no pad like this before . . . damn. . . . This be righteous . . . outta sight righteous.

Moishe looked at him for a moment, I take already a look at your face before you fall asleep. Its hurting a lot? Bobby shrugged, just slightly, having learned just how much movement he could tolerate before the pain kicked his ass. Your body, is hurting too? Bobby suddenly seemed deflated and appeared to be just a little shorter as he sat in the bright red wagon. Moishe pulled the wagon next to a chair in the kitchen, then gently touched Bobbys arms until he found spots that werent too tender, then helped him out of the wagon and onto a chair, Moishe watching him intently, seeing the severe pain registering on Bobbys face, the mouth starting to move to complain or moan, then stopping before a sound came out, able to see that Bobby wanted to keep his eyes open but closing in pain in spite of all his inner resolve. When he was seated Moishe put a pillow behind his back and Bobby slowly eased himself against it. Moishe watched for another moment . . . then got his first aid supplies and equipment and laid them out on the table. He clipped magnifying lenses over his glasses and put on latex gloves before carefully examining Bobbys face, gently probing here and there, Bobby wincing or jerking, but not complaining, Moishe dabbing at areas with cotton and peroxide, cleaning little pieces of grit from some of the deeper cuts, stopping from time to time and standing erect, allowing Bobby to catch his breath and when he could see from Bobbys face that the severity of the pain had passed he continued cleaning the wounds on Bobbys face. When he finished covering everything with antiseptic, he once again stood up and looked at Bobby for a second. . . . Youre having 2 very deep cuts. One on your cheek I can be closing with special bandage, butterfly, so maybe no scar . . . but would hurt having it on sore skin. Sheeit, I doan care about no scar. Maybe so, but one day maybe is different. Other one on jaw should be sewn. Is very deep. Not certain is closing with just bandage. Bobby frowned, Caint you be doin somethin? Moishe shrugged, Plumber, painter, carpenter, handyman . . . but no doctor. You should be going already to the hospital, let a doctor stitch your jaw. Bobby kept shaking his head, Damn, I caint be goin to no hopsital. Aint this a muthafuckin shame, I gotta be lettin some ol honky name Mushie patch me up like he be Dr. Frankenstein. Damn them spics!!!!

Moishe smiled gently at Bobby, sensitive to his dilemma and pain.

Sheeit, I dont be havin no choice.

So . . . Im careful Dr. Frankenstein is not making a monster already.

Bobby looked up at Moishe with the magnifying glasses over his lenses, his eyes looking monstrous. Damn, you be lookin more like Dr. Cyclops.

Moishe grinned, So . . . a doctors a doctor, ya?

Bobby just looked at Moishe and started to shrug, but quickly stopped, then closed his eyes as Moishe started treating his face. He carefully put the bandages on with gentle expertise, and when he finished he carefully scrutinized his work and nodded approvingly, Goot . . . goot. Could be maybe better if I kept open my eyes – looking at Bobby with a serious face, Bobby blinking, staring for a moment, then smiling and Moishe laughed. So . . . youre resting for a minute then we/re seeing how is the rest of you. Then I give to you something for the pain and you rest, ya?

Moishe separated the things that needed sterilizing, then very carefully started cutting Bobbys shirt off – Whach you doin man?! Moishe stopped, Is best way not to hurt you – Bobby staring at him – And anyway, is all torn – smiling reassuringly at Bobby – you cant be wearing it anymore. But what I be wearin man? Moishe waved his hand, I have lots of shirts . . . soft and clean, ya? Bobby looked down at his shirt, Yeah . . . guess so.

Moishe finished cutting Bobbys shirt off, then examined Bobbys torso and though there were no cuts, and Bobbys dark skin hid the severity of the bruises, it was obvious that he was basically one big bruise with some areas much worse than others. He gently touched here and there, held Bobbys ribcage with his hands and had him breathe as deep as possible, probed a few of the more severally bruised areas, eventually stepping back and smiling, So . . . lots of bruises but no broken bones. Lucky. Lucky?!!!! How the fuck you be sayin I lucky, Those mutha – then pain quickly silenced him.

Ya – Moishe nodding his head energetically – lucky.

Sheeit. . . .

Moishe shrugged and continued to look at Bobby who was now paying the price for talking so energetically, for moving suddenly, Ya, lucky. No eyes cut out, no concussion, no broken head, no broken bones, no teeth knocked out, everything, good chance, okay inside. . . . Ya, a very bad beating, but soon you be alright not dead, not busted. . . . Moishe smiled empathetically and tenderly, a sense of gratitude flowing through him. . . . Ya, lucky . . . very lucky. Bobby looked at him, and spoke slowly, quietly, Maybe so, but I be gettin them muthafuckas – the vehemence deadly, tangible – They be history man. Moishes glowing expression suddenly darkened with a profound sadness that came from so deep within him he felt as if he would pass out and he had to steady himself by leaning on the back of the chair and closing his eyes for a moment, fighting the darkness that felt as if it would not only cut off his breath, but totally consume him and spit him out as a little ball of screaming pain. . . . Moishe had no idea how long the struggle continued, but in time he became aware of breathing and his eyes opened and he looked around at the familiar surroundings, blinked his eyes several times then looked at Bobby with love and compassion, wanting for a moment to hug him close to his chest, to gently rub his head, to soothe away all his pain, but all he could do was continue to lean against the chair until he was able to speak. Im giving you for the pain something and youll rest. . . . Ya, rest. Moishe handed Bobby a couple of capsules and two pills and a glass of water. Bobby looked at them, then at Moishe, What you givin me man? Antibiotics and pain pills. Where you be gettin these? Bobby squinting at Moishe. From a friend . . . a doctor. Its alright – they looked at each other for a moment, then Moishe shrugged and his smile broadened, You think maybe its not good you dont take them . . . but its bad you get infection, very bad. You dont mind the pain, dont take the pills. And anyway, we can go to the hospital if you get worse, so dont take — Moishe extending his hand and Bobby tossed the pills in his mouth and drank a mouthfull of water. Moishe felt a profound sense of relief and nodded approvingly, Ya, is best.

Moishe prepared a bed for Bobby with a spare mattress on a low platform so he shouldnt hurt himself if he fell out of bed. When he came back to the kitchen he looked at Bobby for a moment as he struggled to keep his eyes open. Youre able to walk to the bedroom, or we/re using the wagon? I be walking. Bobby started wobbling to his feet and Moishe quickly grabbed his elbows and supported him. They walked slowly to the bedroom. When Bobby saw the bed with the clean sheets and pillow, he became aware of just how exhausted he really was, how deep the pain and fatigue went. Moishe eased him onto the bed, and helped him off with his shoes and pants, then covered him. You feel a chill and Im giving you more blankets. Bobby nodded slightly and stretched out, suddenly overwhelmed with how comfortable the sheets felt and how totally exhausted he was. He had been struggling for a long time to keep his eyes open and now he could close them, and keep them closed, and just go to sleep . . . and though he hadnt thought of it, he felt safe, inspite of everything that had happened that day, he felt safe with this weird old man who lived in this really cool apartment so deep under the ground of the most desolate part of New York City, and probably the entire country. In seconds he was asleep.

Moishe stood watching Bobby, smiling as he noticed Bobbys breathing change as he fell asleep, almost able to see the tension drain from his bruised body, relieved that there was nothing abnormal about his breathing . . . considering the circumstances. After a few minutes he became aware that thoughts were trying to intrude themselves into his mind so he made a more conscious effort to be aware of Bobbys breathing, but the thoughts were insistent so he left the bedroom and went to the living room and sat in his chair.

He looked at his finger tips, the design in the rug, tracing it from the center to the edges and then around the border, tracing intricate scrolls and curlicues, trying to count the crystals of the chandelier, staring at the light as it reflected from them, trying to see hidden shapes in the clouds of a landscape on the far wall . . . but in time he could no longer ignore the question in his mind . . . in all of his being . . . What is this all about? Is Bobby finding his way here just a coincidence? But I dont believe in coincidence. Do I now search and hunt for meaning in this? Ahhh, such a long day. Im fuzzy. Just like Bobby. . . . Bobby. Why is he here? Tell me. Dont be so silent. Why do you always keep such secrets? Tell me is he a curse or a blessing? Will he be gone tomorrow? Is this . . . me . . . a stop on the way from there to there? Why do I believe him? Why do I trust him? Why am I so sure hes not a thief, a gang member, a drug user or seller? O, whats the difference. Is there a real importance to all this speculation, these endless and unanswerable questions? They always lead to madness. Sometime I/ll know, but not now. Its never, now, but only later that I learn these things. Now hes here. Now Im taking care of him. Now we are both alright. Right here, right now . . . we/re fine. Tomorrow??? who knows???? If it comes. Maybe tomorrow wont even bother coming and Im worrying today. So I/ll leave it alone. Hes here. I did a little doctoring and hes fine. . . . Now. And Im fine. . . . Now!

Moishe got up and went to the kitchen and filled a bowl with ice cream and covered it with chocolate sauce, then went back to his chair.

But tomorrow always does come. So far, anyway. Who knows, tomorrow he might leave and Im worrying now. Leave? How could he leave? The day after a beating is always worse. No longer protected by shock. Really feel the pain. Just sit and hurt. Ya . . . just sit and hurt. So what am I, some magician? So what do you want from me? to make him better? You want him better you fix him. Im too old to do this again. No more. How many days do I have? Let them be peaceful. . . . Yes, peaceful. Its not too much to ask. Peace. And what about him? Can I be his only source of help? Millions of people here and Im the only one? Who can believe that? Yes, yes, I know, its for me. So whats he going to teach me???? Yes, yes, I guess so . . . I guess I/ll find that out too, but not now.

Moishe noticed that the bowl was empty and felt a smile on his face, Life should be as easy as eating ice cream. . . . But I dont remember eating it. Im sure it was delicious, but where was I when I ate it? So . . . life is a bowl of ice cream . . . you dont remember living it — Moishe shook his head — If only you could forget . . . but even if you forget you remember, no, no, no, no philosophy today. . . .

But I thought whatever time was left would be peaceful . . . I sit, I read, I listen to music, I go for a walk, I ride to Prospect Park and sit under the Willow Tree, I remember, I forget, I look at pictures, I do, I do, I do . . . or I dont do, but its peaceful . . . only me . . . no worries.

Moishe got up and went to the kitchen and started washing his bowl, I dont mind if time flies by unnoticed while Im washing the dishes, but how long does it take to wash 2 bowls, 2 bowls??? how long since I washed anything more than one????

He wiped out the sink with a sponge, looked at the porcelain for a while, then at the bowl in the drain rack, sighed loud and long then went back to the living room and sat in his chair. The cat strolled over and sat at his feet for a moment, looking up, then tapped his leg and Moishe looked at her for a moment, then nodded his head and tapped his lap and the cat jumped up and made herself at home, turning in a few circles first, then eventually nestling into the spot she wanted, curled her tail around her and closed her eyes as Moishe rubbed her head and scratched her behind the ears, You I dont have to worry about, a rub, a scratch, food and water . . . and love, cant forget that, can I? I love you but I dont have to worry, its so easy to give you everything you need . . . and you give me so much comfort, dont you — rubbing her head with both hands and leaning over and kissing the cat on the nose, the cat opening her eyes for a moment and looking at Moishe, rubbing her nose with a paw, then closing her eyes and adjusting herself again on Moishes lap. . . . Oh, this is craziness. In a few days . . . well a little longer . . . and he/ll be gone. What have I to do with a young boy, and what does he have to do with me? Soon, soon he/ll be better and he/ll leave and Im sitting here worrying. . . . Oh, leave it alone . . . leave it alone and soon no worries like before. Peaceful.

Moishe looked down at the cat, an almost perfect circle of fur, and smiled as he rubbed her from the top of her head, down along her body, to the end of her body, the cat reflexly moving muscles, riding with the rubbing as a cork on gentle currents, then the cat stood, humped her back, stretched, turned in a few circles, then once again settled into a ball on Moishes lap.

Maria gradually awoke in the middle of the night, moaning through a narcotic haze, and pain, her eyes intermittently opening and closing as she swayed back and forth between sleep and consciousness, being dragged in both directions until her eyes stayed open and she looked around the unfamiliar room, as much as possible, her terror as well as her physical condition limiting her movement. She was aware of the glow in the hallway but couldnt remember what had happened and as the paralysis of fear twisted her she was only aware of not being home, at that moment that was the only thing she knew, and she had never been away from home before and didnt know if she was dead, and though her voice was silent from fear, within her head she screamed for her mother, her body becoming increasingly rigid the more she awakened, so she lay still, frozen, trying not to breathe, hoping she could become invisible so that whatever was near her wouldnt see her and maybe she could escape but she didnt know what she had to escape from or escape to, a terrified whimper starting deep within her, beyond the depths of her heart and she could hear and feel it grow and roar its way up from some unknown place pinching her heart, constricting her throat, twisting her windpipe and strangling her with all the agony of the darkest of nights, the most hideous fears of the human soul, the darkness that unleashes all the demons everyone who has ever walked or crawled across the planets surface has feared, the monsters defying all the angels of heaven, wrapping this little girl in their grotesque cloaks of darkness, sinking their ragged teeth and claws into her burned flesh and stripping it piece by piece, slowly and torturously, from her body and tossing her never dying body into the pits of eternal fire where cold soothing water was dripped on hot rocks so she could always see her salvation beyond reach, flaming serpents spitting tongues of fire close enough for her to feel their heat, but never touching, never bringing the relief of death . . . she kept crying for her mommy, mommy, her fear continuing to increase until she broke the paralysis and a faint whimper came from her throat and the sound startled her into a slight movement and she blinked her eyes several times and very carefully, very, very slowly, rolled her head to the side and as she did her memory of the day gradually opened and she remembered being on the stretcher and being treated and being put in a bed and then she almost yelled as she remembered her mother and grandmother being there with her and eventually she remembered she was in a hospital but she still didnt know what to do or where her mother was and she moved a little more as she became aware of the pain, and the whimpering became louder and low moans gurgled from her throat and now that the paralysis was broken she moved her body, twisting around in the bed yet keeping her head almost immobile, all her fear seeming to center there to protect her from increasing the pain but the more she moved, the more awake she became, the more aware of the pain, and her whimpering and moaning increased and then she started sobbing and could actually hear the word, mommy, coming from her mouth and she clutched her hands into fists, tighter and tighter and soon her moaning and restlessness awakened the woman in the bed next to her and she lay there for a moment, listening, then asked her if she needed something, but Maria was unable to speak and continued crying and sobbing, hearing the word, mommy, over and over and the woman watched her for a moment, then asked her if she wanted the nurse and when Maria continued sobbing the woman pushed the call button and in a short time a nurse came into the room and the woman told her she should check out that little girl, She sounds bad, and the nurse looked at Maria for a moment, her fingernails deeply imbedded in the palms of her hands, her arms rigid, her body trembling as she continued sobbing and moaning and staring up at the ceiling, You in pain? and Maria tried to say something, anything, but her throat, too, was rigid and all she could do was moan a little louder and the nurse looked a little closer and could see tears in her eyes, You in pain? and the woman in the next bed propped herself up on an elbow, Shes frightened real bad . . . real bad, and the nurse nodded her head and watched Maria for another moment, then took her blood pressure and left the room, returned in a moment and gave Maria an injection, then watched her until it took effect and Maria slowly opened her fists and the nurse rubbed Marias hands and legs until she stopped trembling and her muscles relaxed and she fell asleep.

Maria survived her first night in the hospital, her first night away from home.


Bobby wakened late in the morning, groggy and confused for a moment, then remembered what had happened and where he was. He realized, after a short time, that he had been laying in bed listening and wondering what was missing, then chuckled silently as he realized he was laying there listening for the scratching of the rats, but Mushie didn have no rats in his wall. Mus be plenty a rats down here, but caint nothin get in here. Sheeit, this be like a fortress an aint nobody knowin this be here . . . wonder why he livin down here? Crazy ol fool . . . but sure be a cool pad but it mus be he into somethin . . . I bes be gettin outta here just as soon as I can – trying to get up and falling back on the bed, every square inch of his body screaming with pain, blinking his eyes to help catch his breath, Sheeit, what the fuck be goin on, seem like everythin feels worse – checking out the different parts of his body by moving, contracting a muscle, touching . . . then slowly sitting up and looking at his hands and arms and then the rest of his body – like the ol fool say, I be black n blue but you caint notice the black – and he started to giggle but stopped and laid back down – what the fuck I be laughin at, I be hurtin . . . but I think about that crazy ol fool an I laugh . . . now what the fuck that be all about. Mus be his craziness rub off on me – Bobby smiled and slowly raised his arms and reached over his head and tapped the wall and smiled broader when there was no response. He was slowly lowering his arms when Moishe came into the room.

So. . . . Bobby blinked his eyes into focus, more aware than before how swollen his face was. Moishe felt Bobbys forehead and nodded, Good, good. For a long time youre sleepin. Thats good. Moishe handed a thermometer to Bobby, Put this under your tongue. Bobby took the thermometer, How come you aint got no rats down here – continuing to look at Moishe as he put the thermometer under his tongue. Moishe smiled, Doesnt ask what time, how long hes asleep, what is going to happen – Moishes smile broadened and he shrugged, He asks about rats. You like rats? Youre having maybe a pet rat? Youre worried maybe youre not having rats to play with? and Moishe laughed out loud, Maybe you are having a concussion already . . . or maybe some of those bumps – tapping Bobby on the head – is where your brains came out – and he laughed louder and looked at Bobby with curiosity and affection – Hey man, this place should be crawlin with those ugly fuckers what – Moishe touched Bobby on the shoulders gently, Put that back under your tongue . . . ya, ya, good. . . . Moishe stood up and continued smiling at Bobby, Just making stupid joke. You look terrible, but you seem alright, okeydokey – and he chuckled and when Bobby opened his mouth to speak he raised a hand and shook his head, Keep under your tongue. More just a minute – smiling when Bobby mumbled but put the thermometer under his tongue and closed his mouth. Good. . . . Cats. Lots of cats. Maybe hundreds. In here Im keeping just four . . . for mice – and

he laughed out loud and Bobby started laughing, not knowing why but something about the old man tickled the shit
out of him, but he stopped laughing almost at once as
Moishe raised a hand, and the pain of his face stabbed him,
Ya . . . its true for mice and tigers – What the fuck you be
talkin about – Shhh, taking the thermometer from Bobby
and reading it, Good – nodding his head emphatically,
*Prima* – shaking it down and putting it back in the small jar
with alcohol. Moishe put his hands, gently, on Bobbys
shoulders, You very strong . . . good health. Yeah, its all
them rats I eat – Bobby giggled then stopped abruptly as the
pain stabbed him again, Damn, that laughins a bitch – and
he smiled and Moishe laughed, nodding his head, feeling
the joy flowing through his body. Now what the fuck this
shit about tigers. Ya . . . is true. You see any tigers here????
Bobby looked at him for a moment, controlling his smile,
and shook his head, giggling, Ah dont see no hippa fuckin
pottamuses either but – Ya, ya, for the first time I see
already they not only keep away the mice and tigers, but
also the hippopotamus . . . ya . . . is good. Bobby shook his
head and smiled as much as he could, shaking his head
gently and giggling, You one crazy muthafucka Mushie, an
you aint on nothin either . . . damn – and he continued
shaking his head and giggling, then put out his left hand,
Gimme 5 Mush. Moishe looked at him quizzically for a
minute – Slap my hand, dontchya know nothing but tigers
and hippofuckinpottamuses – and Bobby giggled louder
and louder bordering on hysteria, the release of tension so
clear and simple Moishe wasnt concerned but simply watched
it happen and touched Bobbys hand, gently – Now turn
your hand over – and Bobby touched his palm then shook
his head – Dontchyall ever watch no basketball – Moishe
shrugged – Bobby continued grinning, We gonna hippen
you up ol man – and they looked at each other for a
moment, smiling, both feeling and enjoying the warmth of
each others smile and the affection flowing between them.
Bobby suddenly frowned, Who feed all those hundreds a
cats you be talkin about? Mice and rats. Bobby looked at
him for a moment, Sure, like they be goin out an buyin Puss

n Boots forim . . . an whach you wantin for dessert? Ya, ya, they have charge card for pussy-cat food – and Moishe laughed so loud and completely that he shook and sat down on a chair and again he and Bobby looked at each other, laughing, shaking their heads, not really certain why they were laughing, knowing what they were saying sure wasnt that funny, but feeling better and better as the laughter flowed through them, each ones laughter and relief bringing something else to the other person and at the same time releasing something from each other . . . eventually they stopped laughing and Moishe wiped the tears away from his eyes. . . . But is true. The cats kill rats and mice and eat them – Moishe shrugged – And sometimes the rats kill cats and eat them. So . . . never too many rats or too many cats. And theres always garbage. Everywhere for miles, plenty of garbage for the cats and rats and mice and – gesturing with his arms – everything else.

They sat quietly for a moment, then Moishe got up, Sit in the chair while Im checking the cuts. Bobby got up, slowly and carefully, no longer concerned about the old man being there while he was in his undershorts. He got up slowly, carefully and sat in the chair and tilted his head back so Moishe could see. Moishe examined the cuts, nodding his head in approval and relief, applying more antibacterial ointment where needed, very carefully touching the various cuts and lacerations to determine the amount of swelling, noticing Bobby, as before, wincing from time to time but saying nothing. Moishe felt a feeling of pride well up in him as he watched Bobby silently sit still while being examined. When he finished he smiled, So . . . is good. *Prima*. Black and blue, ya, but – Yeah, but the black be there anyways . . . damn, you a crazy ol man Mushie. So. . . . But crazy old man makes a good soup, O, Im buying new clothes. Moishe handed Bobby a pair of cotton pants and a cotton shirt, Theyre soft so wont scratch the bruises – and he also handed him a pair of soft slipper-like shoes. Bobby put them on then stepped in front of the mirror, Damn, those muthafuckas really be fuckin me up, look like they be tryin to kill my ass. DAMN!!!! look at that . . . an I aint be doin nothin to those muthafuckin spics. But I be gettin them – So . . . how youre liking the clothes? Huh???? What you think? Bobby looked at himself for a moment, then shook his head. I sure be glad aint no mutha be seein me dress like this. So??? you look good. Bobby smiled at Moishe, You be thinkin I be lookin good I know I be fucked.

Bobby followed Moishe into the kitchen walking slowly and very carefully at first, but soon he relaxed knowing his legs would hold him up, but he was still careful, not wanting to knock into anything, hurting enough without that. Moishe pulled out a chair at the table and Bobby sat and looked around while Moishe heated the soup then served it, putting a box of crackers and a loaf of dark bread and a bowl of butter on the table. Moishe cut a slice of bread and covered it with butter. Bobby looked at it for a minute, How come its so hard – nodding toward the butter. Moishe looked at him, not understanding why he asked the question, Butter is always hard from the refrigerator – Bobby looked at him and nodded his head slowly, O . . . butter – Bobby took a bite of bread and chewed slowly, tentatively, at first, then enthusiastically, Aint never seen no bread like this . . . and never had no butter . . . Sheeit, this be good man – smiling at Moishe who quickly cut another piece and started buttering it as Bobby attacked the soup with a spoon in one hand and the bread in another. Damn, this be good soup Mush, where you buy this? What buy? I make it. What store is making soup like this, echhh. Right the fuck on, this be somethin else. Moishe smiled, Chicken noodle soup . . . few bowls and already the blue is disappearing and youre all black. Moishe laughed and Bobby shook his head and smiled then giggled, You one far out mutha Mush . . . lookit here – extending his hand, Moishe tapping it then turning his over and Bobby tapping his, and they both laughed for many wonderful minutes, Bobby holding the spoon and the bread.

Marias mother and grandmother were with her when she started coming to, their hands on their little girls legs and arms as before. The memory of the night quickly assaulted Maria and before she opened her eyes she stiffened suddenly, and her little body was rigid and as hard as concrete

Maria – squeezing her tighter – we are here . . . Maria, Maria – standing and leaning close to her, seeing the tears in her eyes, seeing the pain struggling in her throat, feeling her body about to crack with tension . . . then watching her head move slightly and the eyes open and look at her and suddenly her little body seemed to crumble and the tension drained as her mother held her and once again absorbed the agony from her little girl, and her mother and grandmother soothed as Maria became more and more aware of their presence and touch, more aware of the light in the room, more aware that what she was seeing and feeling, now, was real and what she had been feeling was a bad dream, a really bad dream, but she was awake and there was light everywhere and she could feel her mother and grandmother and hear their voices and even other sounds and she knew she was alright that her mother was there so she must be alive and alright and the light must be real and it must be daytime and Mommy . . . Mommy – tears swelling and throbbing throughout her little body, flowing through her throat and head and chest, seeming to sweep every thought before them, yet just the merest trickle flowed from her eyes as she reached to touch her mommy, to hug, to feel her breath, to smell her throat and hear her grandmother mumbling prayers, a tiny voice within her growing, nurtured by the tears, and joining her mothers voice and her grandmothers prayers, and sang within her and through her and around her, a voice of safety, a song that gently replaced all fear, a song she heard all her life even when the tune was different, a song that came from so many different places but always bubbled in her heart, and now it came from her mommy and grandmother and she hugged her mommy so hard it hurt her face and chest but she hugged and hugged and clung and listened to the song and tried to kiss her mommy but something was wrapped around her and mommy told her to be careful and gentle, that she was hurt but would be alright, her mommys words joining with the song and her heart became so light it almost floated from her chest and mommy laid her back on the bed and soothed her and brushed her hair back from her face like she used to do when she was a little girl, and she lay on the bed allowing her body to be quieted by the song and gradually her breathing slowed to keep time with the song and soon, in time, she gave up the struggle completely and lay quietly as her mommy dabbed, gently, at the tears with a tissue, telling her it was alright, that she was going to be well soon and Maria just lay there, quiet, peaceful, silent, simply hearing and feeling the song. . . .

and once again mother and grandmother sat with their little girl, trying to soothe and pray away her pain, the two sitting at the side of the bed each in her own way sighing with relief with every breath, unable to see their little girls face but feeling her relax beneath their touch, feeling her sense of safety, thanking God she was alive and would somehow be alright, unable to understand what the doctor had said, but knowing that the doctors would somehow make everything alright for their little one, that the doctors had great knowledge and many devices to help those that have illness and though it all seemed like a great mystery to them they knew that somewhere in this monster of a hospital, this hospital that was so big you could not walk through it in many days, so big that not even those who worked here would ever know each other, and while the old woman sat holding the thin legs of her granddaughter, she knew that her prayers would be answered by some unknown force hidden somewhere in the hospital, this place that so baffled and confused her, a woman who had lived for many years but had never before been in a hospital, all her children having been delivered at home in a village that was smaller than this world of people in many different uniforms, pushing many different machines and others carrying trays filled with bottles and cups and needles and people walking around pulling stands with bottles and tubes and needles in their arms and it was all beyond her understanding but she knew it would all help her granddaughter and she sat, praying, and looking at the bandaged face with two little slits for her eyes and one for her mouth, and Maria lay within her bandages, feeling herself breathe in and out, in and out, mommys here, mommys here. . . .

and so passed the minutes and hours of the morning, the comings and goings, the bangings and clangings, the moaning and crying, all sitting quietly, word-lessly. . . .

until, in time, the food cart came. The food server put Marias tray on the bedside stand and when the two women looked at her questioningly she showed them how to place the tray over the bed and how to crank up the bed so Maria could sit up and eat, But there dont be nothin much there to tell you the truth honey, jus some broth and jello . . . an the milk — She looked at Marias bandaged face — Guess you caint handle much anyway — she turned to the 2 women and lowered her voice, You bes be bringin much food you can from home. A person could be gettin mighty hungry they try an live on the food here — an she winked and continued distributing the trays. The woman in the bed next to Maria looked over at them, An you can believe it — toying with the food on her tray, shaking her head, wrinkling her nose, closing her eyes and sighing — If you can survive this food you can survive anythin — she smiled at them — Makes people want to leave as soon as possible — and she laughed and held her nose with one hand and picked up a piece of food with her fork. Marias mother smiled and nodded her head and told her mother that tomorrow they would bring soup for Maria and later she would go get something she would like. She and Maria looked at the soup, smelled it, looked at each other and smiled and the grandmother got up and stretched over to look at the tray, and then at them, then sat down and blessed herself and returned to praying.

Marias mother looked at her daughter for a moment, forcing herself to smile, Are you comfortable like that? Should I make you higher in the bed? Maria nodded and her mother raised the back of the bed and the woman next to her said, Raise the bottom a little too, so you wont slide down, know what I mean? She looked at the woman for a moment, then nodded, *Si, si* – and raised the bottom a little so Maria could sit comfortably in the bed. Her mother blessed the food and started feeding Maria, the woman in the next bed laughing, It take more than that – and Marias mother carefully fitted the spoon into Marias mouth, watching her as she swallowed, watching her eyes blink and the bandages move, What is it? Marias voice almost inaudible, vibrating with fear and pain. They say it is soup – she shrugged, I will bring something from home . . . tomorrow. Later I can buy what you want . . . ice cream you would like ice cream???? – and she smiled at her daughter as she carefully raised another spoon of soup, Maria turning her head slightly, I cant eat momma . . . I feel bad. I know, but the soup will strengthen you . . . please, one more. . . . Maria slowly turned toward her mother and opened her mouth just enough for her to get the spoon in and Maria clutched her hands as she swallowed and shook her head, No more momma . . . my stomach is bad – and she laid her hands on her abdomen and her mother looked at her for a moment, then put the spoon down and opened the container of milk and put the straw in, then held it close enough for Maria to put the straw in her mouth. She took a few sips of milk then leaned back and rested, once again clutching her hands into fists, her mother watching carefully, This tastes better? – smiling – Yes . . . but it too hurts – once again putting her hands on her abdomen. Perhaps some jello? Maybe . . . one minute.

Suddenly there was mumbling from across the room and a voice that was obviously upset though the words were unintelligible. The grandmother got up and walked over to the bed and spoke to the woman in Spanish who looked at her as she continued to reach toward her bed-side table, Caint get the gauddamn piss pot, doan know why they always be puttin it where, O damn this pain – The old woman watched for a moment then started picking up various objects on the table, No . . . No . . . damn, how you say piss pot in Spanish – and continued until she picked up the urinal and the woman nodded enthusiastically, Thas it honey, O thank God – quickly putting it under the sheets, You dont fine that we all be in trouble, I be tellin you. The old woman watched the deep sense of relief on the womans face, smiled, then returned to her chair and prayers.

From time to time Maria would take a few sips of milk or a bite of jello, clenching her hands each time, and everytime she swallowed her mother thanked God for nourishing her baby, asking that the hurt in her stomach be gone so she could eat and feel good and be strong and leave the hospital soon and be home where she could take care of her as she needed, and, from time to time, Maria would laboriously roll her head toward her mother and tell her, It hurts mommy – her voice filled with tears and her mother would nod, Yes, but soon it will go and you will be home – and she rubbed her stomach gently, stopping only to once again offer her a little jello or milk, the painful time seeming immobile to Maria, yet time seeming to go too rapidly for the mother who stiffened each time someone entered the room, afraid it might be a nurse telling her she had to leave. She sighed inwardly when the little container of milk was empty and she held Marias hands between hers and smiled at her daughter, That was very good. Milk is very healthy – squeezing her daughters hands, Maria feeling exhausted, the pain in her face continually increasing so that she was almost on the verge of tears, I hurt really bad momma – and she started whimpering, It hurts so bad – starting to roll her head back and forth, The fire is starting again . . . make it stop momma – and once again the tears dropped from the edge of the bandages onto their hands and Marias mother looked at her with an expression and feeling of utter hopelessness, not knowing what to do, who to see, looking around the room panicking, she and the grandmother staring at each other for a moment, Marias crying and sobbing becoming louder, and the woman in the bed next to her asked her what was wrong, You in pain honey? and Maria nodded and squeezed her mothers hands tighter and tighter, Its all burnin – and the tears continued to drop and the woman told her to push the button, The one I showed you, remember? That gets the nurse, at least it supposed to depending whos on. You tell her it hurts. She/ll give you something . . . go ahead honey – Maria fumbling around for the button – Its a little higher . . . thats it – finding it and pushing the button, the woman looking at the mother reassuringly, A nursell be here soon an give her something – the mother nodding but still uncertain what was happening knowing only her little girl was in pain and needed help and she squeezed her hands and soon a nurses aide came in and asked what was wrong and Maria tried to talk but the tears drowned out her voice and the aide asked if she was in pain and Maria nodded and again tried to speak but only sobbing moans came from her throat and the aide turned off the call bell, The nursell be in just a minute with somethin – and she left and mother and grandmother looked at each other, once again lost in the mystery of the workings of the hospital and an uncomfortable language and again prayed that soon someone would take their little girls pain away and in time a nurse came in and gave her an injection – the two women watching intently – then left and the women now knew that soon Marias little eyes would stop dropping the tears of pain and would close and she would go to sleep, a sleep far away from pain . . . for now.

Moishe leaned against the counter and smiled at Bobby, So. . . . You eat, good. How you feel? Sheeit, ah feel like every muthafucka in the Bronx been kickin mah ass . . . but my belly be comin out mah ears. Thas some fine soup an braid. Ya . . . is good for everything. Moishe continued smiling at Bobby, then moved away from the counter, So . . . first we took care of the belly, now the rest already. Jacuzzi make you feel good, all over. What the fuck be that? Jacuzzi??? – shrugging -- is like a whirlpool . . . a bath tub where the water spins around – suddenly lifting his head and shoulders in recognition – like in baseball and football . . . they get hurt they sit in the whirlpool, ya? O yeah, I can dig it. Far out. You got yourself onea those suckers down here? Moishe grinned, Ya.

Moishe took Bobby to a room with a whirlpool bath and a large shower stall with a dozen nozzles. Bobby looked around at everything and shook his head, Man they aint even got things like this in the movies. This be far fuckin out – walking around and looking and shaking his head. . . .

So, Im filling the tub and youre getting undressed. What you mean, undressed? What do I mean undressed, you take a bath with your clothes on already? what do I mean? Hey man, I dont go around nakid in front of no strangers. Stranger. . . . Im a stranger already. So youre afraid maybe Im grabbing your *schwarzer schlung*, its so gorgeous I cant stay away???? Man, sometimes you be runnin off at the mouth an I caint understan nothin. Achh, so sit in the tub with your clothes on – shrugging, shaking his head – naked . . . stranger – and he turned on the nozzles and the heat, You see this button, it gets too hot you push, the lights going off . . . so, Im helping you in so you shouldnt slip – extending his hand, Bobby looking at him for a minute, then shrugging, Damn, you got your feelings hurt Mush. . . . I still dont know what I be doin here, but you seem to be a righteous dude – shrugging and looking around as he started unbuttoning his shirt – Where I put these things? Give to me – taking the clothes – Bobby standing awkwardly, self consciously, looking around, almost covering his crotch with his hands – hanging them on hooks across the room. Im helping you in, Bobby letting him hold his hand as he stepped over the side of the tub. Sit . . . there – nodding toward the seat, Bobby lowering himself slowly, a smile changing his expression, the smile growing into a large open-mouthed grin, Damn, this be far fuckin out Mush . . . damn – moving his arms slightly, looking at them, his hands, his feet, the whirling water with wonder and amazement – far fuckin out Mush . . . damn, those muthas get to sit in one a these jus for playin baseball . . . sheeit, an they gettin paid too – Bobby giggled then laughed loud, Hey baby, this be crazy Mush . . . damn. . . .

Moishe grinned and just watched Bobby for a moment. . . . Theres a railing. . . .

Yeah, I see it man.

Good. Dont slip. You need me push this already . . . rings a bell. This turns off heat.

Yeah, I got that one baby, but this be fine. Sheeit, can ya dig havin one a these muthas when your ass be freezin . . . damn . . . damn Mushie you be livin in a muthafuckin palace. Aint even no dope dealers be livin this good – and Bobby giggled and laughed and pretended his hand was a boat and skimmed it along the surface of the water.

Moishe continued watching for a moment, then stepped back from the tub, Im doing some work.

Okay my man. I be here gettin my skinny little ass unbruised, Hey Mush, I sit here long enough I get rid of *all* the black n blue – an he laughed so loud and hard he almost slipped off the ledge – Damn, this muthafucka gonna make a gauddamn honky outta me – and he roared again with laughter, shaking his head, tears rolling from his eyes, Caint be the muthafuckin Bronx man – and the laughter continued roaring from him as he sat back, held onto the railing, and allowed himself to almost float around the tub, feeling the warm swirling water relaxing not only his muscles, but his mind, and suddenly all of life . . . all of the past, and all of the future, and the present was a bright sunny day, and everything was cool and he didnt have to hassle anything, and no one or no things hassled him, and he jus be alone with the warm sun and the fine music he be hearing in his mine, Damn, this be far fuckin out man . . . far fuckin out. . . .

Bobby was leaning back in the tub, his eyes closed, and smiling through his cuts and bruises when Moishe returned to get him out. He stood by the side with a thick terry cloth robe and turned off the jets.

Hey man, whach you doin?

For today is over.

Ova? I was jus startin to groove behin this thing man.

Too much is not good. Now you have a cold shower and relax. Tomorrow we/ll do it again. Moishe helped Bobby out of the tub, and helped him into the shower stall and turned on the cold water. Bobby almost jumped out of his skin and yelled, Hey, what the fuck you doin man – and Moishe chuckled, Thats how youre getting rid of all the black and blue — and he kept the door closed as Bobby continued yelling and calling him a crazy mutha fucka as all 12 nozzles directed cold water at every part of Bobbys body, and when he thought Bobby had enough he turned off the water and helped him put on the robe, then gently put the hood on his head, So. . . . You tryin to kill me Mush? Damn!

Moishe laughed, You feel good, no? all alive all over, ya?

Yeah man, that be — Moishe laughed loud, Far fucking out, ya? — and he laughed louder and louder and Bobby looked at him and started laughing so hard and loud it hurt but he couldnt stop and both of them were shaking their heads, tears rolling from their eyes, their laughter echoing off the tiled walls, the ceiling, the floor and back up through their feet and into their ears and through their bodies coming out again in bursts of joyous sound, and as they continued laughing they slowly started leaning more and more toward each other and soon Bobby was leaning on Moishe who held him gently until there just wasnt any energy left for laughter but the joy was still there and they tapered off and down with short bursts of laughter and periods of chuckling, snorting and giggling until they were relatively silent and wiping their eyes with their fingers and their noses with the backs of their hands. Bobby was leaning heavily on Moishe and shaking his head, You a crazy muthafucka, I doan even know why Im laughin — which started a new round of laugher which quickly tapered to silence and they sat on the bench, eventually Bobby raising his head and looking around, his awe and wonder obvious, I wish my girl Maria could be here, man she sure be diggin this. Sheeit, I should be lettin her know Im cool, she mus be wonderin where I at and whats happenin.

Soon. You be stronger later. And you not looking so good yet.

Sheeit, that be true. Anyways, sometime I gotta see her.

Moishe smiled tenderly, Ya. . . .


Marias mother and grandmother walked the streets, rode the bus, then climbed the stairs to their apartment. The grandmother collapsed in a chair, O, mother of God, my

bones feel like dough, my legs dont want to hold me up –
the mother going directly to the kitchen to start cooking
food for everyone . . . herself, the old one, and her children
who had stayed with friends, and to start the soup to take to
Maria the next day, a strong soup with a good bone and
beans, a soup to strengthen her daughter. The grandmother
relaxed more and more until she felt as though she were
disappearing into the inner parts of the chair, inwardly
shaking her head and trying to understand a life that brought
her from a small village quietness to the madness of millions
of people and tenements, and exhaust fumes that smell like
death and burned her eyes and nose. Perhaps tomorrow she
would stay home with the children, such a long journey to
the hospital . . . but three little children were even worse
than the walking and the ugly monsters breathing smoke in
the streets. There seemed to be so few choices left . . . or it
might be that there are none . . . anywhere. She would walk
with ease down the stairs tomorrow, ride the bus and walk
through endless roads in the hospital, but sitting all day with
the pain. . . . O dear Jesus, Blessed savior Jesus, that is too
heavy a burden for these old bones. . . . I am not like you,
I cannot bear the sorrows of the world on my shoulders. . . .
I do not wear your robe, but sometimes I feel like it is the
crown of thorns that sits on my head. You are God and what
am I???? I am only an old woman in a strange land filled
with much sorrow and pain. O . . . mother of God, what am
I to do? Am I to sit at the foot of the cross and try to take
Marias pain??? and my daughters??? is Isabellas pain mine
too? I am just old . . . only old and weary, I am not the
mother of God and need to find some rest for bones so
much older than those smoking demons. Take my sorrow,
dear mother of God, dear Mary, take my sorrow, and that of
all of us. . . .

Here mother – she slowly raised her head and
looked at her daughter as she put a cup of coffee on her lap,
carefully placing the saucer first, then making certain her
mothers hand was steadying the cup – A cup of real coffee
will lift your spirits.

Raise my spirits?

Yes. You look sad and worn – looking at her mother for a moment then smiling at her and kissing her on the top of her head – It is such a tiring day. You need rest and food. But first – broadening her smile – a cup of real coffee, not the machine.

The old woman almost smiled and bent over as much as possible and carefully lifted the cup to her lips and took a sip, licked her lips then took a small mouthful and closed her eyes as she swallowed, then took a larger mouthful and raised her head and leaned back in the chair and sighed, Ohhh, what a blessing – smiling up at her daughter, the sadness still clearly etched on her face, momentarily obscured by her smile. Isabella returned her mothers smile, Rest. Soon we will eat and then we will talk – smiling – when the children are sleeping.

The old woman nodded her head and finished her coffee and held out the cup to her daughter.

Good. . . . Another cup . . . good.

Her mother leaned against the back of the chair and smiled up at her.


Maria lay quietly on the bed. Unmoving. A dull pain in her right hip slowly radiating out. Getting worse. Thinking move to stop the pain. Mommy gone. Grandmother gone. Bobby gone . . . somewhere. Still sounds . . . noises. From time to time opens eyes . . . lights. More pain. Eyes sting, leg hurts. Cant move. Cant will to move. Cant force movement away from pain. Crack in ceiling moving. . . . Ceiling falling, eyes shut, body tense, waiting . . . waiting for impact . . . to be crushed . . . *the clock lost its hands* . . . mommy . . . mommy . . . alone alone alone O mommy mommy . . .

darkness sudden, safe from ceiling. . . . It hurts. Really bad. Mommy it hurts. Mommy move me. Stop the pain. Terror freezes body, stiff, rigid, cracking and splintering and little pieces falling off and rolling from bed to hungry demon mouth devouring, grinding, laughing, moaning, moaning, moaning, MOANING, MOANING

Maria. Maria. You in pain?

Tears soak bandage, body shatters in million pieces, a million demon shattered pieces, bones, flesh, the sunrise, all swallowed, swallowed and disappearing into whatever is beyond darkness

mommy. . . . mommy

I have the nurse bring you somethin – o mommy – tears of terror soaking gauze and sheets – o mommy – a tiny plea from a small mouth and a huge pain, a tiny plea in an infinite threat, a thin, frail body pleading, reaching, reaching, reaching beyond itself to the unknown for something to touch, something to hold it, to comfort it, trying to force the darkness to give up a little glimmer of light as the darkness continues to consume and rend and torture and devour and torment and twist and grind and grind and spit the powdered bones of the tiny body into its crying eyes – mommy, mommy – the fires of fear and pain burning the tiny shell, the tears hot and red – o mommy, mommmmmmmy please . . . o please. . . .

The nurse gave her an injection, and left the room . . . and planes of soft gray slowly wrapped itself around the demon and absorbed its venom . . . and Maria was gently lowered into the peace of sleep where the handless clock of pain would begin once more to tick away godless hours and would, hopefully, keep its hands and their movement, until the night was once again turned away with the coming of light.

Isabella sat with her mother at the table. The children were in bed, the dishes washed, and they sat, with their coffee, a breeze coming in the kitchen window along with the sounds, noise and smells of the street.

You look very tired momma.

I am worried . . . I am tired – shrugging – I am sad. I do not know why we are here, why we –

Please momma. We have talked so many times. We are here. This is where we are. There was no place to go when Roberto died. We are here momma.

Yes, yes – nodding her head – We are here, in this land of noise and smoke – turning toward the window – it comes in, smell it? Listen –

Please momma. No more. My heart too is filled with pain. I too live in this same strange land as you with a language that is like mumblings to my ears. Everything sounds so bad so terrible, but we are here and –

But we should not be here. We should be where the sun does not have to fight with smoke to reach your face.

Isabella took a drink of coffee, looked at the light reflecting in the coffee and the sides of the cup for a moment, then looked at her mother, seeing the age in the lines on her face and the tiredness in her eyes, Perhaps you should stay home tomorrow momma. It is such a long trip, it tires you.

The trip is long. True – nodding her head – but to be here all the day with the children and the noise is also very tiring. Even more.

The children will not be here. They can go as today to the homes of friends. They are kind.

Yes, yes, I know, I thank God for the kindness of our friends. But what would you have me do, sit under a palm tree? Should I walk to the beach and stick my feet in the wet sand and listen to the water. Should I collect shells from the beach? – *Isabella stared at her coffee cup wishing she could wish all this away . . . all the pain all the unhappiness, but what could she do? Can she wake up in the morning and find a pot of gold on the table and take the family home? Is this a childs fairy tale where she can rub something and angels bring pieces of heaven on velvet pillows?* – Should I wade out into the water and smell the fresh breeze that moves over the water and through the tree tops? Should I bake a chicken? Sh –

Momma – Isabellas eyes and voice heavy with sadness – no more momma. It is enough. I am filled with the same sadness. Maria is my flesh . . . my blood – And mine – Yes momma, and yours, and we will do whatever we need to do to make her better. I too worry. I too try to understand the mysteries of what they say to us and leave in fear and ignorance. I hear words . . . sounds . . . and see my babys face wrapped in bandages, only little slits to look into to see her eyes, a little slit to feed food to her body. All the pain and sadness is the same for me momma.

The old woman stared at her folded hands on her lap for many silent moments, then nodded her head, Yes. . . . Yes. . . . she sighed and lifted her head and looked with great sadness at her daughter, Tomorrow we will go and see her and we will bring the soup and we will sit endlessly at the side of her bed and we will struggle with her pain and their language and feed her the soup, and milk, and hold her and pray to the Blessed Virgin to protect her and send her safe to her home with us – she sighed again and turned over her hands – We know we will do this . . . what else can we do?

Nothing else momma. God will see us through. And we will again ride the bus and find our way through all those hallways to her bed. She will be safe as long as we can see her . . . touch her – she looked at her mother and almost smiled – and feed her soup.

Isabella continued to look at her mother, her smile slowly absorbed by her feeling of concern, hearing the voices of children playing on the street, running up and down the stairs of their building, the sudden screeching after a ball, the yelling of arguments, the sudden burst of laughing, from time to time all the sounds blending into a vague and familiar noise that filled the background of her life that was so familiar it offered a degree of comfort, and she toyed with her coffee cup and looked out the window at the buildings across the street, the clothes lines stretched across the alley, the fire escapes heavily loaded with plants, rugs, boxes, crates, children, adults, cats, dogs and god only knows how many unidentifiable objects, sipping her now cool coffee and continuing to hold the cup with both hands after replacing it on the table, unable to avoid acknowledging the worm of fear crawling around within her and she blinked her eyes several times until she was able to turn her eyes from the window back to her mother and look at the lines of age etched in her face but seeing years of sadness rather than simply years of living as her mother rubbed her fingertips around the edge of her cup, feeling it as she would her beads, hearing the painful screeching of brakes, the grinding of motors, the crunch of wheels, frowning as she tasted the smoke and fumes, her coffee no longer able to penetrate the foulness they created in her mouth, foulness that burned her throat and chewed her tongue, one that she wanted to spit out, to spit into the dirt of the streets to be free of its venom but even if she did, actually, spit the poison into the streets the foulness remained always in her mouth, as the monsters screaming never left her ears, and they too ached from the smoke and shadows of this terrible place, and everyday she tried to think of some way to shut out the noises that attacked her, but even hiding her ears behind cupped hands was useless and futile, so she sat rubbing the edge of her coffee cup with her fingertips, wondering how she ever ended up living so high off the ground, and if she would ever sit in clear sunshine again

and mother and daughter sat in the midst of each others fear and grief as time did not stand still but moved with such agonizing slowness they felt crushed by the hands embrace, and the mother continued rubbing her cup and looking at the edge of the window, And what happens if Maria does not get well?

Isabella remained immobile, her hands around the coffee cup unmoving, her glance steady as a breeze waved a shirt on a line. . . . She must get better . . . shes my baby. . . .

Yes, yes. . . . But if she doesnt????

Isabella was rigid, seemingly not breathing.

These operations they will give her skin . . . from other parts of the body to hide scars. . . . What is it our Maria looks like???? I see only bandages. How is it she needs operations? How is it we know the doctors are true? What is it we know about them? Are they any different than everyone else . . . here . . . in this . . . *place????*

Isabella still rigid, her breathing inaudible and unnoticeable, eyes widening, knuckles getting whiter and whiter

Why dont we see whats behind the bandage? What is it they hide from us? Why do they not talk to us? Why is it they look at us as if we do not exist and walk away? Why is it they look at us as if we are going to steal from them? We are not animals . . . nor are we thieves yet they always run from us when all it is we ask is how is our Maria??? what is going to happen to our Maria??? Why do – MOMMA – suddenly grasping her head with her hands and squeezing as hard as possible, squeezing her eyes painfully shut against the hot tears pounding in her head, feeling the pain of her toes pushing against the bottoms of her shoes, her knotted calves, her burning throat – No more momma . . . please . . . please . . . so many questions – shaking her head – I cannot find the answers either. I look in their faces and try to see . . . to ask . . . to know . . . but I dont know what their eyes or words say – You know what their eyes say – looking Isabella in the eyes, her stare unwavering – it is what their eyes always say to us. O momma . . . momma – tears slowly seeping from her eyes – I dont care what their eyes say, I care only about my baby – But their eyes speak about Maria too, they say they do not care, that she is of no importance to them, she is only a pile of bandages in a bed. . . .

Isabellas chin almost rested on her chest. She watched the tears dropping on her lap, there seeming to be so few falling compared to those she felt rolling from her eyes . . . Where do they all go??? where do they all come from???? She felt her breath on her wrists as she spoke, I pray they will think she is one of theirs and will make her better, as she was the morning she left here and walked down the stairs with her school books in her hand.

I pray too – shrugs – what else is there . . . for us?

I pray . . . I pray and pray but there is only silence from the Blessed Virgin . . . I pray and pray and hear only the beating of my heart – Isabella slowly raised her head a few inches – I am frightened momma – raising her head a little more and staring into her mothers face, clasping her hands and squeezing hard – I am frightened for my little girl. Her mother looked back at her daughter, her expression stern, hard, unrelenting, watching the tears slowly roll down her daughters cheeks, her expression softening with each tear, in time a feeling of reassurance in her eyes as she reached over and put her hands on her daughters, My prayers, too, are spoken to deaf ears . . . perhaps it is that God cannot hear our tiny voices here . . . perhaps it is that the monsters in the streets . . . and the demons in the hearts of these crazy people, chew up the prayers before she hears them. . . .

they looked in each others eyes with as much love as possible, frightened of their fear, each hoping to see, or hear, in the other the answer to their own personal fears and the threat to Maria, Isabellas eyes eventually closing, too heavily burdened with grief to remain open, Perhaps you are right momma. It is possible it is as you say. But we will light a candle anyway . . . what else can we do?

their hands as one between them, slowly leaning toward each other, the air coming through the open window still alive with noise and fumes.


Moishe cautioned Bobby about moving around too much, You are needing to rest already . . . get strong.

Hey Mush, I dont be a ol man like you – throwing his shoulders back, but stopping in mid motion as the pain shot through him, but continuing to smile at Moshie.

Moishe smiled, and nodded his head, Its since a long time Im your age. Now, I find any excuse to rest.

Bobby looked around and frowned, How you get all this shit down here? You got some big shit here Mush.

Thats happening a long time ago. A long time I spent doing this – looking around – but I had lots of time.

Bobby started walking around the apartment and Moishe reached out to steady him from time to time, but held back and let Bobby find his own sense of balance. They went into a room that was filled with carts, wagons, hand trucks, dollies, a couple of work benches, and tools hanging on all the walls, My workshop – Moishe looking around proudly.

Damn, where you get all this stuff?

Long, long time – smiling at Bobby – so much older than you.

Bobby looked at Moishe, Thats for damn sure.

Moishe smiled and shrugged as they continued their tour. Bobby was amazed by what he saw, never having imagined anyone actually living in such luxury . . . all this space to move around, and lights everywhere but they didnt hurt your eyes, you could just see everything so clearly. And the food, a big freezer stuffed with food, huge refrigerator filled with food and more ice cream than he had ever seen in one place. At least that was how it seemed. Bobby kept looking at Moishe and shaking his head as he looked around then started walking toward the front door, This the door we be comin in, the pretty muthafucka? Moishe nodded and followed Bobby to the door who tried to open it and Moishe stepped in front of him and unlocked it, You want it should be opened? Yeah. Moishe opened the door and Bobby looked out, then shook his head and closed the door, Moishe looking at him quizzically, I was so fucked up I thought it might not be real like I remembered, but it be real − shaking his head − Damn, I still dont believe all this shit Mush.

Moishe looked at him, smiling, noticing the signs of fatigue around his eyes, Come, we go back to the kitchen, time for some more soup.

Bobby nodded and followed him back to the kitchen and sat gratefully at the table, closing his eyes for a moment as he felt the effects of the exertion.

Moishe started warming the soup and put the bread back on the table, with the cutting board and knife, and took the butter from the refrigerator. He motioned toward the bread and Bobby nodded so Moishe cut a couple of slices and pushed the bread and butter to Bobby. Right on Mush.

Moishe went back to the stove and poured the soup into a bowl and put it in front of Bobby and once again smiled and felt warm and glowing as he watched Bobby devouring the soup and bread. Bobby suddenly stared at Moishes wrist, What that tattoo − looking up at Moishe?

Moishe stared at the numbers on his wrist for a moment, then looked at Bobby, Ya . . . you dont know about this. Bobby shook his head and continued to look at Moishe who took a deep breath and exhaled noisily, A concentration camp . . . such a long time ago – closing his eyes for a moment – another world, another life. . . .

O yeah, I heard of them – frowning – I thought they was for jews. You dont look like no jew.

Moishe smiled, So. . . . What do I look like?

Just another old honky.

Moishe chuckled, Ya. . . . Well, true mostly jews, but others too.

I hear they be bad ass joints.

Moishe ruminated the words, Bad ass joints. . . . Ya, very bad . . . very bad. . . . I was not jew, but. . . .

Moishe was silent for a moment, Bobby glancing up at him as he continued to eat, So . . . someday Im telling you the story – and Moishe smiled, his thoughts obviously elsewhere. He became aware of the table and Bobby when Bobby dropped his spoon in the empty bowl and leaned back, Man my belly be so full I caint move – wiping the bowl with a finger, then licking it. Moishe watched sleepiness start to weigh Bobbys eyes and smiled, Maybe its a good idea youre lying down and resting.

Yeah . . . I be one tired dude man.

Moishe stood close to Bobby as he got up and started walking to the bedroom. After Bobby laid down Moishe went into the living room and sat in his chair. After a few moments he looked at his wrist, seeing the numbers he could never forget. . . .

So . . . what is the tattoo???? So many years I let the memory rest, sleep some place far away. The numbers are always on my wrist . . . and in my mind, but the memory I struggled so long to forget . . . at least the nightmare of it. I know I can never forget, never be free of those years, but does the nightmare need to be reawakened? Now? How many years can I have left? Shouldnt they be peaceful? Is he here to reawaken the demons? Or are you the demon that cant stand to see me enjoy peace of mind???? O, what is this boy to me? I help him because that is what I do, simply because it is there to be done and I am able to do it . . . he needs help and I can give it . . . he needs bandaids and I have bandaids. Thats enough. Hes hungry and I feed him. Simple. We are all brothers in hunger. Enough Werner, enough . . . enough. Youre a plumber, an electrician, a handyman not a philosopher. Yes, Im a very handy man, a man who is obviously afraid . . . yes afraid. Im afraid. So . . . it is all very simple, I am afraid of getting attached to this boy . . . a grandson (yes, the grandson I never had) and then he leaves and once again I have a broken heart . . . a heart that has been broken many times, yes, yes, it has been mended each time, but no more sorrow, I cannot survive another broken heart . . . the grief, the sorrow . . . I have long since run out of tomorrows in which to be healed. . . . Yes, yes, I know, with each broken heart my heart broke open, more and more each time . . . more light coming in and more love going out, but I was able to endure the pain, then, I can no longer endure . . . my heart hangs by the merest of threads, it beats, but to an old drum. My pain is mine and does no one any good, just as my madness was mine and no one could break the bars for me. I have lived . . . I have died . . . I did the best I could and here I am, an old man getting ready to die and a life . . . a wounded life, an animal from the streets over my head comes into my life and in his need brings with him my past. . . .

Moishe bent over and covered his face with his hands

I cant go back there . . . not again. The camps are gone, let the memories of them sleep in their ashes. I am old and weak and have a heart only for keeping this body alive, not for reliving the horrors of hell − Moishe jerked himself up − Ahhh, whats the use. I will do what I will do and all this craziness, all this talk, talk, talk, words to fill the air and my head and always I do what I do − Moishe shook his head and smiled and filled a bowl with ice cream and poured chocolate sauce over it − Maybe its better to eat ice cream than torture myself, either way Im going to do what Im going to do . . . what else is there?

*

It seemed to Isabella, and her mother, that the doctors were always running through the corridors, and the nurses rushing from one bed to the next, and so could not ask the questions that would not leave their minds and hearts. But one day a nurse smiled at them after giving Maria an injection and saw the fear and confusion in their eyes and faces and reassured them that Maria was going to be alright, that their little girls life was not in danger – She will live? Oh yes, she will definitely live. There is no infection, and she is responding very well to treatment, feeling a sigh go through her as her words registered within the two women and their expressions radiated their relief and gratitude and they held tight to the nurses statement that Marias life was not in danger, that she was going to live and though talk of surgery and scars frightened them they were able to concentrate on the fact that Maria would live and no matter what else may happen that was the most important thing and so they left that day with a lightness of heart they hadnt felt since first this terrible thing happened. The breeze that brushed their faces as they left the hospital was friendly and seemed to be a caressing message from God that He was looking over Maria and would take care of her, that as He filled her little heart with love He also filled His heart with Maria and no harm could come to . . . yes, yes, that was the message of the breeze, the promise of the breeze, and they rode the bus, walked the street and climbed the stairs to their apartment knowing Maria was safe and soon all her troubles would be over and she would be home, with them, safe in their arms. Isabella gathered up her children and started cooking, but first made a pot of coffee. She put a cup of coffee on the table in front of her mother who leaned over the cup and closed her eyes and inhaled the aroma, the sounds from the street muffled and dulled.

And so the trips to and from the hospital were easier, less exhausting to the old woman and less fearful for Isabella. Maria still cried and sobbed but now they knew the pain did not mean Maria was going to die. They could see the pain was bad, very bad, but that would pass and her life wouldnt, and so they did what they could to soothe, to reassure her, to feed her healthy soup, and not worry about their little baby because the nurse had said she would live.

One day Marias bed was empty when they got there and panic made speech impossible for a moment as they stared at each other, blessing themselves, the grandmother muttering prayers, Isabella frantically looking around, and the patient in the next bed told her that Maria was in the treatment room, and both women folded on chairs and sat motionless for many minutes, almost afraid to breathe, then moved slightly and allowed the information to ease away the rigidity of their bodies and they sat quietly, glancing at each other from time to time, each counting their breaths until Maria returned and they could see for themselves that she was alive and alright and they would feed her and touch her and watch her breathe and feel the beating of her heart in her chest.

Then Maria appeared on the other side of the bed in a wheelchair, their gasps audible as their senses were assaulted by Maria sitting in a wheel chair, her face wrapped in bandages, just the same 2 slits for eyes and 1 for the mouth, the hole for her breathing not at first visible and as she looked at them they felt she was suffocating and might at any moment die and that was why she was in a wheelchair because they knew only very sick or old people were in a wheelchair and Maria must be dying, the nurse must have been wrong or why was she being wheeled around and suddenly Isabella almost leaped across the bed as the attendant locked the wheelchair and helped Maria stand, Now, aint that nice honey yo family be here with some soup – chuckling and shaking her head – now dont that be a nice surprise – helping Maria get into bed then smiling at Isabella and her mother, She doin jus fine, yo little honey here – continuing to look at them as she noticed the look of panic on their faces, frowning, wondering what was wrong, then realizing they were staring at the wheelchair and smiled again, No . . . no, it be alright. Patient go anywheres they got to go in a wheelchair and thats the rules . . . you tellem chile. Maria leaned against the raised top of the bed and spoke very slowly, painfully, to the women, explaining quickly, but clearly that she had her bandages changed in the treatment room and you have to go in a wheelchair, and instantly their expressions changed and their relief was tangible and a silent sigh flowed from their bodies. Maria sat quietly, and silently, for many moments and the attendant asked her if she wanted anything and Maria shook her head and the attendant smiled and said to enjoy the soup and pushed the chair out of the room.

The women watched Maria for a moment, seeing the clean bandages, the slightly larger slits for eyes and mouth, seeing this as further signs of recovery and guarantees that Maria would indeed be alright.

Bobbys mother sat on the side of his bed bouncing her youngest on her knee, unmindful of the scratching and squealing behind the wall. The child was silent yet the sounds of its crying were still in her ears, her head, and pulsed throughout all her body. She drank from the coke can and toyed with it for a moment until her fingertips were cold then put it on the floor. She heard her throat swallowing the soda, heard the can on the floor, heard the noise from the rest of the house, the streets, and the walls, but it was like the air surrounding her ... there and unnoticed. The child started whimpering and she unconsciously increased the rate of bouncing until the baby quieted and she just continued staring at the walls, through the doorway, out the window across the living room, unaware of anything except the ache in her heart that had been there so long it was as much a part of her as its beating, not really knowing she lived with this ache for many, many years, only aware of a vague sense that something was missing inside her and that no matter what happened in her life she always, from time to time, became aware of this ache, and would open another coke or light a cigarette or yell at one of her noisy kids, or just stare. . . .

or sometimes she would lean out the window and yell down to her friends sitting on the stoop, or knock on their door, and they would sit and talk and laugh and poke fun and play the dozen and drink soda and smoke cigarettes and for a while she would be unaware of the ache, the vague sense of discontent, but always, sooner or later, it would descend on her and the all pervading feeling of hopelessness and uselessness of being trapped in a life of overwhelming despair, and she would rock back and forth until everything disappeared ... the apartment, the noise, the kids, the rats, her body, her mind and all her feelings and all she knew was the absence of all these things and it somehow seemed to be the way it should be ... but it was impossible to maintain so she always drifted back into her mind and body, and every other aspect of her life, and opening a can of coke, perhaps changing the babys diapers and allowing the wall to descend, the wall she had been building almost all her life and had to work to keep in repair, the wall that cut her off from being drowned by her feelings and surroundings, by the simple reality of her life, and she/d put the baby on her hip and yell at the kids to shut up or go visit some and laugh.

The child was still quiet, riding peacefully on her knee, its head nestled against its mothers arm and side, snug, safe, free. She finished the soda and frowned for a moment, trying to remember exactly how long it be since she be seein Bobby. Sometime it seem like jus a short time, like maybe couple hours ... then sometime it seem like forever since she be seeinim. It be strange. She be seeinim for 13 years now seem like everyday, an now he be gone somewheres an she not knowin where or how he is, only that he be hurt an she caint remember how long it be an it dont seem to make no difference anyhow cause gone be gone but it do feel like jus a couple days ... like could be 2 days since he be here an it sure feel like somethin missin ... somethin jus gone like if you be losin a arm or somethin ... but dont make no never mine cause gone is gone an he be seein me sometime ... yes, he surely will be seein his momma soon he can an then the kids stop yellin at me where he be???? where Bobby this an where Bobby that???? an I tells them over an over I dont be knowin where he be. ...

an
that sure enough be the truth ... I dont be knowin where he be

but he mus be alright or I/d be hearin somethin

yeah, yeah, he mus be alright

She picked up the empty soda can and shook a drop or two into her mouth, looked at the can for a moment, blinked her eyes a few times then looked around the room for a while, seeing the beds, the sheets and blankets, the clothes, doorknob on the closet, the peeling paint and cracks in the wall and ceiling, hearing the rats and the groan of the bed as she stood and walked slowly from the room, Guess I bes be movin Jesse in Bobbys bed, lease for now . . . he be liken that. He all the time talkin bout how cool Bobby be an axin moren anyone where he is. Guess thas the bes thing I be doin, move Jesse into Bobbys bed . . . lease ways for now.

From time to time Moishe would look at Bobbys eyes to see how he was feeling. If he asked Bobby always said he was fine, but Moishe knew his eyes revealed the truth. So, from time to time he would give him a couple of aspirin and suggest he lie down for a while and Bobby would shrug and say, I be doin it if you think I should. You the doctor Mush – and Bobby would giggle and stretch out on his bed and Moishe could see his eyes sigh a loud sigh of relief and gratitude to be lying down and not have to look cool as he forced his bruised and painful body to move around.

Moishe didnt bother with meal times, but just kept putting bowls of chicken soup in front of Bobby, along with bread and butter which Bobby devoured with such joy it almost made Moishe cry. He also gave him bowls of ice cream with chocolate sauce which Moishe said was even healthier than chicken soup and penicillin put together, Its making already the angels to sing in your heart and your stomach to feel like your best friend.

Moishe also knew when Bobby was feeling strong, not only by his eyes, but when he started talking about how he was going to get those spic muthafuckas an get up side their heads. When Bobby said this his eyes would flare and his entire body stiffen with rage and Moishe would feel the coldness of death inside himself and would stare at Bobby for a moment, then be forced to walk away and putter with something to help him keep from saying anything, and to keep himself from crying.

Even as he moved away from Bobby he could feel the tension and venom, and when he started to relax Moishe could feel that too, and knew Bobby would then start talking about Maria, and his mother, They mus both be wonderin where I be. Damn, I gotta be gettin outta here Mush an be seein my girlfren and the Moms. Bobby looked into a mirror at his face, then gently touched a few parts of his rib cage, then looked at Moishe, But you be right Mush, I go lookin like this they be screamin and hollerin all up an down. I bes be waitin. . . . How long you be thinkin before this face be lookin better?

Moishe frowned and pursed his lips, deliberately taking as much time as possible before answering, needing to desperately free himself from the cold anxiety knotting his gut, We see how it heals – shrugging – The cuts they look like they heal very good, but bruises . . . who knows? We see. Maybe only a week an – Week? What the fuck you mean a muthafuckin week? I need to be gettin back to the hood Mush, I caint be stayin here no week, I – Bobby – touching him gently on the shoulders – Its always at least a week a cut takes to heal . . . something deep like that . . . maybe more – looking into Bobbys eyes, his expression gentle, compassionate – You want already to look well when you see them . . . is only a few days more. . . .

they looked at each other . . . then Bobbys shoulders suddenly sagged as he let go of his defiance and tension, Sheeit. . . . Sheeit – walking away and sitting at the kitchen table, Moishe watching him for a moment, wanting to allow him all the time he needed to adjust to his disappointment, to dissipate his anger . . .

then filled two bowls with ice cream and sat at the table with Bobby. Moishe watched Bobby as he toyed with the spoon for a moment, then started eating absent mindedly, then when he was about half finished he turned his head toward the bowl and concentrated on what he was doing. Moishe started eating his ice cream too, Im all out of chocolate sauce . . . its a terrible thing I know, but Im getting more later. I think maybe Im buying a six pack – grinning at Bobby who fought laughter for a moment, then grinned back at Moishe, You sure be a crazy muthafucka Mush – smiling and licking his spoon – but you be a righteous dude. They continued grinning at each other as Bobby wiped the bowl with his finger.


Marias fear lessened when she held her mothers hands and felt the warmth of her grandmothers on her legs, hearing the soothing sound of the barely audible prayers. But sometimes, at night, especially in the dark if it suddenly got silent, completely and totally silent even for a moment, she shivered with panic and grabbed at the sheet with her hands and twisted and squeezed until it felt as if her fingernails would pierce her palms, and she would instantly be covered with cold sweat and her face would rage with pain and she would try to remember how to call the nurse, how to get something for the pain, but all she could do was lie rigid, stiff to the point of shattering, her head trembling so violently it felt as if her neck would snap and then there would be the inevitable sound from the hall or the moan of pain from another patient or the conversation of employees floating from some distant place and she would just as suddenly let go of the sheet and her body would feel as if it crumbled into a little pile on the bed and she would hear and feel the air rushing into her lungs and shots and shocks of light would pierce her closed eyes and she would lose herself in the sounds, the noise, of the hospital and something within her would remind her where she was and that her mommy and grandmother had been there just a short time ago and would be back the next day and spend the day sitting and talking to her and that this place was safe and they told her she would be alright that she didnt have to worry, that they would take care of her and she would live a long life and some of the women working here were very nice and smiled at her and reassured her and she remembered that she woke up each morning and that the goblins of the night never chewed her up and sooner or later the lights came on and sooner or later there was daylight outside the window and sooner or later they gave her something and the pain went away and sooner or later her mommy and grandmother would be there sitting by her bed and she would know that she had survived another night in a strange place, a place away from her home, a place away from her family, and though she still didnt understand what had happened or why, she slowly accepted the fact that she had to be here, like her mommy said, and soon she would be able to leave and go home, but for now she had to be here and they would take care of her, and maybe the confusion would go away and she wouldnt have all the things going around in her mind, wondering why Raul was so mad he did this to her and why Bobby didnt come see her but maybe no one was allowed to see her only her mommy and grandmother, yes, thats what it must be or Bobby would be here, and she would look from the darkness of her closed, pinched eyes to the darkness of the room, and the room seemed to get so much brighter, and soon she could see things like the end of her bed, the door, the wall, and the little pile of crumblings on the bed would form into 'her', and she would lie there blinking her eyes, seeing the edge of the bandage, and soon the nurse would come into the room and give her an injection and turn off her light and she would realize that she had pushed the button, and she would lie there with her eyes closed, feeling warm and safe and know nothing else until she awoke the next morning, and started the routine of another day, anxiously waiting to see her mommy and grandmother come into the room.

Maria was also able to talk briefly with the woman in the bed next to her who had burns on her back and had to lie on her side facing Maria. She asked Maria how old she was and she told her 13 going on 14.

Geez, just a kid, uh? Pretty lousy bein in here, eh?

Maria nodded her head slightly, I dont like it . . . I want to go home really bad.

Yeah, I bet. That ya mother and grandmother comes each day?

Yes — Maria already feeling the strain of talking.

Hurts when ya talk, eh?

Maria nodded her head.

I figured. You a porto?

Huh?

Porto . . . Porto Rican

She nodded again.

Yeah, I figured. The way ya talk, you know? I can usually tell those things — She looked toward the door, then lowered her voice — You know that nurse thats on nights sometimes, the one with the blond hair??? ya gotta look out forer, she a real nasty bitch . . . ya know, like she thinks who she is. Theres a lot ofem like that in here. But some ofem are all right. Theyre nice. I was here once for appendix. This time I got burned on the job. You can bet Im gonna sue the shit outta them. A chance to get some money. What happened to you, looks like ya got a face full a somethin.

Somebody threw something in my face

Oooo, thats awful. Like what?

Maria was struggling but felt obligated to answer and her words came out slowly, almost inaudible, They say lye.

Lye? Geez, what a rotten thing to do. I hope they kill the son of a bitch did that to ya.

Maria tried to continue the conversation but was unable and just closed her eyes, still hearing the womans voice but unable to respond. In time the woman noticed that Maria was asleep and stopped talking and went back to silently waiting for each minute to pass and for some break in the monotony.


Bobby checked out his face a couple of times each day, carefully inspecting it, doing what he could to convince himself that it was healed enough to go see Maria and his family, but when he touched it he had to accept that he was kidding himself and would go lie down for a while, just being up for a few hours and talking with Moishe tiring him.

Moishe would watch him look in the mirror and smile, Its better you dont look so much, you cant notice when its different.

Hey man, I/ll be seein when its ready.

Ya . . . but in meantime you worry. In same time it will heal if you look always or not.

Bobby was quiet for a moment . . . You mean like I dont see my kid brother grown none, but see his clothes too small.

Moishe chuckled, Ya, ya, like children growing.

But you got kids in the house how you not look atem?

Moishe laughed and nodded his head, So dont think about a white monkey, ya, ya —

White monkey?

Moishe waved his arms and shook his head in dismissal, Nothing, nothing. You look. I/ll get for you a bigger mirror, a three way so youre seeing too the back of your head — Moishe laughed louder — So simple, how do you not look at your own face — still laughing, tears forming in his eyes — So . . . sometimes I dont see — and he continued laughing, Bobby staring at him and shaking his head, smiling. Moishe was shaking his head energetically, laughing, crying, all of his body seeming to be having a good time, and Bobby watched, smiling, shaking his head until he too was laughing as loud and hard as Moishe.

Bobby spent more time out of bed each day, Moishes heart feeling more and more filled with gratitude at the speed and strength of Bobbys recovery. Bobby loved the whirlpool bath and spent more and more time in it, then screaming and hollering when Moishe would force him into the cold shower, calling him a torturing muthafucka, weirdo and sicko . . . and Moishe would laugh so hard he would double up. . . . I thought you were a man . . . why you snivel like little boy???? Gaudamn Mush it be fuckin cold in here yo — So how else your getting better so you can go home? By lockin you in this muthafucka till you lookin like

Santa fuckin Claus – Moishe leaning against the door immobilized with laughter – no matter how many times Bobby said, Santa fuckin Claus, Moishe always crumbled with laughter, not knowing why, but it was just about the funniest thing he had ever heard, Santa fuckin Claus, and he was always doubled over when Bobby got out of the shower, stretching his arms up as far as possible so Bobby could put on the robe and Bobby would try to shiver his way into the sleeves, Gaudahm Mush, caint you hold this mutha up so I can get in the muthafucka, and he would look at Moishe all bent and laughing, arms up holding the robe, tears falling from his eyes. . . .

Eventually Moishe would stand erect and Bobby would put his arms into the sleeves of the robe and hug it around him and tie the belt and they would stagger into the kitchen and collapse at the table and wait until the hysteria passed so Moishe could heat the soup.


Moishe had a table set up in the living room for putting picture puzzles together. He dumped the pieces of a 1,000 piece puzzle on the table, Damn Mush, how we ever gonna be puttin that thing together?

Moishe smiled and shrugged, One piece at a time . . . soon we have this picture – pointing to the picture on the cover of the box.

Sheeit . . . where we start, this be a big mutha.

You never before put together a puzzle?

Sheeit, where I be gettin a puzzle?

Okay. So . . . first we turn all the pieces face up, so – turning a few over – and put over here the outside pieces, ya?

Outside?

Like so, with the straight edge.

O yeah . . . okay, so we sit here like a couple a nuts and turn little pieces a cardboard upside down . . . man, I dont get it.

Moishe smiled, Time passes . . . you see, sometimes youre not wanting to stop.

Seem like simple minded bool shit to me, but – shrugging – what the fuck.

Time did pass and soon Bobby got caught up in putting the puzzle together, feeling more and more challenged by the dumb pieces of cardboard and the impossibility of finding a particular piece in the huge pile of pieces scattered on the table. Moishe silently laughed with joy as he watched Bobby becoming more and more involved in putting the puzzle together, watching Bobbys face, the increasing excitement as Bobby found pieces that fit together, Damn, lookit that, dont even look like they should fit but they do.

Ya, it takes a good eye.

These muthafuckas tryin to run a scam on us Mush, but we be settinem straight – holding out his hand and Moishe slapping it and turning his palm over, laughing, Bobby grinning as he slapped Moishes palm, Right the fuck on Mush.

They continued and soon Bobby was totally immersed and addicted to putting the puzzle together. From time to time he would put a piece in and sit back for a moment, See that Mush, that be a key piece, now we really be cookin – and they would continue to sit there, staring at the pieces, picking one up here and there, time disappearing much faster than the puzzle was being put together, and soon Bobby was studying the pieces, scrutinizing them meticulously, and much to Moishes glee would suddenly lunge at a piece and attach it to another and lean back and look at Moishe with a big grin on his face, There ya go Mush, it be nothin to it now with that key piece in . . . damn Mush, I caint be doin this all by my own self, you gotta be helpin some – and Bobby would tap Moishe on the shoulder, Guess your eyes aint be doin too well you crazy muthafucka – and he would giggle louder and go back to scrutinizing the pieces and all of Moishes being would rejoice, the warm glow on Bobbys face filling Moishe with happiness.

Maria continued to spend most of the time lying rigidly in

bed. She still focused primarily on her fear and pain, the rushing about of people, the clanging of wagons and gurneys and stretchers, the sharp clash of voices, the squeak of shoe on linoleum, reminding her of the chaos of the streets and so was familiar, her life seeming to always have been surrounded with noise, noise that seemed an almost pleasant distraction from her surroundings, just as the endless noise of the hospital seemed to lessen her pain and fear, its familiarity having a sense of comfort.

The personnel, too, reflected the streets, her neighborhood. One woman who wheeled her to the treatment room was very nice, but there was another woman who wouldnt hold the chair while she got up and would make her wait in the hall a long time before taking her back to her room. And there were some who wouldnt help anyone do anything, who would look at you as you asked them for help then walk away and Maria would watch them and wonder why they were like that, and when it happened to her she wondered what she had done for them to be that way.

Each time she was in the treatment room she tried to force herself to ask them how she was doing, if everything was alright, but she was unable, frozen into silence by the angry stare of the nurse who unwound her bandages and helped the doctor when he got there. An aide was taking the bandages and throwing them away and noticed Maria wincing as the nurse roughly unwound the remaining strips from her face, You alright?

The nurse glared at her, Shes doing just fine – looking at Maria with contempt.

Maria tried to answer but was completely subdued by the nurses attitude and sat trembling and frightened.

The aide looked at Marias face and shivered, the flesh a searing red, twisted and swollen, almost covering her eyes, the burns so severe her face looked as if many layers of skin had been ripped away exposing the inner flesh and had been raked with a grater so that it looked as if it were constantly screaming. Maria blinked at the aide who eventually realized she was staring at Marias face and averted her eyes, desperately trying to think of something she could say or do, but, nothing came out of her mouth until she finally touched Maria on the shoulder and said, It will be alright – then quickly turned her back so she wouldnt get sick.

The nurse noticed the procedure and glared at the aide before applying the medication, Dont worry, theyll patch her up . . . at our expense of course – wrapping the bandages around Marias face – drug addicts and street whores, and god knows what else, while still in their teens . . . while decent people have to work hard to pay for all this. Makes a person wonder if theres any justice in this world. If I had my way. . . .

When Maria was back in her bed she lay still for hours, seemingly not breathing, seeing the nurses face and hearing her words. She understood the words, but she didnt know what she meant, but she did know what the nurse meant by the tone of her voice and the look on her face. From time to time a shiver would go through Maria as the nurses face came right up to hers and silently laughed in her face and Maria could feel a whimper in her chest but everything remained silent even as the nurses words continued to go through her head, time after time, after time, and her face continued to remain in front of her, from time to time threatening to suffocate her, everything else disappearing, there being only Maria and the nurses face and words, and Maria trying to understand what she had done, why the nurse said the things she had and what they meant about Marias face . . . would she get better? The doctor said she would be alright, she wouldnt die . . . ugly . . . street dirt . . . cant patch up . . . and Maria wondered what she looked like, ever since it happened she wondered what she looked like, but now she was frozen with fear, nobody had said anything, but she said, Ugly, ugly, ugly. . . . Ugly like what? What was she ugly like? The old woman in the Bodega with all the moles and hairs and warts???? But she was old. Older even than the bario, how could she be that ugly???? She was a big girl, but would never be so old and ugly. . . .

and
Marias thoughts went round and round in confusion and

terror, wondering what the nurse meant when she said she was a whore, she was no whore, not street dirt, she lived in an apartment with her mommy and everyone. What had she done to the nurse????

and the internal sobbing continued to grow as Maria tried to somehow free herself from the onslaught of thoughts and images that were torturing her and she struggled to call to her mommy or god or something, anything to help her and somehow she started to slowly become aware of another sound in the room, an unfamiliar sound, one she had not noticed before and as she struggled with her pain, to break free of the images and words, the sound became louder and it finally forced her to move and she rolled over slightly and noticed the woman in the bed next to her struggling, moaning, trying to reach something and Maria squinted and tried to focus on her, to stare through the image of the nurse to see the woman and finally she could see she was trying to reach her water pitcher and was in a lot of pain each time she reached. Maria stared for a moment, her head still clouded with confusion, not knowing what she could do, not sure she was supposed to get out of bed, that if she did they might yell at her, but the longer she watched the woman struggling the more all the fears and concerns fell away and she slowly got up and leaned against her bed for a moment, then went over to the womans bed and picked up the water pitcher, This what you want? Yeah. Maria filled the womans glass with water and handed it to her, and put the pitcher where she could reach it. The woman took the pill from the cup on the table and swallowed it with the water then laid down and closed her eyes. Maria looked at her for a moment then hurried back to bed not wanting anyone to see her out of it.

The woman continued to lay quietly, eyes closed, then eventually opened them and forced a smile on her face as she looked at Maria and thanked her. That bitch of a nurse just dropped the pain pill and wouldnt move the pitcher so I could reach it . . . and she knows how much it hurts for me to reach . . . it just tears my back apart . . . rotten bitch — Maria could feel her head nodding slightly but though she knew what the woman was saying she wasnt really aware of it, nothing seemed to be registering – I/d like to take a cigarette lighter to that bitches tits, let her see what its like . . . jesus. . . . Sometimes it just doesnt pay to be nice, I should teller what I think of her. . . .

the woman was quiet for a moment, adjusting her body to try and find a comfortable position, then looked at Maria, How you doin kid?

Maria wondered how she was? She couldnt seem to figure that out. She felt very scared, like something terrible was going to happen to her, but she didnt know what, just that terrible scared feeling in her stomach like when she didnt have her homework ready but only much, much worse. She tried to answer but didnt know what to say, seeming to be disconnected from herself and all the familiar surroundings looked strange somehow and she couldnt really figure anything out, like even where the bathroom was. She stared at the woman, blinking her eyes, I dont know.

How you feel?

My stomach hurts.

Yeah?

Its all fluttery like.

O. . . . You scared kid?

I want to go home.

Somethin happen before . . . or anythin? They hurt ya when they changed your bandages? Sometimes they can be kindda rough on ya, ya know?

Whats plastic surgery? One day the doctor he said they give me plastic surgery.

Well, thats sorta like when they fix up ya skin, ya know after its been burned, or somethin, like you . . . you know, so it looks nice. Like the movie stars are always gettin it so they look young.

With plastic?

Huh? Plastic? – frowning at Maria, wishing she could see her expression, or at least her eyes so she could figure out what she was talking about – O, you mean like in plastic bags and stuff?

*Si.*

Naa — the woman smiled then chuckled — Naa, not that kindda plastic. Its kindda like . . . well . . . its kindda like stuff they put in ya skin an sometimes they sorta take skin from one place an stick it in another . . . ya know, like they borrow Peter to pay Paul. That sortta thing. But they dont use no plastic.

I dont know what my face looks like. Can it be very ugly? I think maybe it is so terrible to see.

Dont worry kid. Did that bitch in the treatment room say anythin to ya?

She look funny at my face — Maria could feel her face pinch, and hurt, as she frowned trying to get through her confusion and fear and all the unknown invisible things that seem to wrap themselves around her — Im not bad . . . mommy say to me I am good girl — Maria shook her head — I dont know what I did to be so ugly.

The woman could hear that Maria was on the verge of tears, Hey, you dont gotta worry, youre a sweet kid. Theyll fix ya up just fine. Really, youll be just as good as new.

I dont know why I am so bad. My mommy, she cries, my grandmother, she cries . . . they beat up my boy friend an — You didn do that, you didnt do nothin, I can tell. Im a good judge a human nature an I know you didn do nothin.

But everyone cries —

Hey, whatta ya think, a mothers not gonna cry when her kids in the hospital? Sure shes gonna cry. A couple a years ago my youngest had tonsils, right here, downstairs, ya think I didn cry? Ya bet ya ass I did. Its alright kid.

I must be bad if —

Hey, thats crazy. Believe me — staring at Maria, her heart aching for the kid, trying to figure out what to say — I know youre alright, a good kid.

No, no, to be so ugly one must be very bad . . . very bad. — Maria rolled over onto her back and closed her eyes, her body filled with her whimperings, her hands clenched, fingernails imbedded in her palms, her quiet sobs interrupting her prayers to jesus and the virgin Mary, trying to remember the act of contrition but only remembering, Forgive me Ive sinned and then trying to talk to Mary and tell her how much she loved the baby jesus, all my life I love the baby jesus, and you holy mother, blessed virgin mother of god O Im bad . . . so bad my mommy cries and I am so terrible ugly like dirt in the street, like all that garbage everywhere, everywhere and the rats that eat the garbage that smells so bad like all the rotten things and I must be a rotten thing to be punished so bad O I dont want to go to hell, Im afraid to die and go to hell and burn in flames but Im so bad I have to hide my face so people dont get sick O help me blessed virgin I always loved the baby jesus, help me help me. . . .

Her mother and grandmother came into the room and Maria rolled over and reached for her mothers hand and instantly a great sorrow took away the smile from the mothers face and the lightness of her heart, Mommy, mommy – and once again Isabella saw the tears coming from the slits in the bandages, the eyes of her daughter that always sparkled with such life from the very moment of her birth 13 years ago, those lovely brown so soft eyes that always looked at her with such love but now they were only slits in white gauze and once again tears flowed from the slits as pain flowed from her little baby and the lightness, the hope of that day flowed away with the tears to be absorbed by the bandages.

Isabella and her mother felt better that morning than they had since first hearing that Maria had been hurt. The night before they smiled over coffee, telling each other in so many ways that their little baby was safe, that she would live, that soon the doctors would fix everything and send their baby home to them and she will be as before. There seemed to be more fresh air coming through the windows, and less noise, than usual. And so again this morning, as well as more light, a light that seemed happier than other mornings with clouds and dampness and heavy odors and screamings from the streets. This morning the smell of coffee overwhelmed everything and the children went yelling down the stairs to school, and mother and grandmother got the soup ready to take to the hospital, and there seemed to be more strength in their legs, especially in those of the old woman, and the trip through the streets, the bus and then the hospital went with ease as they looked forward to once more sitting by the bed of their baby, their Maria.

And then they were in her room and were instantly aware of her pain, feeling it wrap itself around them as they struggled to her bedside, the rigid, motionless little body on the bed seeming to scream and when it became aware of their presence it rolled and Marias agony could be heard as she called out to her mommy, reaching toward the frightened, confused women taking an eternity to reach her bed, their seeming to be a wave that kept pushing them back and no matter how much Maria reached they didnt seem to get any closer and she hung over the side of the bed as they reached to her but she seemed to be moving away just as they seemed to be fading away from Maria and time suddenly stopped but Marias folding over the edge continued but they could not get closer despite the stopping of time and they heard her tiny, pained voice crying like wind over waves, Mommy . . . mommy, mommy, mommy, mommy and Isabella called to her baby as the grandmothers prayers became louder and the woman in the next bed stared as moving bodies seemed to take forever to cross such a short distance, looking like a slow motion movie, their voices sounding scared even though she couldnt understand the words, but she kept blinking and shaking her head and then suddenly the mother was hugging the kid and the old woman was sort of hugging both of them and mumbling out loud and then the kid was back in the middle of the bed and the women were sitting down and it looked like it did all those other days, except now they were all talking at once and the kid was crying but soon they slowed down their talking and it got quiet and the woman once again closed her eyes and allowed the pain pill to ease her into a shallow sleep.

Maria clung to her mommys arm, sobbing, telling her she was sorry, she would never do it again and her mother held her as close as she could and told her she had done nothing, confused and shocked by Marias fear and pain, not knowing what had suddenly happened and filled with fear that her baby was going to die and Maria kept talking abut how ugly she was and she must have done something wrong and Isabella kept telling her the doctor said she would be alright, they will make you look just as you always looked, the doctor said they will do this when you are healed from the burns. Is that what he said? Yes – turning to her mother – Isnt that so momma? The old woman nodded, Yes, it is so. See, it is true, he said you will be alright. And I am not ugly? No, my little sweetheart. You are my pretty one. Maria continued to hold her mothers hands and blink away tears, and her mother continued to soothe, comfort and reassure her, relaxing more and more herself as she told Maria, over and over, that she was alright, the doctor said they will fix everything. . . .

in time a nurse came in and gave Maria an injection and soon her eyes were closing, mostly quiet, though mumbling from time to time, an occasional shudder going through her body as unused tears and fear worked themselves free; and Isabella and her mother continued to sit, touching Maria and praying, the shock continuing to wear off as they continued to reassure each other that their little girl was fine and would soon be home with them, just like they had seen in that television story when someone threw something in a womans face and she looked just as pretty as ever.

Moishe examined Bobbys face very carefully and thoroughly, then expertly took the butterfly bandage off the smaller cut. He gently touched the area around the cut. . . . So – pursing his lips slightly – is looking very good, should heal without a scar . . . well, maybe a little one to make you look mysterious.

Bobby laughed, Mysterious? Mush, you really be somethin else.

Moishe laughed, totally absorbed by the smile on Bobbys face and the sound of laughter in his voice, Well, maybe its being a dueling scar . . . very important.

Dueling scar, now what the fuck you be talkin about?

Moishe replied with another burst of laugher and shook his head, Forget, forget. Something from old country.

Bobby shook his head at Moishe, smiling. Moishe stopped laughing and took a deep breath. So . . . now the big one. Moishe worked a corner of the bandage loose, then started slowly peeling the tape off. He knew it would be easier to just pull it off, but he wanted to be certain he didnt do any damage. When he finished he cleaned up both areas, and rubbed them with salve, then looked at Bobby and smiled, So . . . couldnt be better if I knew what I was doing – and he laughed with mirth and a great sense of relief and gratitude that the cuts had healed, that his simple ministrations were effective and Bobby did not get any serious infections because Moishe did not know what he would have done if he had because he knew Bobby would not go to a hospital and he would have been powerless to help him and now all the tension that had built up over these days, 7, 8, however many it was, suddenly poured from him with laughter and his legs actually felt weak with relief, but it was okay because the cuts were healing fine, just fine, and the salve would help them continue to heal and Bobby wouldnt have a scar on his cheek, maybe only a thin, small line like he said and he felt like he should sing or dance or do something so he raised his right hand and said, Right on already, and held out his hand and he and Bobby gave each other five and Bobby shook his head and once again laughed so hard tears rolled from his eyes, Damn if you aint the craziest muthafucka I ever see – shaking his head – Damn . . . and the laughter continued until Bobby had to stop because his head was hurting, so Moishe forced himself to stop and they went to the kitchen.

Moishe finally forced himself to silence while they ate the ice cream, and when they finished Bobby got up to look in the mirror. He examined his face as carefully as possible, Moishe watching over Bobbys shoulder, his expression becoming more and more filled with amazement, Damn Mush, you be a regular croaker. That be a hell of a job you be doin. Guess it be cool to go see the moms an Maria. Course I aint seen it before, but I sure be knowin what it feel like. Look like it being stayin fixed too. . . . damn, you sure be one righteous dude Mush.

Moishes smile was like a 250 watt bulb, Ya. . . . Dr. Werner Schultz.

Bobby turned and looked at him, Who he?

Moishe tapped himself on the chest, Me . . . my name is Werner Schultz.

Then what the fuck all this Mushie shit be about?

Moishe took a deep breath and suddenly the beaming smile was replaced with a sense of nostalgia and grief, Its like what you call nickname . . . ahh . . . honorary title.

Werner Schultz. Sheeit, sure dont see no Mushie in that.

Moishe smiled gently and was quiet for a moment . . . Youre wanting to rest?

Naa, I doan think so Mush.

They sat around the table holding a large puzzle about half put together, Bobby almost instantly grabbing a piece and attaching it to another, See that Mush, key piece, even you be able to finish it now – and Bobby chuckled continuing to look at the pieces for a moment, then looked at Moishe, a simple expression of deep respect on his face, So howd you get Mushie??? with the tattoo?

Moishe blinked inspite of himself and stared at Bobby for a moment, Ya . . . ya – nodding his head – The tattoo . . . How you know?

O, I be digginya Mush – shrugging – I see how you be sometime and how you be lookin. No big thing.

Moishe smiled with delight, inwardly amazed at how bright Bobby was, or as he would say, hip.

You say sometime you be tellin me about that constration camp thing – a gentle smile on his face as he once again shrugged – seem like this be a good time. Whach you think????

Moishe looked up at the ceiling for a moment wondering if he had the courage to relive it, to reach back to the agony it would resurrect, but he had already given this possibility as much thought as he could and now it was right in front of him and no reason came to mind to deny telling Bobby the story, it seeming almost natural that it be told to him, now, and that it would be alright, that somehow, for some reason it would be safe. Yet he continued to try and find a reason, any reason, good or otherwise, acceptable or otherwise, but nothing came to mind and the only thing he could see, even as he looked up to the ceiling, closing his eyes from time to time, was Bobbys smiling face and the gentleness and belief in his eyes, the simple honesty behind that smile. Eventually he breathed deeply, exhaled slowly and loudly, and looked at Bobby, So . . . we go to the living room.

Maria felt crushed by the sudden quiet. Mommy and grandmother had gone, the dinner trays had been collected, the shifts had changed, and the sudden lack of activity brought a silence that crushed the cells in Marias body and she seemed to disappear into the bed, just the merest and faintest outline, felt more than seen under the sheet. The silence and pressure it brought seemed to rage at Maria, demanding to know why she was like dirt, demanding to know what she had done, the questions being twisted through her mind as if they would scoop out the entire contents of her skull and there would remain just bone, not a hint of flesh or brain or blood but only a thin layer of bone that was rapidly turning black from the inside out and soon whatever was left of Maria would be black, and if she looked in the mirror, and still had eyes to see, she would see only blackness inside her skull and her entire body. The darkness outside the window seemed to increase with every breath she took, seemed to be oozing through the window and down the wall and across the floor, disappearing under her bed, but she knew it was crawling up her bed and the blackness would consume her from the outside as well as the inside, (the woman in the bed next to her blinked her eyes and frowned wondering if Maria was really in the bed, her shape being so vague, almost as if the mattress was enveloping her, and she stared for a few moments before clearly seeing Marias bandages and knowing she was there, then went back to sleep) and Maria stared at the lines in the ceiling as they moved and floated and spread and over-lapped and seemed to disappear into each other and she felt her arms trembling as she clutched the covers watching the darkness descend upon the room and her, trying to will the light from the hall to push back the darkness as long as possible because she knew with the darkness would come the terrible awful pain on her face and from some terrible place inside her would come that scary voice telling her how bad she is and no matter what she said to herself the voice would convince her she was bad, bad because she must be bad to be so ugly, to have such a terrible thing happen to her, things like this just dont happen to nice people . . . decent people . . . and she didnt know why god didnt help her or the baby jesus let her know what she did so she could confess and do an act of contrition but the darkness would, in time, become heavy, so terribly heavy she wouldnt be able to breathe and she would feel it crush her and she would really know, really and truly know she was bad and mommy wouldnt be there to help her and she would be all alone, just hanging in the darkness waiting to be thrown into an even darker hole but she wouldnt know when it was going to happen, it would just happen and she clutched the covers tighter and tighter until the pain in her muscles forced her to relax, at least a little, and she knew if she could just be good enough she would be alright, that the baby jesus and Mary would save her but she didnt know how to be good enough and now the bed under her back was starting to press on her spine and the many little lumps and bumps that came with the night started jamming them-selves into her back and her throat rattled with moans of pain but her mouth remained clamped shut, teeth and jaw clenched to cracking, but maybe the nurse would be in soon and put that medicine in her arm and she would sleep or maybe she should push the bell and ask but she couldnt unclench her fists, could not let go of the covers, could not move a finger no less all of her arm to reach out to the button but maybe she wasnt supposed to push the button, maybe she is being punished for pushing her baby brother down that time and he cut his lip a little and cried and cried and mommy got all upset and started yelling but she didnt mean to hurt him, not really *hurt* him, she only wanted to get her crayon back so she could finish coloring in her book and she was really sorry she scared him so much and made his mouth bleed like that but Im sorry, dear baby jesus Im sorry, I promise I/ll never do that again, honest, I promise, I know I did that to the cat, I know he screeched when I pulled his tail and Im sorry Im such a bad girl O please forgive me, please dont send me to hell I dont want to burn O baby jesus wheres my mommy O I know its too late for mommy that a whole black night has to go but I dont want to burn, please, please dont send me to be burned . . . but Im really sorry, honest to god, cross my heart and hope to die sorry . . . but I/ll be good really I will, I/ll be good . . . yes, yes, I/ll go to confession and say hail marys every night and I/ll be good — her face getting warmer and hotter, feeling as if someone was pouring hot oil over it, the fumes from her burning flesh singeing her nose and still the nurse didnt come and she thought again of moving her hand to ring the bell but it wouldnt move, feeling nailed to the bed and no matter how hard she thought she couldnt unpin it or ask the woman in the next bed to ring her bell or even cry out loud, all she could do was allow herself to be swallowed up by the darkness and allow it to squeeze her and squeeze her until all her bones felt like they would splinter and snap and her face got hotter and now all of her body was getting hotter and her crying grew louder and louder yet no sound came out of her mouth, her tears simply screaming in her head and seeming to fuel the fires that burned her face and the rest of her body and she promised to never do it with Bobby anymore but still the flames continued to consume her and it felt like all her body was trembling with tears and moans and she was so hot she felt like she was over a fire and her skin would burst open like a potato and still no sound would come from her lips and suddenly she started breathing again and got dizzy with the first rush of air yet still the nurse hadnt come in the room and her face and body were being consumed by the flames, burned to a painful pile of dirt and her breath was cut off and she could no longer plead or beg for mercy and her eyes were staring as wide as they could, seeing the edge of the bandage outlining the darkness of the room and as if from a far-away place she heard her voice saying she didnt know why she was so bad but she would be good, she honest to god would be a good girl and she swore on her heart that for ever and ever she would be a good girl and she felt the hint of a cool breeze on her face and felt her body being elevated and seeming to float above the bed as she slowly slid down the side and stood for a moment against the bed, her body still stiff, but now she knew how to cool it, how to get away from the flames that tormented her and she walked without sound across the room, not seeing, moving stiffly but easily, touching nothing, knocking into nothing, eyes closing for long moments at a time, until she stopped and stood for a moment, just a moment, by the open window, pushing it up as far as it would go, almost crying with relief as she felt the cool air penetrate the bandages, cooling her face and all her body almost instantly, the flames gone, totally gone as was the smell of her burning flesh and all she could feel was the cool, refreshing air and the smell of trees and flowers and she stood for a moment, one little breath of time, then sat on the sill and reached out and bathed her arms and face in the cool, flowing air . . . reaching deeper and deeper into the soft, cool wondrous air, leaning over the sill waving her arms, feeling an almost forgotten happiness flowing through mind and body, feeling like a little girl twirling around in a light summer shower, feeling like all the hugs and kisses in the world, reaching further and further into the comfort of the air that made her feel so alive, her body slowly rolling over the edge. . . .

then starting the descent through the cool refreshing air, feeling an exquisite ecstasy as she floated free of the flames and ugliness. . . .

and all was quiet, even the air rushing past her silent, the streets below tranquil, and most blessed of all was the quietness in her head . . . no screams of pain and anguish, no defending against the onslaught of demons too many in number and fury to be defended against, just simple, peaceful quiet, so happy to know that the flames were out, that she wouldnt have to spend eternity in hell, that the baby jesus had forgiven her for being so ugly and bad like dirt and she would sing a song to him, she promised, she would sing a song to him, all she wanted to do was sing and sing and sing . . . now and forever. . . .

Moishe sat in his chair, hands tented against his lips, staring in front of him for many minutes, Bobby sitting a few feet away, quiet, watching, waiting, then Moishe tapped his mouth with his hands and lowered them and adjusted himself in the chair, So – looking at Bobby – the tattoo . . . ya, the tattoo. . . . They continued looking at each other, but Moishe was obviously also looking past Bobby, past his apartment, past the Bronx. . . . Bobby watching Moishes face, mostly his eyes, knowing Moishe was gettin some things sorted out, doing his thing like he always do, and he just leaned forward, arms resting on thighs, looking at Moishe, occasionally blinking his eyes, not wanting to rush him but giveim his space. . . .

In time Moishe lowered his gaze and looked at Bobby for a moment, seeming to absorb the friendliness and understanding in Bobbys expression, then smiled softly, tenderly, from deep within his heart, a smile so filled with acceptance it could only come from overcoming great pain. So . . . the tattoo – he was quiet for a moment, then leaned forward slightly and spoke directly to Bobby – You know what was a Concentration Camp?

Bobby shrugged, I see some things on television, like in movies and stuff.

Moishe nodded his head, Ya – Moishes eyes rolled back in his head for a moment – There was always the smell of death . . . always in the nose, even walking through snow, always the smell of death – Bobby watched and in a moment Moishe shook his head – everyone is having a tattoo, you become a number . . . thats all, a number only . . .

no name, no person, no heart, no memories, no life . . . no you . . . only just a number on your wrist . . . and also some place on a piece of paper and so its like paper being thrown in the trash, nothing more because its only a number thats burned with the rest of the trash and − Moishe shook his head and waved what he was saying away − Enough, enough − Moishe redirected his gaze toward Bobby to help him concentrate, You know what they call World War Two and the Nazis?

Yeah − nodding his head − like I said, the movies.

Ya. . . . But that wasnt always my country. But I didnt notice the change. I hear the Nazis are growing, but − shrugging − in my town not much is changing. Me and my partner − Moishe suddenly hesitated and his eyes clouded over momentarily − my partner Klaus had small business . . . what you call . . . contractor . . . plumber, electrical, we do little jobs . . . in homes, but we have also a truck so is good the business. We do fine. I have lovely wife and son and Klaus and. . . then suddenly theyre coming in uniforms and arm bands and taking me away. I dont know why. Then they tell me Im a jew − Moishe shakes his head, looks vaguely mystified and shrugs − Just like that Im suddenly a jew, an enemy of my country. I tell them, everyone, Im a German, Im loving my country, how can I be a jew, but they knock me down and drag me away and soon Im stuffed in a cattle car on my way − Bobby squinted and leaned forward more as once again Moishe retreated within himself for a moment, tilted his head back and closed his eyes. . . . Many days we/re on that train, just only a little food . . . and so hot and no water and soon the smell so bad it burns like fire and no room even for the dead to fall down − Moishe slowly opened his eyes and stared at the wall behind Bobby as if he were trying to free his mind from the horror by burning it into the wall − so theyre just standing there, eyes staring like alive, but no tears from their eyes . . . shit, piss, but no tears O God, and we are so many days on the train, no food, no water, no air just bodies cramped and jammed together puking on each other − Moishe shook his head in pain and disbelief − who knows how long on that train. When it stops we dont even know, our bodies are still crushing into each other — Moishe was silent for a moment, Bobby staring, mouth open — we/re there so long . . . and when suddenly they finally opened the door the light is like barbed wire ripping our eyeballs . . . we try to raise our hands to shield our eyes but we cant move we/re so close pinned against each other and just closing eyes doesnt stop the pain ach such pain . . . such pain — Moishes voice weak and mournful — the light, I cant say how much pain, and when they dragged us out, those not living started falling over . . . one, sometimes two at a time like tenpins . . . slow as if the body wants to deny, even now, that it is dead and as long as it stands it can believe. . . . Moishe was quiet for a moment as if in mourning — then we were jammed into trucks and again men are puking on each other, vomit oozing down necks and so much pain from the bouncing throwing us around like kittens in an iron maiden. . . . Moishe slumped in his chair, staring at the floor between his feet

O god, and we hadnt even reached the camp . . . the camp — Bobby continued to stare at Moishe, crushed with disbelief, trying to understand the horror of what Moishe had said, and the expression on his face, An you mean like you aint never been no jew? They just railroad your ass???? Moishe looked at Bobby for a moment, I dont know what is railroad — shaking his head. You know man, like they framed your ass — Moishe still looking quizzically at Bobby — like the man, he dont like your ass he bus you an say you did somethin you dont do an you goes to jail. Moishe continued looking at Bobby and then started nodding his head slowly, Ya . . . ya, is all lies. Bobby was shaking his head, Damn . . . damn! Aint that some shit!!!! An they jus haul yo ass away an fuck you over? Moishe nodded his head . . . They took everything . . . house, business . . . everything . . . and send away my wife and son. She has brother who lets them live with him — Moishes face is pinched with pain — For years Im not knowing if theyre alive . . . 8 years Im thinking theyre dead. Wow! aint that a muthafucka. Damn! An you be locked up all that time. Moishe nodded his head. Bobby was still shaking his head in total disbelief, Damn, that be a muthafucka Mush. They jus be draggin yo ass away an take everythin . . . damn!!!! Moishe took a deep breath, Klaus is having a cousin in the Party and they want the business for themselves, so. . . . They were both silent for a moment, Moishe overwhelmed by his memories, Bobby by the monstrous injustice . . . losing everything because somebody say you be a jew. He glanced up at Moishe from time to time, then inwardly shrugged again trying to believe that that could happen to a white man even if he were a jew. Bobby was confused but he knew Moishe be straight, that he wasnt bool shittinim. In time Moishe raised his head slightly and looked at Bobby, So, I survive the trip and become a number, a blue number on white skin. Bobby blinks as he stares at the numbers, Yeah, aint that some shit . . . on white skin. . . .

Marias casket was closed. Sealed. Inside were her remains . . . the bones, hair, burned flesh, covered in her newest dress, rosary beads wrapped around her fingers. Impossible to know if she was still singing.

Isabella stared at the wood, knowing her baby was inside but still not believing . . . not totally, not that any death, even expected, is believed with the awareness of the simple fact of death. How much knowledge must change in the blood? How many facts purged through kidneys and liver . . . and time . . . long, relentless, interminable and torturous time???? Can a mother, or anyone, look at a piece of wood and tell themselves their 13 year old daughter is inside and will never scream, laugh or . . . or. . . . What is flesh of flesh when the flesh is sealed away from sight??? packaged in a tight fitting wooden box that reflects the dim light of the room but knows nothing of what it contains? Bones, flesh, bones flesh. . . . Yes, Marias bones and flesh, but what of Isabellas dreams . . . what of Marias dreams . . . those little bubbles of train rides, of tv and alone with Bobby, and some vague tomorrow that would make everything alright and make everyone happy . . . life as a christmas tree with eternal tinsel and lights and colorful decorations that shimmer and dazzle, and the Angel on the top, the very tippy top looking down on everything . . . everything . . . the tree, the presents, the people, the Baby Jesus and his Blessed Mother Mary, the baby jesus who would make everything alright and even the snow flakes falling from the sky like slices of coconut would sing and Maria would sing and dance and sing and dance and sing and sing and sing, but now her song is muffled, baffled by the box that Isabella and her mother stare at trying to find their baby and Isabella stares, paralyzed, a few feet from the box, Marias box, her last box and not the one Isabella was thinking of when she thought of giving Maria a present, perhaps this Christmas she would buy her a little stereo and put it in a box, she wouldnt know, but Isabella knew what was in this box but how can she believe, how can she believe she is going to bury her baby? How can that be???? I buried my young husband, isnt that enough for one life – she closed her eyes for a moment, feeling the tears, trying to see the Blessed Virgin who knew how it felt to see her own child dead . . . but yours returned, only three days you were alone with no child to cling to your hands . . . only three days so what do you know about me??? what can you know about me??? and the old one who no longer mutters the prayers of a lifetime. We did not even see our Maria a last time, nor will we ever. We sat for endless hours, days in a strange place of much moving and noise and held her little hands, feeling her flesh on my flesh, hearing her tears and cries, but seeing only bandages. I stare at the box and think, think really hard about Maria, but I cannot remember when last I looked into her eyes . . . when last I saw the smile on her face. What is it I have done to bury my own child . . . to not have seen her one last time as she was, to have no memory of her smile, her sparkling eyes??? to see only bandages wrapped around and around that sweet face O God, God, God, God, God . . . – Isabella finally started falling forward and was able to move her feet so she could fall across the box, cleaning it with her tears, hugging it with her arms and warming it with her breast, hearing her sobs pound against the wood, feeling the wetness of her cheek, trying to hear her daughter, to feel her daughter, to somehow know that Maria was inside this box, this piece of wood that didnt care who was lying across it or was locked within it, it was just there to keep mother and daughter separated for ever . . . for all eternity . . . no last look, no last word or touch, shes just gone O GOD GOD GOD GOD HOW CAN THIS BE . . . how can this be??? and Isabellas words were muffled as she tried to bury her face in the wood, hoping desperately that if she hugged the wood hard enough her baby would feel it, her baby would know that her mommy was here just like always, that her mommy loved her . . . O God, she loved her baby, but I dont know what I did to have her taken from me like this . . . what can a mother do to have her baby yanked from her arms by first the madness of children then the curse of death? Am I to be punished for all eternity because I could not feed my children and I came here so we could live . . . we could at least have food? Is that my crime in the face of God? Is it like the old one forever says to me, We should not have come to this land of ugly words and madness? Does Maria pay for my sins???? O Blessed Virgin let my child live as yours did. Dont leave me alone, deserted in the jungle of noise and craziness. Bring Maria back to me. She is just a baby. She needs her mommy O dear God . . . GOD, GOD!!!! – pounding on the box, her tears splashing on the shiny finish, shimmering in the light, rolling over the sides and to the floor like tiny pearls,

her mother standing stiff, mouth clenched tight, closed to whatever may come in and to whatever might come out, the silence going deep, deep within her, to the core of her heart and beyond, the coldness of silence eating its way through her. She listened to her daughters screams, watched her pound the box, heard the tears hit the box over and over and remained unmoved and unmoving, retreating deeper and deeper within herself, the silence consuming her. In time friends took Isabella off the coffin and led her out of the room and soon the old woman was alone still standing in the same place, hearing the muffled sobs and voices in the distance, but unaware, aware only of the cold, deep silence within her, a silence she vowed never to break.

Bobby stood in front of the mirror inspecting his face carefully, tentatively, gently touching the bruised and cut areas, his hand leaping away as if from a hot stove when he felt an extremely tender spot (looking in the mirror to see if Moishe noticed), and when he finished prodding he just stood and looked, turning his face this way, then that way, then this way, over and over, then nodded and turned to face Moishe, This face be doin real fine Mush. I be in good shape to go see my girl and the moms.

Moishe looked at him for a minute, then went over to him and squinted at his face, gently turning it, tilting it, examining it from various angles, then smiled, Dr. Schultz is doing a good job, ya?

You righteous Mush.

The healing is very good . . . ya, very good – Bobby smiling broadly, very pleased – But youre still having many bruises, still a little swelling some places . . . some very ugly marks, ya?

Bobby broadened his smile, his eyes twinkling as he looked into Moishes face, But Im so pretty Mush, aint no amount a bruises be hidin that – Moishe returning his look, nodding slightly – an I gotta see my girl an let the moms know I be alright.

Moishe continued looking into Bobbys eyes, forcing a smile on his face, reached up and gently, tenderly . . . lovingly touched Bobbys cheek for a moment, just for the eye wink of a moment and nodded briefly, Ya – then suddenly turned and started walking to the kitchen, looking back over his shoulder, Come . . . we talk first. He sat at the kitchen table and Bobby joined him. Moishe looked at him for a moment. . . . So . . . youre coming back?

Bobby blinked for a moment. . . . Sheeit, I didn even think of that Mush – Moishe looking at Bobby, his expression gentle, not reflecting the terrible turmoil going on within him – I guess I dont be knowin . . . you know what I mean, like I dont know whats happenin out there . . . like what the moms be up to and Maria an the cops an those muthafuckin spics – shrugs – I jus doan know. . . . Aint that somethin, all this time an I never figured that one out. Guess I figured when I be leaving I be leavin, but now. . . . Sheeit Mush, I jus doan know – he suddenly leaned forward and smiled – but I be comin back some time anyway to be seein you, like a doctors visit, yo dig? Moishe nodded and forced a smile on his face, Ya. . . . You come back so I give to you the bill, ya? Right on Mush – Bobby laughing and he and Moishe giving each other five. Moishe was quiet for a moment, then took a deep breath and exhaled noisily, Youre needing a map to get back. Man, that be true. Aint no body findin this place ceptin you, sheeit, I doan even know where I am. Moishe chuckled, You here – then laughed as Bobby shook his head, Damn Mush, sometime you be one corny mutha. Ya, ya – getting paper and pencil – sometimes so bad I laugh. Im making some maps. Maps? To get home . . . and to get back here when youre coming back.

Right on.

Moishe drew parrell and perpendicular lines on one of the pieces of paper, a big X for the entrance to the cellar. He then drew a map showing Bobby how to get from the entrance to Moishes apartment. Moishe showed the maps to Bobby, Im coming with you to the entrance so Im showing you landmarks, ya? We/ll take flashlight and hide it for when you come back. Bobby nodded and Moishe showed him the other map, showing Bobby how to get back to his neighborhood. Damn, I come all the way over here? Now aint that a bitch, Im not rememberin hardly any of that . . . matter fact Im not rememberin hardly anythin after those mutha fuckas jump my ass – his expression suddenly hardening, Moishes eyes closing slightly as he studied Bobbys face. Anyway, I be gettin them. Some day I be gettin their asses – looking up at Moishe and smiling – but not tonight Mush, right now Im jus seein my girl and the moms, right Mush? Moishe shrugged, Maybe you should forget them . . . see your girl friend and mother . . . be happy. Mush –

looking at him as if he really didnt understand – You cant be doin that. They kick my ass I got to be kickin theirs, thas the way it is Mush, I got to get up side their heads, Hey, I dont even be knowin if its day or night out there. Night – looking at his watch – 8:23. You be safe – smiling mischievously at Bobby – They cant see you in the dark, only the blue spots – and Moishe laughed, Bobby shaking his head and smiling, Thats why we won the war Mush, we be natural born night fighters. Moishe stopped laughing and leaned back, his palms on the table top, So. . . . Yeah, lets go man. It be a long time since I see my girl.

They stepped out the door of Moishes apartment into the darkness of the cellar. Moishe locked the door, then opened a haphazard door in a pile of old wood and debris a few feet away. When they passed through that Bobby looked around and his eyes bugged out of his head, Damn Mush, you cant even be seein your pad, alls you see is all this ol junk – Bobby shook his head and continued to stare in wonder how you couldnt know there was anything there, yet he had just left the hippest pad he/d ever seen, and he stood for many minutes just looking around and shaking his head in astonishment and disbelief. Finally he turned and saw only darkness, darkness so thick he could feel it brushing against his face. Damn Mush, how you be seein anythin? I can see in the dark – turning on a flashlight, the beam severing the darkness. Wow, that be a mutha.

Moishe led Bobby slowly through the endless darkness of the cellars, showing him various landmarks and pointing them out on the map, walking very slowly so Bobby could familiarize himself with the surroundings, the map and the direction he was walking. Bobby kept shaking his head, wondering when they would get to the street, feeling like he had been walking for hours, Moishe asking from time to time how he was feeling, Youre not tired? No man, I be fine, and they continued walking, Moishe making certain Bobby recognized every landmark at each turn and eventually they could feel a difference in the air and soon they were at the foot of the stairs leading up to the street. So . . . the flashlight is here, behind this pole and under this pile, like so. I dig it. When youre going up be careful, look first so no one there. Yeah, I got it Mush. And youre walking slow, ya, youre still already a little weak. I be fine Mush, but I take it easy. I ain about to run no race man. Good O – reaching into his pocket – youre needing some money. Hey man, I cant take your bread. Moishe shrugged and Bobby could see his smile in the almost total darkness, You eat already my bread and you cant take it? – and he giggled as he knew Bobby would be shaking his head and smiling. Bobby put the money in his pocket, Okay Mush, I catch ya later. Bobby turned to go up the stairs, then stopped for a moment, then turned and tapped Moishe on the shoulder, You be one righteous dude Mush – holding up his right hand, Moishe slapping it and then they squeezed each others hand. Bobby turned and went up the stairs, stopped near the top and carefully looked around, allowing his eyes to adjust before moving, then turned and looked back down the steps, We be the best night fighters around, right Mush – then giggled and put his head out a little more, then stepped up the remaining few stairs, turned left, and disappeared from Moishes sight. Moishe stood there for a couple of seconds, then slowly walked back to his apartment.

Though he saw no one Bobby kept looking around, checking out what was behind him. Bobby wasnt sure how long he had been at Moishes, but he knew it couldnt be too long, but it felt like years since hed been walking the streets, specially a hood he aint never seen before. But he kept walking, aware of the sound of cars in the distance, gradually slowing down until he was forced to stop after walking a few blocks. He leaned against the wall for a moment surprised, Damn, ol Mush be right, I not so strong as I thought. That whippin draggin my ass. He continued walking through the devastation, the abandoned and half crumbling buildings, the area looking like those war movies he told Moishe hed seen. He rested again for a moment, then continued, trying to remember to walk more slowly, and soon he started seeing an occasional car, then an occasional person, mostly street people, winos and bums, and the light from the street lamps seemed eerie, making him feel that there was something under every piece of rock, every bit of paper, every piece of garbage, that he didnt want to see, that if it saw him it would follow him and maybe worm its way inside his bones or his brain and he wouldnt even know it but it would kill him in some way, maybe eat him through the throat, the skull or maybe chew up his stomach and hed be left here in the rubble just a little pile of dried out skin and every time he looked away from the ground he became more aware of the light, that eerie, almost solid light that seemed to come from some dark place and not the street lamp and so the air he was walking through, the air surrounding him was threatening, it too becoming something he couldnt see or feel but could get him and he wouldnt know about it and he wished he had that big ass flashlight of Moishes so he could shine away this ugly mutha fucka that was creepin up on him. . . .

but the sounds of traffic and people got louder and louder and he became increasingly aware of them and everything became less threatening as the buildings became lived in and mostly had windows and all their walls and there was just the usual garbage on the streets and all the people walking and the kids running broke up the weird light and the tension drained from his mind and body and he felt more comfortable as everything became increasingly familiar. He also became aware of the stores and the smells and realized he was hungry, as well as tired, and also remembered the money Moishe had given him so he stopped in for a hamburger and a cup of coffee and a big piece of sweet potato pie. Mushie be a good cook, but he didnt have no sweet potato pie and Bobby felt like one, big smile as he chomped it away, piece by piece, then sipped the last of his coffee, enjoying the smells and the rest, and enjoying knowing he only had a few more blocks to go before he be seein his homeboys.

Yeah, he be seein his homeboys, but he might also be seein those spics an right now there was no way he could whip they ass. He run into them now he be fucked, those muthafuckas kill him for sure, he jus plain whipped. He just wanted to walk around, feel all the busyness, all the runnin and yellin and bad mouthin, but knew he couldnt, that he bes be cool if he wanted to stay alive. He suddenly realized he hadnt been thinking like this all the time he be at Mushies. He jus lay back an take it easy an not worry about nothin, certainly not bout stayin alive. . . . Yeah, thas right, even right away I somehow know he not be hurtin me . . . aint that some shit? Damn. . . . Now I be back in the hood an I gotta be doin all this worryin about stayin alive. Aint that some weird shit! I guess maybe he be knowin about stayin alive in that constration camp an everything. Sheeit, what the fuck I be doin now? Feel like I could lay down an sleep some. . . . maybe all night. Mus be all this fresh air — and he laughed to himself and shook his head and continued walking, checking out every dude who wasnt black, totally black, checking out every doorway, every fire escape, every window, every car, staying close to the walls of buildings, walking slowly around the area he knew his brother hung out, stopping from time to time to rest, catch his breath, and look at everything more carefully. . . . and then he saw his brother Jesse walking down the street and he almost jumped on him, but waited until he was close and called him over. Jesse looked at him for a moment, surprised, blinking his eyes, then grabbed him, Bobby, jeez . . . where you been? How ya doin Jess? Bobby, where you been, whats happenin? I be in your bed now. Aint no body know where you be. Didnt know if you be dead or what like they do to Maria an — Maria? What happen to Maria? You aint heard? Bobby shook his head, eyes staring, his expression dazed, Whats happenin? She be dead Bobby. Damn, I thinkin you know. . . . or you be dead too. O sheeit, I be sorry Bobby — looking at the color draining from his brothers face, Bobby leaning heavily on Jesse, suddenly very weak, very sick, staggering back into the wall as he held himself up by leaning on his brothers shoulders, his eyes glazed as he stared at Jesse, How can she be dead, she cant be dead. . . . how she be dead???? She kill herself. What the fuck you mean, she kill her self? Jesse looked at his brother for a moment, You dont know nothin about what happen with the spics? Only they whip my ass with a muthafuckin chain. Jessies eyes widen, Sheeit, they do that? Bobby nodded then shook his head bewildered, But what the fuck happen Jesse – shaking his brother – what the fuck you be talkin about???? You need be sittin Bobby. Les go in Jimmys. They went into the coffee shop and sat at a table in the back, Bobby ordering a cup of coffee and telling Jesse to get himself some ice cream or something. Jesse squinted as he looked at Bobby in the harsh light of the shop, You dont be lookin to good bro. Where you been all this time? Bobby blinked and shook his head, dazed, Some ol man, what you be sayin Jess, how Maria be killin her self – still shaking his head, the rumbling shock twisting through his body. Jesse looked at his brother for a moment, Damn bro, you be lookin all fucked up. Bobby waved his comments away, his expression becoming more and more agonized. You dont be knowin theys throwin lye in Marias face? Bobby stared opened mouthed and bug eyed and slowly shook his head, I doan see nothin but the muthafucka wailin on me with the chain. Yeah, I can be diggin that. Yeah, they throwd lye inner face and she go the hospital. Seem like she be gettin better an one night she go out the window – looking at Bobby, watchin the bruises getting darker – it be 9 stories – Bobbys eyes suddenly slammed shut and he leaned forward and moaned and he looked like he was going to double over or throw up or scream or something but he just hung there, Jesse watching, wondering what was happening, then slowly sat more erect, still clutching his gut and the counter man called over to them and asked them what they was wantin and Jesse said he be havin a bowl of strawberry ice cream, then he turned back to Bobby and looked at him and Bobby nodded, Two. They were silent for a moment, then Bobby asked, Why she be killin her own self? Jesse shook his head, Nobody be knowin that bro. She jus be doin it. The counter man called for them to get their ice cream and Jesse brought them back to the table. Bobby looked at his for a moment as if he were staring through it then started picking at it as if in a trance, Jesse watching him as he scraped off large pieces of ice cream. Maria fall 9 floors . . . damn – Bobbys voice low and mournful, his expression reflecting his intense sadness. Man, I dont. . . . He shook his head and stared at a spot on the table between him and his brother, Where them muthafuckas now? Who that? That mutha fuckin punk Raul an them. . . . Jesse looked at his brother for a moment. . . . Dont be seein much a them bro. They not showin their face aroun here none. Bobby was still staring, talking and nodding unconsciously. What you be doin now, bro? Bobbys head was shaking and he put another piece of ice cream in his mouth, Dont know. Guess I bes be gettin back to the ol man. Gotta figure this. Nine muthafuckin stories. Bobbys head was still shaking and his eyes suddenly slammed shut again and he leaned back in his chair, I cant be doin nothin yet Jess, Im still too bus up. Gonna come see the moms? Bobby shook his head, No . . . no . . . bes not. You be telliner Im alright, hear? Jesse nodded, feeling a sense of importance, feeling much older than his 9 years, I be takin care a that. How about Mr. Franklin down at school? They be wantin to know where you is. Bobby shook his head, Jus be cool with that. They be forgettin soon enough. Jesse laughed, That be true. How I be gettin a hold a you I be needin you? No way Jess. I/ll be aroun. I be gettin back together soon enough then I be aroun. You jus be tellin I be aroun. Let them muthafuckin spics be thinkin about them 9 stories — once more staring at the spot on the table until his eyes started blinking and he once again looked at his brother, They really threw that shit in her face — Jesse nodding — in her face. . . . Maria. . . .

Bobby stared at the spot and Jesse stared at his brother, in silence, then Jesse started scraping the liquid in his dish and licking the spoon. Bobby leaned back and pushed his ice cream to Jesse, still looking dazed, but his color had returned yet the bruises blazed even more angrily than before. He suddenly stood, I gotta go Jess an be thinkin this shit through, O — taking some money from his pocket and handing Jesse a few bills — Here. Jesse paid for the ice cream then walked his brother to the corner, feeling really big and important as Bobby put his hand on his shoulder,

An dont be tellin the moms how I be lookin. I gotcha bro. I just teller you be fine an got things to do. Right on. Jesse grinned and grabbed Bobbys hand after he gave him five, Be cool bro.

Jesse watched Bobby walk down the street for a moment, then turned and ran back to his house to tell his mother, and everyone else, he had seen Bobby.

Bobby instinctively walked as close to the buildings as possible, trying to be a thin shadow, alert and paying attention to what was happening in the streets, something he usually had no problem with, but now he kept seeing an image of Maria falling those 9 fuckin stories, groaning deep inside himself as the image insisted on torturing him and then exploding as he suddenly heard the splat of a ball against a wall, or garbage thrown on the ground and he would suddenly freeze and lean against the wall for a moment . . . rigid . . . then force himself to breathe and continue walking and it suddenly seemed that it was quiet, only the sound of distant traffic and even that was becoming fainter and more occasional but still the image of Maria falling through the air haunted him and he couldnt cut it loose no matter what he did, but even so he continued to look around carefully, checking out all the doorways and shadows even though he knew Raul and those other muthafuckas wouldnt be here, but he didnt know who might be following him, waiting to get his ass alone in a deserted street, or one of the gangs that roamed around looking for someone to take out just for the hell of it, so he continued to walk through the now dark and deserted streets, through the war-torn rubble of the south Bronx, instincts energized and alert even though he seemed to be totally absorbed by the image of Maria floating down 9 stories to the street, the hard ass concrete, and he kept shaking his head to clear the image from his mind until he found himself stopped before the entrance to Moishes cellar, having no recollection of having traveled the distance from Jimmys to here, how he remembered to make the right turns, to cross the right lots, just suddenly being here, standing still, looking down at the steps and the total, tangible darkness just beyond. . . .

And still the image of Maria falling insisted on assaulting him.


Moishe too was being haunted, haunted by memories he thought he had buried, and now reawakened like some creature from the past who had been in suspended animation for centuries, awakened in a new world, bringing its fear and venom to a world it didnt know existed when it laid down to sleep. He wants to know about the tattoo and I dont say, Its nothing, or its a joke, I talk about that train . . . O God help us, does he really need to know about that ride???? True, true, I dont know what he needs, or I need, or anyone needs O Werner, enough, enough. No philosophy. Or is it Moishe that ruminates and ponders???? Who knows? And what difference does it make? Im the one with the memories. . . . Im the one with the pain. . . . Im the one caught between Werner and Moishe . . . Im the one the boy talks to. . . . And Im the one who sits and worries about a young *schwartzer*. . . . Yes. . . . Yes . . . it is true, Im the one who sees him as the grandson Ive never had because my son was killed in a land I had never heard of . . . fighting for a country he had only lived in for a few years. . . . A haven . . . a land of hope . . . yes, hope. From the ashes of death . . . yes, literally, ashes of death, we come together, Gertrude, Karl-Heinz and me . . . we find each other after all those years . . . and ashes . . . and we cry with so much happiness after all those years of thinking each other is dead, our hearts so heavy with grief and death and simple dreams of a bowl of hot soup, never knowing if it is possible for the gates of hell to be burned and then we are together. . . . O my God such joy. When first Im told they are alive Im afraid to believe, to hope and Gertrude had the same fears too and then we see each other . . . 7 years, 3 months, 16 days . . . Im so skinny my bones are embarrassed, still after being liberated all that time, but we recognize each other and drown each other in tears of happiness and Karl-Heinz is staring at us not knowing who this man is hugging his mother or why we/re crying and we sit and eat together after such a long time, we sit and eat and laugh and cry. . . .

          And then they say we can go to America and we are so grateful again we cry and we leave behind the rubble, the pain, the hunger, the constant reminders of the screaming hideousness of the past and start over . . . yes, over . . . and then Vietnam and suddenly Gertrude and I are alone . . . as we once started . . . alone. . . . We never heard of Vietnam. How can a place you never knew existed take the life of your son, your only child ??? the land of hope . . . a new life, So whats with that tattoo Mush? Yes, whats that tattoo Moishe? Numbers, simple numbers . . . numbers that cant be erased, a bridge to the past that cant be destroyed . . . not the bridge, not the past Oooo, such madness – bending over for a moment and holding his head, staring at the floor between his feet then closing his eyes, his mind assaulted by the grotesque, overlapping images . . . then opening his eyes, blinking and sitting up and taking a deep breath . . . I went in Werner Schultz and I came out Moishe . . . but I came out. Thats good . . . I guess. . . .


When Jesse told his mother that he had seen Bobby and he was alright she sat down and started rocking back and forth very gently. . . . What he say?

That he be fine an you got no cause to worry.

She continued rocking back and forth, An I be fine an he shouldnt worry. Thats nice, we all be fine. No worries . . . no neverminds.

Jesse was still smiling, still feeling big . . . important.

He say when he comin home?

Uh uh. He worry about them spics. He be taken care a them firs he say.

She nodded as she rocked, He worry about the spics an I worry about him. Seems like there be nothin but worrin goin on – rocking, staring at a roach and ignoring it.

Seem so. . . . He didnt know nothin about Maria. He thought they jus beat up on him an – She suddenly raised her head and looked at Jesse, They hurt my boy?

Jesse stood taller, stuck his chest out, He be fine. Aint no spics hurtin Bobby. They givem a few licks with a chain, but he jus fine.

She seemed to suddenly become aware of her two young ones yelling and crying, Now what you be fussin about? All the time cryin and screamin a body cant get no res you just all the time be wantin somethin with yellin – Jesse edging out of the room, knowing the conversation was over and anyway, he delivered the message and werent no more to be tellin but if she wanted to talk more she know where he be – Yuall jus be swollowin me up alive – rocking faster and harder, her young daughter toddling into the room, Mommy, mommy, Billys crying – yanking her leg – Billys crying – and she slapped at the hand as if it were a fly and continued rocking – He be fine – No he not, he cryin – Go way chile, goddamn caint you see I be busy, Jesse stood in the doorway, smiling, then turned to run back to the street to tell his friends about his big brother an what he be goin to do to the spics what whipped his ass, and the mother continued to rock and rock until the sound of the crying was absorbed by the sounds coming from the rest of the apartment, the building and the street . . . and soon they were all absorbed by silence and she hugged herself, rocking back and forth, closing her eyes and soon she was peaceful and in time Billy was quiet and one of the kids peeked in the room and realized what was happening and went back to the other kids and reported that it be okay and they went back to their game and their laughing and giggling and yelling and slapping each others hands, unconsciously keeping an ear alert to their mothers voice, but for now all was peaceful and they were free and would make the most of it.

Bobby sat on the top step for a moment catching his breath. He felt as if he had been running for miles . . . no, even worse. His gut was knotted with the hollow pain of exhaustion, the muscles and bones in his legs painfully jellied. He tried to clear his head, but no matter what he did, no matter how often and hard he blinked or shook his head or tried taking a deep breath he couldnt seem to understand what had happened or how he felt or why he was panting because he knew he hadnt been running . . . or had he? and when he tried to take a deep breath the pain in his sides stopped him instantly. Now that he thought about it it seemed when he hit the deserted area he started trotting and maybe even running some . . . wasnt sure but it seemed that way so maybe that was why he was panting but it did seem like maybe his breathing was slowing down some, like maybe hed be able to get his ass up and start gettin to Mushies . . . but the cellar looked really dark and he wasnt sure he could find his way, even with the map and flashlight, yeah the flashlight, sheeit, bes not be forgettin the flashlight, damn near did forget that sucker, good thing that be poppin up in my mine or I/d never would be findin ol Mush . . . but that be one dark mutha down there, bes be takin it easy. . . . Bobby suddenly looked around, carefully, studying the distant as well as the close shadows for any hint of movement, wanting to be absolutely certain no one saw him go down the stairs and not come up, not wantin anyone checkin him out an maybe findin Mushies pad . . . Sheeit, I dont know if I be findin it with a flashlight an map so how some poor ass gonna jus be findin it???? I bes be gettin on . . . .

Bobby stood and looked around again, then descended the stairs. He reached for the flashlight and couldnt find it and started to panic, What the fuck be goin on, somebody be takin the mutha fucka, sheeit, mus be someone aroun here watchin me and waitin to jump my ass O damn that sonofabitch how the fuck they know the fucker be here an where the fuck — his hand touched the flashlight and he almost crumpled with relief, needing to lean against the damp, filthy wall for a moment, feeling the grime on his hand but not caring, just so filled with relief that he found the flashlight and there really wasnt someone waiting in the shadows to hitim side the head and take his clothes or maybe jus hitim cause they feelin like it. . . . In time he stood away from the wall, waited until he stopped wobbling, then started walking very slowly.

He waited as long as possible before turning on the light,

not wanting to take a chance on being seen from the street. He walked unthinkingly for a moment, just automatically making the first two turns, then stopped and realized he didnt know what he was doing and started to panic, turned around in a circle several times, almost totally disorienting himself, then he stopped and blinked against the terror and the darkness and the image of Maria falling that suddenly reappeared and assaulted his mind, and fought through the pain to take a slow, deep breath like Mushie said, and reminded himself that he had been here before, that it was okay, that there werent nothin here that be gettinim and then he became aware of sounds that it seemed werent there before, but he forced himself to take the map from his pocket and look at it, then shined the light around, pushing back the darkness and the fear, and soon recognized a landmark on the map and waited for just a moment, thinking, remembering, then started off in the indicated direction, walking slowly, from time to time shining the light in as wide an arc as possible to push back the demons, then continuing, occasionally tripping over a piece of debris, a bottle cap that felt like a boulder and a threat to his life, trying to be careful where and how he placed his feet as if he were walking through a mine field, never knowing what his feet might discover . . . and he checked the map again and again, sometimes panicking as he didnt see a landmark clearly drawn on the map, but then somehow remembering what Moishe said about stopping and taking a slow, deep breath and relaxing, then looking again and there it would be, right where he had already looked, as if someone had suddenly put it there while he was taking the deep breath and then his eyes started to sting with sweat and he could feel sweat rolling down his sides, his back, even his legs and he continued walking slowly, carefully, attacking the darkness with the light beam . . . and then he thought he saw a light in the distance and he quickly turned his off and stared but couldnt see anything, thinking maybe it was a rat running around a corner . . . but how could he see only one eye? If it be a rat there be 2 eyes, not one . . . an anyways, that be too big to be a rat, if that be a rat that muthafucka biggeren a fuckin tiger and he continued staring and Marias image was suddenly shimmering in the darkness, but her face was all burned and her mouth was open in a silent scream and Bobby was frozen with terror . . . and then the light was there again, bigger, brighter, and moving up an down and a little sideways and he knew it had to be somebody but who the fuck could it be? Who the fuck could be down here an what the fuck they be wantin, and he tried to think of how he could hide so he could see them but he couldnt see anything unless he turned on his light and then they be seein him an the muthafucka might be blowin his ass away and he – Bobby . . . Bobby. . . .

Bobby almost collapsed with relief. It was Mushie, that muthafucka Mushie, and Bobby tried to reply but his mouth was dry and nothing audible came out until he moistened his mouth and lips with his tongue, Mushie! MUSHIE MUSHIE!!!! The panic in his voice obvious to him but he didnt care he was so happy to hear Mushies voice he almost shit his pants an fell on his knees, MUSHIE, HERE, HERE!!!! Turn on your light already. O sheeit, yeah – turning on his flashlight and feeling his face crack into a grin – Im here Mush. Bobby watched the light get closer and closer, feeling his face still in a shit-eatin grin but not caring, knowing he was trembling, but not caring . . . knowing he had to pee so bad he be tastin it, but not caring he so muthafuckin happy to be seein Mushie . . . so mutha fuckin happy he feel like huggin and kissinim all over his head . . . then Moishe was standing in front of him, So. . . . Bobby just stared, grinning and trembling, Moishe noticing and smiling, Youre looking alright. Yeah . . . I be alright Mush. Moishe smiled warmly with overwhelming relief, Good. Good. . . . They stood in the blackness, flashlights pointed to the ground, vaguely yet overwhelmingly aware of each others presence and an infinite sense of relief within themselves. The momentary silence was unbroken by any sound. . . . Then Moishe grinned, So . . . we go home, ya? Right the fuck on Mush.

They walked faster, the 2 lights seeming to be a late sun to the thick darkness, Bobby following Moishe, his fear

absorbed by the light of Moishes presence. Im sure glad to
be seein you Mush. Whach you doin out here? Goin
somewheres? Moishe shrugged, Im suddenly thinking youre
here needin me, so. . . . No shit? I/11 be damn. . . . Ain that
somethin . . . damn. You really thinkin that? Damn. . . . Ain
that somethin. . . . I – Bobby suddenly stopped, silent,
staring as an image of Maria falling swiftly, fleetingly,
floated through his minds eye then disappeared. Moishe
peered at Bobby, Youre alright? Bobby nodded, leaned
forward slightly, Moishe almost reaching out to hold him,
then started walking. Moishe kept glancing at Bobby, careful to keep his pace with his, Bobbys feeling of relief and
hysteria continuing, yet he was silent. . . . .

When
they entered Moishes apartment Bobby walked, dazed, to
the kitchen and sat down at the table. The heavy silence
prevailed as he sat looking at the table blinking his eyes,
then at his hands, the floor, around the kitchen, seeming to
be familiarizing himself yet appearing to not be seeing
anything. In time he took a deep breath, the pain showing
on his face, and exhaled slowly, Moishe happy to see him
following his suggestion, Damn Mush, you really be wonderin
if Im okay? Moishe nodded. Aint nobody ever wonderin
that before far as I know. Damn! You really be wonderin. . . .
You one righteous mutha fucka Mush. Bobby looked at
Moishe, more light seeming to come from him, especially
his eyes, than the fixtures, and tried to smile but suddenly
his eyes filled up and his throat was closed with knotted
agony that rose from his gut, and he looked at Moishe, his
mouth open for a moment, then shook his head and stared
at his feet. . . . She be dead Mush . . . a few tears rolled from
his eyes and splattered on his sneakers, O Mush, she be
dead, out the window Mush, out the window, 9 stories
down, O Mush down to the muthafuckin groun Mush splat
on the sidewalk Mush O Mush – covering his face with his
hands for a moment, tears oozing between his fingers . . .
then looking at Moishe, his face wet, the tears seeming to
have blended the shades of color of the bruises with the
blackness of his skin and the light reflected from the moisture

and he looked as if he were glowing as his eyes reflected all the pain and misery of his life, his world, as he looked at Moishe, What Im gonna do Mush???? She be dead – shaking his head – Like she aint never gonna be gettin up off that sidewalk Mush – shaking his head and muttering, O God, an they aint never gonna be gettin her outta that sidewalk, you know that? they aint never be gettin all a Maria outta that sidewalk, 9 stories Mush, they always gonna be some part a her groun into that sidewalk an all them peoples be walkin on little bits a Maria an they aint even be knowener – shaking his head once more, his voice and attitude reflecting his amazement – you know that Mush, they dont even be knowen there be little bitty pieces a her in the muthafuckin groun, they dont even be seein its a different color there an what the fuck they care about Maria it aint their ass be steppin on an grindin deeper an deeper into the muthafuckin ceement, aint no muthafuckin skin off their muthafuckin noses what the fuck they be carin about – Moishe having to blink his eyes against Bobbys pain and despair from time to time, feeling Bobbys pain grind around in his gut stirring up more of the pain he had been experiencing with the memories that had been reawakened, his heart aching and crying as he watched Bobby becoming more and more angry and enraged with grief and the total senseless bestiality of Marias death, a little girl, for some reason, fell to the earth into death and Bobby was trying to find the pieces and nobody would know why this happened, nobody would be able to point to this or that and say, Ah, here is the cause, no more will this happen . . . nobody . . . not Bobby, not Moishe, not Marias mother or father . . . nobody, but everybody will suffer and grieve and be overwhelmed with grief and regret and confusion just as Bobby is now – they all the time be walkin all over us anyways what the fuck we be here for but for those muthafuckas to be walkin all over our ass an she be so sweet Mush, like dippin your finger in the sugar bowl an now she jus a sidewalk stain an everybody be goin about they business an – Bobby grabbed his head and bent over, his arms on the table, and Moishe sat, quietly, listening to Bobbys breathing, watching the occasional spasms in his back, listening to his own heart and momentarily feeling overwhelmed by his powerlessness, wanting to hug Bobby but knowing he had to allow Bobby the dignity of his grief for another moment so Bobby could empty his heart of its pain for a moment, just the briefest moment, but an absolutely necessary one, so Moishe sat, watching, almost losing himself with empathy.

In time Bobby raised his head, slowly, and looked at Moishe with a wet face and red eyes, briefly, then shook his head for a moment, his eyes closed, then looked up at the ceiling, closed his eyes half way, I be gettin those muthafuckin spics they be history – Moishe feeling a sudden and sharp stab in his heart, his mouth starting to open, but quickly closing – Aint no way they be gettin away with what they did – suddenly looking towards Moishe and staring, hard, heartless, at him – When they be whippin my ass they be throwin lye in her face . . . thats what they be doin . . . burn her all up . . . the people what be there say she be burned all up – Bobby continuing to stare as Moishe blinked back his tears, wanting to reach out to Bobby, to say something – they be burning her face all up an she go out the window 9 stories up an she still fallin when she hit the groun O Mush – looking at Moishe with an expression of bewilderment and confusion, a sense of being lost flowing from him, lost in so much more than his own pain and rage, so obviously overwhelmed by the sudden events in his life that he didnt know what to ask though it was obvious to Moishe that Bobby wanted to ask him something but the words simply were not available and Moishe was grateful they werent because he had none himself right now – Im tellin you Mush, I be gettin them muthafuckas. Maria cant be dead an they be alive – an Moishes heart twisted with pain and he felt his head nodding and heard himself say, Ya, I know Bobby. . . . Ya, I know . . . and they continued to look at each other, Bobby staring, Moishe looking into Bobbys eyes and even if there had been the ticking of a clock it would have gone unnoticed just as the clicking on and off of the refrigerator was unheard

and eventually Bobby stood

slowly, very slowly, agonizingly slowly, and walked trance-like to the living room and sat at the table with the puzzle and toyed with a few pieces. Moishe followed him and he too toyed with the pieces and put one in, Is key piece? – Bobby nodding his head, continuing to toy with the pieces, still moving his fingers even after dropping the pieces, Moishe trying to smile, Is easy now – but Bobby simply stared and Moishe was unable to force himself to try and make Bobby smile and so they sat in silence, Bobby staring at the table, Moishe glancing at Bobby from time to time. Bobby blinked his eyes, careful not to allow them to stay closed too long for fear of seeing the image of Maria falling through the air, from time to time Moishe thinking he should get bowls of ice cream for them but his inertia was too intense and in his heart he knew Bobby wouldnt even know it was there, so he sat in silence toying with puzzle pieces reminding himself that this would pass . . . yes, it would pass as all things pass, but now Moishe realized he was more worried about what would follow than what was happening at that moment. Bobby would survive the pain of Marias death, even the shock of the injustice, this Moishe knew, Bobby was strong, resilient, but would he survive the hate that was now poisoning his heart? To survive hatred and the cancer of revenge is not easy when justified by all the evidence you see. Who will tell Bobby hes not justified? His friends??? her family? Who is telling him this???? True . . . Sol told me, but how long before I heard??? how long before I believed???? And . . . how long before I was willing to let it go? Does Bobby have that much time? Can I now touch him on the shoulder and say Bobby I have to talk to you, I have to tell you to let go of your hate, that it will destroy you . . . what nonsense. I have to sit, quiet, say nothing, and . . . and what? What is it you are going to do Werner???? Nothing, just hope. Maybe my tongue will be guided? Yes, what other hope is there, only that my tongue will be silent so my heart can speak.

Isabella sat with her mother at the table, relieved her

mother was still silent. Perhaps some day she would want to hear her voice, ask her to speak to her, maybe even beg her to talk, but now her silence was a blessing, a great blessing . . . a great comfort. Since Marias death there had been questions . . . many questions and all somehow the same, over and over, from her children, other children, friends, neighbors, storekeepers . . . endless questions and agonizing replies . . . over and over, each one digging up the pain and twisting even wider the break in her heart . . . but no answers. Sometimes she wanted to scream but where could she go!? Where was there a door she could lock to keep out the world so she could scream away her agony? And would it help? Her begging, her prayers did not help. Her endless tears did not help. Maria is dead . . . and buried . . . and nothing will change that . . . no, nothing will ever change that. All she could do was pray to the Blessed Mother for comfort and ask for a time of peace where every breath, every word would not torture her . . . a little soothing silence that would somehow ease her pain and make it possible for her to sleep . . . to just sleep . . . no nightmares, no dreams, only sleep and help in getting up in the morning to face another day knowing the children would be running and yelling and screaming but Maria would not be heard, Maria would not be there. Another day of washing, cleaning, cooking, feeding, shopping, of going up and down the stairs . . . and crying, in her heart always crying but now her eyes are dry, no tears left to flow down her cheeks, but always the crying in her heart, the sadness that rolled and twisted around within her and choked at her throat so she could not eat, at times could not breath, but always there, her constant companion, and though there were times she wished she could go to sleep and not wake up, she knew that she would and that she would do everything necessary to take care of her family, the family without Maria, to keep doing what she had always been doing even though everything now seemed so hopeless, that maybe the old one was right and all the children would go the way of Maria, one by one, but she could not believe that, could not believe that all her children would be ripped from her bosom as was Maria.

No. The Blessed Mother would not allow that to happen. She knows too well a mothers sorrow at the death of her child. So Isabella sat in the comforting silence, aware of the presence of her mother, but not looking at her, just grateful for the quietness and the tiredness growing in her body. Soon she would be able to sleep. Soon, another day after the death of her Maria will have passed.

Bobbys mother clung to the body on top of her as it moved, grunted, sweated, smelling of old wine and cigarettes, her own hot breath reflected into her face from his neck, vaguely aware of her voice, the groaning coming from her throat seeming distant and almost disconnected from her, clutching the warmth of a body that wanted to be with her, telling her things she had to hear, making her feel important, special, absorbing some of the loneliness and longing she lived with, filling the dark emptiness within her if only for a moment, yet the voice sounded distant, grunting through a haze, wondering will he really be gettin her tv fixed like he promise an how long it be takin, she wanted to see her game shows an the kids be yellin about their cartoons an all and anyways they always be yellen but the tv be keepinem quiet an she wonder what Bobby be doin about now, if he really okay like Jesse say an if he really be tryin to kill the spics and what might happen if he does, specially he be by his own self and how he goin to do somethin an maybe the poeleece be gettin him an what be happenin toim then, o lord, she just didnt know what was happenin to her boy – *the guy stopped moving and just lay heavily on top of her, breathing hard and it seemed like he was saying, O baby, O baby, and she hugged him tighter and told him he was so good, You the bes man I ever had. He smiled in the dark, Yeah baby* – and suppose he really killem what be happenen toim then? Suppose my boy be goin to prison what chance he got up there with all them bad mens??? they be hurtin my boy and he caint help hisself none with them, he jus a boy, he aint no man yet an they aint got no right sendin my boy to prison with them mens he aint did nothin wrong, he only protectin hisself, they aint got no right be hittin on him with no chain an be hurtin his gurl frien so she kill herself, what for they be wantin to do that? my Bobby caint be gettin no more hurt than he is, he need be goin to school an get hisself a good job he jus dont need no pain with them spics that whippedim an they got no business anyway doin that to my boy. . . .

and her eyes slowly moistened and a couple of tears wet her cheeks, mixing with the warm wine-sour breath, the breath chuckling, You sure be admirin my big dick, dont you baby – and the breath chuckled some more – It be all for you baby, jus take as much as you want, hahaha. . . . You be fixin my tv wont you baby? Huh? You be fixin my tv????

Bobby slept. Moishe sat in his chair. When Bobby had finally gotten up from the table and went to the bedroom, Moishe could still see the demons that haunted Bobby in his eyes. Moishe had started to get up, but something kept him in his chair so he just watched Bobby move to the bedroom seemingly inanimate in all areas except movement, a terrible lifelessness saturating Bobbys body yet Moishe painfully aware of the hatred flowing through and from him.

Moishe listened to Bobby getting undressed, then getting into bed, the sounds of settling into a comfortable position loudly missing, Moishe waiting many moments to hear those sounds, but the silence continued . . . and Moishe continued to sit at the table, unaware of time, feeling only the ache in his heart. Eventually he sought the comfort of his chair and all the happiness and contentment it had absorbed all those years, but still he could not get free of the horrors of the days before his chair, the years he wanted to forget, all the pain and fear Bobbys presence had brought back. . . . Yes . . . true, he did come back. Am I glad? Is it a joy in my life to have here a boy with such pain? Werner stop. You should sleep. You sit here and torture yourself. You can see he is haunted by images . . . demons, thats enough for one house. . . . Yes, true, this is one house and he is part of the house and his torment is enough, I dont need to add mine . . . mine from the past, which at least is real . . . but the future . . . why should I suffer today for something that hasnt happened yet? Isnt there enough pain today, do I need to borrow tomorrows? Ahhh . . . he is not my son . . . or my sons son. I accepted my loss . . . my many losses, and each time more of me died, yet I still live. Yes . . . I still remain with this flesh and bones . . . for what? To suffer? I bury my son . . . my wife, just to suffer longer? That cant be . . . no, cant be. I live because I live. Dont make a big mishagosh of this Werner. Lets not philosophize. Remember who you are. Yes, who I am. Im here, hes here, because we/re here. O, I weary myself with talk and angst. When I need to know I will know, as always . . . I will know. And now I know I should stop. Just relax so I can sleep. So Werner, let it go . . . let it all go and crumble into a little ball that just floats, a little speck of light that just is and doesnt think, just shines and smiles and laughs and moves on the air and through the air . . . just a little dot of light that doesnt know what darkness is . . . that has no dreams, no hopes, just all the light of the stars right here right now . . . no past no future, just bright and peaceful now . . . the eternal now. . . .

and Moishe sat in his chair, barely breathing, looking as if the air was forcing itself into his body, his hands on his lap, sitting totally immobile, his eyes closed in a restful comfort. . . .

eventually he slowly opened his eyes, blinked a few times, looked around for several minutes, then slowly stood and went to the bedroom. He looked at Bobby for a moment, hoping Bobby was having a dreamless sleep, then shrugged and got undressed and went to bed. He lay on his back for a moment feeling the soothing softness of the darkness, then closed his eyes and slept.

Bobby was still dazed the next morning, seeming to be trying to push himself into something but always being forced to be where he was and not liking it. He just nodded or grunted almost inaudibly when Moishe would ask him if he wanted a cup of coffee . . . some juice . . . eggs, toast, and remained silent as they ate breakfast, and when they finished Bobby sat with his hands around his coffee cup staring in front of him, eventually focusing on the tattoo on Moishes wrist. Moishe could feel Bobbys eyes staring at the numbers and wanted to cover them with his other hand, but rather kept his wrist where it was, unmoving, uncovered, trying not to allow Bobby to know he was watching him. Eventually he heard Bobbys voice though he didnt notice Bobbys lips moving, but the words were clearly spoken, You aint no jew Mush how come you got jew numbers an a jew name?

Moishe looked down at his wrist for a moment, then at Bobby who still hadnt moved, Is funny how you are always asking questions I dont want to hear. Bobby blinked several times and slowly looked up at Moishe who tried to smile, finally succeeding as he looked into Bobbys eyes, The questions are simple, but the answers . . . the answers are taking time. Bobby blinked again and nodded, Spect so. . . . Why are you wanting to know? Bobby looked at Moishe for a moment, then shrugged, Dont know. Jus seems like I got to be knowin. They looked at each other for a moment, then Moishe leaned forward and rested his arms on the table, consciously ignoring the tattoo.

When first we/re in the camp Im still in a rage, how can I be locked up with jews, Im a good German . . . how can Klaus do this just to steal the business . . . how can this be allowed to happen???? This just cant be happening to me. . . . And all the time Im thinking already about my wife and son, about if theyre alive and in my heart afraid theyre dead . . . over and over, day and night Im thinking about my wife and son . . . I close my eyes and I see them, I open my eyes and I see them, no matter where I am Im seeing my wife and son . . . and then Im seeing them dead . . . I dont know how theyre dead, but dead . . . and even if Im not seeing Im knowing . . . theyre dead and I want to kill someone but I cant do anything. If Klaus is there Im for sure killing him, but theres no Klaus so who Im killing, the guards? Im taking from them their guns and shooting them? All I do is think of killing till Im sick from thinking but I still think, I/ll get him, I/ll kill him — Moishe leaned back in his chair — But then I thought of killing the jews . . . If the guards saw I hated the jews they would let me go home and if I killed the jews they would know I hated them, so I thought I/ll kill them, all of them in my barrack its their fault Im here, and I tell them every day I hate them, theyre scum, if it wasnt for them there would be no camps and I would be with my family. And every day we got weaker from hard work and so little food, now only thin potato soup with mostly skins . . . a little bread. And it kept getting colder and colder . . . winter winds, snow, ice and we had to march to work in the cold and march back to the camp every day and it, Ach . . . Moishe sighed and his body sagged, We/re walking back from work, the sky is heavy and ugly like dirty lead, the wind stabs like ice razors. I look around at these jews and they look so dirty, ragged . . . And they smell . . . and Im thinking, there must be something wrong with these people or this wouldnt happen to them . . . things like this just dont happen to decent people — and Moishes and Bobbys eyes looked into each others for many seconds — Ya — nodding his head — I was there with them . . . a good German . . . ya, a good German who loves his Fatherland and loves his wife and son and makes for them a good home . . . a good home . . . warm in the winter with plants and flowers in the window box and a garden. Good food. We were happy and laughed a lot and had a big tree at Christmas . . . good, decent people. So — still looking into Bobbys eyes and shrugging and turning his hands palm up — So . . . even sleeping Im having terrible pains in stomach, big knots in my gut and all the time screaming in my head to get them, to kill the jews, and more and more I think of killing Klaus and his cousin, of making them live in a camp, making them wear these uniforms, to smell the shit and death day and night — Ya, maybe the hating in the beginning is keeping me alive — Bobby peering, obviously agreeing as he nods his head — ya . . . in the beginning is maybe keeping me alive. But then it starts to kill me, the pain, the poison ya, poison, I can feel it flow through me, terrible poison, worse than the food or the cold . . . and inside all I hear is the screaming of the poison — looking piercingly at Bobby for a moment, then nodding his head and sighing — Ya, Im having only the hate and it gets all the time worse so I cant stand straight — Moishe suddenly relaxed and his body seemed to slump slightly in his chair and a sense of affection and tenderness seemed to flow from him as he held Bobbys hands in his for a moment — That was already the worst, the hate . . . it didnt go anywhere, it just stayed inside me and ate me up . . . like a cancer, I was being devoured by my own hate — Moishe looked at Bobby for another moment, then let go of his hands and leaned back in his chair. . . . So . . . we/re walking back from work area, everything hangs like dirty lead . . . even the trees are looking like dirty lead . . . Ahhhccchh such a cold day, such cold . . . freezing . . . and this old man falls, no, it wasnt like he fell, its like he crumbled . . . I can still now see so clearly that day so long ago . . . Oh . . . so many lifetimes ago . . . and Im seeing so clearly we/re walking along and all of a sudden this old man is crumbling and hes on the ground and I know, somehow Im knowing he will not move, that even as the sergeant comes and tells him to get up he will say nothing and not move that he has nothing inside and the sergeant will shoot him in the head and yell at us to keep moving and we will walk and stumble and try to convince ourselves that nothing happened, that it is best, he was old and would soon anyway be dying and hes no more cold and hungry but something inside is not believing and suddenly Im picking up this old man — looking at Bobby with an expression of amazement and surprise — Im not thinking to do this, is just happening and I have an arm around him and am trying to drag him along and a guard comes up to me and hes whispering loud and scared in my ear, Quick, before the sergeant sees him, quick!!! and he stood just behind us to block the view and others made a circle and I somehow dragged/carried him, his one arm over my shoulder and Im hanging on it, my other arm around his waist and somehow Im breathing but not knowing how. Hes a thin, little old man, but he feels like so big a man but I keep holding him, keep us moving, my hands and arms so stiff, so

cold, their pain screaming louder than the hate and somehow we/re getting back to the barracks and I drop him on
his bunk and others are laying on him and warming him and
hes breathing, his heart keeps beating, and Im unable to
open my hands or move my arms, its like Im being sprayed
with cement, Im all stiff and I just stand there and Im feeling
my eyes stare at the old man and someone puts over me a
blanket, and someone else is rubbing me and soon I start to
feel my arms and hands and the pain is making me cry . . .
the blood is rushing through my hands and arms and is
making me cry so bad is the pain – Moishe looked up
toward the ceiling, obviously involved with memories and
thoughts, then lowered his gaze and once again looked at
Bobby, but this time his expression was glowing, soft and
overflowing with compassion – Bobby staring at Moishe,
fascinated, overwhelmed and speechless, being able only to
shake his head – And Im not even at the beginning knowing
Im doing this. We/re walking and I realize I have already
this old man so I just keep walking – Moishe throws up his
arms and leans back and shakes his head – Im not understanding, but its happening. And he lives. He lives a year,
then, like millions, dies – Moishe shrugs – But maybe Im
living because I carried him, maybe my hate would kill me
before the camp – Moishe shrugs again – So anyway, they
rub my arms and Im almost screaming with pain, but its
passing and too is passing the hate for them, O, not all, not
for Klaus, but I see the other prisoners differently, something is happening to how Im seeing them. And theyre
having in the barracks a meeting and one comes over to me
after they whisper a long time in the corner and saying
theyre making me a honorary jew and giving me the name
Moishe, may I have the name and be blessed – Moishe
spread his arms and smiled – Im cursing them, hating them,
and now they make me one of them and so Im a part of the
world around me and something is happening inside . . .
like a new feeling – Moishe was obviously struggling to find
the right words – a closeness to those men I never felt
before, like I truly was one of them like if Im a jew or not is
meaning nothing, but we are all, *men*, somehow together. If

Klaus is there then Im still killing him, still strangling him with my bare hands, but . . . now something is different . . . like something inside moved. Before Im not talking to them, Im pleading with the guards to get me away from the jews, Im not a jew I shouldnt be here, and theyre laughing so Im stopping, but still Im not talking to these men and now Im one of them, Im one with them, like Im them and theyre me – Moishe leaned back and closed his eyes briefly, a look of joy and utter detachment on his face for a moment, then he opened his eyes, looked at Bobby and spread his arms – And thats how Im becoming Moishe. Bobby smiled and shook his head, That be some deep shit Mush – and they continued to smile at each other until Moishe got up, I think we/re needing some ice cream. Hey, dont be forgettin the chocolate sauce Mush – and Bobby laughed and Moishe nodded his head and chuckled.

When Moishe finished cleaning the bowls Bobby got up from the table and asked Moishe to show him how to use the row machine, It be time I got me some exercise, get my strengt back. Moishe felt his insides instantly knot and the smile twist off his face. He stared at Bobby for a moment. . . . I be too weak man. . . . Moishe nodded his head and followed Bobby out of the kitchen. Bobby sat in the machine and pulled back on the oars, having difficulty moving them, Damn, they be some tough suckers Mush. You be pulling like this? Moishe nodded his head and Bobby shook his in admiration, You be a strong ol man Mush, damn.

Moishe showed him how to adjust the tension and to seat himself properly. But is important you start easy, to take time. Your muscles are still bruised, very tender. You must go very, very slow. Is very important.

I cant be waitin Mush. I gotta be gettin my strengt back now. Them muthafuckin spics aint callin no time out while I get my ass in gear, no fuckin way Mush.

But too much strain youre getting weaker, and if youre hurting your muscles maybe you never get strong. Do it like so – Moishe reduced the tension all the way, and Bobby started pulling on the oars slowly – this way you loosen muscles first. Is best.

Moishe nodded when he was satisfied that Bobby knew how to use the machine then went to the living room and sat in his chair.

So . . . I go to the grave to dig up the past, and he wants his strength to kill – Moishe closed his eyes and shook his head in sadness and defeat – and now I care about this boy . . . I knew I would, and you knew I would and now again salt is rubbed into my open wounds. Is there some law against an old man living in peace? O God – holding his head and resting his arms on his legs – why cant I just tell him to leave? Why cant I just tell him it is time for him to go home to his family? Im not his father or his keeper. Why do I do these things? Why cant I simply feed a hungry mouth without loving it and being involved with its heart? Why must I give my heart and soul with my bread? He builds his strength to kill who he sees as responsible for his girl friends death and his pain. This has always been the way of the world. Fine. Let it be so. Im not here to change the world. Why cant I let him do what he is going to do without having my heart broken . . . over and over? Hes no concern of mine . . . no flesh of my flesh, no blood of my blood. . . . Hes free to do what he must, I dont deny him that, but why must I die with his enemies? Why must I always die to be reborn to die again and again. Its enough! Its. . . . O, why do I yell so loud in my head? I know I will sit and ache and die a thousand times before he even leaves to find them . . . this I know . . . oh, how well I know. So help me to just accept that this is what I will do and will be here with my arms and heart open . . . always . . . what else is there for me to do?

Bobby pulled the oars gently and slowly, aware of the severe tenderness in his muscles, yet building up a rhythm that slowly, imperceptibly increased until he had to suddenly stop and ease his arms off the oars and catch his breath, Damn, this sucker like to kill me . . . I bes be doin it like Mushie say, he be right on about everything else, guess he know about this shit too. Bobby rested for a few minutes, then started again, slowly, until he was once again rowing too fast and was forced to stop, Damn, this muthafucka seem like it got a mine of its own, cant seem to be doin like Mushie say. Again he rested a moment, then started rowing, continuing the process until he just hung on the oars. . . . He thought of doing a few push-ups, but figured there was no way he could be doin that, so he laid on the floor and did sit-ups until he was exhausted, ending up hugging his knees, head on arms and panting, until the dizziness stopped and he got up and went into the whirlpool and finally the shower, the process relaxing and rejuvenating, but his expression reflected his depressed feelings. He wrapped himself in the thick robe and went into the living room and looked at Moishe for a moment.

Moishe continued to stare at the cat he was petting, then felt Bobbys presence and looked up, instantly aware that Bobby was troubled by something new, something other than Maria . . . or perhaps it was in addition to it. Moishe continued to pet the cat as he waited for Bobby to tell him what was wrong. . . .

I be hurtin Mush — Moishe opening his eyes wide and mutely asking what was wrong — I dont mean like there be something wrong, but I be sore . . . real sore — Bobby was obviously building up to something and Moishe waited, trying to encourage him with his expression — I cant hardly move that sucker Mush — A shroud of sadness seeming to cover Bobby — I guess I really be weak Mush. . . . You be right . . . it gonna take some time fore I get strong, but I keep pullin them muthafuckas, I dont be whimpin out, no fuckin way. — Moishe nodded his head and his face reflected his pride and satisfaction in Bobbys attitude, his courage, even though he dreaded what Bobby wanted to do with his strength — Its taking time, but its coming — Moishes expression so filled with understanding and acceptance and empathy that Bobby stared into his eyes for many minutes before smiling and nodding and going to get dressed.

Moishe watched Bobby leave the room, then nodded his head as he accepted a decision. When Bobby came back he put the cat on the floor and got up, So, youre strong enough to take a ride?

Bobby nodded and pulled his shoulders back.

Good – nodding his head – Ya . . . is good.

They walked to the subway slowly, mostly silent, Bobby looking around and surprised at how differently everything looked today, in the sunlight. In many ways it was so much uglier, the light shining on every crack and broken bottle, illuminating every chink in the tumbling walls, every broken window, but it wasnt threatening, you could see there was no one hiding in the shadows, your muscles werent tense with expectation everytime you turned a corner. It be a ugly muthafucka but you could shine it on.

As always, the area reminded Moishe of his final years in Europe when it seemed like the entire continent was rubble, occasionally walls standing until they were torn down, in time the rubble cleared away, grass planted sometimes until another building took the place of the one that had been bombed. But here the rubble was never cleared away, just added to and piled on by the survivors in little, impotent acts of defiance. Every day Moishe would look around and be reminded of so many years ago, but at least here he wasnt assaulted with the smell of the camps, the stench from the furnaces. There was no pain here for Moishe because there was no search for loved ones, no despair over the past or hope for the future. He was simply walking through a devastated and deserted area of the south Bronx with Bobby and soon they would be on a subway train in the midst of people and noise.

As they stood on the platform waiting for the train Bobby asked Moishe where they were going?

Brooklyn.

Brooklyn? No shit? I aint never been to Brooklyn.

Moishe looked at him and smiled, All this time you have never been to Brooklyn?

Bobby shrugged, Why bother?

Moishe grinned and shrugged, Ya – he started laughing – Ya, why bother. . . .

The longer they were on the train, the more nervous Bobby became. He had never been this far from the hood in his life. Being at Moishes was bad enough, but he knew he was safe there, but here . . . wherever he was at this moment, was too far away, especially when he was too weak to fight or even run, but that was something he never did have to worry about because he was no runnin wimp . . . but right now he could just about be liftin his arms and so he looked around cautiously, seein who looked like trouble, who might be wantin to get up side some suckers head, but everythin seemed to be cool . . . least ways he be hopin so. . . . But even with the jerkin of the train and the noise that was giving him a headache, and knowing he was far away from the hood, he still be feelin safe with Mushie an that be a funny thing how jus bein with an old honky like Mushie could make him feel safe when Mushie not be knockin no heads together, but he be a strong sucker, Bobby seen that, but he jus aint no fightin man, Bobby could see that too, but he feel all powerful safe with Mushie, more safe than any time in his life and Bobby looked at Moishe for a moment, wondering how this old man made him feel safe, and inwardly shook his head, just not able to figure that one out.

When they came up out of the subway the street was wide and bright and felt so different than his hood Bobby stopped for a minute and looked around. The streets were jammed with people and cars and trucks, just like the hood, but somehow it was different, like it was easier here somehow. In the distance he saw a huge open space with a tall stone something going up pretty high and a lot of trees and when they started walking they walked in that direction.

Where we goin Mush.

Moishe nodded in front of him, The park. . . . Prospect Park.

Prospec Park. . . . Bobby thought for a second. . . . What we be doin in Prospec Park? How far we from home, we be on that train a long time Mush?

Moishe shrugged, whose knowing? 45 minutes – Moishe chuckled, On the way back Im measuring . . . every clickety is 1 meter, every clackity 2 meters . . . clickity, clackity, clickity clackity – and Moishe suddenly started laughing and Bobby stared at him for a moment, surprised, then started laughing too, Moishes laugh so happy it just swept

Bobby up and they both laughed for a few minutes as they walked to Prospect Park.

It was a park day: warm, sunny, light breeze, the park filled with people of all ages, from weeks to years old, and there was every human noise known coming from the trees and the sloping grass-covered ground. They were walking by the bridle path and Bobby suddenly stopped as he heard an unfamiliar noise, then stared at the slight bend in the path and watched as a trio of horsemen came into sight: a man, a woman and a young girl, evidently a family, and Bobby just stared, transfixed, especially by the young girl who was wearing a complete riding habit, remaining riveted to the spot, moving only his head as he watched them ride by, still staring until they were hidden by the trees. Moishe was amused as he watched Bobby, You never before see riders?

Bobby shook his head, Uh uh. What the fuck they be doin?

Moishe laughed, Riding elephants, what else? You never see people ride elephants? — And Moishe continued laughing, obviously having such a good time that again Bobby started laughing as he shook his head, Mus be somethin here be gettin you high Mush. I aint seen you smokin nothin, but you sure be outta your head — and Bobby continued shaking his head and laughing.

After a few minutes Moishe stopped and he put an arm around Bobbys shoulder and hugged him slightly, Bobby being startled, but standing still and not shaking Moishes hand off but feeling all warm inside and safe like his hand was alive with something, feeling so safe that it didnt even occur to him he felt safe, just that Moishes hand was like magic and Bobby felt good. Soon they were just smiling and continued walking, Moishe pointing to the bridle path, Thats a riding path.

People really ride horses here?

Moishe nodded.

Bobby shook his head, Man, this Brooklyn be a far out place Mush.

Moishe was smiling, You never see before?

Uh uh, least ways not in the street, jus tv.

So. . . . Now youre seeing Brooklyn cowboys.

Again they laughed, Bobby grinning from ear to ear, I be gettin as high as you are Mush I be livin in this muthafuckin park.

Ya, ya, is good. But the elephants theyre tramping me?

O man, you too much. You be one crazy dude Mush — shaking his head, grinning, and feeling like huggin Moishe.

They continued walking, Bobby stopping occasionally to watch a kid flying a kite or model plane, or a group throwing a Frisbee, the look of wonder on his face filling Moishe with an overwhelming sense of gratitude and affection.

Bobby had never spent so much time walking on grass and from time to time he would bounce up and down on the balls of his feet, the softness of the earth under him delighting and amusing him. They continued walking, avoiding being run over by the running kids and dogs, until Moishe stopped. Bobby looked at him, then around and back at Moishe, Why we stoppin Mush?

Thats the tree — nodding toward a huge willow tree a hundred yards away on the edge of the lake.

The tree?

Ya.

Bobby continued to look at Moishe.

Our tree. Gertrude and me . . . and our son — He looked at Bobby and smiled — Our family tree.

Bobby just looked at Moishe not understanding what he was talking about. Moishe started walking again until they reached the tree and Moishe sat and leaned against the trunk, Bobby sitting beside him.

The branches reached out almost 30 feet at the broadest and the tips dipped to the ground, the sunlight dancing on the leaves waving slightly in the breeze, and reflecting off the rippling water of the lake a few feet away. Sitting under the tree, looking at the lake through the branches, the sounds of laughter coming from the boats on the lake as people rowed or paddled, the dancing light, the moist coolness coming from the ground, the smell of the grass and earth and water, the air easing on his face as it worked its way through the branches and leaves, the presence of Moishe and the memory of his hand on his shoulder, the sky highlighted with clouds glimpsed through the tree . . . all created a new world for Bobby, a world that seemed to have no walls or corners or shadows, a world where you never had to look over your shoulder and it almost made Bobby want to run because there seemed to be nothing to lean against, nothing familiar, nothing in his experience to help him feel safe, but somehow Moishe solved all that just by sort of being there and grinning that stupid grin of his. . . . Yeah, it was alright, and he leaned back against the trunk of the tree and took a deep breath and closed his eyes for a moment, then opened them and looked around and everything was still there, just as it had been a minute ago, and he looked at Moishe who was looking out at the water, an occasional duck bobbing on the surface, an expression of such peaceful contentment on his face Bobby felt his face smiling too. Moishe continued to look at the water as he spoke,

In old country we have like this a tree too. When I was a young man and just started working for Mr. Kreiger Im coming here, haha, going there, with Gertrude. Our first date is picnic by the lake and we/re sitting under tree, Gertrude and I. She has for us a basket of food and Im bringing wine – Moishe looks at Bobby, a beautiful sense of softness about him while remembering vividly the times of his youth, Bobby not really knowing what he was talking about, just picking up on Moishes feelings – And we sit there and eat and laugh and talk and look at the water and the ducks and row around the lake and come back and just are stretching out on the grass. . . .

Im not even kissing her – Moishes smile broadened, then he chuckled for a moment as Bobbys eyes widened – Is true . . . we hold hands a little while we talk, a little bit sometimes, but Im so scared to kiss her but all the time in my chest my heart is pounding and my stomach, Achhh, mine stomach is already in my throat, O Bobby you should see my Gertrude –

Moishes eyes filling with such love and affection they were brighter than the sun on the leaves – and everyday is being like today . . . even when one day it rains after we/re spreading the blanket and shes unpacking the food. . . . Ya, everyday like now with music in the air . . . and shes loving me like the tree is loving the sun – Moishe grins almost self-consciously, continuing to glow with love, Bobby totally transfixed, mesmerized, by Moishes story, but more by his feelings – Ya Bobby, you should be seeing her with the sun spinning around in her hair . . . it was so golden Bobby like more than any flower . . . like honey and always when we/re there a butterfly is flying around her head, ya, ya, is true, always, I dont know we go there how many times and always a butterfly, always, even up to the last time we/re there . . . a butterfly dancing in the golden sunlight of her hair and such a happy dance O Bobby who is thinking trouble??? who is thinking like what was going to happen, ya theres trouble, ya, ya, in all life theres trouble, but Bobby who is thinking with the butterfly dancing in the golden light, the water sparkling, the birds singing and we/re hugging, eating, drinking wine and telling each other such things O Bobby such things of love and all true from our heart so whos thinking that some day the birds and the butterflies and even the flowers turn into beasts, maddened, crazed beasts of prey who devour the land ach Bobby, you should see . . . you should see our little boy running after the ducks and geese, hes falling and getting up and falling and we/re laughing and he stumbles and the ducks quack and waddle a few feet at a time – Moishes head back, laughing, Bobby grinning – and then is biting his foot a big goose and hes yelling and is so funny. . . . O Bobby . . . is so funny . . . and always when there, before we/re married, married after and with our son always is coming the butter-fly . . . is true Bobby, always is coming the butterfly – Bobby staring at Moishe whose expression was almost angelic, obviously so happy in just remembering those days, the memories bringing not only the joy of then, but also replacing all the pain that followed in the days, and years since . . . and Bobby continued to stare, never having been around anyone like Moishe, never feeling the way he did at this moment, nothing in his life comparable to what Moishe was talking about because Bobby could see by the way Moishe looked that this was different than anything he knew or could remember, for damn sure the moms never had no look on her face like Mushie be having now . . . but suddenly Bobby did remember something that made him feel good all over at the time and in the remembering, when he was a little kid and it was one of those really hot summers and they turned on the hydrant and all the kids were running through and in the water yelling and screeching . . . it was Bobbys first time with a hydrant open like that and it suddenly became another world. He had seen hydrants, and especially that one on his block, and heard the word, hydrant, but never really knew what they were for and now all of a sudden instead of burning up with the heat he was feeling cool and running and screaming with the other kids and the hydrant became a magicians wand transforming the blazing street into a cool wonderland and the air was suddenly free of the stink of garbage and big folks yellin at little kids, and the little kids yellin at the littler kids and even some of the old sourpusses was laughing as the kids screeched their way through the powerful stream, playing every game they could think of with the stream of water, sometimes standing to the side and jumping up and down on the wet streets, their sneakers squishing and squeaking, older kids shoving younger kids into the water, younger kids showing off for the older kids, 'watch me, watch me'!!!! the cars coming down the street stopping, closing their windows, cursing the water and the kids but only some and anyway, Bobby didnt hear the ones that were pissed off, too delighted to be aware of anything but having fun, and the cars would crawl, barely moving through the area, windshield wipers whacking back and forth, drivers nervous because they were afraid of hitting the kids as they ran and yelled not paying attention to where they were going, then continuing down the street but sooner or later another one would come through the stream and the kids would yell at the driver to hurry up, hurry up . . . and even after the water was turned off they continued running in the wet streets, the air still so different, so unfamiliarly clean, and then the ice pushcart came around and he got a ice with strawberry and he sucked it and chewed it, feeling the cold almost numb his throat and stomach and then he sat on the curb by the hydrant, reaching over and touching it from time to time, thinking of it as his friend, wanting to talk to it but knowing if he did everybody would make fun of him so he just talked to it to himself, and that night in bed and many other times when it was so hot and sticky he couldnt hardly move through the air. He sat on the curb very aware of how his wet clothes felt on his body, his wet sneakers on his feet, the wet ground under his butt and the incredible magic of the hydrant that had changed his world of smells and heat and grouchy and crabby big people to one of just a whole lot of fun and something else he didnt understand, but something that made him feel good and he never forgot, he never forgot how one minute he felt crushed and squeezed by the street and then all of a sudden it no longer had walls but was wide open, like the hydrant, and became a really great, great place, like some kind of fairy tale and he felt like he never felt before . . . all just like that, out of nowhere, and he hadnt even hoped for anything like that, it just happened out of nowhere . . . just like that. . . .

and that was sort of how being with Moishe made him feel, now, like all of a sudden everything that was always the same had changed but he knew it was all the same, but somehow. . . .

he knew, mostly anyway, how the water made him feel good that day, but how does being with Moishe make him feel good???? Bobby shook his head and grinned and let go trying to understand what was happening, he just looked at Moishe with that look on his face like he never saw on anyone before and felt all those good feelings go through him and enjoyed it, figurin he best enjoy it as much as he can right now because sooner or later the street be squeezing in on him but for now he wasnt going to give that a thought but just sit with Moishe under the willow tree and look at Moishes face wondering how anyone can look so happy, and remembering the hydrant, the strawberry ice and how his wet sneakers felt when he walked like there was a big squishy cushion between his feet and the street . . . and, from time to time, seeing the sun wiggling around the leaves of the tree and hunching over the ripples in the water as boats glided by, ducks getting nonchalantly out of their way, and all the yells and screams of kids, kids, kids, and above all the various and sundry noises there was laughter . . . all kinds, all volumes, all laughter. . . .

So — still looking through the hanging branches at the water — We come from old country to America and friend brings us here. They too are having child, little girl, and we/re coming here and riding in boat and we/re seeing this tree . . . from over there, near that little island. Gertrude is first seeing it and yelling to me, The tree, the tree, and is almost tipping over the boat — Moishe suddenly laughed, moving his head for the first time in many, many minutes — Its like shes thinking she can walk on the water and is going to run to the tree — Moishe stopped laughing and closed his eyes for a moment, his face continuing to reflect his joy — Im rowing right here, that same little chink in the wall, and we/re getting out and sitting right away under the tree and all the years we/re coming here and sitting, we/re walking and rowing too, but always were sitting for a while here under the tree, just like this, and looking and hugging and yelling at Karl-Heinz to stay away from the edge, dont fall in, and Gertrude is telling me, always, to relax, hes alright . . . ya, she was so good a mother . . . and everytime we/re sitting here Im looking for a butterfly but never a butterfly here . . . but still her hair its like honey and the sun twinkled in it . . . always twinkled like lights on a Christmas tree . . . ya, the sun on her hair was always like Christmas. . . .

Moishe leaned back against the tree and closed his eyes, again his reverie so clearly and lovingly reflected on his face, and Bobby sat beside the old man feeling as if he were sitting in the sun and it was twinkling in his hair, feeling so relaxed by whatever was coming from Moishe and so aware of the clean smell of the earth beneath him, the water, the air, the tree and still feeling the joy of his hydrant and squishy sneakers . . . watching a family of ducks bobbing up and down on the water, making their way to where the hanging limbs of the willow tree met the lake. . . .

In time Moishe opened his eyes and looked at Bobby with the same look of peace and reverie on his face, So . . . youre liking my tree?

Bobby smiled and shook his head, It be righteous Mush — touching him on the shoulder — You be righteous bro — continuing to look at Moishe, feeling a sense of strength and softness flowing through him and around him, again, something he had no experience with, a feeling alien to him yet not frightening, not even questioning it, but simply experiencing it and knowing it was safe to allow it to happen, that the feeling was alright, that he was alright and it was fine to be touching Moishe like he was, leaving his hand on Moishes shoulder and feeling the warmth and safety that came from him, feeling somehow simply a part of the moment, void of self-consciousness, aware only of being there with Moishe and touching him and that it was alright, that everything was alright . . . yeah, that was it, everything was alright

and Moishe looked into Bobbys eyes, aware of the change, aware of Bobbys place in what was happening at that moment, feeling, in turn, something coming from Bobby, Moishe realizing he was a part of Bobbys experience and rejoiced with a thousand hallelujahs, so happy to feel Bobbys contentment at and with the moment and feeling himself as much of the old happiness as was possible and that was as it should be, if resurrecting the past meant he had to again feel the crush of the camp and smell its deadly air, then he also should be able to feel the joy of love, the cleansing, healing happiness of their love under the willow tree and all other times because they carried that joy with them wherever they went . . . even under a building, lying in filth and fixing a pipe . . . of course, at that time he was more involved with other things, other feelings so maybe he was not as aware of the feelings of love, and didnt think about the butterfly, but always the love was there. . . .

Ya Bobby, we/re married 25 years and sometimes Im coming home from work and as Im starting already up the stairs I think of Gertrude and feel like I cant wait to see her . . . sometimes the pain is first tearing me apart, but always is there the love . . . always . . . O Bobby – placing his hand on top of Bobbys hand on his shoulder – sometimes Im so angry shes leaving me, alone, but eventually Im remembering the 53 years we/re having together and not always its the peaches and cream, after all, she was a woman – grinning – even now Im having to make stupid joke . . . but always the love Bobby . . . always – tapping Bobbys hand a few times, then leaning back against the tree and staring up through the branches at the sky . . . Bobby watching a little kid, being held by the arm by a parent, throwing bread crumbs to the ducks, the kid bouncing up and down and screeching, the ducks swimming around and gobbling the crumbs, from time to time diving under the surface for the ones that were slowly sinking.

They stayed under the tree until the sun moved far enough to the west to bring a chill to the shaded, damp air under the tree. The change in the air and temperature was so great when they stepped from the shadows into the sunlight they both stopped for a moment to experience the warm air brushing against their skin.

They continued walking through the park, Moishe deliberately avoiding the zoo where animals were locked in tiny, foul smelling cages, staying with the rolling grassy ground, the children yelling and running, the people lying on the grass, some hugging and kissing, a thousand and two radios playing all different stations and all melting into a noise Moishe chuckled at but was so happy he didnt have to live with, thinking it was nice he could go home and play what he would play, but for now they could rock their craziness.

They stopped at one of the pushcart vendors, Moishe still smiling, So, maybe Im talking you into having some hot dogs?

O Mush, how the fuck you ever figure that one out? you

be one smart sonofabitch . . . damn, you be right on Mush—
raising his right hand and waiting a moment until Moishe
understood what was happening, then raised his, then gave
Moishe a high five and Moishe laughed and gave it right
back.

They stayed at the hot dog push cart for many minutes,
and when Bobby finished his second one, and his Pepsi,
they started walking again.

Mush, you best be gettin that wagon an wheelin me
home, Im not makin it, uh, uh, no way Im walking all the
way to the muthafuckin subway — shaking his head and
laughing, Moishe grinning and still feeling the sensation in
his chest when he heard Bobby say, 'home', a feeling of
absolute joy, but also one of fear, fear of losing another son,
another person he loved and held dear, but he decided to
postpone the pain until later and enjoy right now, just
enjoy . . . enjoy. He looked at Bobby, Is long time since Ive
been here.

Yeah?

Ya . . . long time. . . . And the first one I show my tree to
is you.

Bobby stopped walking and so did Moishe, No shit? I be
the firs one you bring to your will tree?

Ya . . . number one . . . is true.

Bobby was smiling and grinning and bouncing up and
down on the balls of his feet, feeling the grass bend and rise,
bend and rise, Damn . . . now aint that somethin. . . . Damn . . .
the firs one. . . . Damn, I caint believe that . . . me . . . the
firs one. Damn Mush, you be somethin else — and Bobby
started walking, shaking his head, beaming, beaming, beaming
and bouncing on the grass, feeling and hearing the grass
squish under his sneakers. He stopped and looked at Moishe,
both with expressions of total joy on their faces, shook his
head, Damn Mush, I really be diggin you. You be one
righteous dude!!!!

They continued to stroll through the park, each within
themselves yet so aware of each other and the day, the sun,
the sky, the people, the sounds, the birds and the grass.
They were quiet on the ride back, each keeping the day

alive in their own way, re-experiencing the joy as much and as deeply as possible.

They were quiet as they ate that night, very few words passing between them, still locked in their reverie. When they finished they both leaned back in their chairs, looking at each other occasionally and grinning, until Bobby got up and said he was going to bed, I be beat Mush. All that fresh air and grass be making me nod out – grinning and giggling – an I aint never been to no Brooklyn before . . . man, that takes a lot out a little ol Bronx boy – both of them smiling and chuckling, Moishe feeling a contentment and joy he hadnt felt in a long time – an I gotta be workin out real hard tomorrow . . . got to get strong as you Mush, so I be rowin that muthafucka . . . got to be gettin strong Mush – Bobby suddenly looking reflective, the smile and joy totally gone from his face – I got to be makin them pay . . . theys the ones killed Maria . . . she be dead . . . dead Mush an they got to be payin for that . . . an I be seein they do – looking down at the floor, nodding in affirmation to his inner voice, reaffirming his conviction and commitment – got to be seein they pay for it . . . thas my job . . . yeah, that be my job – still looking at the floor and nodding his head as he turned and went to the bedroom.

Moishe died a thousand deaths as he listened to Bobby and saw the change on his face, saw, and heard, the conviction in his voice, feeling an endless flow of tears hammering at his eyes as he watched Bobby leave the room, staring at the doorway long after Bobby had left, the empty doorway seeming to have some sort of substance, a message . . . an omen that Moishe could clearly see but was unable to accept . . . or believe. . . . The thought passed through his mind that he should get up and go to the living room and sit in his chair and maybe the cat would jump up on his lap and he could lose himself in petting her; or a bowl of ice cream might soothe him or even washing the dishes might help him forget his pain, he could clean up the kitchen, tidy up a little . . . scrub the sink . . . something, but he could only sit at the table immobilized by the twisting pain and sense of betrayal . . . betrayal not by Bobby, but himself for allow-

ing Bobby to fill his heart and to once again find happiness
in another human being . . . betrayed by his memories . . .
betrayed by his need to hope he could change Bobbys
mind. How could he allow this to happen???? O God –
holding his head – How could he allow this to happen????
He sat holding his head, staring at the table, feeling the
kitchen getting smaller and smaller until he suddenly lifted
his head and looked around and decided to go out. He left
a note for Bobby in case he woke up and wondered where
he was, and quietly left the apartment.

The sky was clear, the moon bright, the light in the
distance eerie, a strange pink glow in the sky almost like
distant fires. He roamed around the endless area of deser-
tion and abandonment, the blocks upon blocks of rubble,
feeling the hard and gritty debris under his feet that was so
different from the grass he had been walking on such a short
time before. He heard shards of glass splinter and occasionally crack sounding like a gunshot, and in time he sat on a
pile of bricks in the shadow of a crumbling wall . . . almost
convulsing as ancient groans ground through his body,
screams of pain, desperation and despair, the heavy, leaden
blackness within and without and the paralyzing stench of
death, the suffocating agony of living – his body jerked
spastically and he wrapped his arms around his head, NO
NO!!!! AHHHRRRR

*the first hideous, endless night in the*
*camp they stood in the leaden air on ground screaming with the*
*torturous tortured voices of those who had preceded them, stood*
*through the leaden day into the leaden, interminable night when*
*suddenly floodlights stabbed their eyes as had the sun, and the*
*putrid, befouled men struggled to stay erect less they be beaten*
*and tossed into a ditch and set on fire as had others, their*
*screams twisting into their brains and scraping the inside of*
*their skulls throughout the night, the screams that would haunt*
*and torment them in the darkest of nights and the brightest of*
*days all through the remainder of their days on earth and per-*
*haps eternity. . . .*

Moishe was bent over so far, as he sat
on the pile of bricks, that he was almost a ball . . . Ya, the

first night ended and so many more nights, and days, yet to live. Achhhh — Moishe stood and looked up at the sky, able to see only an occasional star and the lights of a few aircraft. The battered and decaying buildings looked eerie in the light from the street lamps, desolate silhouettes in the darkness. Shadows animated the garbage and debris filling the streets and empty lots. The silence leaden, broken occasionally by the squealing of a rat or screech of a cat. There was nothing he could do. Bobby was here so Moishe had to help . . . he had to do what he had to do. And thats to suffer? Is that what Im supposed to do? Sit and watch hate eat up so young a life . . . again . . . as I have over and over? O what is this all about? O whats the use. There is never an answer . . . only questions . . . questions . . . but always we do what we do — Moishe shook his head and started back to the entrance to the cellars.

Bobby spent as much time as possible exercising and working out. He knew exactly where the tension had been set for Moishe and was determined to be able to do at least 25 at that setting and 50 pushups real fast, justlikethat, before going after the spics. His body was tense with anticipation, his mind with impatience, but he knew hed be wasted if he didnt get in shape, so he tugged and yanked at the oars, and exercised his arms and legs.

Bobby finished working out, showered and was sitting at the kitchen table, Moishe bringing 2 bowls of ice cream and chocolate sauce. Moishe forced himself to keep smiling through his pain and conflict, finding such joy in the way Bobby closed his eyes from time to time as he ate the ice cream, licking his lips and, hmmmmming, eventually to clean the bowl with his finger and licking it.

Moishe leaned forward and scrutinized Bobbys face, Youre looking like new, even the bruises almost all gone.

You mean I be pretty jus like before?

Pretty? — Moishe shrugged and smiled a real smile — This Im not saying.

They smiled at each other for a moment, then went back

to eating their ice cream. When he finished Bobby leaned back in his chair and looked over Moishes head for a moment

An you be in the constration camp four years?

Ya . . . more.

Bobby shook his head, Damn, that sure be a muthafucka. – Bobby looked at his bowl for a moment, then raised his eyes, You goin in there a German an comes out a jew . . . damn.

Moishe nodded his head.

Dont seem to me they be doin you no favor makin you a jew Mush. Firs you caint move your arms then they starve your ass. – shaking his head and chuckling – But you really be talkin to them jews after that, eh?

Ya, ya. No longer I stay in the corner hating them . . . not talking. Im a – smiling – brother . . . a family.

But you still got them Germans to hate, right Mush?

The guards . . . the Nazis . . . and Klaus, always I hate Klaus, ya . . . O ya, I still hate, Bobby, and its killing me.

Seem like them muthafuckas aint given no hate a chance to be killin ya the way they be beaten and starvin your ass.

Moishes smile was soft and filled with understanding, Ya thats what Im saying, but I learn the hate was truly the killer.

Sheeit, hate be keepin your ass alive bro, you be hatin strong enough you keep movin, you keep breathin, you keep livin so long you can be hatin, no way uh uh, no way you be makin it in this muthafuckin world you aint hatin somethin . . . somebody . . . uh uh, no fuckin way.

A thousand lifetimes of pain passed through Moishes mind and heart, the million memories of shattered dreams, decimated hopes, a thousand and one disappointments in a day twisted and ravaged his tortured body and soul, each and every cell of his being screaming with tortured memories . . . and a sadness so profound for a moment it felt as if he would sink right through the floor into the bowels of the earth that gave him birth . . . not because he identified with what Bobby was saying, it was not only the words, the feelings, the broken and busted dreams they represented, but the lack of anger behind them . . . their simple calmness, acceptance, something so simple it had long ago been accepted as an immutable truth in the very marrow of Bobbys bones, it had been said with the same emotion and ready recognition as if he were saying you stop on red and go on green, and for that startled moment in time Moishe felt as if he were dying and any moment he would be able to leave his body, but almost instantly he was back at the table, experiencing a lifetime of torment and he had to lick his lips and swallow many times as he looked at Bobby who was still smiling as if nothing startling had occurred, as if the world hadnt suddenly ceased to be for a moment and they both hung, suspended but animated, in an eternal and agonizing purgatory, but now they were both at the table and Moishe struggled to return Bobbys smile. . . . Ya — nodding his head — Ya, is true. Hate makes the muscles bulge . . . can survive almost anything . . . ya. . . . But Bobby . . . in the end Bobby we dont survive our hate — closing his eyes for a moment so his past could quickly pass — We die Bobby . . . even while we stay alive we/re dying.

Bobby shrugged, I aint seein that Mush — Bobby frowned and looked at Moishe, hard, in the eyes for a few moments — You aint hatin Mush? Tell me straight Mush, you aint be hatin those muthafuckas.

Moishe looked as deeply as possible into Bobbys eyes, Is true Bobby, Im not hating now.

Bobby continued to stare for a moment. . . . You jus up an stop hatin them muthafuckas?

Moishe shook his head and smiled, No way. I hate so much I got muscles in my gut — and he laughed and Bobby looked at him for a moment, then laughed too. Moishe stopped, took a deep breath, Is there a man named Sol. Im standing, arms stiff . . . just standing. . . . Some are warming old man, others warming me. So. . . Im standing there in the middle of the barracks, arms stiff, like so . . . and I start to shake, and then a man is hugging me . . . ya, just like that hes hugging me . . . and then someone is putting around me blankets and the man keeps hugging and pushing gently on my arms and I can still feel the scratch of the blankets and the warmth of this man as hes hugging me and somehow the pain isnt killing me though Im feeling like Im going to crack. . . . Ya, like Im cracking like piece of ice into little pieces but soon Im still . . . and warm, and he steps back and looks at me as he keeps on my shoulders his hands. And so, like that we/re standing until he helps me walk to his bunk and we/re sitting — Moishes voice trailed off and Bobby continued staring at him, blinking his eyes from time to time, almost saying something several times, but nothing coming out of his mouth, so they sat in silence for a few minutes until Moishe started speaking again, So then he talks to me, and — Moishe smiles and spreads his hands — and we talk for years.

An you still here — Bobbys voice filled with amazement and admiration.

Ya . . . still here — Moishe smiled at Bobby for a moment, then obviously came to a sudden decision, So, you want to get strong . . . okay. Youre getting dressed and we go to the store.

Where we goin?

We/re gettin some dumbells.

Dumbells? How we be gettinem back here?

The red wagon, ya? Is carrying one dumbell can carry more.

Mush, its them jokes gonna be killin your ass . . . sheeit.

When they got back with the weights Bobby started playing with them and Moishe laughed and showed Bobby how to use them, demonstrating the exercises, Bobby once again amazed at how strong Moishe was when he tried to do the same exercise as effortlessly as Moishe and had to struggle. Moishe reassured him when he saw how much it upset Bobby to be having so much trouble, Youre still weak and not used to exercise. Soon youre lifting like paper-weights, ya?

Right the fuck on Mush. . . . And soon I be liftin those spics heads like the piece of shit they are — instantly Moishe experiencing the ripping in his heart and sudden lack of breath. He continued to watch Bobby for a few minutes, not certain he was really seeing him, then left him alone to continue the workout and found the cat and sat in his chair, the cat on his lap, but it was restless and jumped down as soon as Moishe let it go. Moishe watched it for a moment, then closed his eyes and leaned back in the chair for a moment wondering if he would ever be free of pain, wondering yet again why Bobby came into his life when he expected these final years to be peaceful and free of the conflict and pain that seemed to haunt him all his life, the agony that always came when he thought he had suffered enough.

But that thing that he could never see, that wonderful thing of love he found within himself, always answered his questions long before he asked them, but in a way he could never anticipate. But he did trust that thing . . . absolutely. Yes. He trusted it. And so when he saw how much Bobby had accepted hate as a necessary part of life he realized, in his gut, (or was it his heart???) that he had to help Bobby become strong, to give him what he had. Wasnt that the answer Sol had given him, and this thing inside him constantly reaffirmed, to share whatever I have. Bobby needs to be strengthened in his body and Moishe knows how to do that . . . so I do that. Is this different? It cant be. Somebody needs something I have so I give it. . . . But why this???? How do I know why? I dont ask. Why? WHY? Its always, eventually, unanswerable, and the more I ask the deeper I go into madness. Why I dont need, just how. So I help him get back the strength he needs to kill young boys, O Werner . . . young? Are they ever young on these streets Werner? Was anyone young in the camps? Young. Is it young to not even question hate? To accept it like breathing? Werner, stop analyzing. Please, no more madness. Simply allow your heart to be open. Dont defend yourself against the pain of loving this boy and having him torn from your life as has happened in the past . . . especially with Karl-Heinz . . . o god . . . our little Heinz. How could he survive those years of hell and then when . . . let your heart embrace this boy, fully and totally. Give him all of it. Dont defend against the pain Werner. If it comes it comes. But if it comes let it come in its own time . . . not now. . . . O

Werner, what madness. You couldnt close your heart if you wanted to. Already its as if youve known him all your life. Hes in your heart and soul . . . in every cell of your body . . . in your genes Werner, in your genes. Dont defend against the pain. If it comes it comes. If it does youll have the answer. You know that. You always have the answer. Do as you do. How many years now Werner? Should we count? — Moishe smiling and shaking his head — Heart and arms open Werner . . . always, heart and arms open . . . and Moishe opened his eyes as he became aware of something tapping his ankle and the sound of meowing, and he looked down at the cat, smiled and tapped his lap, Come on — and the cat jumped up on his lap and spent a few minutes kneading, then turned in a circle a few times before snuggling into Moishes lap in a tight ball, tail wrapped alongside its body, one paw over its eyes, sighing softly, contentedly, and going to sleep as Moishe rubbed its head and behind its ears. Moishe continued to pet the cat, smiling at its purring, and continuing to smile as he also heard Bobby struggling with the weights.

The days and weeks followed a routine that Moishe laid out for Bobby and Bobby followed exactly. He worked out in the morning before he ate, then showered and drank a large body builders drink Moishe prepared for him. When Moishe first filled a glass from the blender Bobby looked at it, frowning, then looked at Moishe mischievously, What this gonna be doin Mush?

Moishe shrugged, Maybe its making your muscles as big as your head — laughing his silly laugh.

Bobby shook his head and smiled, Mush, you sure be a sad assed dude.

Moishe shrugged and grinned, Is maybe adding 3 inches and 2 lbs to your wiener, ya?

Hey, right the fuck on man! — shaking his head and grinning as wide as possible — Wiener can ya dig it???? A muthafuckin wiener, hehehe. Mush . . . you be sick . . . damn . . . you be a sick dude.

Bobby sipped the drink, then opened his eyes wide and looked at the glass, then Moishe, Hey, this be righteous Mush. Bobby took a long drink, looked at the glass again, then emptied it and licked his lips, That be tastin fine. . . . Damn, an it be puttin some bad weight on my pretty dick! Sheeit, you be alright Mush.

They looked at each other, smiling happily, Bobby wiping his mouth with the back of his hand, I be fixin to axe you Mush what be happenin to the dude what be huggin you?

Moishe looked at Bobby not understanding, So????

You know, the dude in the camp that be huggin your arms down after you –

O ya, ya . . . Sol.

Sol? That be his name?

Ya, Sol – Moishes expression changing to one of reverie and reverence – Ya . . . Sol. . . .

Bobby studied Moishes face for a moment, always loving it when he got that look on his face, whatever he was feeling making Bobby feel good, and, too, Bobby knew it meant that whatever they were talking about, or he was thinking about, meant something really special to Moishe and he really liked to see the old man so happy, really groovin behind it, it jus be turnin his ass on, He be makin it?

So????

You know, he live?

O ya, ya. Sol lived. Who knows – shrugging – maybe hes still living. I hope.

You see him after you split the camp?

No . . . no. Last time Im seeing Sol is couple days after camp is liberated.

Bobby was still turned on by Moishes expression and manner and was smiling from deep within himself, He be your main man, huh?

Main man? – looking bewildered.

Bobby started laughing, Man, it sure do tickle me when you lookin that way.

So?

Bobby smiled all over his face, I mean like you two was really tight . . . bes friens.

O ya, O so . . . so . . . Im not knowing how much best friends. Sol was . . . O, so important . . . like – shrugging, groping for words – like god, like breathing.

Like he hip ya to the camp . . . like show ya how to make it . . . run a scam or somethin.

Moishe looked at Bobby for a few long moments, that reverential expression on his face, Bobby feeling it sweep over him. Moishe looked at Bobby with such overwhelming tenderness and love Bobbys knees started to weaken . . . Im not knowing from scam, but ya, Sol showed me how to survive . . . not just stay alive . . . survive – gently tapping his chest – in the heart.

Bobbys expression asked the unspoken question, How?

O Sol, such a simple man . . . a nobody, a clerk or bookkeeper – shrugging – who knows, but such a person – Once again that faraway look crossed Moishes face as if he were somewhere else – You know Bobby, sometimes Im thinking all those years ago did Sol really be, is he really there or am I imagining – smiling, grinning – Sometimes Im even thinking it was an angel whose talking to me . . . Im thinking if I talk, today, with other men in that barracks are they seeing Sol too? Are they hearing him?

Bobby watched, smiling. . . . Soun like he save your ass for sure.

Ya – laughing – for sure . . . for sure.

What he be doin, showin you how to be gettin extra food an stay hid from the muthafuckin man?

Man? – again shaking his head and smiling.

Bobby shook his head laughing happily, just loving to watch Moishe, Damn Mush, how you get so square? The guards.

O ya . . . ya, the guards. No . . . and anyway, how can you hide? No. Sol is showing me how not to hate –

Not to hate? In that muthafuckin joint? Soun like bull shit.

Ya, ya, I say to him the same thing.

I doan know Mush – shaking his head – Soun like some deep shit to me! Anyway, I bes be gettin dressed.

Suddenly Moishe was alone in the kitchen looking at the doorway, hearing Bobby moving around in the bedroom.

Eventually he got up from the table and washed the glass, and the blender, and remained at the sink for a moment remembering how patient Sol was with him, how Sol always let him yell and curse Klaus, and the Nazis, Moishe feeling his face flush, knowing it was getting redder and redder as it got hotter and hotter, but not caring, just wanting to scream his hatred into the rotten, foul air, wishing he could scream it into the brains of the guards then scoop their brains out of their skulls and scream them into oblivion and always he would reach the point where he could no longer yell, his throat almost closed, feeling a large lump, hearing the hoarseness, his voice starting to fade and always . . . always, without ever one exception he would end up on Sols bunk, his arms wrapped around his head, moaning and crying from deep in his soul, from some place he had never known existed, never having been so violated by life . . . so shattered by the circumstances of his existence . . . never having the ability to imagine being in a situation like the one he was in at that moment . . . and always Sol would let him have the dignity of his pain. . . .

and when Moishes turmoil would subside Sol would put a hand on his shoulder and reassure him that it was alright to feel as he felt. Just feel Moishe and dont judge . . . thats all. You are a loving man Moishe, you cant stop the love forever, it is more powerful than the camp.

Sol — tearfully looking at him — How can you say these things? How can you look around and say these things? There is nothing but hate here. There is nothing but blind stupid hatred here and you want me to love these . . . these . . . crazed beasts?

I want only that you treat yourself with respect. They wont so you should. Is that not so?

Words Sol . . . words. It is only hate that keeps me alive.

Is that so? Perhaps, but I think not.

I live only to someday get Klaus and all the rest of them — waving his arm in a wide arc.

Moishe my friend, we all need a reason to live. If yours is hate, to kill, then so it is — shrugging and looking at Moishe with profound understanding – but what do you end up with? a poisoned heart and in the end hate will kill you.

Kill me? Hate is not killing me. I will stay alive to . . . to . . . O god. . . .

Sol was quiet for a moment . . . My friend, we have more chance of surviving this place than our own hate. Hate always destroys the hater, that can not be avoided. But some of us will survive this place, that is always the way. I dont know why, but there is always those who survive. Maybe life wants it like that so we can tell others what happened, so all this will not happen again.

You sit here in this place, this putrid miserable hell, and spout this . . . this . . . shit, this pure unadulterated SHIT!!!!

There was a faint hint of a smile on Sols face, Where can I go my friend? Yes I sit here and say what I say.

But how can you talk such shit?!

How? Because no one has suffered more from hate than me. Hate killed me, my friend, so I know.

Ahhhhhhh. . . . Moishe jerked up from the bunk and waved his arm in dismissal and went to his own bunk and sat, hunched over, his arms wrapped around his head. . . .

How many times did I run away from Sol? – Moishe smiled – until I died. Yes, like Sol said, hate killed me. So Werner, now we let Bobby die. So maybe hate will kill him so he can live. We will see. I just dont interfere with life . . . Ya, just like that – smiling and shaking his head – just like that.


At night they went out for walks. Moishe would buy a few pieces of fruit and they would eat them as they strolled along the streets, sooner or later always stopping at a pushcart and Bobby loading up on hot dogs.

They were mostly silent as they walked through the deserted, rubble strewn area, not by conscious intent or decision, but primarily because the area created such oppressive feelings within them, each for their own reasons and in their own way, that conversation was impossible. . . . Moishe remembering the years he lived here, first with his wife and son, then with just Gertrude, remembering the people that used to live here when this was still a family neighborhood, when children ran the streets and women pushed baby carriages and a night like tonight all the strollers would be out and they would walk or just stand and talk, neighbor to neighbor, friend to friend, sometimes just strangers smiling at little children and complementing mothers: Such nice chubby cheeks, oh I could just eat them up – pinching cheeks and waving their heads in the childrens faces. . . . Yes, so many people . . . and smells, the smells of life like cabbage soup, chicken, all kinds of chicken, brisket, pastrami, bagels, biali, bread, all the smells and all the people and all the stores . . . one after the other, all touching . . . stores for blocks and blocks, and on any block you could get everything you need, food, clothes, pots, pans, ice cream. And all those years they lived in the same apartment over the dry goods store . . . the sun coming in the kitchen in the morning like a canary bird . . . ya, thats what Gertrude said, like a canary bird. Who knows why it was like a canary bird, but it was there and so was the window that you could open and close, just like all the windows and doors, in and out, up and down. When Moishe had to get up early some mornings he would sit at the table drinking coffee, watching the sun come up and always it excited him to know that the sun would be there for another day, that the darkness would be penetrated then absorbed, and on those mornings he would count his breaths from the first hint of light until the last hint of darkness, seeing how much brighter it got with every breath he took as if he was willing the sun up for another day just by breathing, and it seemed to bring a hint of light to his memories of the camp and the years he thought his family was dead. They were good mornings, yes, very good mornings. Now the same buildings were crumbling, shattering, the once crowded streets strewn with rusted cans, broken bottles, bricks, rocks and rats and it sounded like a million lives were being crushed under his feet as he heard each step crunch through the debris. So hard to believe that once there was so much life right here, in this place, and now only shadows and death . . . and dying. Silence was needed for Moishe as he walked through the symbol of his life . . . life always followed by crumbling death as if everytime he watched the sun rise he was willing its descent. . . . But that too was lovely sometimes when they sat in the living room of their railroad flat watching the sunset, not that they could actually see it set, but they could see glimpses of sky between buildings and watch it change color, he and Gertrude always fascinated by the play of light and color in the sky and on the buildings, fascinated by how parts of certain buildings seemed to be softened and altered by the changing light. And each time he walked through here with Bobby he wanted to point out where he had lived, where a certain store had been, the school, the park, a playground but always the crunching underfoot rendered him mute and they walked in silence, Moishe anticipating the turning of a corner where they would be surrounded by life and leave the decay behind.

Bobby always walked close to Moishe, feeling safe if he could reach out and touch him. It wasnt something he figured out, or tried to understand, it was simply something he knew instinctively, the streets having sharpened his instincts for staying alive. So he stayed close to Moishe, yet always alert, checking out every movement, every sound, sensing what was around a corner before turning, making sure he stayed clear of any spots where someone could be hiding. He knew no one knew he was here, but this was not only a no mans land where anything was possible, a place nobody really knew except maybe Moishe, but even he didnt know if some crazy person with a hatchet or butcher knife might be hiding in one of these buildings, and there were so many of them, miles and miles of them, even Moishe couldnt know what was happening in all of them at the same time, and even if he did it could change in a minute, no, this wasnt Bobbys hood. This was like a different country, a different language, none of it understood. He knew his hood, knew the faces, the doorways, the cars, a couple of blocks were his turf and the familiarity brought with it a sense of safety, that was why they never left the hood. Born, live and die all within the same couple of blocks. You knew nothing could really be trusted, especially people, so you walk on the balls of your feet behind a bad look. But even that doesnt always work, especially when you dont know if some dudes are looking to kick your ass. Bobby knew. If that could happen then anything could happen here and he had seen on tv how indians hid under snow or twigs . . . and some dudes in the war hid under the ground, too, and they suddenly jump up and get up side the head of some poor sucker, they just cut his throat, or something, and this sure as hell was a place where somebody could be hiding under the garbage and you wouldnt know it or there could even be a land-mine like on the tv and blow your legs off or jump up in your crotch and blow your dick off and Bobby sure as hell didnt want that to happen so he walked cautiously, always within reach of Moishe, noticing that Moishe always seemed to know exactly where he was going, always knew exactly how to get through the rubble, always sure of what he was doing, never seeming to be uncertain where he was going to put his foot next, and he never seemed to be nervous, never worried about what was happening the way Bobby was, he just kept walking and when he turned he just turned, he didnt stop and look around and wonder, he just made the turn and kept on walking and Bobby just followed but always marking landmarks in his head, trying to remember which way Moishe went, how he angled off here and there, what kind of mark was on the building where he went left, where he went right, and though he stayed close and kept an eye on Moishe, he was as aware as possible of where he was and what his surroundings looked like, and how it changed in the dark.

Then, as always, it seemed like there was suddenly a few people on the streets, cars moving by and in another couple of blocks they would be in a neighborhood alive with people and traffic and though Bobby remained alert he felt good to be surrounded by people, and Moishe seemed to be more at home, more relaxed, and he extended the bag of fruit to Bobby and he reached in and grabbed a peach and started eating, You ever kill anyone Mush?

Moishe stopped and looked at Bobby, blinking his eyes in surprise, Kill???? Kill someone?

Yeah Mush, kill someone.

Moishe shook his head, No. . . . For long time Im wanting to . . . but no, I never kill anyone.

They stood in the middle of the sidewalk, people passing in every direction, all the activity and sounds of the summer evening continuing, Moishe looking intently at Bobby as he stared off in the distance, obviously sorting something in his head. Eventually he turned toward Moishe, Wondering what it be feelin like. I seed guys get snuffed, an they all the time wastin dudes on tv, but I dont be knowin how it feels, whach yo think Mush?

Moishe was silent for a moment, then shook his head, I dont know. Am thinking many times what its like . . . sometimes Im feeling my hands around Klaus' throat and its feeling good to squeeze and see his eyes bulge — Moishe closed his eyes and took a deep breath, exhaled slowly and opened his eyes and shook his head again — No, how it feels I dont know.

Bobby nodded and they started walking again, Was wonderin is all. I figured a guys been fucked with much as you maybe did some dude in.

They continued walking, Bobby obviously still turning things over in his mind as he almost absently chewed a peach. After walking a few blocks they reached a playground and sat on a bench in the park area surrounding it. The yelling of kids was louder here but didnt annoy them, Bobby involved in his thoughts and Moishe waiting for the next question, but Bobby kept chewing until there was nothing left but the pit and tossed that in the bag. He watched the people walking by then asked Moishe, How you think I should be gettin the spics?

Moishes immediate reaction was to tell Bobby he should not try to get them, to forget revenge, but he knew that was not what he needed to say, that it would simply reinforce his determination to get them and create a distance between Bobby and himself. He shook his head, I wouldnt know. Plumbing, wiring, Im doing. Killing I dont know. Moishe smiled at Bobby, TV is showing you maybe. They all the time killing, ya?

Bobby was too preoccupied to get the humor in Moishes voice, but simply thought about what Moishe had said for a moment, then shook his head, The tv aint worth shit Mush. Im talkin some serious shit. I sure cant takem all on at once, got to be gettinem alone . . . only way. Bobby pinched his mouth for a moment, then rubbed his chin, Seem like the bes thing be make them suckers sweat, right Mush? — Moishe shrugging — Let them know I be after they ass. Yeah . . . they must be wonderin where the fuck I be. I be tellin Jesse to spread the word, they be hearin. Yeah, I jus keep checkin with Jesse an he be lettin me know. When Im ready I jus be seein whats goin on an sooner or later I be catchin them suckers alone. Yeah, thas the way, be puttin the big scare inem. For now I jus be stayin with you Mush. Moishe continued looking at Bobby as he tilted his head back for a moment, thinking, then nodded in agreement with himself, then looked at Moishe, Be soundin good to me Mush. Let them suckers be worryin they asses off. Hey Mush, how about us gettin some hot dogs, I be hongry.

Moishe smiled and got up, For you a hot dog, for me heart burn. No thanks.

Mush, sometimes you be unamerican.


Bobby continued with the exercises, pushing himself as much as possible, sometimes pushing so hard he would be unable to move for a minute, but he always continued. Soon he was going out at night, back to the hood. He didnt find his brother the first 2 nights, but he did walk around carefully, staying always in the shadows, avoiding open areas and familiar faces. He carefully studied the familiar streets, trying to notice everything he had always taken for granted, checking out this stoop and that, this staircase to the cellar, where the lamppost was and who had what garbage cans where, the entrance to alleys and did they dead-end or lead to another street or was there a fence at the end and could he get over it easy, or was there a wall and did it have a door or fire escape and what roofs were easy to get to and down from, checking out every doorway, every store in the limited area of his hood. He eased himself across streets and hustled up 4 and 5 flights of stairs as fast as possible, standing on the roof panting and not moving for a few minutes, glad he had made it up the stairs, but annoyed he was still so weak he was unable to move for a couple of minutes, knowing that right then he was defenseless, that the spics find him now, like this, theyd throw his ass off the roof and he breathed deeper, trying to catch his breath faster so he could check out the roof and get his ass where it was safe. He didnt want those muthafuckas surprising him. He had to pick the time and the place. So he checked out the roof, looking at the distance between one building and another, wondering if he could jump if he had to, and how could he be sure until he actually jumped, and he sure as hell couldnt check it out now, so he just eyed it carefully, hoping hed never have to find out because it looked like a hell of a jump, especially since there was a ledge around the edge so he couldnt be gettin a runnin start, but maybe he wouldnt have to try, maybe he could pick them off one at a time on the street, but if he could get them up here wouldnt be no one around to help them, it would just be Bobby and them, one at time and he would pick the time, and they wouldnt know until he had his blade on their neck. He had caught his breath, and had checked out the roof, but lingered a few more minutes savoring the thought of catching one of those muthafuckas up here and hanging his ass over the side of the building, letting him hang over the edge until he could see every little person all that way down and it start looking like a thousand feet an hed be pissin in his pants he be so scared and Bobby would laugh at the sucker and twist his head around an look into his fuckin face so he be seein Bobby, seein him real good and know who it was who was droppin his ass over the side so he could be fallin through the air jus like Maria did, but firs he be fuckin up they face like they did Maria an he fuck withem so bad they be beggin him to throw them off the roof but he/d fuck withem some more the rotten muthafuckas . . . they gonna be payin for what they did to Maria, you muthafuckin pricks, you goin be payin GODDAMN YOU MUTHAFUCKAS! Whach you be doin that for? Muthafuck. . . . She be so fine . . . so sweet. She be laughin an makin me feel good all ova — sitting on the edge of the roof, looking down at the cracked and tattered tar paper, head hanging from neck, arms resting on thighs — She so funny sometime. She laugh at jus about anythin an be havin a good time laughin. . . . Damn! Why they do that to you baby? Why they kill you? You be such a sweet young thing an you be my girl they have no right to fuck with you O fuck!!!! O Maria, why you go out that window? What the fuck be happenin baby? I wish I be holding you so you cant go out no window. . . . O baby . . . the spot between his sneakers was darkened with dots of tears, one after the other rolling slowly down his cheek and hanging for a moment, then falling to the roof and looking back up at the one about to join it. Bobby watched them splat on the black rooftop, flatten and spread out until they were absorbed by the years of dirt, knowing he should wipe his eyes, that he had no business sitting there like that, so defenseless, unable to see more than a few feet because of the tears in his eyes, yet he was so totally and absolutely powerless to move that he had to stay there watching the tears fall the monstrous distance from his face to the rooftop because if he moved he might never be able to hear Marias voice again and right now, sitting there totally exposed to every danger he had been trying to avoid, he was hearing her voice . . . her sweet girl voice all around him telling him all those fine things she used to say and sometimes it was whispering in his ear, jus like she used to do, and he could not only hear her voice, but feel her breath on his ear, and the tip of her tongue as she brushed his ear with it and giggled, and he closed his eyes and listened, and felt, and saw her as she walked up the street to meet him, smiling, waving, hip hopping and kindda jumpin against his chest and hanging around his neck and she looked so pretty and sounded so nice he jus didnt want to lose it cause it might never be there again, she might go away and never come back an just didnt want to take that chance so he stayed seated on the edge of the roof, eyes closed, tears falling, until he became aware of the sounds coming up from the street, and in the air and sky, and opened his eyes, blinked away a few tears, then wiped his face with the back of his hand and lifted his head and looked around for a few minutes, listening as hard as he could, wanting to be certain she was really gone, then got up and went down to the street.

He stood in the shadow of the fire escape, leaning against the wall, still a little disoriented, knowing where he was, that he had no business standing there like that, that he knew a thousand people on this block, and they knew him, that any second someone would be coming by and recognize him an maybe they wouldnt be a friend, yet he couldnt move but continued leaning against the wall, trying to will himself to move, to keep moving, but it was as if he was paralyzed and then suddenly the door of the building just a few feet away slammed open and a kid ran out but stopped after a few feet and turned and looked at Bobby, eyes wide, mouth starting to open and Bobby started kicking himself in the ass, knowing Sheltin wouldnt be doin him no harm, but he be yellin his ass off about him standin there an Bobby wished ta fuck he could hide but he knew it was too late so he smiled, chopped a short wave at Sheltin, and walked away hoping ta fuck that Sheltin be keepin his mouth shut long enough for Bobby to be getting round the fuckin corner an haulin ass and as he turned the corner all he heard was the same old street sounds and he ran the short block to the next corner and through an alley he knew would take him to a building with heavy shadows where he stopped for a minute to catch his breath, then started walking as fast as he could, stayin close to the buildings, following the shadows, cursing his stupid ass for gettin caught like that, now everybody be knowing he was back and by now them spics probably knowin too and he had to get his ass back to Mushies, and he continued walking as fast as possible, running and trotting as often as possible until he was once again aware of the silence around him, the only sounds those in the distance. He sat down on the remnants of a barrel in the shadows and caught his breath, so pissed off at himself he couldnt stop panting and being aware of every ache and pain in his body, his chest still feeling like it was going to explode, not having run so much and so fast in a long time, just more evidence he was out of shape, but better than he had been, but still he needed to work out some more and not be so goddamn stupid to let something like that happen, and again his head hung from his neck as he shook it in regret and bewilderment until his breathing eased, and then he suddenly realized that what had happened was perfect, absolutely perfect. The spics be knowin he aroun an they be knowin he after they ass, an Sheltin be the right the fuck on one to be tellin peoples cause they know he not tight with me, jus neighborhood . . . yeah . . . yeah. . . . Gauddamn!!!! THAT BE RIGHT THE FUCK ON!!!! ALRIGHT!!! they be thinkin Im some kindda ghos or somethin, just hangin my teeth out at Sheltin like that an disappearin . . . yeah, that be really fuckin with they mines — Bobby laughed out loud and jumped — I just be goin aroun the hood every onct in a while an grin the fool at some dude an splittin like a ghos. Bobby raised his fist in a victory salute and bopped back to Moishes on the balls of his feet.

Marias mother trudged up the stairs, her legs heavy, body weary, spirit anguished. Another day survived, a night brooding ahead. At work her mind was not tormented . . . praise God for the need to concentrate . . . *si*, praise God. But the spirit is always anguished. Still, those hours free of the torment . . . yes free, but the sadness, the desperate and eternal grieving always chilled her stomach and spoke to her heart O Maria, Maria . . . Blessed Mother of God where is my baby, where are her sparkling eyes and — NO, NO!!! Enough. I will accept what God has given me. No need to seek more. Enough I walk the same stairs my baby ran up and down shouting to her friends, laughing, through the door to her mommys arms. O Sacred Heart, I walk those same stairs, I walk in my babys steps, can you feel that little angel? can you feel my steps upon yours, my heart beating in — Isabella stood before the door of her apartment. Vaguely aware of the perpetual noises around her. Were they loud? Were they heavier than the sadness in her heart? Noise . . . noise. Can the clatter of people and tv's silence, or even dim, the ravages of a tortured mind . . . a tormented heart????

Her mother was at the sink. The children had been fed and sent to do what they do. Isabella sat. At the table. Did she sigh with the movement? Perhaps . . . perhaps. Her head slowly raised, the ticking of a clock somewhere gently lifting her chin. But the ticking could not force her lips to smile. The children are fed . . . thank you momma.

You are well?

They are studying?

Yes. And you?

Me? — staring at her mother.

Isabella almost shrugged, almost shrugged her shoulders . . . almost looked at her mother.

The old woman dried her hands and filled a cup with coffee and placed it gently in front of her daughter. Isabella stared at the cup. Her mother sat.

In time Isabellas head raised and she looked at her mothers hands. . . . You can go home if that is your wish momma.

Home?

To the Island, the place of your birth, our birth.

Place of our birth. Yes, many hundreds of years we are born there, and buried. Our bones take up much space. Very much.

Isabella raised her head and looked at her mothers eyes, then into them. . . . There is history there. Yes. . . . You said many times you want to leave this madness.

Yes . . . many times — The woman closed her eyes for a moment, tilted her head — Yes, without doubt I have said many times I want to leave this madness. But my blood is here. Can I leave my blood for old bones, even if the breeze from the ocean whispers to me? No, I think not Isabella. I must stay with my blood. There are yet 2 more to grow. Blood goes on . . . and on . . . does it not?

Yes. . . . Yes momma . . . and on. But — suddenly Isabellas shoulders sagged. They were silent. In time the old woman moved her hands through the grief to Isabellas cup and gently nudged it toward her daughter.


Moishe was aware that he was becoming increasingly restless each time Bobby left to 'check out the scene'. A bowl of ice cream, with chocolate sauce, didnt really help, nor did sitting and petting the cat. Perhaps it did take the edge off a little, but he always ended up sitting and getting up, sitting and getting up, going to this room, going to that room, listening to the radio, listening to music, reading, but no matter what he did, or didnt do, he was always thinking about Bobby, doing all he could to keep his mind from worrying, but he couldnt keep from thinking about him and what he was doing and what he was planning on doing, and he is just a boy, just a boy, a young boy who shouldnt be thinking about doing those things. . . . But hasnt it always been that way? Hasnt every generation taken young boys and trained them to kill? And is he really so young here? Is this so much different from a war??? and Moishe would shake his head in wonder at a world that does these things YOURE CRAZY SOL — standing close to him, leaning forward, his face inches from Sols — YOURE CRAZY!!!! — Moishes eyes bulging, his face red and bloated with rage, his body so rigid it looked like it was threatening to snap, his hands clutching at air, trying to find something to squeeze, to choke, to wrap around and brutally strangle the life from, feeling himself gloat and salivate, his spittle dripping into the bulging eyes of Klaus as he squeezed a little tighter, ever so slightly tighter and tighter, wanting Klaus to live as long as possible, to suffer as much as possible, to squeeze into his miserable throat all the suffering he and his family had endured because of him, and so he would increase the pressure just the faintest bit, rejoicing in the reflection of pain and pleading in Klaus' eyes, the mute please dribbling from his lips, the wild impotent flailing of his arms, feeling and hearing the ligaments, muscles, tendons and bones crackle and shift and throb under his hands, overwhelmed with the glorious knowledge and awareness that he was forcing the life out of Klaus, not a disease nor court of law, no vengeful god, but him, Werner Schultz was judge, jury and god and slowly squeezing the life out of this vermin and every cell of his being was rejoicing and celebrating knowing he was doing it, he was causing the life to slowly, O how beautifully slowly, half breath by half breath, ebb from this man he hated more than the guards that prodded and taunted them, the officers that abused and killed them . . . more even than the god that allowed all this to happen, and as he watched Klaus' eyes film over and his arms start to hang limp from lack of air he knew he was killing all the evil in the universe and as Klaus hung limp in his hands he released his throat and watched Klaus' body jerk with spasms as it reacted to the sudden influx of air and he groveled and gasped, eyes seeming even wider than before, as he gulped the air into his lungs, the blood rushing feverishly to free itself of the carbon dioxide and take in the life-sustaining oxygen and as Klaus' breathing started to normalize and he was actually able to move just a little, Werner leaned over, close to Klaus' face and smiled with all the hatred he had in his mind, speaking slowly and clearly with such vehemence it almost took the breath from Klaus' body, I hate you you son of a bitch. . . . I am going to kill you a thousand times . . . slowly clutching his hands around Klaus' throat, waiting until he heard Klaus cry and scream with a voice that was so thick, so hoarse from a crushed windpipe it sounded more like a groan from the bowels of the earth, before he squeezed hard enough to choke off all sound and once again rejoice in seeing the inner terror and struggle in his eyes as well as feeling the still living life force trying to combat Moishes strength and determination and Moishe laughed out loud, very loud, louder and louder as he felt the resistance and played with it, opening his hands slightly from time to time to only once again squeeze, squeeze — Moishe laughing and laughing, squeezing and laughing. . . .

MADNESS
SOL . . . WHAT YOU ASK IS MADNESS – Moishe increasingly aware of the clutching of his hands as they hung at his
sides, Sol looking at him with compassion and understanding, Moishe immobilized by his rage, feeling as if he would
explode, leaning inches from Sols face, hands strangling the
air around them, until he suddenly screamed and started
pounding the wooden post, and soon stopped screaming
and simply clung with rigid desperation to the post and
sobbed, and once again Sol hugged Moishe, saying only, It
is alright my friend . . . it is alright . . . rubbing his shoulders until Moishe collapsed into Sols arms and his head
dropped on Sols shoulder, Moishes tears soaking through
the striped fabric of Sols shirt, Sols tears wetting the striped
fabric of Moishes shirt as he hugged him, repeating gently
in Moishes ear, It is alright my friend . . . it is alright. . . .

Bobby was still bopping along on the balls of his feet
as he walked through the rubble, past the deserted and
decaying buildings, swerving to avoid a hole, stepping
over broken bottles and pieces of metal, avoiding wire that
could wrap around his ankles and cut right through his
sneakers, feeling his way around about as good as in the
hood, maybe better because he didnt take anything for
granted around here, no way, so he bopped along, spring-
ing, bouncing, feeling good, real good, cause a plan was
falling in place and now hed make him a schedule and go
back there every now and then an let someone see him
and he have them spics going crazy and sooner or later
they be alone, O man this be fine – and he moved easily
through the rubble, stopping only rarely to check something out, right up to the stairs leading down to Moishes
cellar and found the flashlight easily and started walking
through the blackness, but now more slowly because this
was some tricky shit, you got to make the right turns or
you be lost forever down here and end up being food for
the rats and he be gauddamned if he was going to be
feeding the rats, least not to keep them alive, and he checked

his map from time to time, first deciding what was the right way, and smiling and giggling when he checked the map and found out he was right and continued along his way, feeling more and more confident because now he had a plan and now he knew how to get through this trap and he was getting stronger, he could feel it in his bones as well as his muscles, and soon he was at the last turn and as he went around the corner he saw a light but instead of panicking he smiled because he knew it was Moishe and he called to him, and Moishe answered, and when he reached Moishe Bobby tapped him on the shoulder, his smile even bigger, Whach you doin out here Mush?

Youre coming Im thinking, so I meet you here – shrugging – I dont know, seems like I should.

Too lazy to meet me back there, eh?

Moishe smiled, I think its the time you find it alone.

Bobby giggled, O yeah, suppose my sweet little ass got lost, whach you be doin then?

Moishe grinned and tapped Bobby on the shoulder, Im knowing youre finding it.

Bobby nodded, You be right on Mush. . . . But what the fuck we be doin standin out here? Lets go on home.

Moishe nodded and opened the lock and they went in. They both headed, automatically, for the kitchen and Bobby sat down and Moishe filled 2 bowls with ice cream and chocolate sauce. Bobby was so excited, and grinning so widely that it made Moishe chuckle, So. . . .

Bobby quickly jammed a couple of spoonsful of ice cream in his mouth, then started telling Moishe about his night, almost bouncing up and down with excitement.

I tellya Mush, I really be doin it cool, jus like them ol mountain mens I be seein on tv. I be checkin it all out an soon I be knowin every inch with my eyes closed, I be knowin what goes where and whats aroun each corner. Like Wyatt Earp with all them shotguns stashed around town, you know?

Moishe grinned and shrugged, So what am I a gunfighter Im knowin these things? Wyatt Earp????

Bobby laughed, You see Mush, that be your trouble. You

jus aint hip to history man. Thas cause you ain got no tv. Caint be knowin all these important things you aint got no tv.

Moishe was still grinning as they sat in silence for a moment, eating ice cream, Bobby eating as rapidly as possible, his spoon clanging against the bowl, So what you think Mush, aint that a cool idea . . . I be drivin them spics crazy.

Moishe swallowed his sadness with a mouthful of ice cream and nodded his head, and Bobby continued rambling on about the night and his plan, Moishe nodding occasionally. Eventually Bobby stopped talking and leaned back in his chair and seemed to almost collapse, Im goin to be gettin to bed Mush, I be beat. Gotta stay in shape. Need lots a rest. See ya in the mornin bro.

Sleep good

Moishe remained at the table after Bobby left, reminding himself to just love him . . . just love him Werner . . . just love him.

Bobby awakened the next morning still feeling excited about his plan. It seemed even better when he thought about it, play a little psychological warfare with those dudes. It all seemed to be working out and it made him feel good, confident, and so he had a little extra energy when he started working out . . . from time to time his shoulders or head moving slightly as if dismissing a thought.

Moishe became aware that he couldnt hear Bobby working out. He sat in silence at the kitchen table for a few moments, then went back to eating his breakfast. Suddenly Bobby was standing in front of him, body still shiny with sweat, a serious expression on his face, What the fuck you mean bout hate!?

Moishe stared at Bobby for a moment, not really understanding, struggling to know the question so he could search for an answer.

You know what I be meanin Mush, all that shit about hate doin in your own self.

Moishe lifted his head in recognition, So. . . .

What the fuck all that bool shit be about — Bobbys indignation growing — What the fuck that be all about man?

Moishe shrugged and turned his hands palms up, It means hate always stays inside like . . . like . . . like a cancer and destroys you.

Well it aint gonna be killin me. I be hatin those muthafuckas an aint nothin be stoppin me from hatinem even after I be finished with them. You be diggin that man!?

Moishe tried to not allow his face to reflect his sudden feeling of sadness, but it was impossible, Ya, I know how you feel — nodding his head with a great degree of understanding and respect — I know how it is feeling Bobby.

Sheeit, aint nobody knowin how I feel about — Bobby stared at Moishe unable to will himself to finish the sentence, unable to even finish the thought. . . .

they looked at each other for many heartbeats, the confusion and conflict on Bobbys face obvious as he tried desperately to find a way to believe that no one . . . NO ONE! knew how he felt, how fucked over he felt not only by the spics but the whole fucking world, how sometimes he felt ground into the cement, the black tar of the streets, the streets covered with shit, spit, piss, oil, dirt, garbage, and an occasional body, that NO ONE knew how it felt to be fucked over because you be black, because you be poor, because you be . . . because you just be . . . and the more he looked into Moishes face the more his frustration intensified and he felt like he was going to explode, that there was nowhere to go with the energy that was building up within him and if he couldnt find a way to justify these feelings that were consuming him he would explode, and his head started shaking and beads of sweat erupted on his face and suddenly he collapsed onto a chair and closed his eyes and grabbed his head. . . .

and all this time Moishe sat remembering the look of compassion on Sols face hoping it was now on his, trying not to allow the terrible aching in his heart to intrude upon Bobbys right to do what he had to do to learn what he had to learn, wanting, as always, to reach out to Bobby and with a magic wave of his hand eliminate all pain from his life, but Moishe could not even remember a fairy tale where that happened. None. There was always the test, the lesson, the victory over our own limitations that had to be won so Moishe put his energy into remembering Sols look and remembering that there was no difference between himself and Bobby. Moishe reminded himself that he had survived the camp, as well as his hate, and hoped in his heart of hearts, that Bobby would survive too, and would more than survive but would prevail over his hate. . . .

and in time Bobby raised his head and looked at Moishe, wiping his face with his hands, staring at Moishes expression for many minutes, hearing the tick and thump of his heart, hearing each breath entering and leaving his body, finding himself being absorbed by the rhythms in his body and the look on Moishes face. . . .

I dont mean you nothin Mush, but I still be hatin them muthafuckas an if it be killin me then it goin kill me, but I damn surell be killinem firs. . . .

There was another silence, each aware of their own and the others breathing. . . .

Ya . . . nodding his head – Ya. . . . Always your friend. So. . . .

Eventually Bobby got up slowly, I bes be showerin Mush, doan want them spics be smellin me comin – and he forced a smile on his face before he left the room. Moishe watched Bobby walk away and his eyes were suddenly singed with the death-smell of the camp and he jerked himself up and waved away the thoughts, Enough, enough. Its better I cook a good breakfast for him and give my head a rest. To the stove Werner . . . to the stove.


Bobby continued his night-time excursions to the hood from time to time. Sometimes he would go back 3 and 4 nights in a row, with a few days off, and then just a night here and there with several nights in between, sometimes making sure someone saw him 2 nights in a row, once 3 in a row, but usually making sure there was at least one night between and always be sure there was no pattern to where he might be seen, where he might show up next. He had to be cool and make sure the spics didnt get him in his trap, layin in wait for him to show up some time and doin his ass in. He didnt know exactly how long he had been with Moishe, but he figured it was a couple of months because he was on his way to school when it happened. An he was gettin strong. All that stuff Moishe was giving him, all those vitamins and stuff, and the food, was really making him feel good and the exercising was working, it was really working, he could see his muscles were bigger. And he was really diggin working out. It hurt so much when he first started he almost wanted to cry, but now it was different. It still hurt but in a different way and he always felt so good when he finished, good in a way he never had before. There was a sense of lightness and strength in his body that was new, and a physical sense of security. He just felt different walking the street. And by the time he finished showering and eating he felt like he had been laughing for a while, or something. Anyway, it was working real good and thats how he felt.

Except when he got to thinking about all that stuff Moishe was talking about, then he would feel like something was troubling him, but he would just think about the look on the spics faces when he got them, one by one, and he would feel a surge of power that chased everything else away.

From time to time he would find himself just looking around when he went back to the hood, and he would instantly stop and hide in the nearest shadow and look around carefully to be sure there wasnt anyone tailing him. He stayed absolutely still for a few moments, blending in with the wall behind him and the shadows, his eyes carefully scrutinizing everything, especially the innocent looking doorways and alleys, and windows and fire escapes and shadows, always the shadows to be sure there wasnt someone in one studying him as he looked around. Whenever this happened, whenever he realized he had just been looking around and forgetting what he was doing was a matter of life and death, he would get on his own back for a minute and tell himself his ass goin be dead fuckin meat if he keep doin that, they spics be liken nothin betta then be findin him jus strollin aroun like he forgot they there to kill his ass an he here to kill them. He knew their hood, the streets they felt safe on, an he checked them out very often. They would never think they could be attacked by one guy on their turf, but that was their big mistake. He had the big advantage . . . he knew where they were, they didnt know where he was. There were 4 of them and only 1 of him, but he could outslick them dumb muthafuckas – and he quickly cut off the thought, I be thinkin they dumb shits an I be the dumb shit. Uh, uh, no way I be outfoxin my own self with that shit.

One night he saw Raul and 2 others outside a Bodega with their girlfriends and decided he would check them out . . . as well as his idea about them not seeing too good on their own turf. He walked down a few streets, crossed the boulevard, went east another block then came back north on the street parallel to where they were, and went through a narrow alley he had already checked out a couple of times from the roofs and on the ground. As always he kept close to the wall, in this alley the south wall because it didnt have any doorways where someone could suddenly come leaping out at him. He also knew what doors on the north wall were open, at least most of the time, in case he had to split. There were also 2 very narrow alleys leading off this one, so narrow they were unseen if you didnt know they were there. One led to a cellar where he could go either east or north and get to a street, the other had a short fence he could easily vault and go east over another short fence and into a cellar where he could get to a street. He walked slowly, his eyes never still, and when he got a few feet from the street he could hear their voices and then he could see Raul holding his girl friend, rubbing her back and laughing and suddenly Bobby was inflamed with rage, sweat instantly bursting on his face and body, his eyes almost sightless with fury and he fell against the wall and caught his breath, forcing himself to remain absolutely still and not do what every muscle in his body wanted him to do, what his head was screaming at him to do. He knew he could cut Rauls throat before they knew what was happening, and maybe be cuttin one of the others, but theyd get him an thered be nothin left of him and there was no way he was goin be lettin them muthafuckas be gettin his ass. He slowed his breathing like Moishe taught him, and stood there, watching, remembering, reminding himself that as long as he didnt lose his cool he had them by the balls, so he continued breathing deeply and slowly, until he was calm, then picked up an empty wine bottle, spun around a few times and got dizzy, then staggered out of the alley forcing himself to try and walk straight like a drunk, passed within a few feet of Raul and the others and continued going north, then turned west at the corner, ran around the block and circled back to where he had been when he first saw them, a matter of just a few minutes, and they were still there, smoking, joking, laughing, hugging . . . and Bobby watched, stared as hard as he could, as hatefully as possible, reminding himself to keep checking everything out. He watched until he knew it was time to go and he slipped along the shadows back the way he came, then back home.

He was still feeling excited the next night when he and Moishe went for a walk and ended up by the river. There was enough traffic on the river to make watching it interesting: small pleasure boats, tug boats with and without barges, derricks, launches, and a few Moishe could not identify. Bobby had only been here a few times in his life and was not familiar with the names of the different kinds of vessels so he listened while Moishe told him what the purpose of some of them were. It didnt really interest Bobby much, but he really liked listening to Moishe talk, chuckling occasionally at the funny way he spoke. Bobby kept giggling, still feeling high from the night before, feeling the power he felt last night when he staggered by them mutha fuckas, and feeling a little anxious to get back to the hood, but wanting to cool it for a couple of nights, not wanting to lose his power, and was not aware that he was now laughing and not just giggling.

Moishe stopped talking and looked at Bobby, So . . . tonight everythings funny?

Bobby shook his head, No Mush, I jus be feelin cool, you dig?

So cool youre laughing when I talk . . . I say hello, youre laughing. I say goodbye, youre laughing. I say is going fast the boat, youre laughing – Moishe shrugged and smiled – so thats cool?

Bobby laughed and shook his head, No man, it jus be funny way you be talkin sometimes is all.

So . . . Im talking funny? Its not English Im speaking?

Yeah man well, its like different man. It dont be soundin like reglar English Mush.

Is not regular?

Man, you know, you got that funny accent Mush. You dont be talkin straight like the rest of us.

Accent?

They looked at each other, smiles getting broader, then they both started laughing and Bobby shook his head as he realized Moishe was putting him on and gave Moishe five.

They continued sitting by the river, eating fruit, Bobby still bouncing on the bench though they were both silent. After a few minutes Moishe asked Bobby why he was jiggling around so much?

Jigglin? What the fuck be jigglin Mush?

Jiggling . . . like you have itchy powder in your underwear. Youre not sitting still.

Bobby giggled, Jigglin – shaking his head – Damn, you sure be a funny dude sometime Mush.

So????

I was fixin to tellya, I see those spics las night . . . an I walk right by the muthas an they not knowin nothin.

Moishe looked at Bobby, his face as expressionless as he could get it, and Bobby told him about the previous night. Moishe was fascinated by the intricasies of Bobbys planning and the ingenuity behind it, and was increasingly caught up in Bobbys narrative, having, from time to time, to remind himself that Bobby was not describing a childrens game, but a contest of life or death.

So I think Im jus about ready Mush. I figure sooner or later they goin be one a them muthafuckas walkin down the street alone an he be mine. Theys got to be lots a peoples done tol them theyd seen me an they mus be wonderin what Im up to. They ass got to be sweatin Mush . . . got to be. You make a man worry an he fuck up . . . they be worryin, I know it. . . . So what you think Mush, I be ready?

Moishe stared at him, feeling blank, lost, trying to shrug but his body shuttered slightly, feeling his throat forming words but knowing he could not speak them, that he could not plead with Bobby to forget his hate . . . , Youre looking strong. . . . Ya, ya, youre looking strong.

Right on Mush. That workout shit be doin a good job. Sheeit, how long I be workin out now, mus be couple months.

Ya, ya, months.

Bobby looked surprised, then started grinning again, Damn it be a long time I be meetin you Mush — looking into Moishes face, suddenly looking serious, grateful, an overwhelming sense of sincerity in his voice — You be a good frien Mush. I sure be all fucked up when you be findin me, an thas for damn sure. I remember. I be feelin all bus up inside like aint nothin in the right place an doin the right thing.

Moishe smiled self-consciously, flushing slightly, and shrugged, I —

I remember how I be feelin when I went down your stairs. I be thinkin Im goin die. Cant hardly breathe. Cant move. No more. I be thinkin maybe Im goin die an they muthafuckin rats eatin my ass. I jus hopin I be dead before they starts eatin on me is all.

Moishe beamed at Bobby, I see how you are and Im wonderin what to do. No doctor he says. No hospital he says. So Im a little bit crazy trying already to patch you up.

But you be doin it bro. Better than the mergency at the hospital. You be lucky you gettin outta that alive. How yo knowin how to do all that shit Mush?

Is no big deal. When little boy for Christmas Im getting doctors set . . . maybe 8 years old, an Im playing doctor ever since – and Moishe burst into laughter, Bobby staring for a minute, confused, then understanding and laughing with Moishe, the two of them sitting on the bench in the cool stillness of a late summer night, only a few stars visible in the sky, but the running lights on the boats on the river looking like diamonds, rubies and emeralds . . . and they continued to laugh, leaning closer and closer toward each other until they reached out and hugged each other, each flooded with the feelings of the other as well as their own, feeling a closeness that Bobby had never experienced before, in a way he didnt know existed, and Moishe felt love and gratitude flowing through him from Bobby, and from within himself. They sat back on the bench looking at the river and the lights on the other side, experiencing a sense of unity that would, like everything else, pass, but for now, right now it soothed every painful memory, bringing with it the sense that all things are possible. The feeling sparkled within them and they relaxed, feeling peaceful and soon the thought of hot dogs drifted through Bobbys mind, and then the ice cream he and Moishe would have when they got home and he stretched his arms and legs, rotated his neck and shoulders, then looked at Moishe, What that dude be sayin to you?

Hmmnmm – looking quizzically at Bobby.

You know, that dude in the camp that be helpin you. What he be sayin to you?

O, Sol. Ya, Sol – Moishe studied Bobby for a moment, trying to think what to say. He took a deep breath telling himself to speak from the heart – Why now you ask?

Bobby shrugged, Dont know Mush. Suddenly seem like I got to know what he say. Ain hardly thought about it, jus be comin out my mouth.

Bobby sat back waiting for Moishe to answer his question knowing he would after he got things sorted out in his head like he always did before he said anything. So Bobby waited.

Sol is such a good man. He always do first what he say I should do. Never do different than what he say.

Like he put his money where his mouth is, eh?

Moishe stared for a moment, then smiled, Ya, ya. Is putting money where mouth is. Ya – nodding his head and chuckling – That is good, ya.

Bobby smiled and shook his head, You funny bro – and went back to waiting.

Sol is saying my hate is killing me quicker than the camp. Look what hate has done to our country . . . these camps are built by hate. Look at the guards my friend, the 'authorities', they have become mad, crazed animals . . . wretched beasts of prey. Sol was quiet for a moment, then spoke quietly, but so . . . strongly I still shiver when I think of it. . . . Then he said: Hold on to your hate my friend and you will become what you hate.

Bobby shrugged, I dont be knowin nothin bout that, but what else he be sayin?

Moishe hesitated for a moment, then took a deep breath, He said I should wish Klaus be happy, that – Bobby peered at Moishe, eyes clouding, disbelief and resistance on his face – He say what? – total disbelief on his face and in his voice, Moishe looking at him sympathetically, knowing it was impossible for Bobby to hear that now, yet knowing, in his heart, that he had to tell him the truth just as simply as it had happened, that love and respect demanded he tell him the truth, that Bobby deserved nothing less in answer to his question – He say you should – Bobby shook his head and jumped up and stepped to the railing a few feet away and looked down at the water, shaking his head, trying to force Moishes words from his head, from his brain, from his mind, his energy coming to the defense of his hatred, yet something within him seeming to be trying to at least listen to what Moishe said and he shook his head as the battle raged, Moishe watching, knowing pain by pain what Bobby was experiencing, though it was so many years ago he went through the same agony he still remembered it . . . pain by pain, breath by breath . . . tear by tear, and he waited for Bobby to go though his process, doing all he could to allow the love in his heart to replace the fear in his mind and body and just love Bobby . . . just love him. . . . Bobby jerked around, still slightly stooped like a fighter stalking his opponent across the ring, but his hands were extended behind him, holding on to the railing – How the fuck he say that? How he fuckin say that? That muthafucka be takin you business an throwin yo ass in a muthafuckin constration camp an fuckin up you family an doin all that shit you be havin – pointing to his tattoo – an you say you caint never be forgettin what be happenin an – Bobby spun around and leaned against the railing, pumping his body back and forth, throwing his head back and shaking it violently – Damn! MUTHAFUCKA!!!! MUTHA FUCKIN FUCKA!!!! – pounding the railing with the side of his hands, then stamping around in a circle, pounding his anger into the pavement – That muthafucka crazy!!!! How he say that to you Mush when you be in that fuckin joint????

Moishe took a breath and spoke as slowly and gently as possible, He was there too Bobby. Same hell.

But he be a real jew!

Moishe filled his words with all the love of his being, No one deserved to be there Bobby. It was the same hell for all of us. No one deserved to be there . . . no person . . . no animal. . . . No one Bobby.

Bobby stared at Moishe for a moment, his agitation and rage making his head vibrate, clouding his vision, Aint no body in the world be sayin that shit! No one! Everyone say get that muthafucka an kill his ass . . . real slow. The whole world be sayin that!!!!

Moishe was quiet for a moment, and silent, concentrating as much as possible on the love he felt for Sol and Bobby . . . and himself. . . . Have you always agreed with the world Bobby? Are you always thinking the world is right? – Bobby suddenly jerking his head around and staring at Moishe – Muthafuck the world man! Thats bull shit!!!! – continuing to stare at Moishe for a moment, but unable to sustain it and jerked his head around again, leaning against the railing, pumping his body back and forth. . . .

Moishe continued looking at Bobby, silently, then spoke with the same gentleness and love, Youre asking me a question . . .

Im answering. Im always answering your question, ya? – Bobby spun around and looked at Moishe – Im asking now you a question, You think always the world is right?

Again Bobby was unable to look into Moishes face, unable to deal with the expression of compassion and love, and after a moment looked down at his feet . . . eventually raising his head and looking at Moishe and shrugging, then shaking his head, No, I dont know if I know what the muthafuckin world be . . . ceptin I think the muthafuckas full a shit – Moishe continued to look at Bobby with the same expression on his face, from time to time Bobby looking down at his feet then up at Moishe . . . then once again at his feet . . . then back at Moishe . . . eventually he shook his head, No, I dont be thinkin the muthafuckin world be right. I be thinkin all them muthafuckas – snapping his head from side to side – out there be bad muthafuckas an be killin my black ass right the fuck now if they even be knowin I alive. No, I dont be believin the world be right, not by any fuckin way! But that doan mean he be right you got to wish that muthafucka be happy!!! shit! I be wishin he be miserable with every little part of me. . . . Gauddamn right I be wishin that! All day an all night I be wishin that, fuck die you rotten muthafucka!!!! – and Bobbys body continued to shake with rage as he stared at Moishe for a moment, then back to pounding the rail, stamping around in circles, slapping his head then once again the railing, until all he could do was collapse on the bench and hang his head and hug it with his hands.

They sat silently, Moishe forcing himself not to reach over and put his hand on Bobbys shoulder, knowing it was not the time . . . not yet. Maybe never. Maybe Bobby never would give up his hate. Maybe it started too soon for him. Maybe that was all he saw, all he knew. Moishe didnt know. He only knew his heart was telling him to just sit, silently, quietly, and to just be there for Bobby, but not to interfere. Moishe became aware that he was toying with the bag they had carried the fruit in, empty now except for the peach pits. Something in him smiled at being aware of a brown paper bag with a couple of peach pits and getting some sort of comfort from feeling it between his fingers. Maybe there was some message there, some profound insight to all the pain of the world, or at least Bobbys, but Moishe had no intention of getting caught in all that. The peaches had tasted good and they had told each other that with every bite as they walked along the street . . . and now the bag felt good between his fingertips. That was all. And Bobby, and he, would survive this night, this talk . . . this anguish. . . . Moishe shook his head and sighed inwardly, this whole eruption over just a few words . . . , Wish him happiness. . . . Such pain over those words. About a man he never knew. . . . O God, such turmoil over something so simple. Can anything be simpler than those words . . . or more impossible? Wish him happiness. . . . And how strange . . . how crazy. . . . I think of Klaus and Im alright. . . . I mention wishing him happiness and look what happens???? How can we ever find happiness? We hunt and we hurt and we do what we do . . . what we have to do. What – enough, enough. Klaus is dead and so is my hatred. But Bobbys hatred kills in little bits and pieces. So young to die of hatred. But how old do you have to be to die??? even slowly????

In time Bobby stopped trembling and he took a deep breath and sighed, becoming aware of the pain in his body, the intense soreness as he started to relax. He sat up slowly and stared at the river for many minutes until he became aware of the boats gliding along the water, visible only by their lights. In time he leaned back and took another deep breath and exhaled slowly, still staring at the water, Looks like I be rememberin that breathin stuff Mush.

Moishe smiled and put his hand on Bobbys shoulder, Ya, is helping. We can use all the help we/re getting, ya?

I guess so Mush. Yeah, I guess so . . . shit, I dont know what the fuck be happenin man – breathing deeply again and leaning his head back and looking straight up at the sky as he exhaled, It be like that muthafucka up there, it all the time the same yet it be different . . . know what I be sayin Mush? Like it always be over ya muthafuckin head but you dont know what the fuck you be seein, shit, I dont know what the fuck. . . .

Ya – smiling in the dark – When we/re looking, Gertrude

and me at the stars we/re not caring about the names, ya?

Bobby nodded his head and looked back at the river, liking the feel of Moishes hand on his shoulder and having him close, but still confused by the night, by trying to figure out what had happened, how they be comin here an him feelin so fine bout las night an what he be goin to do an all at onct everythin seem all fucked up. Bobby shook his head, to even try and sort it all out hurt. He remembered thinking about hot dogs and ice cream and now that seemed like a thousand years ago, almost like it had happened to someone else. But somehow that river be lookin. . . . The lights seem to be wigglin acrost the water, doan they Mush, specially around the boats . . . be like the lights comin up outta the water and boogie acrost it. . . . Be lookin nice, eh?

Moishe started looking at the lights when Bobby started speaking and was mesmerized for a moment, then blinked himself into speech, Having more stars in the water than the sky. . . . Nice breeze — lifting his face to feel it — Soon is winter. Ya. . . . Thanksgiving . . . Christmas. On the river snow and ice maybe. On the lake here an —

Lake?

Ya, Prospect Park.

O . . . yeah.

And the old country. Freezing. Snow on trees all around lake. People skating. Sleigh rides. Same here. Lots of red noses. All bundled up. Scarves all wrapped around many times, so much longer than here — smiling — here is stingy scarves. Bobby started to say something but suddenly stopped as he saw the expression on Moishes face suddenly become so sad and pained Bobby felt like he had been hit in the stomach and he looked, wide-eyed, as Moishe struggled with a sudden memory — In the camp theres no boots, afraid toes are snapping off so we/re walking and stamping feet, only keep moving, keep moving — his voice getting louder and louder — keep moving, keep moving, keep. . . .

Moishe was suddenly silent, eyes closed, Bobby aware of his own heart pounding in his chest and ears, and Moishes chest heaving for a moment. . . . then Moishe opened his eyes and looked at the river for a moment . . . shook his head, then looked at Bobby, Im almost forgetting, Im thinking – shrugs and strains a smile.

I damn near be getting my feets frozen, I remember. My sneakers be all ripped an it be snowin an then the wind come rippin aroun like a muthafucka. . . . When I get home I be huggin and rubbin them fuckers for a hour.

Moishe stared at Bobby for a moment, What youre doing?

I boos me a new pair very next day man.

Boos????

Yeah – smiling, then giggling – You sure be havin a problem with the language Mush – Moishe smiling a real smile as he looked at Bobby and listened to him – I stole me some muthafuckin sneakers man, an some socks. Sheeit, I be warm the whole rest of the winter.

Ya . . . if only theres something to steal . . . O well – shrugging and pushing the memories from his mind. – One thing is very nice in winter

Yeah?

Having already a cold nose and going in warm house.

Yeah, that be cool.

They grinned at each other and sat silently for a few minutes. Eventually Bobby turned back to Moishe.

An this guy he be marchin too an he say, Wish he be happy?

Moishe nodded his head, Ya.

What you be sayin?

Moishe laughed, Same like you. I tell him hes crazy, out of his fucking mind! Ya, like you.

Bobby grinned then started chuckling, You be puttin me on?

Moishe shook his head, No. Im telling him.

Again they were silent, grinning at each other, enjoying the moment.

What you be doin?

Eventually Im having no choice. . . . Im doing what Sol is saying.

No fuckin way. You be wishin that – O shit, I cant be

believin – after all the shit that muthafucka be puttin your ass in??? how you???? Bobby trailed off into silence and shook his head.

Moishe waited for a moment . . . Im fighting. . . . Im fighting. Inside something is knowing Sol is right, but Im fighting . . . hate is what Im needing. And maybe Im right – shrugging – Maybe hate is keeping me alive, is giving me reason to live . . . but soon its killing me.

How that be, it be killin you? Sheeit, this world be one big muthafuckin hate machine man an there be peoples all over the place, it doan look like it be dyin.

Moishe tilted his head to one side and beamed at Bobby, So . . . youre calling this living – and laughed, Bobby staring at him for a moment, then laughing too – The hate is so bad one day Im collapsing on march back to camp. Im getting up but Im dizzy, some men are helping me, and in my heart Im knowing 2 things – Moishe stopped for a moment and looked at Bobby with profound kindness and compassion – for absolute certain – tapping heart – in here. . . . All of a sudden Im knowing that Im dying . . . that simple, Im dying and tomorrow or next day, Im not getting up from ground and before is setting the sun Im food for wolves. Absolute! – He was quiet for another moment watching Bobby absorb the information – And Im also knowing, same way almost same time, that Sol is right – getting more excited – Im knowing in all of me, Sol is right . . . and I start to cry. . . . Why??? – Bobby shaking his head – Because Im knowing both things are right . . . and I then know 2 more things . . . I dont want to die, I want to live . . . and I cant give up my hate, so Im standing there trembling, sweating, wanting to live but I cant stop killing me!!!! I cant tell you what Im feeling then . . . so terrible . . . like being already in a nightmare and youre knowing you should wake up but youre saying no and you cant stop yourself . . . youre saying no, no, no. . . . Ya, maybe hate was reason to live for while . . . maybe even its keepin me alive. But now. . . . But I cant stop. . . . Im dying. . . . I cant hate, and I cant not hate. They looked at each other, silent, the sounds of the streets and the river continuing yet each aware only of the beating of their own hearts. . . .

Bobbys voice was quiet, concerned, So what be happenin Mush?

I keep crying, like . . . sob, you know? I keep sobbing . . . not loud, not much tears, and Im dizzy, everything is moving a little bit, is not too much, but Im dizzy. So Sol is again hugging me and telling me his hate – Moishe shook his head and moved his hands – Hes telling me a long time but is happening to him worse then me, his wife and 2 daughters were betrayed by a friend, are taken to camp and hes hearing theyre dead – the sounds of the streets and river were a backdrop to their silence, their thoughts, the intensity of their feelings, a simple indication that life was continuing all around them, as it was continuing within them, as they talked about the many deaths some people share, experience – Hes being told he has to be willing to wish that man happy – Bobbys eyes suddenly popped open and bulged, his mouth opening but he remained silent – and so same like me a prisoner is holding him and saying same as to me. Sol is saying he cant . . . even if he wanted to he cant, and man is saying thats true, but if hes willing to give up the hate something in him will show him how to do it, will do what he cant do – Moishe looked out at the river, allowing the lights, the movement, to push aside the pain of the memories. . . .

Bobby continued shaking his head, still unable to speak, his disbelief and conflict obvious.

In time Bobby stood and leaned on the railing, then turned and looked at Moishe for a moment before speaking, I dont know Mush. I dont think you be lyin to me, I know you be straight bro, but I caint believe that shit . . . uh uh, no way can I be believin that shit. It be like I dont be doin nothin an the man come up to me an bus open my head, then the moms, an who else, an I supposed to say merry xmas muthafucka, whach you wantin for xmas I can give ya????

Moishe smiled, then grinned and nodded his head, Im not thinking so, but. . . .

As always Moishes smile put a grin on Bobbys face, I dont know where you be comin from, but you do be knowin what it be to be hurtin. Ain no bool shit about that bro, you be knowin about that. But that other shit – shaking his head – no way . . . uh, uh, no way man. . . .

They remained silent for a few minutes, then Bobby stood straight, adjusted his pants and shirt, What say we be gettin some hot dogs Mush, I be starvin. All this fat mouthin make me hongry – smiling and waiting for Moishe to get up before starting walking in the direction of home.

The next morning Moishe had a strange feeling as he sat at the breakfast table, frowning and confused, until he realized that Bobby usually was finished working out by now, but he could still hear him working with the dumb-bells, which meant he still would be using the rowing machine. Moishe wondered, briefly, why he was spending so much time with them today, but soon shrugged it off, telling himself it wasnt important, that he couldnt hurt himself doing this for one day, and also knowing that if he thought about things too long he ended up worrying . . . no matter what he started thinking about, worry always fol-lowed. So he poured himself another cup of coffee, covered another piece of bread with butter and jam, and thought about the previous evening and all the changes of emotions they both experienced. It was an overwhelming thought, so much having happened Moishe could not absorb it all yet. Anyway, he was content to remember the walk home, the peaceful feeling he had which somehow surprised him, and the joy he always felt in watching Bobby devour hot dogs, wham, wham, wham, gone . . . onions, sauerkraut, red pep-per, mustard, wham, wham, wham.

He had long finished the coffee and bread when he heard the shower and knew Bobby would be out in a few minutes so he started cooking the bacon and sausages.

Bobby was quiet while eating and was quiet during the rest of the day. A few times Moishe tried to start a conver-sation and though he could see Bobby actually tried to talk he was just in a quiet mood so he left him alone. Moishe kept himself busy in his workshop, but became increasingly uncomfortable during the day. He told himself there was nothing to be uncomfortable about, its a day like any day . . . just a day . . . and some days people are quiet, thats the way it is. But he had difficulty believing his own reasoning as the day went into night, and then his gut tumbled when Bobby said he was going out much earlier than usual, and checked his jacket several times, tapped his pockets making mental notes and nodding to himself, putting on his gloves and saying so long, See ya in a little while Mush.

Moishe looked at him for a moment, feeling anxiety roiling around inside him.

Moishe started to say something, but suddenly closed his mouth and just nodded and watched him leave. He sat for a long time listening to his heart beat, feeling the turmoil . . . the fear . . . trying to deny that he knew what Bobby was going to do tonight, but tried only for a minute, knowing much too well the futility of denying the obvious.

Bobby had gone to bed the previous night feeling fine. . . . Hot dogs, with everything, ice cream and chocolate sauce, all made him feel good. But he woke up with a sense of urgency, he had to get things going. He knew he had to get the first spic tonight if everything worked out. He was going to be cool, he wasnt going to take any chances. He knew what to do and was going to do it. He was going to wait until the set-up was just right and he could call all the shots. He had been checking everything out for a long time and wasnt going to blow it, wasnt about to do anything stupid, he was going to stay cool, but he wasnt going to go for no walk with Moishe tonight. He had to go to the hood. He could feel it in his bones. No more showing his face and splitting. Not now. That part was over. Every other part had been taken care of, and taken care of right. Now he was going to get them on their own turf, the one place they wouldnt be expecting him. They knew he never be fool enough to hit them on their turf so thats what he was going to do.

He walked fast enough to keep warm, but not too fast to tire him. There was a cold breeze and he wished he had worn the scarf, but knew that would be crazy, you cant be putting a noose around your neck like that, he was no fool. As always, he kept to the shadows when he got to the hood and went to the roof of a 4 story building to watch what was happening. One of those spics always walked down this street past a very narrow alley. He was sure that would be the perfect place to get him . . . if there was no one around. It was getting colder and fewer and fewer people were on the streets, staying in the bars, candy stores, coffee shops, wherever it was warm. Bobby studied the streets, the movement of traffic, people, checking out his feelings about what was happening. He went down to the street and went south, then west to a place he knew there was a fence he could climb and work his way to the alley by the bar. He stood in the shadow feeling something alive within him, feeling alert, feeling the piece of brick in his hand, knowing it seemed crazy to be here with just a brick in his hand and a knife in his pocket, but that was why he was sure it would work . . . at least once. And he checked this out a hundred times and that one dude walked by here a couple of times a night, he was always walking up and down this block, and he always came walking west, then south down past the alley and Bobby knew all he had to do was wait and sometime, some night, he would walk right past him, it sure was getting cold just standing there but Bobby was willing to wait forever to get those muthafuckas, all he had to do was wait and keep his head clear and if it got too cold and he got fuzzy hed wait until another night, but tonight he was waiting, right now, breathing slow, staying aware of his breathing like Moishe showed him, moving his toes around in his sneakers as much as possible so he will always be aware of them and not suddenly find out theyre too cold to move when he was face to face with his enemy . . . reviewing his plan in his mind from time to time, doing everything Moishe showed him to concentrate, to be aware of what he was doing, reminding himself of what he already knew and he knew these streets just as good as any one and he kept his eyes wide his mind alert, reminding himself that his eyes were accustomed to the dark and he could see the alley clearly, but someone walking down the street would only see a narrow wall of blackness and hed be invisible to them, so he stayed in the shadows knowing he was secure and waiting . . . waiting. . . .

and then he saw him crossing the street . . . alone . . . and he started counting the guys steps as he squeezed the brick tighter, checking out his hands and feet, rotating his shoulders, reassuring himself that every part of his body was working properly, reminding himself that he had been working out all these months and was stronger than ever, being aware of his breathing, making sure he didnt allow himself to hold his breath, but to continue to breathe normally, quietly, watching him cross the street and suddenly was out of sight as he reached Bobbys side of the street, and Bobby continued counting steps, focusing his eyes on the first spot by the curb that was visible from where he stood, knowing that the bars light would cast the guys shadow when he was exactly 3 steps from Bobby and that would be the signal for Bobby to stagger out of the alley and pretend to stumble and fall onto the guy and he continued counting and at exactly the anticipated second he saw the shadow and staggered from the alley and bumped into the guy and before he could say, Hey, Bobby had rolled him along the wall into the alley and hit him as hard as he could between the shoulder blades with the brick, and the guy let out a low grunt like air suddenly leaving a container and Bobby hit him again with all his strength, wanting to scream in his face, wanting to call him every kind of muthafucka he could think of, wanting to rip him apart, but kept his mouth closed, silent, and hit him a third time, the thud of the brick the sweetest music Bobby had ever heard and with each smashing of the brick into his back he felt him crumble more and more and Bobby felt incredible strength and excitement surging through him, knowing how right he had been that if he hit the muthafucka right in that spot hard enough he couldnt make a sound, and the prick sagged like dirty rags to his knees and then to the ground, making strange, gurgling sounds, sounding like he was dying, almost silently gasping for air, and Bobby quickly rolled him behind the el-shaped corner completely out of sight of not only the street but anyone in the alley, and he yanked him by the hair and put his knee in the middle of his back and banged his face into the cold, filthy ground . . . then again and again, wanting to continue to keep smashing the muthafuckas face into the concrete . . . but reminded himself of what Moishe said about being aware of what he was doing and not let the blood pounding in his head and the excitement in his body make him forget his plan so he quickly felt the guys pockets and found his knife and put his knee in the guys back and held his arm by the wrist and pressed his hand against a block of wood and shoved his face against the ground with his knee as he thrust the knife through his hand into the wood, then pounded it to the hilt with the brick, keeping his knee on the back of the guys neck, grinding as much as possible, continually re-minding himself what Moishe had said about breathing and being aware so he didnt get drunk on what he was doing and maybe have some dude come up behind him without him knowing it, and when he finished hammering the knife into the wood he took his own knife out and grabbed the guy by the hair and showed him the blade and the guy tried to speak but Bobby had his head pulled back at such an extreme angle he was unable to speak and Bobby stared at him for a moment, his head back and to the side as much as possible, eyes staring, spittle dribbling from his mouth and Bobby let his hate get a little out of hand and slowly passed the blade under the guys nose and briefly thought of slowly slicing his nose off, and then cutting his eyes out and . . . Bobby quickly took a slow, deep breath, then exhaled slowly reminding himself where he was and what he was doing, then leaned over and put his mouth next to the guys ear, Jus so you be knowin, Im the nigga you be whippin with the chain . . . I be the nigga you doan like . . . I be the nigga you be killin Maria cause of. I hope you be rememberin me cause I aint never forgettin you muthafucka . . . you be hearin me? You be killin Maria you muthafucka . . . Bobby stared at him for a moment, then reached over and twisted the knife in as wide a circle as possible, agonizing groans struggling in the guys throat, I hope you be hearin me good cause I want all you muthafuckas be knowin Im comin back an gettin all you scum bag muthafuckas . . . you jus be sure you be tellinem Im gonna be gettinem, thas why I be lettin you live. You be sure you be tellin Raul he be seein Maria real soon . . . real soon, you be hearin me spic — twisting the knife again and yanking harder on his head — an I be makin sure that message be stayin in your head, you be hearin me, I dont want no chanct it be slippin out so I be cuttin this muthafuckin ear off — the look of panic on the guys face increased and Bobby became aware that the guy was pissing in his pants — now aint this a bitch, you be pissin in your pants. Might be your dick be freezin to the ground an you be loosin that too. Whach you think, think maybe I should be cuttin you useless dick of *maricone*? — and Bobby stared into his face for a few seconds, getting off on the look of uncontrolled terror in the guys eyes, then slowly started slicing his ear off, leaning to the side to avoid getting blood on himself, his eyes bulging as he stared at the knife going deeper from top to bottom, hearing then smelling the guys shit as he lost control of everything and his eyes rolled back in his head as Bobby stared at the knife, momentarily unaware of anything else, then suddenly there was no resistance to the knife and the ear was in his hand and Bobby stared at it until he again reminded himself to stay aware and took another slow, deep, breath, exhaling the same way, and repeated the process several times before taking his attention away from the ear and back to the guys face. His face was covered with blood and water and dirt and Bobby couldnt tell if he was conscious or not and he leaned over and waved the ear in front of the guys face, noticing that his eyes registered awareness, I sure hope they be findin you before you be bleedin to death, but if they not might be theys gettin the message anyways. Whach you think spic — Bobby started to say something else, wanting to tantalize, torment and torture the muthafucka as long as possible, but stopped in spite of his desire and just looked at him for a moment, then twisted his face with disgust, Ah, fuck you muthafuckas, you aint even worth my shit. . . .

Less see how loud you be yellin with your own ear in your mouth — and he shoved the ear in the guys mouth and gradually released his head and listened for a second to the faint and pathetic groans coming from his throat, then blinked his eyes rapidly for a second, wiped his knife off on the guys jacket, then stood and backed away a few feet, stopped for a second, then turned and disappeared into the darkness, knowing exactly what route he would take back home, and also what alternative routes he could take if something unexpected happened. Bobbys adrenaline and blood were pounding and his exhilaration was so intense he was unaware of his feet touching the ground, but he automatically followed the route, over a couple of fences, through a few alleys, south on one street, east on another, then back west for a couple of streets, always in the shadows, always moving at the same pace as those around him, always invisible to the casual eye, unnoticed by walkers and drivers alike, just another dude hustling through the chilled night to get his ass home, the exhilaration seeming to increase, yet he stayed aware, constantly checking everything out, making sure he never came up behind anyone too fast or too close, not wanting some dude to think he had to defend himself against him, always looking alone and purposeless, always adjusting his speed to his surroundings until he was the only person on the street and he trotted, faster and faster, punching the air in front of him harder and harder, turning and running backward as fast as possible like a defensive back then jerking around and leaping high in the air to knock down the pass or intercept and run on down the field, straight-arming every sucker that came near him, occasionally stopping and picking up a couple of rocks and throwing them at imaginary targets and hitting the bullseye everytime, then back to running and punching and leaping until he got to the steps to the cellar then stopped and leaned against the railing for a moment, then leaped in the air, his fist reaching for the stars, Right the fuck on!!!!

Moishe was still sitting in the same chair, feeling weighted down after Bobby left. He tried to leave himself alone, but was forced to accept the simple truth: he was afraid of another loss, to once again love someone and have them torn out of his life. He told himself to relax, you have seen the truth of him even if he hasnt. We all do what we can do and right now you sit and relax and maybe read a book or listen to music. . . .

but when Bobby returned he was still sitting in the same chair, in the same position, in the midst of the same discussion, but his mind stopped suddenly when Bobby opened the door, locked it and leaned against it, staring at Moishe, his face wet, eyes wide, very wide, all of him seeming to be jumping up and down and running at top speed while standing still. There was so much adrenaline and energy coming from him that Moishe felt the impact in his own chest and was shocked for a moment. . . .

Eventually Bobby moved and sat a few feet from Moishe, sweat dripping from his face, panting, staring . . . and Moishe forced a smile on his face and silence from his mouth though he wanted to ask a dozen questions, but he just looked at him, inwardly sighing and happy that he was alright, carefully noticing that there were no rips or tears in his clothing and only sweat on his face, no cuts, gashes or bruises and no scrapes on his hands and his knuckles were not split and he was sweating but had obviously been running so he did all he could to remain calm and silent. . . .

and finally Bobby began talking, his words thrown out in lumps until he calmed his breathing, then smiled, That breathin shit really be workin Mush. It be savin my ass from fuckin up — Moishe started to relax slightly, feeling a warm glow start inside him, expecting Bobby to tell him how he decided to not get revenge, but the glow stopped growing as Bobby related the events of the night to him, in detail, telling him every move he made and how he kept reminding himself to relax and be aware, relax and be aware, and soon the glow was replaced with apprehension as Bobby told him of finally seeing the guy and how he waited, and then the apprehension turned to fear as Bobby continued to tell him what had happened, step by step, feeling sick that he had inadvertently helped him, that the simple exercises he had shown him were being used to hurt another person, but when Bobby had finished his story Moishe was at least grateful that Bobby hadnt killed him though he felt sick and wanted to throw up or hide somewhere but he sat and listened as attentively as possible and when he finished Bobby leaned forward and asked Moishe what he thought, Cool, eh Mush? I outslick them muthafuckas an you know that muthafucka Raul be sweatin his ass off bout now. Yeah. . . . Whach you think Mush?

Moishe looked at him for a moment, trying desperately to get at least a semblance of a smile on his face, feeling himself struggling but having no idea what he looked like, whether he was smiling or crying. . . . Why you dont take off your jacket and stay for a while?

Bobby stared at him for a second, then laughed, Yeah, right the fuck on — taking off his jacket and gloves and wiping his face with his hand — Bobby suddenly jerked up and walked around the room, a few feet in one direction, then a couple in another, Man, I cant be tellinya how good I be feelin, like I can take them muthas an be choppinem up in little bitty pieces . . . but I think I bes be coolin it for while, whach you think bro? wait till they be gettin careless again, I aint about to be lettin them be gettin behin me, right bro? they aint got no idea where I be or when I be gettin ready to get up side their head, uh,uh, no way they know where I be or when I be on they ass an aint nobody goin to keep lookin over his own shoulder all the time, right Mush? some time you jus aint doin it no more no matter what be happenin an thas when I get the muthafucka, wham, right Mush? I just be letten them tell me when I be gettin them, sheeit, alls they know I might be fixin to crawl through they window right bout now an slittin they throat while they be sleepin, sheeit they doan know what I be thinkin of doin, but I be lettin them know, right bro? I be lettin them know — Moishe couldnt hear any more. He kept his face smiling as

much as possible, but tuned out the words and their meaning, trying to fill his mind with anything but what Bobby
was saying . . . and when he was aware that Bobby had
stopped talking he got up and filled bowls with ice cream
with chocolate sauce, even more grateful that Bobby had
not killed anyone. . . .

So whach you think
bro? Moishe looked across the table at Bobby as he scooped
ice cream into his mouth, and shrugged. Bobby didnt seem
to notice but just continued talking, Like I say, I figure I got
all the time, time be on my side. I just be stayin here an goin
out when I wants to an see what they be up to, damn, they
never know what be happenin . . . damn, heheeh !!!! Bobby
tried to be quiet and, from time to time, would be silent for
a moment, but it was impossible for him to remain that way
so he just kept talking no longer aware of what was coming
out of his mouth, but just talking off the energy and excitement, Moishe nodding when it seemed he should, until
Bobby said he was going to clean up and took a long
shower, a very long shower, and when he returned he
walked much slower and was quiet, suddenly seeming
drained, Man, that shower like to take all my energy Mush.
Think I be gettin to bed. Mus be gettin late anyway –
glancing up at the clock – Damn, it be after 3 . . . we mus be
talkin a long time – Bobby grinned – Guess I be doin the
talkin, eh bro? Moishe smiled and nodded. Bobby giggled,
Look like I be talkin my sweet little ass to sleep – getting up
and stretching – You goin to bed Mush . . . pass your
bedtime.

Moishe smiled, A few minutes – nodding his head – Ya,
a few minutes.

Bobby went to the bedroom and Moishe sat at the table,
wishing he could simply fall asleep and wake up and all the
questions would be answered or not exist, but he knew he
would be unable to sleep if he went to bed, that he had to
allow the thoughts pounding in his head to dissipate so he
could relax. He inhaled and exhaled slowly and deeply a
few times and allowed his body to relax then watched his
thoughts bounce around and left them alone, from time to

time reminding himself that there was nothing he could do, things are as they are and he could think all night or not think all night, could sleep, stay awake, scream, be quiet or eat more ice cream and things still would be as they are.

Moishe awoke later than usual and sat on the side of the bed for a few minutes, feeling disoriented having gone to bed so much later than usual. He looked at Bobby for a moment, still sleeping, clutching the edge of the covers. He briefly wondered what Bobby may be dreaming, then tried to remember his own, but gave up almost instantly. He felt sluggish . . . no, it was more a feeling of sadness. The resolve he had gone to bed with had been mangled by dreams and he had to talk himself into getting up and washing and getting the day started.

Bobby had gone to bed exhausted but excited, determined to get up his regular time even if he was going to bed hours later than usual, it didnt matter because he felt energized, turned on, and he wanted to get up and hit the weights and get a good workout. He awoke several times in the morning, each time telling himself it was too early to get up and went back to sleep. Eventually he could no longer sleep, but still he refused to get up, but covered his head with his arm from force of habit even though there was no daylight to hide from. He refused to look at the clock, but kept trying to convince himself that it was too early to get up, but he couldnt convince his body which felt awake and just would not go back to sleep and he tried to reach back to the previous night to grab some of the exhilaration and determination he had been feeling, but it was gone, totally disappeared, at best a vague memory and he was confused by his feelings as if there was something a little off somewhere, something wrong but he couldnt figure out what it was and no matter how he tried to figure it there didnt seem to be any answer, just this dragged feeling like he didnt want to get up but just sleep all day but he couldnt and laying in bed trying to was becoming more uncomfortable than the thought of getting up, but still he wished he could just pull the covers over his head and just sleep for a couple of days, but why should he feel like that when he was feeling so great about today last night, but he guessed it didnt make any difference, but somehow it did and he knew it was ridiculous, that that spic deserved what he did to him and anyway, it wasnt shit compared to what they did to Maria, they killed her and she going to be dead for all time, aint nothing going to fix that like a doctor fix his hand, an fuck that dude with his wishing them happy, I aint about to be wishin them happy an who be wishin Maria happy? Show me who be wishin her happy? She cold stoned dead and all the wishin in the world dont be doing her no good

swinging his feet over the side of the bed, then sitting up and looking at Moishes empty bed, looking dully at the clock, it slowly registering that it was late morning and he should get his ass in gear and hit the weights and the machine and the rest of it but somehow he just couldnt find the energy to even think of working out and maybe he shouldnt, might be a good idea to take a day off and let his body rest, it seemed like Moishe had said something like that one time that he should take a day off once in a while, something about building up the body so this was as good a day as any to do that, probably the best thing he could do today and maybe just hang out or ah shit, what the fuck, just any fucking thing and fuck you Sol and those muthafuckin spics too. . . .

and he put on some clothes and went to the kitchen and sat at the table and told Moishe he wasnt working out that day, Figure I give my muscles a res, you know, like you be sayin – suddenly quiet, looking at Moishe who just stared for a moment, then got up and got the coffee.

They sat in silence, Bobby clutching his cup with both hands, sipping at the hot coffee, feeling the heat on his face, closing his eyes from time to time and just bathing in the heat, moving his face a little from side to side, eventually putting the cup down and buttering some bread and covering it with jelly, keeping his head lowered, not looking Moishe in the eye, but glancing at him from the corner of his eyes. . . .

So . . . youre sleeping good?

Bobby nodded, opened his mouth, closed it and nodded harder, unable to raise his head. He squirmed around in his chair, eating the bread as fast as possible then draining his cup, got up abruptly, still not looking at Moishe, Guess I be takin me a shower, and left the room.

Bobby sat in the whirlpool as long as possible, trying to visualize something melting away . . . not knowing what, but whatever it was that was dragging his ass, and when he started getting weak he forced himself to stay longer, but eventually left and got in the shower. He stood in the middle of the stall, all the streams of water pounding him, until the same sense of futility that got him out of bed got him to finally turn the water off, staying in the shower for many minutes in the same position, then getting out.

When Bobby got back to the kitchen Moishe was still sitting at the table. When Bobby sat down he asked him if he wanted breakfast.

Bobby felt like telling him to fuck off, but just shrugged and nodded.

When Bobby finished eating he leaned back and sipped at his coffee until it was finished, and sat quietly, looking pensive, Moishe watching him, he too silent, waiting.

Eventually Bobby asked him how he wish that dude happy? I mean like what you say?

Moishe remained silent for a few more moments, looking at Bobby. . . . Thats all I say . . . I wish he should be happy.

Nothin else?

Moishe shook his head, Not at first.

Not at firs? What be happen later?

First Im wishing only he should be happy. . . . I dont know, its going on for months maybe. Then Im wishin I mean it — grinning and suddenly bursting into laughter.

Bobby laughed, You what???? Sheeit — shaking his head.

Ya — chuckling — Then each day Im having to say again and wishing I mean it.

Bobby looked at Moishe for a minute, then asked him what happened?

Im living. Soon Im moving. . . . Ya, I live — Moishe looked serious for a moment — But later I see how Im feeling different inside . . . like the knots are untied . . . a little anyway.

Bobby looked at him sceptically, An you dont be hatin that joint no more?

Ohhh, that Im not saying — shaking his head — No, that Im not saying. I cant be there all those years without sometimes Im having such a pain — holding his stomach — But eventually somehow Im not hating Klaus — nodding his head — ya, somehow Im not killing myself by wanting to kill him — smiling at Bobby — but also Im looking at the other men sometimes, the jews I cursed, and thinking, they should all be happy . . . we should all be happy, and later the hate goes . . . but it comes back, over and over is coming back . . . leaning on table and leaning toward Bobby — but I no longer want to hold on to it because now Im feeling difference when Im letting it go. . . . Sols right, my hate was killing me. . . .

Moishe was silent, looking up at the ceiling, obviously remembering. . . . But I only see that later, *after* Im wishing.

Bobby continued working out and exercising each day, pushing himself as much as possible, each day trying to do just a little more, sometimes pushing himself close to the point of exhaustion, from time to time gasping for breath, unable to move for a few minutes, but always doing at least one more before stopping, within himself leaping in the air with his fist raised in victory even if he was slumped over unable to move a finger.

When he was able to move he sat in the whirlpool, allowing his body to relax and his mind to wander, leisurely drifting . . . drifting . . . feeling the hot water whirling around him, feeling as if he were floating in the water, as if his body had no weight, that he could simply float out of the tub and through the ceiling and beyond the clouds . . . and he could see the clouds below him, feel the air around him, and he had no idea how long he was in the tub, floating around, time seeming to have stopped. . . .

When he finished with the tub he dressed and went to the

kitchen and had coffee and something to eat. He always got a nice feeling when he saw Moishe, and he liked hanging out with Moishe, he just sort of felt laid back sitting at the table, drinking something, eating something and listening to Moishe talk, Bobby chuckling at the funny way he spoke, and sometimes absolutely fascinated by the stories of the camp and the old country. When he thought about it Bobby frowned and shook his head and smiled because he even liked doing those dumb puzzles with Moishe. Bobby couldnt figure any of this out, it just didnt make any sense so he just didnt try anymore but would just sit and sip his coffee and look at Moishes funny grin, listening to his funny way of talking, from time to time surprised and amazed that he was content to just be there all this time and not want to split.

Moishe was putting the dinner dishes in the sink when Bobby got up and said he was going out. He wrapped himself up as warm as possible, putting on a turtle-neck sweater and a knitted hat. As always Moishe just stood, silently, when Bobby said, See you later Mush, and left.

As always Moishe stared at the empty doorway for several minutes after hearing the click of the locks on the outside door, blinking his eyes against the sudden onslaught of thoughts and worries, until he was able to move and start washing the dishes.

Bobby stood in the shadow for a minute after coming out of the cellar, getting used to the sudden cold wind. It seemed to be colder than last night when he and Moishe went for their walk, but maybe it was just the wind was blowing harder. He didnt decide whichway to go back to the hood until he came to a corner and then went which ever way his instinct led him, always making sure he was aware of what he was doing, which direction he was going, always watching each shadow. He checked the familiar territory making sure nothing had changed, taking nothing for granted, continually testing himself to see if he remembered every crack, every stone every twist and turn, wanting always to be ready for any unforeseen circumstance.

He hadnt checked out the hood for a couple of weeks, not since he got the first spic, so he was exceptionally cautious as he figured if he bumped into any of them they would be together, that it was still too soon to catch another one alone. But he knew that some night he would. It was impossible to always be together, that they were alone when they left their houses, were going home or seeing a girl friend, and would getim and be that much closer to getting Raul who would be last and have a lot of time to sweat.

The wind was blowing from the east and he knew everyone would be huddled in their jackets trying to avoid the wind and would be on the north/south streets as much as possible so he stayed on the east/west as much as possible. Although he looked as if his head was bent as much as the few other people on the street as they struggled against the wind, he kept it up enough to give him a complete view of the streets knowing everyone else was seeing only the tips of their shoes.

His eyes were watering slightly when he turned a corner, facing north, and thought he saw a friend of Rauls walking toward him. He backed in a doorway, wiped his eyes and quickly evaluated the scene and in a second knew what he would do and almost laughed when the entire scene suddenly appeared in his mind. He knew that a few hundred yards north of where he stood there was a doorway that led to a building that had a storage area under the staircase with a panel that was loose and he could kick it out and go into the air-shaft between the buildings and over a short fence, through the cellar in the east building on the west side and be on the street 1 block south of this one before the guy knew what happened. From there he could decide which way to go, there were a half dozen options at least. He started walking north, pacing himself to meet the guy just south of the doorway knowing the guy would be so startled he wouldnt even know Bobby went into the doorway. Bobby kept his head lowered, but his eyes kept him in view the entire time as they approached each other. Bobby gave the appearance of being huddled in his jacket, hands deep in his pockets, but his hands were out and he was flexing them, keeping the circulation going so they wouldnt numb up on him, and as they approached each other he slowed his approach just a little so they would meet exactly where Bobby wanted them to and when they were almost side by side Bobby raised his head and grabbed the guy by the jacket and pulled him close to his face so he could see who he was and stared at him for a couple of seconds, absolutely silent and still, then grinned and stared into the guys eyes, stared right through the guy, grinning, silent, still, grinning . . . grinning . . .

then suddenly let him go and before the guy could react was through the doorway, running quietly down the hall, under the staircase, through the panel to the airshaft, over the fence, out the other building to the street then turning north until he almost reached the corner then, during a break in the traffic, continuing east, running between cars, and in less than a minute was a world away from the guy who was still processing the information, spinning around, backing down the street, then running to tell Raul what had happened.

Bobby quickly slowed his pace to a fast walk and lost himself in the people on the street, staying as much as possible in the shadows. He figured the guy would tell Raul what had happened and he chuckled to himself thinking of the look on the guys face and the one that would be on Rauls and how pissed off he would be as they ran around the hood trying to find him, but he didnt laugh even though he sure as hell wanted to because he knew laughing would make him careless for a moment, so he kept swallowing his laughter and hustled as fast as possible away from the hood and soon he was once again in the safety of the deserted streets with the ugly shadows cast by abandoned and crumbling buildings, the shadows flat, lifeless, yet seeming to reflect the agony of not only the buildings but the people who lived there, the people who passed by, or the shadows of people that were left behind, the shadows of people too despairing and weak to carry their shadows with them and so they stayed as the people moved on to find some other shelter, but Bobby only felt elation as he passed them, the exhilaration of another victory, allowing himself to start feeling that elation now that he knew he was safe and in a matter of minutes would be in his cellar on his way to Moishes, sitting back being cool eating a bowl of ice cream and chocolate sauce while the muthafuckin spics were running they asses off lookin forim. . . .

And, as always, Moishe sat and wondered when he would accept things as they are and stop deceiving himself that maybe Bobby would give up the idea of revenge. Everytime he asks me questions and nods his head I think Ive changed his mind, that now he will give up the madness of revenge and live happily ever after. . . . How can I do this – shaking his head – How can I keep doing this? All the years I have lived and all the months hes been here and I still deceive myself into thinking . . . thinking??? hoping . . . ya, hoping I have changed his mind and always he says, See ya later Mush. Always! And I go through this over and over. Well, maybe I should accept the fact that Im going to continue doing what Im doing. . . . But how sweet it would have been to be living with my son now . . . or close to him. I could babysit while they went out. I could teach them things. I could hug my son and kiss him on the cheek. I could hug his wife and their children. I could buy Christmas presents and wrap them and put them under the tree and we would turn on the lights and play music and . . . O Werner, for gods sake stop – blinking the tears from his eyes, feeling them roll down his cheeks and falling from his chin to his shirt – allow the past to sleep . . . please Werner, no more unnecessary sadness . . . no more unnecessary tears – He heard the door being opened and felt a sigh of relief flow through him and his body bent forward slightly. He pushed himself back in his chair and smiled when he saw Bobbys face, flushed with excitement and the cold wind. He yanked his jacket and hat and gloves off and sat down, his breathing rapid with excitement, Check this out Mush, It be sweet . . . yeah man, it be righteous and sweet. O man, you really gonna be diggin this – his eyes still wide with excitement, bouncing around on the chair as he told Moishe how he checked everything out, Moishe nodding and smiling, always relieved when Bobby returned safely from his trips, Bobbys eyes flashing with a mischievous expression, and when he got to the part of seeing the guy coming along the street he stopped, rubbed the top of his head and looked at Moishe for a moment, How bout some ice cream Mush?

Moishe got them bowls of ice cream and Bobby started scooping the ice cream in his mouth as he bounced on the chair and told his story . . . Moishe getting more and more caught up in Bobbys excitement . . . So anyway, like I say, I got this all figured so I step in fronta this dude and grabim – illustrating with his hands – like this, ya dig, and I grin atim . . . thas all, I jus be grinnin like a damn fool an I be right in this suckers face man, I mean right the fuck there, an I grin this dude right the fuck outta his mine then Im gone . . . jus like that, Im gone . . . history, an I doan be lookin back, but I got these eyes in the back of my haid, right? an I be seein this sucker standin there wonderin what the fuck be goin on an by the time he move Im gone, I mean Im outta there man an that muthafucka still doan know what be happenin toim . . . sheeit, I coulda reached in his pocket an be takin his money he so paralyze, damn, you shouldda seen that poor dumb muthafucka bro, I bet he be standin there so long he catch hisself a cole, an they still not knowin where I be – scooping furiously at the ice cream, spoon clanging against the bowl – an they never be knowin – and Moishe continued to look at Bobby, smiling, still consciously involved with his sense of relief which grew when he realized that no one was hurt, that Bobby simply outthought them and was sitting there wolfing down ice cream – I bet they be freezin they dicks off right now tryin to find my ass – shaking his head and grinning at Moishe – Thas how I be lookin at the dude man, jus like this . . . all my teeth hangin out . . . grinnin like a damn fool . . . I be tellin you Mush, if I wasnt so pretty I be scarin that muthafucka to deth – giggling and scraping the bowl with the spoon, then his finger, then leaning forward and grinning again at Moishe – Thas what I do bro – staring, grinning, Moishe smiling then laughing, whatever tension was left draining from him as he laughed, then shook his head and looked at Bobby – Why you be lookin like that Mush? Like what? Like a wino what jus got a bottle a thunderbird – making a silly face and shaking his head, Moishe looking startled for a second, then bursting out laughing – Im thinking, if its dark hes seeing only the teeth – clicking his teeth at Bobby – and the two of them sat grinning at each other, Moishe, from time to time clicking his teeth . . . until they both started laughing so hard they were crying and shaking their heads, begging each other to stop . . . until they were able to start breathing normally and, from time to time, look at each other for a moment without laughing . . . then sat in silence catching their breath and rubbing their stomachs . . . eventually they each took a deep breath and sighed, again sitting quietly and gradually turning more and more toward each other until they were looking at each other, a hint of a smile on their faces . . . then Moishe picked up the bowls, slowly, and rinsed them and put them in the sink, then sat down, the silence continuing until Moishe asked Bobby if his parents knew he was alright?

Bobby jerked up slightly and frowned, Parents????

Ya, mother and father, theyre worried? Is many months youre here.

Its just us and the moms – Moishe nodding – And I be takin care a that the firs time I go back, an I be sure I see Jesse every onct in a while, you know, tellim I be cool an find out whats happenin in the hood . . . like that.

Ya, ya – nodding his head, the concerned look still on his face – Its a long time and Im thinking maybe they – she – worries.

Its cool Bro. Aint no big thing a kid doan come home for a while. An anyway, she be havin enough kids to be buggin her. One less be jus fine cept I doan be no trouble anyways, but even so, it be cool Mush – looking at him for a moment, then smiling – You really be wonderin about that, eh?

Moishe shrugged as offhandedly as possible and returned the smile.

Aint that somethin, you really be worrin about someone you doan even know. . . . Damn – shaking his head, still smiling, then slowly getting up, I be wipe out Mush. Im gonna be gettin some sleep.

Ya, is good idea.

The NE wind stopped the next morning, followed by a warming trend and there was a late second Indian summer, prompting people to leave their homes, even unnecessarily, after having assumed they would be inside for the duration, not coming out except for food or drink until the spring thaw, but now everyone was out for what they knew to be the last time to enjoy just standing, or sitting, in the sun, enjoying its warmth even more than usual knowing that at any moment it might be the last moment of the year.

Moishe and Bobby were among the people who were on the street enjoying the warm sunshine, enjoying the sudden and frantic activity on the streets.

They continued strolling the streets, eventually ending up by the river shortly before sunset, enjoying the stillness of the air and the unseasonable warmth. Bobby and Moishe sat in silence for a few minutes, then Bobby turned to Moishe, You say you aint see Sol since you be gettin out the camp?

Moishe nodded and smiled, Ya. The day we/re being liberated. Such a day − shaking his head − like you never see.

Bet you guys are jumpin all up an down, eh?

Moishe shook his head, a look of sadness on his face, No . . . only a few of us can stand. . . . One morning we see the guards are gone and is everything open, but we cant move.

You mean you just stay in the muthafuckin camp Mush? Only so few can move. . . . And where we/re going????

then we/re hearing a car and soon a jeep with 4 American soldiers is there. We just look and stare. Im thinking I want to go to them, maybe Im thinking I should be hugging them, I dont know, but Im not moving like no one else is moving. They stop in the middle of the compound and look . . . look at the pile of bodies and you can see theyre not believing what they see . . . or what they smell. Bobby, these are men who many, many years, are fighting, seeing so much blood, so much bodies, but they look at us and cry . . . ya . . . they cry and throw up. Men so long fighting, killing, and they cry and throw up. A few of us stagger out and they are afraid to touch us.

No shit????

Ya . . . I could see theyre wanting to touch us but afraid theyre hurting us O Bobby, Im still seeing so clearly this young man looking at me, tears all over his face, arms reaching and just laying his hand on my shoulder like Im a butterfly and hes not wanting to hurt me . . . just like — gesturing with his hand, then touching Bobby on the shoulder — just like so and Im wanting to say something or cry but Im only looking and feeling on my shoulder his hand and all for ever Im not forgetting his face . . . tired, dirty, young but aged with so much pain, and the tears streaking his dusty face and its like Im seeing his heart beat in his eyes but Im not saying a word and its not till later, maybe days, Im realizing it was long time since Im saying a word . . . how many days Im not knowing, but many days. Maybe Im forgetting . . . maybe my throat is not knowing — shrugging — I dont know, but Im looking at his face and in his eyes and hes putting so light a hand on my shoulder and says . . . Komrade. Ya . . . hes saying Komrade and my heart is saying, Komrade, but out of my mouth is coming nothing, but Im seeing in his eyes he knows what my heart is saying . . . he knows Bobby . . . he knows. . . .

Moishe took a slow, deep breath and let it go. . . . I dont know how long Im not seeing Sol. Finally we/re seeing each other and we/re just standing, looking . . . its almost like when Im looking at the soldier and Im not saying anything. So finally we/re hugging and crying and Im not knowing, even now, if we/re saying anything to each other. Maybe no. We/re hugging and then. . . .

An you aint be seeinim since?

Moishe shook his head slowly, No. No more. Well, a couple of times Im dreaming of Sol, thats all. But not even that maybe ten years now.

Ten years . . . sheeit, that be a long time.

Ya — nodding his head — Is maybe ten years.

Bobby looked at Moishe for a moment. . . . An you be comin here?

No. Is couple years later. We have more years of camps . . . DP camps.

DP?

Ya. Displaced Persons. Millions of people. All over Europe. No home. Family lost — shaking his head — Is terrible. So many people looking for families. Is such madness . . . so many records destroyed with bombings and millions of people looking for each other . . . millions. People try to help, but so many millions. . . . I fill in forms, I answer questions and all the time Im hoping and afraid of hoping.

Bobby looked at Moishe for a moment.. . . Yeah, I can dig it. You be hopin for somethin an the world fuck withya.

Moishe was silent for a moment, still hearing Bobbys words. . . . Ya, Im afraid to hope. But I think, is it true Gertrude and Karl-Heinz can be alive???? So, anyway, we/re finding each other and there we are, the three of us . . . together . . . Karl-Heinz isnt knowing who I am, but Gertrude and I are knowing — laughing, Bobby shaking his head and smiling — And finally so many years later we/re together . . . almost 9 years.

Alright!!!! Goddamn Mush, that be cool . . . yeah, right the fuck on bro.

So things be pretty cool since then, eh? You an your family be swingin?

Thats what Im thinking. So many years of such pain an misery like no one is knowing . . . but we/re together . . . thats enough pain for us an —

Right on bro. I be withyall.

Moishe smiled faintly and nodded his head, Ya, Im thinking enough. Then Karl-Heinz is dead and Im wondering can there really be a God . . . can this really be????

silence. . . .

Bobby staring at Moishe. . . . Moishe shaking his head in bewilderment. . . . We/re becoming citizens and celebrating, now we/re belonging someplace, now we have a country, *our* country. We/re so proud . . . so happy. Even my busi-

ness, Im having a little store with MOISHE CONTRACT-
ING on the window – wistful, nostalgic smile on his face,
Bobby grinning – So again Im having my own business . . .
and we even are having a willow tree. . . .

So . . . we/re
becoming Americans – smiling at Bobby, eyes bright –
we/re happy

suddenly Moishe bent over, covering his face
with his hands, O Bobby – his voice muffled, wet, his body
twitching with a sob, silent, only the sound of his breath
between his fingers, his body jerking periodically, Bobby
staring wide eyed, leaning toward Moishe, his hands reaching out, his mind confused. . . .

eventually Moishe took his hands
away from his face, Its not Im expecting no troubles, who
can live without trouble . . . no pain? Life is life. But we/re
thinking so much suffering and now we/re living a normal
life, pain, ya, but. . . .

Moishe took a deep
breath and closed his eyes and shook his head, How such a
thing can happen. We/re not even knowing Vietnam. We
hear sometimes on the radio, but wheres Vietnam? We/re
not thinking, war, me and Gertrude, we/re thinking life,
happiness . . . we work hard. Then Karl-Heinz is being
drafted and still we/re not thinking something can happen.
How can it? All thats in the past. We cant be again in the
suffering – Moishes eyes pleading as he looks at Bobby –
But we/re wrong . . . all is wrong and Karl-Heinz is dead.
Gertrude is getting the telegram . . . 2:37 in afternoon. After
6 Im coming home and shes sitting in chair, staring at wall
and on floor is telegram and her arm is hanging like so . . .
just like so . . . and inside me everything is big knot and
pain like Im not knowing for so many years . . . like everything is gone . . . like heaven and earth gone . . . like air
gone . . . like theres nothing just something so black and
terrible inside and I see the telegram on the floor and I fall
into chair and Im sitting, looking at Gertrude . . . Im not
knowing how long Im sitting so, but is so dark Im only
seeing Gertrude not clear and I lift her arm and hold her

hand and kneel on the floor beside her . . . I dont know Bobby, maybe hours Im kneeling there holding her hand and Im not understanding, havent we suffered enough? Everything was ripped from our lives and we struggled to make a new life and now our only child is dead . . . dead. Troubles, yes, but not to bury our child. No. NO!!!! O Bobby I scream at god and tell him No, NO! But still after screaming we/re burying our child and all our tomorrows are in a box buried in the ground . . . just a box in the ground – shaking his head, staring at the ground, Bobby still leaning toward him, bewildered, confused, wanting to do something but able only to stare at him and feel like reaching to him – Im thinking there cant be a god. I have to think there cant be a god. If theres god what kind of god???? What kind of god is allowing this . . . is taking from us our child? And then Im thinking god is allowing the camps hes allowing our son to die. Theres a difference????

The sun was almost completely set and the boats on the water had turned on their running lights and they were reflected in the water as were the lights from the buildings near the river. The sky was streaked with color that was disappearing into the dark blue that would soon be the evening sky. Moishe took another deep breath and raised his head, I dont know how long we/re not talking, me and Gertrude. Maybe only few words for days . . . whos knowing, maybe weeks – shrugging – who knows. Im thinking to kill myself, that Im not standing the pain. Is impossible to be living in this world. But Im killing myself and Gertrudes alone so somehow I live. For so long a time Im not working but friends are helping . . . bring food, hugging, talking . . . Here, eat a little soup – Moishes pain made Bobby speechless even though he felt so many things within him struggling to be said.

Moishe and Bobby looked at each other with compassion, seeming to nod at each other though their heads were still. . . .

Ya. . . . Ya . . . then again Gertrude is cooking . . . and Im working. Still we/re not talking much – shrugging – maybe little bit nothing talk, and I work I say nothing. Im doing the job and Im leaving. . . . Ya, doing the job and Im leaving. But still is terrible thing inside just like in camp and Im remembering Sol but who Im wishing happy? Who Im pointing to and hating and wishing happy? Im sitting in my workshop, is maybe months later, Im wondering how long is this pain and Im realizing maybe forever. . . . Ya, maybe is forever the pain, like before. So who Im wishing happy? I wish happy the president? the army? Im wishing happy Vietnam? Im beating my head with my fists and Im not knowing who to wish happy, I dont know even who to hate – shrugging and tossing his hand in the air – and all I hear is the sound of my fists on my head, over and over. Who knows again how long? I stop and Im seeing puddle of water on floor and realize Im crying. My face is wet and stiff and on floor is a puddle. Tears. All my tears. Achhh – bolting up and waving his arms – Time is again stopping and Im not knowing is late. I look at clock on wall Im thinking its saying 8 oclock, but – shrugs and shakes head – So Im telling myself I should go home. Inside Im knowing I should go home but Im feeling like Im tied to the chair, but I move, Bobby, I dont know how long to get up from chair. Its like a horrible dream to get to the door, but I go home. Gertrude is frantic, all trembling, crying, Im not knowing what shes saying and shes hitting me and hugging me and Im dying inside and I hold her and shes calming down and Im wondering what is happening. . . . Im even looking for a telegram, something. . . . but soon shes only crying then shes looking at me and saying Im late. Ya, shes saying Im late and shes calling the store and Im not there and shes thinking something is happening to me and all of a sudden shes alone . . . O God, how terrible . . . shes feeling like Im dead and shes alone in a strange house in a foreign country, and she doesnt know what to do or who to call or where to go, shes just sitting trembling and crying being all alone and how shes going to bury now me and be coming home to here, this place and Bobby Im suddenly realizing how shes feeling, how everything inside is hollow and pain and shes so terrified O Bobby Im just holding her and kissing her and telling her I love her and Im knowing in my heart who to wish happy. Its only then Im knowing who I want should be happy . . . only then when Im seeing in her eyes the hand of death . . . ya, then I know . . .

and so again I have a reason to live. . . .

So . . . somehow we/re surviving – tilts his head back in reminiscence and smiles – but always Im seeing in my picture mind we/re holding hands . . . ya we/re sitting in the kitchen, maybe morning, maybe night, and sometimes we/re not talking, just sitting and holding hands . . . and sometimes we/re looking at each other and smiling, and one day we/re laughing and then its already a couple of years Karl-Heinz is dead and we go on. . . . Ya, we got through together me and Gertrude, and. . . .

Moishe smiled warmly at Bobby who was looking at Moishe with admiration, respect and confusion, and they both huddled deeper into their jackets as the wind became stronger and cooler, and after standing for a few moments they started walking home, huddled against the wind, but still experiencing the warmth coming from each other.

Bobby pushed a little harder during his workout the next morning . . . and he sat on the rowing machine, gasping, panting, forcing himself to go the extra length by visualizing Maria . . . his sweet little Maria who was so cool and could outslick every chick on the block . . . oooo she was so sweet and knew how to hug him so he felt good all over . . . and some more . . . and summoning up all his hatred for Raul and seeing his fist smashing his face over and over . . . and even as he hung on the oars waiting to be able to move, he continued to see Rauls battered face.

In the whirlpool he once more relaxed and let go of his body, and the image, and simply felt free as he floated, weightless, his eyes closed, a sense of freedom from everything flowing through him. . . .

until he once again became aware of the warm, whirling water.

When Bobby sat at the kitchen table Moishe noticed he had a pensive, reflective expression on his face, the same look he always had when he was mulling over something. He watched him for a moment, then went to the stove.

Bobby started buttering the fresh rolls, You be out early, eh Mush?

Ya. Is good the rolls, ya?

Right on Mush.

Moishe sat at the table as Bobby ate, Is really changing the weather. Is winter time. Snowing but all wet and everything slides.

Yeah, it figures. Get a couple nice days an soon the wind be whippin your ass an the snow goin down your neck.

Moishe smiled, Ya.

They were quiet for several minutes, Moishe noticing the old look had returned to Bobbys face. Eventually Bobby looked at Moishe, You really be lovin your woman, eh Mush?

Gertrude? Ya, we are loving . . . all those years we are loving. Is never stopping. Im always loving my Gertrude and shes always loving me.

Bobby closed his eyes and shook his head, That be cool Mush, that — he suddenly stopped and stared at the wall across the room then looked at Moishe, You say it be snowin?

Moishe stared at him, bewildered, Ya . . . wet. Everyone slide.

Bobby nodded slightly in response, then stared at the wall again for a moment, nodding his head to some inner thought, then suddenly stood up — Yeah — and quickly left the room.

Moishe blinked and stared, and was still sitting in the same position when Bobby came back into the room dressed to go outside, bundled up with gloves and boots. Moishe started to remind him to put on a scarf, then closed his mouth and swallowed as he felt, again, that terrible pain in his gut, the horrible hole chewing its way up to his throat and wrapping it self around his heart.

I gotta be goin out Mush. See you later.

And he was gone. Just like that he was gone and Moishe remained immobile, remembering it was just a few minutes ago, it seemed, Bobby sat down at the table and they were talking and he felt something in his spine and could feel himself trying to explain something and all of a sudden hes gone . . . gone without his scarf . . . today with wind and snow hes going out, again, without his scarf . . . and this time its daylight . . . daylight . . . and no scarf around his neck to be used as a weapon against him. Daytime.

They never be expecting me in daytime, no fuckin way. They be so busy tryin to keep they ass warm and dry they not be seein me comin up onem. . . . Yeah, muthafucka number 2 goin be eatin some shit today. . . .

moving quickly and silently through the deserted lots, peering into the wet snow just enough to protect his eyes but still aware of everything around him, always alert to what may be around the next corner, behind him or just out of sight, aware that his enemies did not know he was tracking them.

He suddenly turned south for a block and went through a deserted building, then turned east until he came to an inhabited part of the area just on the fringe of his hood, changing directions as often, and suddenly, as possible until he reached their hood, then kept the breeze at his back as much as possible, constantly checking everything out around him and especially behind him, but wanting to be certain that if he suddenly met someone they would have the snow and breeze in their eyes and face, knowing they would always be looking at the ground. He checked out all the places he knew they hung out, but didnt stay in the area long, always ducking into a known doorway and emerging on another street, sometimes a few streets distant, circling in another direction, knowing that sooner or later he would see one of them and all he had to be was patient and he would have his chance . . . just be cool and keep checking everything out. It was still early in the day and someone would be going to the store for something . . . milk, bread, something and all he had to do was stay alert and keep looking through the snow and remind himself that they wouldnt see him until it was too late, but he would be checking them out as soon as they showed their face . . . and again he turned west and went through an alley and over a fence to come back north then turn west with the breeze and snow at his back, and after a couple of hours of circling and concentrating on his mission to ward of the cold, he saw Luis going into the bodega and stopped in a doorway across the street where he could see the check-out counter, and when Luis was at the register, he started across the street and let him walk a few feet north before rushing across the street and coming up beside him just as he was passing a doorway and Bobby slammed into him and threw him through the doorway and banged Luis' forehead against the wall, then did it again and again until he was almost unconscious, then quickly dragged him down the hallway and out through the air-shaft to the alley and slammed him against the wall again and allowed him to slump to the ground, still silent, concentrating with all his will and energy on what he was doing, quickly going through Luis' pockets and taking his knife, then pulling his pants down around his ankles, shoving his face into the ground when he started to moan, then dragging him over a couple of feet when he noticed a pile of shit covered with flies and shoved his face in it, then pulled his head up by the hair and jammed it back in the pile of shit, feeling Luis almost losing consciousness, and slicing a message for Raul on the back of Luis' jacket: YOU BE DEAD RAUL and started to leave but his hate continued to boil and he struggled to keep aware of what was going on around him but got caught in feeding his hate and was immobilized for a fraction of a second then Luis started to moan and Bobby quickly looked around to see if anyone was behind him, then shoved Luis face back into the shit and stuck the knife in his buttocks and quickly turned and vaulted the fence and ran through the adjoining building and through its cellar until he came back to the street south and west of the alley, not rushing too fast along the street, but again becoming a part of the traffic, knowing Luis would be unable to move for a few minutes and when he tried to stand he would trip over his pants and fall down and by then Bobby would be long gone as he was right now, turning a corner and once more keeping the breeze at his back and going down an alley that took him in a southeasterly direction and would terminate by an empty lot with a large outdoor advertising sign and piles of rubbish and large cardboard cartons and packing crates that bums lived in from time to time, then turned west until once more the sounds of traffic were distant and he was the only one walking the streets.

Most of the snow melted instantly upon hitting the street, but there was a thin layer of white on the cold ground of the deserted area and the abandoned buildings had a fairy tale quality to them perceived through the falling snow, splotches of white on cracks, ledges and protruding bricks and piles of debris and Bobby continued rushing through the snow, still feeling excited, exhilarated and sweating from his encounter with Luis, continuing to look around, alert and aware of his surroundings, and the more he looked around the more he slackened his pace until he stopped, about a block away from Moishes, and stood still feeling the snow brushing against his face, refreshing him, looking at the buildings through this same snow, feeling slowly more and more detached from his surroundings, feeling absorbed by the scene that surrounded him, how it made everything that had just happened seem so distant, so far away, so unreal, like it was all some sort of kids cartoon and everything was soft and quiet and happy ever after and they just cant never be no rats in those walls . . . not now or ever . . . just no rats in the walls. . . .

continuing to walk slowly through the snow, feeling as if each flake was brushing his cheek then moving aside to let him through, as if each flake was his friend and there to help him do whatever he had to do and he stopped again and tilted his head back and opened his mouth and let the snow drift down to his throat or lay on his tongue, blinking his eyes against the flakes, and feeling as if there was music going through him, music that he wasnt hearing, but somehow feeling, some sort of easy music like some of those far out gospel singers, those really righteous groups and he could feel himself humming something as he once again started moving, feeling safe in the open spaces between the crumbling and deserted buildings, knowing there was nothing for anyone to be hiding behind, no way anyone could be running from the nearest building to where he was without him seeing them and knowing exactly what to do and exactly where to go. He was in the wide open spaces, the most wide open space left in the city, completely visible to anyone who might be looking, even in the falling snow, but even if there was someone looking he was absolutely safe so he walked slowly towards Moishes, from time to time tilting his head back and opening his mouth to the falling snow, feeling it go down his neck but not caring because he knew he would soon be home where it was warm and dry, yet increasingly aware of how the cold had penetrated him to the bone, now that he wasnt using his energy to ignore it and accomplish his mission, and now the breeze was becoming a wind and every breath was even more chilling, but still he stopped occasionally and tilted his head and felt and tasted the snow, until he was going down the stairs to the cellar. After taking a couple of steps, he stopped, for a second, then turned and went back to the stairs and looked out at the snow and the buildings that were visible, buildings he knew were a dirty red but looked sort of rosy through the pale gray whiteness of the snow-filled air. He stared at the snow, the buildings, watching the flakes drift the final few feet to the ground or the railing by the steps, and sometimes disappear, then raised his eyes again to watch another snow flake flutter its way to the ground, fascinated by the whole procedure, thinking of a snow flake starting way in the hell up there wherever they come from and travel all that way just to disappear into the ground, or some day melt and flow to the sewers, but right now it was nice to look at, so peaceful and quiet and made the air feel like a feather against your cheek an make everything look so nice, so different than the way you know it looks but it was nice to have it look this way for a while . . . at least for a while. . . .

eventually he turned and went back to the apartment.

*

Moishe was determined not to sit and think about Bobby while he was gone. He went to his workshop and kept busy putting together some shelving for a friend and customer, playing the radio a little louder than usual hoping to drown out his thoughts, reminding himself to concentrate, that his friend deserved the very best Moishe could do, and so he worked carefully, methodically.

It went well for a couple of hours but soon his stomach reminded him of the passage of time, but was afraid to stop to eat lunch for fear without distractions he would fall into the pit of worry and never get out and so he continued working, suddenly dropping the sanding block and jerking around when he heard the door opening.

Moishe reached the kitchen after Bobby had taken off his wet clothes and hung them by the door and he could hear him in the workout room. . . . and recognized the sound of water going into the whirlpool. He looked at the wet jacket and hat for a second, then went into the other room. Bobby was in the tub, the water still coming in and rising up his chest. Moishe noticed instantly that he was sweating.

Youre alright?

Yeah, sure Mush. I be fine.

Moishe looked at him for a moment, nodding his head, Needing another whirlpool, ya?

Yeah. I need be gettin warm an this be the bes way.

Ya – nodding his head – Ya – staring at Bobby, not knowing what to say but feeling the need to say something – Im making us some hot soup, ya?

That be good Mush. Yeah, I be goin for that.

Moishe struggled with his feelings as he started heating soup, not wanting them to force him to say or do something he had no business doing or saying, keeping as deeply involved as possible in what he was doing at the moment.

Bobby sat in the warm water, feeling it rise higher and higher, feeling the heat penetrate deeper and deeper into his body. . . . waiting for it to get high enough to turn on the jets . . . feeling his body get lighter and lighter as the water continued to rise . . . and then he turned them on and the water started flowing around him and all the remaining chill left his body, as did the tension, and he leaned back and allowed the water to relax him and for a moment he concentrated on the smell of the soup, but soon he was becoming less and less aware of his surroundings, less and less aware of his body . . . more and more detached from it and everything else, that lovely state he sometimes experienced when he sat in the whirling warm water, that state of knowing he was Bobby, but some other Bobby that seemed like he was more Bobby than the one he was familiar with, and all the trips of each day seemed to be gone, like there were no streets, no alleys, no rats, not even any walls or sky, like things just, were, and so he allowed the water to lift his body and he simply allowed himself to go where he went, hoping he could stay there as long as possible. . . .

Eventually he felt himself becoming more and more aware of his surroundings, feeling the water, smelling the soup, and, eventually, his butt feeling tender from sitting in the tub, and aware of thoughts going through his head. . . . that no one would be expecting him to go back tonight, that all he had to do was fill up on some hot soup, cool it for a couple of hours, then go back just about sunset. . . . or maybe a little before, and grab Antonio . . . yeah, he had the strongest feeling it would work out perfect, that he would be able to get Antonio alone somewhere in his hood, he knew it, he just knew it in his bones. . . . Yeah, there was no doubt it would all work out perfectly. He would be able to just grab him before he knew what was happening and fuckim over and then let Raul sweat for a while . . . yeah . . . thats the way it was. Perfect. He leaned back in the tub and smiled, raising his right fist in the air.

Moishe watched Bobby silently eating, aware that he was constantly glancing at the clock as if he had some important appointment to keep . . . and the expression on his face obviously meant Bobby was thinking of something, planning something, and was totally preoccupied with it and Moishe was going to have to struggle not to ask what he was thinking, determined to keep his mouth shut and —

Good soup Mush . . . it be nice an hot.

Good. Im glad youre liking — embarrassed by the hysteria he heard in his own voice.

It be cold out there. Thought my ass never be gettin warm.

Ya — straining to control his voice — Youre going a long time.

Yeah — pursing his lips and looking over Moishes head — But it be worth it — smiling, eyes narrowing — Two muthafuckas taken care of . . . 2 more . . . actually one more then I be gettin Raul — peering at the joint of wall and ceiling — He be thinkin he outsmart me, but I knows what I be doin. . . .

Moishe stared at Bobby, as he stared at the clock for a moment, then nodded his head, Jus about be dark about now . . . specially with the snow cant hardly be seein anythin about now — nodding his head again and slowly getting up from the table. He put on his jacket and knitted hat and gloves and opened the door, Be seein you later Mush, and left.

Just like that he leaves and Im sitting here hoping O Bobby . . . Bobby. . . .

Bobby had only walked a few hundred yards when he became aware of the cold, the wind blowing much stronger now, the temperature dropping, and the snow being whipped around by the cross currents of wind blowing through the buildings and down the canyons of streets. He cupped his hands over his nose from time to time, being assaulted not only by the cold wind, but the memory of how cold he had gotten earlier in the day, how it had started getting painful to just keep moving, his nose and ears starting to feel like they were going to fall off, having to pound his hands together or hug himself to keep warm, and fight the temptation to stay in a warm hallway, if he found one, so now, only a few hundred yards, and a few minutes, from home, he felt the chill of the night penetrating his bones.

There was still a hint of light in the western sky and he figured it would be a good time to get back where he had been, nobody sees so good this time of night, very easy to make little mistakes in what you see, and they sure as hell would not be expecting him to show his face jus a few hours after taking care of Luis and Bobby chuckled to himself at the image of Luis laying in the alley, his pants down around his ankles and his own knife stuck in the cheek of his skinny ass. But that was before and this is now and he had to be careful and not fuck up or hed be dead meat, no doubt about that. He had to really check everything out no matter how cold he got, and he couldnt help thinking that if he was this cold now how cold would he be in half an hour, or an hour, or more if he had to stay out that long . . . but he knew he had to go back tonight, he knew it in his gut and in his bones, that this was the perfect time to get Alfredo, there was no doubt about that so he pushed himself a little more to keep walking and to keep his eyes open and moving all the time, utilizing his advantage to the fullest, the advantage of being the hunter. Yeah, he had a big advantage, but it wouldnt mean shit if he didnt stay aware and keep checking out every shadow, every corner, every angle.

It was a little easier when he got to the populated part of town where the buildings cut down on some of the wind, and he could lose himself more easily in the traffic of the streets, people ignoring moving bodies in this kind of weather, and he was going to take full advantage of the weather and his knowledge. He was saving Alfredo for now because he knew his routine . . . always being home between 5 and 7 during the week to eat with his family. His old man would whack the shit out of him if he wasnt there to eat. Once, a couple of years ago when he was just a kid, his old man came down to the candy store where he hung out and slapped the shit out of him in front of all his homies and dragged him home by the ear, twisting the fucking thing like he was trying to yank it off, Alfredo screaming and crying and pleading and not coming back to the store for a week, staying in the house because he was so humiliated. Bobby had checked him out everytime he came back to the hood and knew he would be home until 7, and so he knew exactly what he was going to do, having reviewed it in his mind, step by step, many, many times.

It was a little after 6 and he walked east on the street across from the candy store and stopped for a moment in a doorway and checked out what was happening. He could see Raul and a couple of others hanging out in the back, talking, waving their hands around like fucking windmills, and almost got lost in staring and hating their asses, but snapped himself back to where he was and what was happening and took a couple of slow, deep breaths, then continued walking east, then turned south at the corner. He had plenty of time to check everything out. He continued south for a couple of blocks, still being alert to his surroundings, even though he knew where Raul and some of his friends were, that this was spic turf and they would all be knowing who he was if he gave them a chance to see him, or let them get behind him, or ambush him around some corner, theyd love nothing more than tearing him apart, but he wasnt going to let that happen, he was going to stay cool and keep digging every muthafucka on the street, checking everyone and everything out, not allowing the smallest shadow avoid his attention.

He turned west and went into the second building and quickly climbed the stairs to the roof. He stood on the roof for a moment, leaning against the door, catching his breath, then walked very lightly and carefully across the roof to the south west corner which had an overhang that was only a few feet from the roof west of it. He jumped across and continued west to the other end then picked up the plank he had stashed against the side of the roof and placed it on the edge connecting to the building south and crossed over, then pulled the plank to that side. The edges of the next roofs were so close he had no trouble simply stepping across until he reached a building then went down the couple of stairs to the top floor where Alfredo lived. He stayed in the dark corner, knowing no one would notice him even if they looked, but no one ever did because the stairs going down were in the opposite direction so he would remain invisible. He figured he only had 10 minutes or so to wait and he breathed slowly and deeply until he was relaxed but alert, then wiggled his toes and fingers to be sure they had all their feeling and wouldnt suddenly numb up if he had to bolt into action, then shrugged all the different parts of his body, continuing to keep up the exercises until he heard footsteps approaching the door of Alfredos apartment only 6 feet away. The music coming from the apartments drifted to the back of his head somewhere and he heard, clearly, every footstep of Alfredos, the voices, Alfredos voice in response, the turning of the doorknob, and when he heard the initial squeak of the door opening he started leaning forward, knowing Alfredo would be facing the door as he closed it and as soon as he heard the squeak again he took his first step and just as he heard the click of the lock he covered Alfredos head and face with his gloved hands, twisted him around and powered his knee into his crotch as hard as possible, feeling more than hearing the groan that came from Alfredos mouth, then powering his knee into Alfredos gut, then again and again, allowing him to bend as he gasped for air through Bobbys hand still clamped tightly against his face, then Bobby quickly dragged him up the steps to the roof and once more kneed him in the crotch and eased him down on the thin layer of snow, being very quiet, silently grinding his face into the tar of the roof, then quickly taking Alfredos knife from his pocket before yanking his pants down and wrapping them around his ankles, then grabbing his hair and yanking his head around and up, Alfredo still gasping for air, and leaned within a few inches of his face, You be tellin that muthafucka Raul he be next, then sliced his cheek, stuck the knife in the roof just a few inches from his nose, then quickly disappeared across the roof, Alfredo still unable to breathe enough to yell, the entire sequence having taken less than a minute, and within 30 seconds after he left, Bobby was across 3 roofs, down the stairs to the air-shaft, through a cellar and up to the street and heading north east toward home, disappearing into the traffic, just another body in the foot traffic on the street, another shadow, same shape, same size, same speed, not thinking of what he had done or how he outsmarted them dumb muthafuckas, but doing what he needed to do right then, aware of every step, every car, every face, every hat, every jacket, checking them all out, until there were no more bodies to check out, no more cars to check out, no moving shadows to check out, just the shadows of the deserted buildings and rubble, only the sounds of the occasional rat or cat, and he turned a corner and leaned against the wall for a moment, listening to his breathing, not worrying about slowing it down, but allowing himself to feel the exhilaration and excitement of outslicking the spics again, of knowing he be playing with Rauls head an he be winning the game. Yeah, he damn sure be winning, and he felt like skipping across the rubble to home, but pulled himself back and finally did take a deep breath then checked out the area before starting home.

Moishe was still in the workshop when he heard the door opening, surprised that Bobby had been gone such a short time, having conditioned himself not to expect him back until early in the morning. He forced himself to finish tightening the 4 screws holding the bottom on a toaster, took a few deep breaths, then went to the kitchen.

Bobby was still standing, blowing on his hands and rubbing them together and cupping them over his face and breathing into them to warm his face and nose. His eyes glowed with exhilaration, his face flushed, and it was obvious he had difficulty standing still, the excitement he had delayed feeling was now safe for him to experience and was obvious in his movements.

In the ol work shop, eh Mush? Screwin aroun, eh? – giggling and rubbing his hands together.

Moishe looked for a moment, then allowed himself to relax and smile.

How about some hot chocolate and ice cream Mush?

They sat with their ice cream and hot chocolate and it was obvious almost instantly to Moishe that he wouldnt have to ask any questions, that all the information he wanted would be bubbling out of Bobbys mouth and he told Moishe how he had outslicked those muthafuckas and how he did it and what he did an how the muthafucka never knew what happened, never said a fuckin word but he make sure he knew who it be was fuckinim up an how he cut his cheek and stick the knife right in front his nose so he cant be missin it but the muthafucka not sayin shit an Bobby jus disappear in the night an he never did hear that muthafucka say shit, he be freezin his balls off for sure up there an now theres only that muthafucka Raul left an when he getsim he be beggin Bobby to killim cause hes gonna fuck with that muthafucka somethin fierce man, an he goin be killinim for a long time, he gonna keep that son bitch alive an makeim suffer for long fuckin time, he be cuttin him all up an down his ass an legs before he be throwin his ass off the roof an hes gonna watch the muthafucka splatter all over the groun jus like Maria an he hopin there be snow on the groun so he can seeim nice an clear an be watchin his blood spread all over the muthafuckin street an he jus goin be hangin over the side a that roof watchin and damn sure be listenin to Raul scream his punk muthafuckin ass off as he be fallin through the air an Bobby goin to like hearin that man it be music to my ear an maybe I be tapein it sos I can be hearin it over an over an I be disappearin before any a them muthafuckas be knowin whats happenin, only Raul be knowin an by then he aint be doin no talkin jus spreadin hisself over the dirty fuckin spic street an maybe I be goin down an pissin on the sonofabitch or maybe jus pissin onim from the roof an all those spic muthafuckas an they can all be sucking my black dick those monkey faced pricks an. . . .

                                        . . . Moishe listened, feeling his head bob up and down, and his gut knot in anguish, his throat fill with tears, his eyes closed to pretend the world didnt exist, and his ears closed so he wouldnt hear what Bobby was saying, and all the time he saw and heard Bobbys excitement he could feel the pain behind it, and all the old pain of his life was resurrected and clawed and ravaged him . . .

in time Moishe became aware of the sound of Bobbys spoon scraping the bowl, empty except for a stain of liquid . . . becoming increasingly aware of himself watching Bobby . . . then of the difference in Bobbys posture, the attitude of his shoulders, the deflated look and feeling coming from Bobby, as well as a sense of confusion. He watched Bobby forcing a smile on his face from time to time, eventually giving up, and, from time to time, shrugging his shoulders as if in response to some inner discussion.

Eventually Bobby got up, still silent, and sat at the table with the puzzle and leaned his head on a hand as he stared at the pieces, from time to time picking one up and looking at it, turning it over and over, lackadaisically trying to fit it into several pieces, then replacing it on the table, his hand lingering on it for several minutes before he eventually started pushing other pieces around, his shoulders slumping more and more. . . . In time he stood and tried to stretch himself straight, but only partially succeeded then turned and looked at Moishe and started to say something, then turned and went to the bedroom.

Moishe wasnt surprised to hear Bobby having a restless night, a couple of times mumbling aloud and flailing his arms, as he did on the first night of finding one of his enemies. Nor was he surprised when he stayed in bed longer than usual the next morning, getting up sluggishly and obviously having to force himself to work out, the session shorter than usual. Moishe left Bobby alone and stayed busy in his workshop.

Bobby wandered around the apartment restlessly, then got dressed and told Moishe he was going out for a while. He wandered around the area aimlessly, feeling the cold breeze and huddling into his jacket, continuously adjusting the scarf around his neck, then thrusting his hands deeply into his pockets. From time to time he would look around, not really aware of anything except the warmth of the sun on his face and the lack of cold air blowing down his neck. He wandered toward the river, strolling across the street and almost getting hit by a car that jammed on its brakes and skidded sideways, stopping just a few feet from him and he stared at the driver who was screaming at him, then sprinted to the sidewalk, confused, not certain where he was, feeling the surge of panic and adrenaline in his gut, rushing down the street, bumping into a couple of people who told him to watch where he was going, You think you own the street you dumb ass son of a bitch – the adrenaline shoving him down the street, confused, until he staggered to the railing by the river and leaned against it, wondering how in the hell he got there and what the fuck he was doing there, suddenly shaking with fear and collapsed on a bench. He sat quietly for a while, then got up when the chill started him shivering, and started walking toward home, trying to continually remind himself to stay alert, but still he would find himself walking down a street unaware of how he got there, more and more frightened until he was almost in a total panic, sweat running down his sides as he walked faster and faster, from time to time breaking into a trot. When he finally reached the steps he rushed down, stumbling and almost falling, and leaned against a wall in the shadows, panting, trembling, afraid someone might come rushing down the stairs and he would be unable to defend himself, yet unable to move deeper into the darkness toward home . . . afraid too that Moishe might see him there and be pissed at him or ashamed of him and he didnt want to be embarrassed by being found leaning against the wall, sweating, unable to move, so he shoved himself off the wall and started stumbling through the darkness. . . .

When he got home he yanked his clothes off and went right into the whirlpool, unable to think of anything else to do, aware his entire body was trembling, and when he felt the hot water swirling around him he started to feel safe and he began to relax and feel a part of the flowing water.

Moishe continued working, sighing audibly when he heard Bobby come in. When he heard the water draining from the whirlpool he glanced at the clock and realized that it was hunger he had been feeling in his stomach.

Bobby was silent and listless the rest of the day and the days following. His head was tilted forward, his shoulders rounded, and he toyed with his food, often leaving some on his plate. He continued to work out but without any real enthusiasm, and definitely without pushing himself as he had.

Moishe spent as much time as possible in his work shop, always battling with his thinking and his tongue, concentrating as hard as possible on his work; sighing, inwardly, from the bottom of his toes when Bobby would wander into the work shop and ask Moishe what he was doing. After the days of silence, Moishe wanted to let his tongue rattle on and on, but spoke very slowly to prevent that from happening, and showed Bobby what was wrong and how he was going to fix it, and Bobby would nod and from time to time pick up a tool and hold it for a while, then put it down, Moishe tempted to ask him if he wanted to fix it, remembering how much he enjoyed showing Bobby how to fix things.

Bobby suddenly became aware that he was holding a pair of pliers and put them down and nodded his head at them then turned around and walked slowly from the work shop.

Moishe had been hoping that Bobby had come out of his depression, but he continued to be silent the remainder of the day and during dinner. Bobby ate, but still without enthusiasm. When they finished eating they both remained at the table, Moishe trying to force himself to put the dishes in the sink, but, for some unknown reason, unable to move so he sat trying not to stare at Bobby, and not to be obvious when he did, his mind seemingly a blank, breathing deeply and slowly, then slowly straightened, Is long time since you see your mother, ya?

Bobby nodded his head as he continued to stare absently.

Moishe continued to look at Bobby for a moment. . . . You think maybe you should be writing a note?

Bobby blinked his eyes and looked at Moishe, confused, Huh????

Just short – Bobby still had the dazed, confused look on his face. Moishe shrugged and smiled slightly, Maybe she worries?

Bobby frowned, You think she be worrin?

Ya, I think maybe so.

You really be thinking so Mush?

Ya –

Bobby continued to stare, then shook his head, Sheeit, I dont want the moms to be worryin, but how I be writen her a letter – looking at Moishe totally puzzled.

Moishe shrugged and smiled, A few words only. Youre alright. Safe.

The same expression was still on Bobbys face, You think the moms be really wantin that?

Ya – nodding his head enthusiastically – O ya.

Bobby continued looking at Moishe . . . I dont know Mush . . . Why she wantin a letter from me?

Shes wanting to know youre safe.

But she be knowin that Mush. I be seein Jesse when I goes to the hood and he be telliner.

Ya, but is not the same thing. I think she also like a letter.

Bobby still looked puzzled and shook his head, Okay, if you sayin so. But what I be writin?

Just a note. Youre telling her everythings fine . . . youre with a friend . . . not to worry — shrugs — Just so shes feeling good and not worry — getting up and getting the paper and pen and placing them in front of Bobby, Is easy. . . .

Mush, I dont. . . . I never wrote no letter . . . I. . . .

Is fine . . . fine. Here, just say, Dear Moma, Im —

I dont know Mush — shrugging and writing it on the paper.

Moishe continued to dictate the short note. When Bobby finished writing he leaned back and looked at it. . . . There it be Mush.

Moishe smiled at him, Ya . . . you do a good job . . . very good.


Bobby got up earlier the next morning, though still later than usual, only lying in bed a relatively short time trying to get back to sleep, and worked out a little more enthusiastically, from time to time attempting to envision Raul and how he would kill him, but unable to resurrect the image, but continued to work out, forcing himself to finish his routine, not certain why he was doing it.

Several days later they walked slowly through the neighborhood, buying a few pieces of fruit, stopping at a vendor for hot roasted chestnuts and went to the river and stood at the railing and watched the traffic on the water, bundled in their warm clothes, scarves around their necks, wool watch hats pulled down around their ears, warm gloves on their hands, silent except for an occasional short comment about something seen, feeling the cold air but also the warm sun, feeling an inner glow that obviously did not come from the sun.

Bobby was puzzled, feeling that something had sort of shifted around inside him, not knowing what, but he knew something was different, that something had moved even if it was a tiny bit like how a booster move jus a touch when he see a mark . . . but whatever it was he felt something new for Moishe . . . not like it be something gone an new thing there, but like something added to what be there . . . like he an Mushie be connected with rope instead a string . . . whatever it be, it be there an it makeim feel gooood. . . .

                                        an some-

how he be seein Mushie different, like how he see those old beat up buildins. Used to be he see them like tumblin down bricks, but now he see they be strong muthafuckas stayin up there like that even when everybody tryin to tear their asses down . . . yeah, they be righteous the way they still standin . . . an Mushie righteous the way he keep standin up. Sheeit, he like some muthafuckin mountain, or that river out there, cant be nothin stoppin it or Mush.

A sense of peace pervaded the apartment the following days, Bobby continuing his routine, Moishe his, Bobby spending hours each day with Moishe in the work shop, relaxed, enjoying fixing things Moishe kept in repair for old friends. One day Moishe gave him an old hot plate to fix and Bobby found the needed part in less than 2 minutes and they celebrated with high fives and a bowl of ice cream with chocolate sauce.

That night they sat around the table talking for a while after dinner. Eventually Bobby looked at the clock and got up, I got to be goin out Mush.

Moishe put a very strong effort into not allowing the sinking feeling in his gut to be reflected on his face, but could feel that he was failing, especially when he noticed he didnt put on his scarf.

I got to see can I find my brother Jesse an see whats happenin — Moishe feeling a great relief as the churning knots in his gut seemed to flow away — You be cool Mush . . . an doan be fuckin up that puzzle. Bobby giggled and left.

Moishe sat at the table for a moment listening to the thoughts rattling around in his head, then shook his head and got up, No, not tonight. No philosophizing. Tonight we/re a reader, we/re a worker, we/re a puzzle putter together, we/re a whatever, but we/re not a philosopher.

The walk through the cellar to the street was like a decompression chamber, a chance to get used to the cold, without the wind, before going up on the street to be hit, literally, with the reality of the weather now that winter was closing in.

When Bobby got up to the street he stood for a moment getting accustomed to the wind, standing straight, shoulders back, allowing the wind to hit his face and get as deep into him as possible before moving. He knew he had to stay alert and you cant do that if youre worried about being cold, or protecting yourself from the wind, so he stood there, breathing deeply and slowly, until he was able to breathe normally with the wind in his face, and not have to hunch over to protect himself just to breathe. No matter what came down he was always going to be at least one up on the spics.

It seemed he walked further than usual before he started seeing people on the streets. Might be he was right, that the only people on the street in this weather be people who had to be there . . . dope fiens and thieves. Seem like everybody else be in a bar or home watching the tv. But the kids be out. They always be out on the street, never wanting to spend too much time in the house, always be out in the street running around an not hearing all those babies and kids yellin an screamin in the houses, either in your own apartment or everyone elses. Bad enough you got to be hearing all that noise in your own house, but when everyone else be screamin too it really be too much, an the streets the only place you can find some peace and quiet, as well as freedom, least aint nobody out in the street asking you to do this or do that. Better you be standing in a doorway with your friens, out of the wind trying to stay warm.

Although he didnt think the spics would come to his

hood, he still took his usual precautions and went to the roof of a building to look over the general area, then crossed the roofs in a haphazard pattern, but knowing where he was heading. After checking out the area for more than a few blocks beyond his turf, he went down to the street and slowly circled in on the area where Jesse hung out, going through buildings, cellars and alleys as usual.

When he got to the candy store Jesse and his friends hung out in he did not look directly into the store, but from the side of his eyes and continued walking until he reached the corner then turned north and continued until he reached a building in the middle of the block then went in and up to the roof and walked back south west and sat on the roof, in the shadow of an abutment, impossible to be seen from anywhere except behind him, and he constantly checked over his shoulder, his ears always alert to any change in sound or feel of the breeze, or behavior of the pigeons who were always walking or flying around.

The abutment blocked the wind, but sitting still was cold so from time to time he would stand and lean against the abutment, or squat, still in the shadows, putting his hands against his face to warm his nose and cheeks. He was doing a couple of slow squats to keep warm when he noticed Tomboy, Jesses number one man, going into the store. He stood still keeping alert and in a few minutes he saw Jesse coming down the street. He wasnt certain if Jesse and Tomboy were going to just hang out or go somewhere so he followed his instinct to rush down to the street right now in case Jesse and Tomboy were going to split right away.

Bobby was in the doorway across from the candy store by the time Jesse pushed the door open and went in. Like everyone else he stopped right away and banged his body and blew on his hands to get warm, before going to the back where his friends were. Before Jesse could sit down, Bobby had gone to the pay phone in the liquor store next to where he was and called the candy store pay phone and when one of the kids picked up the phone he asked for Jesse. Jesse thought he was joking and at first didnt get up, but when the guy insisted he went to the phone booth and laughed into the phone, Yeah, sure, what you want sucker?

Bobby spoke slowly, quietly and clearly, Dont be yellin out my name Jess.

Bob —

Now what the fuck I be sayin!

Yeah, sure — closing the phone booth door, back to friends.

How you doin?

I be fine man. Where you at?

Dont be makin no difference Jess.

Hey, how you be knowin this number? You dont be hangin here.

Hey, I make it my business to be knowin lots a things.

Damn, that be slick bro.

You okay though, right?

Yeah. I be cool. Everybody cool.

Whach you be hearin about them spics?

Jesse started laughing then quickly stopped but continued chuckling, They be goin crazy bro. I hear they be callin you the phantom and be scared shitless. They really be fucked up.

They dont bother you?

Sheeit, they aint nowheres round here man, you know that.

Jus checkin Jess. How the moms?

She be cool bro, like always. But she be gettin a letter, hey, hey, you be writin the moms a letter? Yeah, I betcha you be writin, eh? I wonderin my ass off about that an it be you right enough I betchya.

Bobby was grinning widely and chuckled but remained silent.

Seem like she read it dozen times bro. Check it out, she doan know but I be seeiner puttin it under her pillow . . . damn, I was wonderin my ass off about that an it be you all the time, aint it? Sheeit, I know it be you.

She like it then.

Man, she jus sit there quiet seem like for hours, no yellin at no one, you dig?

Bobby was nodding his head, Yeah. . . .

She sure enough dig it bro.

Right on. Dont be tellin no one it be me on the phone, you dig?

Hey. . . .

I gotta split.

Damn, you be too much bro . . . muthafuckin phantom . . . sheeit! right the fuck on!

I be talkin to you again Jess. Be cool.

You righteous bro. You be right the fuck on righteous. Muthafuckin phantom . . . Jesse was giggling and shaking his head as Bobby hung up and stepped out the door an into the midst of the people walking the street, turning south at the corner and weaving his way home, smiling all the way.


Bobbys mother sat by the window, looking at the street as she always did, seeing the lights and traffic, but unaware of anything in particular. Seemed like she spent most of her life sitting and looking out this window, freetime anyways. Most of the time the youngins be frettin over somethin, but right now they were quiet cept for some gigglin and stuff. She wonder how long her Bobby be gone? Long time seems like. But Jesse keep tellin her he be alright, but she dont be seein that for her ownself but he wrote her a letter an say he love her. Dont nobody ever be writin her that before. Some say it, but she knows what they be meanin. The youngins be sayin it, but this be the first time somebody be writin it . . . to her, an it be her Bobby who wrote it. She be readin the letter everytime there be no one hangin on her arm, an it be makin her face feel funny. She be wondering why until she realized she was smiling. She be likin that. She like how her face feel when she be smiling. Firs time it be hard, like her face dont know it can smile, like it be afraid. But eventually the smile came naturally to her face, and then she became aware of how nice it felt, sort of soothing, making her feel pretty, or at least reminding her of how she looked as a very young girl before Bobby was born, sort of free to dance around and spin, always wanting a wide skirt like in the old movies so she could twirl and have her skirt follow her like a large circle swishing through the air . . . it sure seemed like there was a time when she ran through the house as a little girl, barefooted on her tippy toes, feeling free and pretty, and sometimes just sitting on a chair, her feet still not reaching to the floor, and wiggling her toes, Lord, it seemed she be doing that for hours, just sitting there watching her toes wigglin and wonderin how all that happen, how she get her toes to wiggle like that? and it felt so good to just sit there wigglin those toes, but it seemed like all of a sudden she be looking at Bobbys itty-bitty toes and she dont be doin no more dancing or even thinking of twirling around and around, her big skirts swishing through the air, and maybe that be when her face forgot how to smile and her toes to wiggle, but she could sit here thinkin how her Bobby say he love her an her face be smilin an it feel good, an she could feel her toes wiggling and wanted to take a peak at them to see if they were the same old toes that used to wiggle, but must be because theys the only toes she ever had, and all these things going through her mind made her smile more and more, it all seemed so silly but that be fine too, anything that make her smile be fine cause it sure did feel good to feel her face smiling, an who cared anyway about the nonsense going through her mind, so she sat leaning over the back of the old, worn-out couch, looking down at the street, feeling her face smiling even more as she thought about when she be goin to bed how she take her Bobbys letter out from under her pillow an be readin it again fore she go to sleep.

Moishe was in the workshop when Bobby returned, surprised he was back so soon, trying to continue to concentrate on what he was repairing, but his hands stopped moving and he leaned his head toward the door, listening to the sounds of Bobby taking off his jacket and hanging it up, straining to hear his footsteps, it seeming to take forever to determine what direction he was walking, then almost shouting when he realized Bobby was walking in his direction . . . and then it seemed like an eternity before he felt him beside him wanting desperately to see the expression on his face, yet frightened of what it might tell him so he just stood there trying to keep his hands moving and his eyes focused on them, remaining silent but after a couple of seconds his mouth started moving seemingly of its own accord, Youre seeing your brother?

We be talkin.

So, how he is?

He be fine.

Moishe sensed something coming from Bobby, and heard something in his voice, and turned and looked at him and something in him opened and blossomed and gave a long, happy sigh of relief when he saw the grin on Bobbys face, So. . . .

Bobby looked at him for a moment . . . You sure be workin a lot lately.

Ya . . . is keeping me out of trouble.

Bobby chuckled, Yeah, we got to be keepin you off the streets. You a bad dude Mush.

Moishe smiled at Bobby, relief continuing to flow through him in waves, Ya, no woman is safe when Im on the loose.

Right on Mush.

They were silent for a moment, both looking at the appliance Moishe was working on.

A grin was working its way into Bobbys smile, Jesse say the moms be gettin a letter.

So????

Yeah. He say she dig it.

Moishe had to blink back tears of gratitude and was silent, just standing still for a moment, then nodded his head feeling as if his heart was overflowing.

Check it out Mush, he say she dont be yellin for a while and be puttin it under her pillow . . . the letter.

Eventually they looked at each other, smiling, grinning, nodding, eyes locked, staring, Moishe feeling warm, tender, and grateful; Bobby filled, again, with unfamiliar feelings, but somehow it was alright, he sort of felt connected with something . . . he knew he was feeling connected to Moishe, but it seemed like there was something else too, like he was a little bigger somehow, but he wasnt sure how. Eventually a few words came out of Bobbys mouth, You be wishin a lot, huh?

Moishe shrugged, A long time Bobby.

You be wishin for a whole lots a people, eh?

Moishe looked at Bobby for a moment, smiling, In so many years – shrugging – whos knowing how many.

They continued looking at each other and eventually Bobby picked up the appliance and looked at it for a moment then replaced it, Who that for?

Ohhh, an old friend. Like everything, ya?

Yeah – continuing to look at it, turning it a few inches this way a few inches that way.

A few days later Moishe and Bobby were working and Moishe told Bobby he would be right back. Bobby continued working on the toaster Moishe had given him to repair. Eventually Moishe came back to the workshop, a grin running all around his face, not from ear to ear, but around his neck too. He started to say something, but giggled instead. Bobby looked at him and smiled, shaking his head, Damn Mush, I aint never seen a shit-eatin grin like you be havin on your face – Moishe chuckling, Bobby laughing, and Moishe tugging him by the arm and leading him to the kitchen. When they turned the corner and were able to see the table Bobby stopped and stared, bug eyed, Moishe looking at him grinning and glowing like he hadnt glowed in years, more light coming from Moishe than the candles on the cake. Finally Bobby turned and looked at Moishe, What the fuck be this Mush?

Moishe had to concentrate to be able to speak, but finally the words came out of his mouth, Im thinking soon it must be your birthday, ya?

Bobby thought for a second . . . Sheeit, guess so. Caint tell what day it be livin down here an all . . . no school or tv tellin what day it is.

November 20 . . . soon is thanksgiving.

Well check that out. It be thanksgivin week, usually, 21st. Sheeit, that be tomorrow. How you be knowin that bro, I aint never said nothin?

Moishes grin seemed to be growing every second as he shrugged, Whose knowing, I figure somehow. Fourteen?

Bobby stared at Moishe for a moment, then looked at the cake and walked over to the table and counted the candles, Right the fuck on Mush, fourteen mutha fuckin candles. Damn! – shaking his head in complete wonderment – You be. . . .

Moishe picked up the cake and held it, So youre making a wish.

What Im wishin for?

Is your wish. Youre not telling me.

Bobby stared at Moishe for a moment, then the cake, then back and forth a few times, then closed his eyes and tilted his head back and after a moment opened his eyes and looked at Moishe, Okay man, I wished.

Good, now, youre blowing out the candles, ya?

Bobby grinned and shook his head as he looked at Moishe, You be lookin like Santa Claus Mush – giggling, then taking a deep breath and blowing all the candles out in one sudden breath.

So, Santa Claus is granting you wish – putting the cake on the table – Now youre sitting down.

Bobby was so caught up in staring at the grin on Moishes face that it was a few moments before he noticed the party favors on the table. He looked at them for a moment, then back at Moishe who was sitting with a party hat on his head. Bobby stared for a moment then started laughing, laughing so hard he almost cried and lost his breath, Moishe pointing to the hat by Bobby and gesturing that he should put it on, the both of them laughing and shaking their heads, Moishe finally getting up and putting Bobbys hat on him and they sat at the kitchen table in an apartment under the streets of the abandoned and deserted south Bronx with party hats on their heads, laughing, shaking, twitching, pointing at each other and laughing harder, louder, blowing the paper horns with the unrolling paper and feather at the end at each other, leaning across the table tickling each others nose, tears dripping down their cheeks, popping the poppers and watching the streamers and confetti float through the air, gasping for air, struggling to speak, Moishe pointing at Bobby and shaking and laughing and it went on and on until they both ran out of energy and fell back against their chairs and it seemed they were approaching a semblance of normality when Moishe started singing happy birthday, Bobby staring, amazed at first, then started laughing and his head fell, literally, on the table with a loud THUMP and that started a new round of laughter and finally Bobby grabbed his crotch with both hands and limped to the bathroom, laughing, shaking his head, and stumbling, losing his balance, uncertain he would get there without wetting his pants, and when he returned he plopped in his chair and tried to speak, but couldnt summon up the necessary energy and they both sat in silence and after a few minutes Moishe served them both ice cream then cut the cake. It was still many minutes before they could speak without bursting into uncontrolled laughter. Finally Bobby stopped chewing long enough to look at Moishe with the deepest of affection.

They smiled at each other for a few minutes, then Moishe pushed a small gift-wrapped box across the table, Happy Birthday.

Bobby stared at it for a moment, then looked at Moishe in disbelief, then picked up the box and looked at it, wondering what it was, glancing from time to time at Moishe who was smiling mischievously and bouncing up and down in his chair impatiently, expectantly, wanting to yell at Bobby to hurry up and open it, but remaining silent and savoring the expression on Bobbys face as he fondled the box, looking at it and Moishe, then slowly peeling the paper off and opening the box and staring at the computer/watch it contained, holding it carefully, lovingly, in his hands as if it were an offering of some kind, looking at it almost as a parent looks at a child there was so much awe, respect and affection in his expression . . . a long time elapsing before he could look at Moishe, but was still unable to speak, so he looked back at the watch cradled in the palms of his hands, feeling as if he had never seen anything so incredible, so miraculous in his life . . . as if he had been waiting all his life, or longer, for this gift and now that he finally had it, holding it in his hands was even more wonderful than the dream of having it . . . as if for the first time in his life the reality exceeded the expectation. . . .

eventually Bobby gently unstrapped the watch from the box and put it on his wrist and turned his wrist this way and that as he looked at it, then took the directions out and started to read them, amazed, and looked at Moishe, Damn Mush, this thing be doin everything – and looked back at the directions with even more astonishment, How you be knowin I be wantin this – Moishe shrugged and smiled – I dont even be knowin this my own self til now . . . damn. This be the farthest out watch I ever heard of. Goddamn bro, you be somethin else . . . I. . . . And again Bobby was speechless and just looked at Moishe with the most loving and tender expression Moishe felt he had ever seen in his life. . . .

On Thanksgiving day Moishe started preparing food early in the morning, literally bouncing up and down. Bobby watched him for a minute before letting him know he was in the room.

In the afternoon Moishe said everything was ready and he put a duck on the table and surrounded it with bowls of food and gravy. Bobby stared at the food arranged around the dark brown duck, every bowl or platter a different color, everything steaming hot and smelling wonderful.

Whats that Mush?

Bavarian duck . . . from old country.

Bobby stared, fascinated, at the table as Moishe carved the duck and fixed Bobbys plate, putting everything just so, carefully dripping the gravy just so, placing the plate in front of Bobby just so, Moishe continuing to stand and lean toward Bobby, So . . . eat . . . try already the food. Bobby smiled and grabbed his knife and fork and got to the duck and looked at the piece on the tip of his fork for a moment, then slid it off with this teeth and closed his eyes as he slowly chewed, then opened his eyes and smiled and nodded his head, Hey Mush, this be righteous – quickly putting another piece in his mouth and Moishe sat down and beamed at Bobby as he chewed and then ventured onto the potato pancakes and cabbage, his eyes opening wider with each bite – God *damn* Mush, you be a righteous cook, hmmmmm . . . real righteous. This be outta sight bro.

They continued talking and leaning back in their chairs for a while after finishing their meal, then Moishe cleared the table and said, So. . . . Now we take a ride, ya?

Where we goin Mush?

Prospect Park

Visit ya tree, eh?

Ya . . . we visit my tree.

A light snow flurry started as they walked to the subway, and by the time they got up to the street in Brooklyn the snow increased but the breeze had almost completely stopped and large, white flakes of snow were drifting to the ground and it seemed to change the color of the air and everything they saw. A thin layer was already sticking to the ground and they could feel it under their feet, and almost convince themselves they could hear it crunch over the noise of the streets, feeling the flakes gently brush against their cheeks, resting on an eye lid until it was blinked off, stopping and opening their mouths and tilting their heads back and allowing the snow to drift into their mouths . . . walking across the same area of the park they had the last time, and though there were no kites being flown, there were still kids running and yelling, an occasional Frisbee floating dream-like, birds suddenly creating little whirlpools of snow, bared tree limbs and evergreens almost losing their identity in the snow-heavy air, green grass still peeking through the thin layer of white, the lake and willow trees in the distance having a fairy tale feeling about them, the sounds of voices and distant traffic muted by the snow, everything soft and gentle, and the closer they got to Moishes tree, the more it dominated their vision, the larger it appeared, its limbs bent from the weight of the snow.

They leaned against the trunk and looked out at the lake, the trees lining the shore, seeing birds suddenly flutter from somewhere within the trees, standing on brown earth that gradually turned white a few feet from where they stood. After a while Bobby squatted and from time to time tossed a small pebble into the lake, the ripples seeming to change colors as they rolled away from the shore. He would wait until the water was still, watching the snow fall and be absorbed by the lake, then toss another pebble, then stopped as he watched a few ducks swim by, then stood up, They be lucky you not gettin ahold a them. They damn sure wouldnt be swimmin they asses off now — smiling at Moishe, who smiled back and put his hand on Bobbys shoulder and squeezed, Bobby standing still and smiling up at him. They stood like that for many minutes, an occasional flake of snow working its way through the limbs of Moishes willow tree and gently brushing a cheek or resting on a nose before melting.

They left the protection of the tree and wandered around the lake for a while, stopping to watch a couple of young kids tug their sleighs, trying to ride down the slopes even though there wasnt enough snow on the ground, but every now and then they would hit a patch and they would glide forward for a few feet and screech with delight, and for a moment Moishe remembered pulling Karl-Heinz on his sleigh, and riding down the hill with him by the willow tree in the old country, but he let the image disappear, to be absorbed by the snow, and the years, knowing how painful it was to hold onto those memories, so he watched them come, enjoyed them for a brief moment in time, then let them go and continued strolling through the snow with Bobby, looking, listening, enjoying. . . .

They both felt so relaxed, so content, so stimulated by the wonderful feast they had had, the festive atmosphere they enjoyed while eating, and now the snow, the voices, the laughter and the tree, that they could have walked for ever . . . but they also knew they would get tired before they got there. So, while the sun was still barely discernible through the snow they started back to the subway, and home.

The next night Bobby decided to go back to the hood. He almost regretted the decision before he left the abandoned area, but he followed his gut feeling. It was cold, windy, and he pulled his jacket as tight as possible around his neck, but the wind continued to blow flakes of wet snow down his neck, but still he kept his head raised enough to always be able to see what was happening. He covered the last half a mile on roof tops and stopped when he was on the fringe of the spic turf. He had nothing definite in mind but, as before, he figured hed know what to do at the right time. He stood out of the wind against a chimney, carefully watching the street below. Suddenly something caught his eye in the distance and he stared to the east a few blocks and recognized the walk of one of Rauls friends and quickly ran down the stairs to the street. He stayed in the shadows of the doorway checking out the street, but part of his mind was still remembering yesterday and the food and the ducks and the kids in the park and the snow and how warm and comfortable he felt standing next to Moishe . . . and safe . . . yeah, safe from everything. Not that there was anything to feel safe from in Prospect Park, or eating the duck, but somehow he felt safe now, but he shook his head clear of all thoughts as he noticed the guy walking down the street, the limp identifying him from almost any distance, and when he was a few yards away Bobby scooped up as much wet snow as possible and suddenly stepped in front of the guy and as he grinned in his face he shoved the snow down the back of the guys neck, Bobby holding him for a couple of seconds, grinning, then let the guy go and quickly disappeared back into the building as the guy jumped up and down, yelling, stamping his feet trying to get rid of the icy snow dripping down his back and Bobby could hear him faintly for a short time as he ran up the stairs to the roof, onto the next few roofs south, then down the stairs, east along the street and long lost in the shadows by the time the guy could connect a name with the face that had grinned at him.

Bobby told Moishe what had happened, laughing the entire time, a genuine smile on Moishes face when Bobby described the look of shock on the guys face when he felt the ice going down his neck.

\*

Moishe and Bobby had gone for a walk, and it was late afternoon when they started home, happy that the wind was at their backs. The air was heavy with dampness, the clouds low, the sky overcast and a faint light made their world seem soft and gentle, giving everything a dreamlike quality as Christmas lights and displays in store windows were softened by the air. Bobby was really digging the way the lights sparkled and shimmered, and kept pointing it out to Moishe.

Ya, is always nice with the lights and displays, Oh, the next street is a card store, you can get your cards.

Sheeit, we be havin a few weeks for Christmas Mush.

Ya, but why not get them now. You wait and each day is something getting in the way and soon . . . too late, ya?

Bobby chuckled, Okay bro, we be gettinem now – shaking his head.

When they left the store Moishe suggested that Bobby might want to get presents for his momma and brothers and sister.

I aint got no braid Mush, how Im gonna be buyin presents?

Im owing you money for the work, ya?

Work? You mean fixin the funky things??? sheeit, that dont be no work bro.

Moishe shrugged, so what I do with my money? You help me so I pay you. Is fair.

Bobby grinned at him, Hey, I aint turnin down no braid. You givin, Im takin.


When they finished eating dinner Bobby started looking at the Christmas cards he had bought that day, When you figure I should be writin these out Mush?

Moishe shrugged, I guess now is good.

Bobby continued to toy with the cards. . . . Yeah . . . guess so. Seem weird be sending cards to my family.

Youre not sending Christmas cards?

Well, we just sorta give cards to each other, know what Im sayin?

O . . . ya.

Bobby looked at the cards of a moment. . . . What I be puttin on here?

Moishe shrugged, Like always. . . .

Bobby nodded, staring at the cards, Hmmmm. . . .

You tell them you love them.

Bobby continued staring at the cards, frowning, then looked at Moishe, Seems different writin it on the card, know what Im sayin? I be handin the moms a card, or Jesse and hugginem an like that . . . but writin somethin on the card. . . .

Moishe looked at him for a minute, smiling, then said, You just say, Dear Mom at the top and Love, Bobby at the bottom.

Bobby looked at Moishe. . . . Yeah, I guess. . . . Somehow mailinem to your own house seems weird – shrugging – but I guess that be cool.

When he finished signing the cards and addressing and stamping the envelopes, Bobby looked at Moishe for a moment, looking embarrassed. . . . You go with me for gettin the Christmas presents Mush?

Moishes face lit up instantly, Ya. . . . Ya, I go with you.

Bobbys eyes were lowered, still embarrassed, Like, this aint my hood Mush an Im not knowin the stores, know what Im sayin?

Moishes smile was tender, loving, and completely understanding, Ya, I know. Its already a lot of fun to go. . . . Like long ago. . . . Ya, ya, we go tomorrow, maybe the stores not too crowded.

Bobby looked as if a thousand ton weight had been lifted from his back and he sat up straight and smiled, Right on bro.

Late in the morning they left the house to start their shopping. Moishe knew he and Bobby would have a good time, and they did. It was different for Bobby this year. He wasnt sure exactly how or why, but it was more fun strolling through the stores with Moishe who seemed to be laughing at everything and enjoying everything and having such a good time Bobby just assumed he was having a good time too, what the hell, why not?

They roamed from store to store, strolling up and down the aisles, spending most of their time looking at toys and games for Bobbys brothers and sister. By the time they were hungry Bobby had bought a couple of presents and felt cool having the bag hang from his hand.

They continued shopping after lunch and though Bobby was more restrained, he was just as enthusiastic and happy and checked out everything he thought someone might like. After buying a few more presents he frowned at Moishe and told him he didnt know what to get his mother.

What it is youre buying before?

Mostly cigarettes . . . like if I had the bread I getter a carton.

Moishe pursed his lips for a moment . . . Maybe shes liking a nice sweater, keep her warm.

You think so Mush?

Ya. I think maybe shes liking a nice pretty sweater . . . keep her warm, ya?

Yeah. Spect you right. She sometimes be shiverin, guess maybe a sweater be right on.

When they reached the womans sweater section Bobby suddenly stopped and stared, confused, when he saw all the different kinds and types of sweaters there were, and Moishe just sort of took over, and when he asked Bobby what was his mommas favorite color Bobby just looked at him and shrugged. Moishe looked through them and finally ended up with a couple of styles and colors and when Bobby couldnt decide Moishe shrugged and held them up and said theyd better take both of them. It took a second for the information to sink in but when it did Bobby smiled, Right on bro, that be a good way solve that problem.

Now that the important purchase had been made they were free to just roam around the stores and look at whatever they were in the mood for and, from time to time, pick up another little gift for one of the kids. Bobby was still excited by just walking around, knowing he wouldnt be hassled by anyone because he was with Moishe. He had never seen so many different things in his life, not even on tv. He didnt even know what some of the stuff was for, but he had a ball strolling around and looking, being in another world, one so different from his he couldnt compare them, and he was safe, this he knew even though he felt conspicuous from time to time.

Moishe allowed his memory to go wherever it wanted even if it would, in time, lead to pain. How long since he had such a wonderful time shopping???? Oh . . . who cares. Right now is the only important time, and right now he was feeling wonderful and enjoying the holiday season, and actually looking forward to Christmas, maybe the last time in his life he would have anything like a family Christmas.

That night Bobby went back to the hood to see Jesse and tell him where and when to meet him so he could give the presents to him for the family.

The next morning Bobby and Moishe went through their usual chattering at breakfast, but when they finished eating their talking sort of dwindled into silence, and they looked at their plates for a moment, then at each other, and eventually their smirks turned into smiles when they realized they were both thinking the same thing, and they got up and got dressed and went back to the stores.

A few days before Christmas they bought a tree. Moishe very carefully unpacked the ornaments and lights and other decorations, some of them from their first Christmas in America. He tested the lights, replacing the bulbs that were burned out.

Is a long time since I used these decorations – smiling at Bobby – Ya, first since Gertrude is dying.

Bobby watched, fascinated, as Moishe unpacked all the decorations, dusting off a large wreath, fluffing the ribbon, then putting it on the outside of the front door. Bobby stared at him speechless, and when he finished Moishe closed the door and looked at Bobby and shrugged, Why not? Bobby just shook his head.

Bobby picked up the ornaments very carefully, for a while, then became less timid in his handling of them, but continued to watch Moishe to see exactly how he was doing it, then felt a sense of excitement as he carefully placed each one on a branch, then stepping back and looking for bare spots, or just looking at the tree and smiling and shaking his head, Damn, it jus keep lookin better n better.

When they finished with the ornaments they started with the tinsel, Bobby starting by putting one strand at a time in carefully selected spots, Moishe smiling as he watched, then more and more on at a time until finally he was standing back and laughing and tossing them at the tree, Moishe joining him as he walked around the tree tossing tinsel.

The tinsel boxes were empty and Moishe turned on the lights and they stepped back and looked at the tree, Moishe looking more at Bobby than the tree. Bobby was smiling, beaming, and shaking his head, Damn bro, I aint never seen no tree like this. This be far out Mush . . . Gauddamn!!!! Damn!!!!

They put the presents under the tree and Bobby sat on the floor a few feet from the tree and just looked, smiling, shaking his head. . . . Damn!!!! That tree be somethin else. I bet the kids be diggin it they see it – looking at Moishe, grinning – I bet they be diggin some ice cream too bro.

Moishe laughed and got them ice cream and put on a record of gospel music. Bobby looked at him surprised, Hey Mush, where you be gettin that?

Same store Im getting the Christmas carols. While Im in the store theyre playing this, so – shrugging and smiling.

Bobby shook his head and laughed, Check it out – moving his body in time to the music.

After a few minutes a different song started playing, and Bobby stopped moving, then stopped smiling. When he handed his empty bowl to Moishe he started frowning and staring at the base of the tree . . . continuing to stare, the sound of his voice reflecting his expression: flat, almost toneless and disconnected, Maria be diggin this song. . . . She really diggin gospel. She be diggin Christmas too, all the time talkin about the baby jesus. Seem like Christmas the day she be lookin for the most. Guess she dont got to worry none bout that now.

Moishe watched Bobby as he got up and went over to the

tree and knelt down next to the presents and started looking at them, picking them up and putting them down, moving as if in a daze. Moishe took the record off and the sudden silence seemed to scream through the room and create a black hole that threatened to suck them into oblivion until he put the carols back on. Bobby continued to move the presents around, checking the name tags, feeling the ribbons, checking out the bows, all his movements detached, dreamlike.

Bobby sat quietly for a moment, then took an ornament off the tree and let it hang from his fingertips for a second, then put it back, touching it with his fingertip, staring at the point of light reflecting from it, lowering his hand and continuing to stare . . . eventually shrugging slightly, then standing, Im beat Mush. Gonna get my ass to bed.

Ya . . . is late and very busy day – watching Bobby force his body into sluggish movement, his shoulders rounded. It seemed like a very long time before Moishe heard the sound of Bobby going to bed, a slight sound as if he had lowered himself slowly and carefully onto the mattress, and then not move except to breathe just barely enough to stay alive, as if he were hiding from a drunken guard with a club who wanted to bash his head in and break all his bones. Moishe leaned for what seemed an eternity against the sink, almost seeing the pain in Bobbys body and mind, struggling with the knots in his gut, the tears struggling to flow from his eyes, the terrible black, cancerous sadness and longing pushing at the back of his throat and churning through his body, a sadness that filled every cell of his body and mind, a pain that forced Moishes eyes closed for a moment, slowly becoming aware of the tears trickling down his cheek, tears that felt so cold and wet as if they came not from within him but from some foreign and alien place of blackness and ice, his head bending lower and lower until he became aware of a groan starting deep within him, ripping his gut, growling in his throat, then slowly forcing itself through his twisted mouth with a deep sense and sound of unbearable anguish and Moishe shoved himself from the sink and staggered across the room to a chair and fell on it, supporting himself by leaning on the table, no longer seeing the tree with the ornaments and tinsel reflecting the lights, the presents seeming to have disappeared and even though he knew the lights were on and he could see the familiar walls and objects of a lifetime, he felt only darkness, a horribly familiar darkness, an impenetrable darkness of such heavy substance it threatened to crush the life from his body, a darkness he had suffered and survived for so many years, so many times, a darkness filled with demons he thought he had left behind many, many years ago in a lifetime past, but now again devouring him in little bits and pieces, one tearful cell at a time crying out for mercy and Moishe cried for Bobby and his pain, and for himself and his pain, a pain not forgotten but thought to have been in the past, a pain he would not wish on anyone yet here he was not only suffering the same pain but witnessing its destruction of a young man he loved as his own child and he shook his head, feeling the tears fall on his hands, wondering why the world had to be so cruel and why he was once again going through this when all he wanted was to live his final days in peace, but he could not allow himself to become enmeshed with that for if he did it would certainly destroy him, and that would be of no help to Bobby, and certainly none to him because he did want to leave this life peacefully and not raging with pain and torment, so he forced himself to sit up, a little at a time, and to breathe deeply and slowly until he could actually hear his breath going in and out, in and out, in and out, and he tilted his head back as he so often did in the sun to feel its warmth, but this time all he felt were the tears rolling down his face, and he cried out to Gertrude, the sound of his voice startling him and he shook his head and remembered, again, the day they got the news about Karl-Heinz, but now Gertrude was no longer here and it was Bobby who was going through the agony of conflict and grief, and there was nothing he could do, nothing, right now, he could say to Bobby, this he knew in his gut, that he had to leave Bobby alone with his suffering, right now, and just be there for him if and when he wanted comforting, but dear god why did he have to suffer with Bobby, hasn't there been enough pain for any one person in his life? And how many times would he ask this question, cry out the same words to some unseen force? Oh enough . . . enough Werner we have gone past the point of no return, past the point of useful grieving over our past, and certainly past any point of reason about worrying about Bobbys future. Over and over . . . we have been here, right here, many times. The only thing is to let it go . . . let it go . . . wish for his happiness Werner, what else is there right now? Wish for his happiness and we/ll see what tomorrow brings. This will pass as does each day and tomorrow will bring itself and thats always enough. Yes, always enough. Just let it all go Werner.

Bobby lay in bed thinking of Maria, feeling how small and smooth her hands were, and how she rubbed up against him and twirled her fingers on the back of his neck, and how the feelin seem to go right down his spine and into his crotch . . . seem like no matter where she touched him the feeling went to his crotch and his dick got hard, and he cupped his crotch with his hands, and felt her tongue between his lips, and how she shoved herself on him and even now he remembered how her eyes always had a sparkle in them, sort of like the lights on the Christmas tree shining off the tinsel and then she was falling through the air, her eyes wide and mouth open but it was quiet and she just kept falling and falling and no matter how hard he tried he couldnt stop her falling or switch back to her tongue or the light in her eyes, she was just falling and then she was on the ground like he was over her and then just standing, but she was bleeding and he was all confused and then he had Raul on the roof and forced him on his knees to look over the edge, down into the alley with all the garbage, broken bottles and winos and he shoved him slowly over the side, Raul struggling but the skinny fuck wasnt worth shit and Bobby twisted his arm behind his back and kept shoving the muthafucka over the side, letting him balance on his gut and rocking him back and forth, back and forth, pushing him a little more each time until he was almost hanging straight over the side and Raul was yelling but his screams were lost in the wind and the snow and who could hear one more scream over the rest of the noise, but Bobby could and loved it but he wished he could just remember Maria and see her eyes and feel her hand but it only lasted a moment and then he was smashing his fist into Rauls face and hanging him over the side of the building, holding him by his ankles and watching him squirm, his head banging against the side of the building and Bobby squeezed his hands together tighter and tighter, his knees slowly drawing up higher, and he could feel the silent groans rumbling in his throat, and tears rolled down his face into his pillow, and his body became increasingly tense as over and over every memory of Maria was replaced with violent thoughts of Raul, and finally he felt his tears on the pillow, and felt a continuing silent scream twist itself though his body and mind as he felt himself caught between Maria and Raul and he knew with more and more certainty that he had to kill the muthafucka, he had to kill him but not too fast, he had to make the fucka know what was happening, he had to know there was no way Maria was just goin be rotten in a grave an that muthafucka walk free, no fuckin way, and soon all there was was Raul, Maria having faded into the shadows and he was unable to reawaken her image, to feel her hands, her lips, her tongue, the warmth of her body, there was only the cold hatred that he pounded into Raul and the feeling of pounding the muthafucka made him feel good, really good . . . it made him feel even better than thinking of Maria, and the frustration of feeling the excitement that memory sent through his body, it just reminding him of what can never be again, shes dead an aint never gettin up outta the grave so why think about her an how she felt and how he felt, but killin that muthafucka Raul made every part of his mind and body come alive, made every part of him pump with energy and hatred that cleared everything else from his mind and he felt like a fuckin king, like no muthafucka nowhere could do him anything, like he was the most powerful dude in the whole world, and he continued to slap the shit outta the muthafucka and pound him with his fists and dangle him over the side of the building and watch him fall to the alley, over and over until he could no longer keep the image going and his body suddenly seemed to curl itself into a ball and he somehow drifted into a darkness without images and he slept, still knotted, hands still in a fist so tight his palms were indented by his fingernails, and his body and mind continued to torture themselves while he slept, not allowing him to rest but only to be unaware of the images going on in his mind.

On Christmas Eve they decided to open their presents before Bobby went to give the presents to Jesse. They had agreed to only give one present each, but there were 4 under the tree. Bobby looked at them, then at Moishe, I know I only be buyin one so whats happenin bro?

Moishe smiled impishly and shrugged, Im seeing already a couple things. . . .

Bobby smiled, nodding his head, You too much Mush . . . but I dont be complainin. You wantin to buy me presents I be takin them, you better believe.

They laughed and looked at each other for a moment, then Moishe picked up a gift and handed it to Bobby. He tore the paper off and yanked out a pair of jeans, Hey, these be sharp Mush . . . far out. . . .

Im thinking youre needing them so it doesnt really count as a present, ya?

Hey, whatever you say Mush — both laughing as Moishe picked up another gift, a very small box. Again Bobby ripped the paper off and fumbled the box open and stared at the contents for a moment, puzzled, then picked up the chain and looked at the medallion hanging from it. He looked at Moishe, What it is bro?

Good luck charm. Is African — smiling — mojo.

Bobby looked at Moishe, grinning, then chuckled, Gauddamn, a muthafuckin mojo. Well alright. Damn. . . .

Moishe grinned, feeling a warmth flowing through him. Bobbys eyes were sparkling and Moishe could see, as well as feel, Bobbys gratitude and affection, as well as his amazement and surprise. He watched as Bobby put it around his neck and looked down trying to see it on his throat. He got up and went to the mirror and stood in front of it for many minutes posing with his mojo, from time to time turning around and showing it to Moishe, Man, this be cool . . . check it out bro, it be cool . . . continuing to look at it in the mirror until he suddenly turned and rejoined Moishe on the floor by the tree, I bes be givin you yours Mush — handing him the present, his eyes filled with the deepest love, Moishe melting into Bobbys expression, the gift wrapping feeling warm and almost alive — It dont be much bro, but I think youll be diggin it. Moishe unwrapped the gift slowly, smiling, savoring every minute of opening a gift from someone who is all excited, waiting for you to open the gift, someone who is watching your face, your eyes, to see your reaction, to see how your heart responds to what they think is a little gift, nothing much, but is always their heart wrapped in pretty paper — Damn Mush, you be unwrappin forever. Lucky thing it not be alive, it be long dead. Ya, ya — chuckling and tearing the paper off and tossing it aside and holding up a picture, framed, of a scene of a lake with trees in the background, ducks on the water, birds flying through the sky and low over the water, and a willow tree in the foreground. Moishe held it at arms length and stared, his heart pounding — I be knowin how you like the tree bro so I figured you be needin one down here — Bobby grinning anxiously, trying to get Moishe to say something, Moishe stunned in silence not only by the gesture of love, the simple fact that Bobby knew how he felt about the tree and probably looked hard for a picture like this, but the thing that Moishe stared at was not the tree but the birds flying in the air, something you never saw in the camps . . . none of them. Birds never flew over the camps. . . .

Well bro, whatchya think? staring anxiously at Moishe, worried that he made a mistake, Moishe suddenly grinning and smiling warmly and looking at Bobby with open and simple love, Its so beautiful gift — shaking his head, unable to stop a few tears from rolling from his eyes — Im loving it so much Bobby, its — again shaking his head and shrugging, unable to speak, but his expression letting Bobby know that he loved the gift and Bobby beamed and squeezed Moishes shoulders, I be hopin you be diggin it bro – and Moishe could see how much it meant to Bobby to have given him a gift he liked, something truly meaningful, Bobbys entire expression telling the story – Ya . . . ya, is something special – looking at Bobby for a moment, both silent, then Moishe gave Bobby the last gift, Something I thought youre needing. Bobby held the gift for a moment, smiling, looking at Moishe, then gently started opening the wrapping and took out a brown, cashmere scarf and held it in his hands, rubbing his fingertips up and down, looking at Moishe with total amazement, Man, this be smooth. Ya, is cashmere. Is very warm too. Catchmere. Damn – putting the scarf around his neck and pulling it back and forth for a moment, then wrapping it around a second time – Damn, I aint never be feelin anythin like this Mush – Moishe beaming and almost jiggling up and down with happiness – This be the softest thing . . . rubbing it against his cheek and shaking his head. . . . Damn – holding up his hand and Moishe slapping it, then continued to sit for a few minutes, Moishe looking at his picture, then the walls thinking of where he wanted to hang it, and Bobby keeping the scarf around his neck and looking at his mojo, eventually putting it back around his neck. He looked at Moishe, Where you be puttin that? Moishe shrugged, Maybe on that wall so Im seeing it from my chair. Thats cool. Moishe nodded his head, Ya, seems like good idea. He banged a nail in the wall and hung the picture and sat in his chair and looked at it for a moment, smiling, Ya . . . ya. . . . Bobby stood behind the chair and looked, Hey, check it out. That be a cool spot bro. They stayed like that for a few minutes, then Moishe stood, So – turning and once more looking at Bobby, both smiling happily – Merry Christmas Bobby. Right on Mush, Merry Christmas. Moishe tentatively reached out and squeezed Bobbys shoulders, and after a moment Bobby did the same to Moishe and they stood there for a moment, then Moishe said, So . . . time to pick up the paper, ya? – laughing and picking up the wrapping paper, from time to time looking at the tree . . . Bobby starting to put his familys gifts in shopping bags, I bes be gettin to see Jesse, damn if they aint gonna be pissin in they pants they be seein all this sheeit – laughing and shaking his head as he carefully put them in the bags. He got dressed, putting the scarf on last and wrapping it around him twice, Check it out Mush, lookin sharp, eh? Is very nice – shaking his head – Ya . . . is looking very nice. Bobby stared at Moishe for a moment . . . then picked up the bags, Seeya later bro.

Moishe walked through the apartment for a few minutes, checking in with every room, feeling like a celebration, still thinking of Bobby wearing his scarf, and ended up sitting in his chair looking at the picture.


Bobby bounced through the barren lots, not really noticing the abandoned and gutted crumbling car bodies, not wondering who might be in them or in the buildings or shadows. He kept rubbin his chin against the scarf and feeling so cool, so mellow, feeling himself walking higher and higher on the balls of his feet, wondering just how high he could stretch himself, the bags of presents feeling weightless in his hands. He could feel his nose getting colder by the seconds, yet he felt warm and comfortable, and even sort of liked his nose feeling cold because it made the rest of him feel even warmer. He walked fast enough to keep himself warm, feeling as if he was going to a party . . . no, he felt as if he was a party, yeah, like he was a party happening right now, and he couldnt wait to see Jesse and give him the presents and see his eyes roll back in his head like they did when he was surprised and excited. Bobby chuckled as he thought of Jesses reactions to the bags of presents and walked faster, becoming increasingly anxious to see him. He unconsciously stopped turning corners at the last minute and doubling back on himself, but took the shortest most direct route. He still more or less looked around, but felt safe and there seemed to be a special kind of feeling in the air so he just walked rapidly through the streets not studying every shadow and doorway, that somehow the feeling in the air, and within him, made it impossible for anything to happen, that everyone must feel the way he did and just wanted to have a good time, and the car lights looked like Christmas lights, and even the cabbies seemed to be laid back, at least for cabbies. The street lights made him think of the Christmas tree they had and all the sparkling lights that blinked off and on, and the ornaments and all the decorations, and he seemed to feel even warmer thinking about it, or maybe it was just that his nose was getting colder, but no difference, he was feeling good thinking about that tree and how so many things were reminding him about it, even the lights in windows, and neon lights in stores, and what the hell that be fine and he suddenly had to swerve from his path as a drunk wrapped himself around a lamppost and started puking, slowly sliding down with each eruption until he was on his knees hanging from the lamppost moaning and mumbling as vomit continued to trickle from his nose and mouth. Bobby swung wide to avoid him and hustled past, fast, shaking his head for a second but leaving the drunk in the past and switching his thoughts back to the tree and Jesse and wishing he could show him their tree, and the moms too and everyone, but might be some other time, but it sure be cool havin a tree like that, sort of makes things different somehow, it do something but it be real cool to have a mess of presents for everyone, that be the thing that be makin it feel good . . . yeah, an makin him feel all warm inside, well what the fuck, even that poor sucka hangin from the lamppost be feelin fine . . . for a while, and Bobby chuckled out loud again and shook his head, still not able to understand how drinkin that wine make you feel good enough to end up hang from a lamppost and pukin your guts out . . . damn, seem like a fucked up way to be happy, and he shrugged and continued walking and bouncing and looking forward to seeing Jesses face when he saw the bags of gifts.

The streets were more and more crowded and people were knocking into each other as they rushed along, eyes lowered trying to get as deep as possible into their clothes, wanting to feel the warmth of Christmas Eve even though the wind was telling them they were freezing and there was no way they were going to survive the weather but they kept moving and knocking into each other hoping theyd get to where they were going soon and be able to relax in a warm room. Bobby didnt even notice the people bumping him, barely hearing their mumbled apologies, if anything at all was even said, and turned the last corner and continued down the east side of the street, noticing Jesse waiting on the inside of the door of the diner, and went into a doorway halfway down the block. Jesse waited a couple of minutes, checking everyone out who was walking along the street, then joined his brother.

Hey bro, whats happenin?

I be cool Jes – smiling and grabbing Jesses hand and rocking it back and forth, holding it much longer than usual.

Hey, doan be yankin the muthafucka off bro.

Bobby was grinning widely, Sorry Jess, guess I be excited, eh?

You aint on somethin are ya? You be lookin cranked bro.

Naw – shaking his head and laughing – Just diggin the scene.

Yeah, I see you got bags. They all for us?

Right on Jess. Theys marked what for who.

Damn – shaking his head in wonder and hefting the bags in his hands – That be a lots a shit bro. Where you gettin all this?

The store, where you think?

Jesse shrugged, still looking at the bags of gifts, Doan know. Jus aint seen nothin like that.

Come from the other side a town bro – tapping him on the shoulder – I think yuall be digginem.

Spects so. . . . Jesse slowly raised his eyes and looked at Bobby, You aint be sellin no drugs is you?

Hey dude, comeon.

Then where you be gettin the braid for this?

I got me a gig bro, hey man, I aint fuckin with you.

Jesse looked at Bobby for a moment, then shrugged, Spects you cool bro.

Sheeit, aint everybody dealin Jess.

Seems so bro, just about. But you sure doan look like you is . . . looking too good.

Well, not this dude. Anyway, how you be?

I be cool bro. The moms got your card on the dresser in her room.

Yeah?

She dont know I see it but she be lookin at it every onct in a while.

Hey, that be cool. You be gettin mine too?

Yeah, we all gotsem. It be real cool gettin Christmas card in the mail, you dig what I be sayin.

Hey . . . why ya think I sendem?

Jesse looked at Bobby, shaking his head, frowning, I doan know whats happenin bro. How come you be sendin cards an buyin all these presents and stuff?

Bobby shrugged, I doan know Jess. Frien mine say to do it. I be workin for im.

You livin with this dude?

Yeah. Real fine pad man, far out, righteous

You be comin home soon?

Shrugging, Dont know Jess. Got somethin to straighten out with Raul.

I hear he be one nervous dude – giggling – Say he always lookin over his shoulder.

Should be, muthafucka. But he aint about seein me.

Jesse suddenly straightened and stretched as tall as possible, looking with pride at Bobby, Right on bro. You be whippin his ass afore he know what be happenin.

I be doin more than whippin his ass – the smile suddenly gone, Bobbys eyes clouding over, He be gettin his haid smashed like a muthafuckin melon bro. . . . He be gettin what he give Maria.

The sudden change in Bobbys appearance and voice startled Jesse, actually scaring him for a moment, then he once more stood tall with pride, Right on bro – giving Bobby a high five.

Bobby continued to stare at the wall for a moment, then blinked his eyes and looked at Jesse, You bes be gettin these gifs over home.

Right on, bro – picking up the bags.

An you be goin right home, you dig?

Whach you thinkin I be doin this weather, cruisin aroun the streets — smiling up at Bobby.

Bobby smiled back and punched him lightly on the shoulder.

You be cool, bro.

Bobby continued smiling at Jesse and raised his right fist. He continued to watch Jesses back as he walked rapidly down the street until he was out of sight.

Bobbys mother waited until the youngins were asleep, then sat in the middle of her bed and surrounded herself with the presents, touching each one, gently sliding her fingertips along the ribbons, watching the itty bitty points of light dance around the pretty paper with all those pretty pictures . . . and she started gently bouncing on the bed feeling like she was clapping her hands and knowing her face was smiling, Oh Lord was it ever smiling so much it be gigglin, she sure nough could hear her face gigglin and see her toes wigglin . . . wiggle, wiggle, wiggle . . . and she bounced a really big bounce and laughed out loud then quickly put her hands over her mouth and sat absolutely still for a second, just a teeny weeny second, but her face still smiled and giggled and she jus about ready to go dancin acrost the floor an jus wait till she tell Tillie what her Bobby done gave themall for Christmas . . . yeah, her Bobby sure enough be a good boy an she remember when he was just a youngin taking the tit and he would snuggle into her with his ittybitty hands and feet all curled up and then he just be working his pretty little head into her neck, right here, and rubbing his face all warm and soft into her cheek and she/d hold him and rock him and he would be all quiet and just sort of gurgle and sometimes his little body would jerk and he would wiggle around like a pussy cat and nuzzle into her even more and she would hum to him, never havin a singing voice which sometimes made her feel a sadness, it seemed like every-body be able to sing but her, least ways black peoples, but she/d hum and he would sort of coo like he was dreaming of something fine . . . so fine . . . and she would drift into some nice peaceful feeling almost like she not be having feelings, least ways what she called feelings, something so nice and soft like maybe they both be having the same dream . . . and sometimes she/d watch him crawl around the floor, going a few feet then stopping and looking up at her and smiling that big silly grin a his, then crawlin some more and she/d laugh and damn if she didnt clap her hands and when he got to where she be she/d pick him up an be huggin him almost to death an hed be laughing that baby laugh, but then squirmed out of her arms so he could be doing some more crawlin and he always be just like a pussy cat crawlin aroun everything, looking under everything, but then they Gauddamn roaches be crawlin around with him and she/d have to pick him up and hed cry and try to get back on the floor like he wanted to play with them ugly little things, but it was the muthafuckin rats that just ruined everything, looking at her Bobby from the corner and she knew they be thinking how theyd like to bite him and rip him apart, and she scream at the evil muthafuckas and chase them away from her Bobby with a broom, and then hed start crying and screaming til she almost be hittin him with the broom, and she had to stand guard over her boy an try to keep him off the floor, but he all the time wantin to be crawlin aroun, and when she pick him up an putim in his crib hed scream until she screamed, and she/d hang over his crib screaming at him to shut up and he screamed louder and she screamed louder and she knew those nasty muthafuckin rats were always waiting and then Jesse come along some time later then Sissy then Billy and how she goin to keep them rats away and all day they be screaming and she be screaming and she saw Tillies youngun after a rat done bit out half its cheek and she be wantin to strangle them damn kids to shutem up and little Bobby on the tit and nuzzlin in her neck was not even a memory but what could she be doin . . . what could she be doin with no man aroun to keep things straight, just her an the screaming kids and those Gauddamn rats an some fool be tellin her to pray to Jesus an she be tellin him to have Jesus come an take care of the rats an slammed the door in his nigga face, but whats a body to do . . . but he was a cute little baby, the first born, very first, and she nothin but a kid her ownself, but she be taking good care of him, and they be doin jus fine . . . for a while . . . yeah, they be doin jus fine . . . but I sure do worry about my boy bein out on those streets an what happen to him even if he be livin with some ol man who be fine. Jesse say Bobby come home soons he gets things straighten with the boys what hurt his gurl frien, Oh Lord my boy not be needin any more trouble, but aint no reason he be wantin to come back here, but he a good boy, my boy, a real fine boy an his eyes be lookin just like they did when he was just a itty bitty baby and he be havin the same grin . . . he be changin . . . he be Bobby, but he be different, but that same itty bitty baby grin be on his face an he be lovin his momma, yeah, he be lovin his momma . . . he be a good boy my Bobby . . . he not be havin a mean bone in his body . . . no, aint no meanness in my boy . . . no way, no meanness an Bobby be lovin her, she knew that, the muthafuckin rats caint be doin nothin to stop that, no way . . . her Bobby be lovin his momma . . . seems like anyways. . . .

After Jesse left Bobby continued to stare through the glass of the door for many minutes, then turned and started to go slowly up the stairs to the roof. He sat behind the ledge, out of the wind, allowing the cold air to clear his head, thinking about how happy he was coming over here, how excited Jesse was to see him, and all the gifts, and how they dug each other an tellin him about moms keepin his card, an how he felt thinking how excited everyone would be when they saw all the presents, and how they would be screechin and yellin as they ripped the paper off, feeling the way he felt tearing open Moishes gifts, and then watching him open his, and the tree and all that . . . all that stuff. . . .

and then he started thinking about Maria and how she would have been excited too about Christmas, but she wasnt opening any presents. Even that drunk puking his ass off may be opening a present, at least he/11 be opening another bottle sooner or later, and that muthafucka Raul will be openin gifts and sittin around a tree or something with his family and theyll be laughin and yellin, tearin paper and boxes and that muthafuckas goin to get something he wants, somethin hed be hoping for and is goin to hoot his ass off just like nothing ever happened, just like he didnt have anything to do with Maria being dead, like he didnt push her out the window so she could smash her head on the sidewalk and hes just going to celebrate all night and tomorrow yellin Merry Christmas and Felice Navifuckindad. Sheeit, that muthafucka probably has a belly full of wine right now and is feeling warm all over and good like Christmas going to last forever, Sheeit! what the fuck that muthafucka doin eatin his belly full an laughin an scratchin muthafuck this sheeit, aint no way he havin a Merry Christmas – getting up and rushing down the stairs to the street, and rushing through the people, not paying any attention to his surroundings, the doorways, the shadows, but walking as fast as possible to Rauls turf, not giving a shit who saw him or who might recognize him, but increasing his pace until he was trotting, then jogging, bumping into a few people and just rushing on, almost knocking over a kid struggling with a skateboard who cursed him in Spanish, Bobby vaguely recognizing him as the kid brother of the first guy he got in the alley, the guy he pinned to the wood, but fuckim, what the fuck that little shit gonna do me, and he ran around a corner and slipped on a patch of ice and almost catapulted into the street but reached out and grabbed the lamppost and hung on it for a minute, his heart pounding in his ears and throat, feeling his eyes bulging but seeing almost nothing, and as he spun around the post he could see the kid staring at him and he pushed himself forward and ran down the street and plunged into a doorway, almost breaking the door as he exploded into it, then ran up the stairs the sounds of celebration and screaming chasing him up the steps until he got to the roof then leaned against the door, panting, sweat dripping down his sides, wiping his face with his scarf, his head raging, the air around him tinged with red, the fire in his brain tensing every muscle in his body, starting to step to the edge of the roof and staggering, his head shaking so violently he couldnt see and he fell against the door not hearing it thud against the metal sheets, sliding down until he was sitting, half lying, on the roof, a cold shock going through his body from the ice, continuing to slide until he was on his side, stretched out on the ice, panting, gasping for air, his eyes jammed shut against his dizziness, rolling his head and face on the ice until his vision started clearing, then rolling over on his back and looking up at the sky, the dull, cataract sky, no stars visible, just a heaviness that seemed to be slowly descending, and a panic shuttered through him and he again squeezed his eyes shut, then slowly opened them, the sky seeming to stay in place, the redness of the air slowly drifting away, and he blinked and forced himself to breathe slowly, deeply, without realizing what he was doing, then suddenly sat up, panicked but alert and looked around and tried to quiet his breathing so he could hear his surroundings but for many minutes all he could hear was the sound of his breath, then slowly the street sounds came up to him and he grabbed the knob of the door and raised himself and leaned against the door putting his ear to the freezing metal, listening . . . listening. . . .

but heard nothing, once again wiping his face with his scarf, then allowing his breathing to slow and quiet, the cold air and the chill going through his body to clear his head and his eyes . . .

then suddenly started trembling as a shock of images assaulted his mind: the kids eyes as he recognized him, the eyes burning into the back of his head as he stumbled down the street, the kid running to tell Raul, all the people he bumped into staring at him, falling on the ice and Raul and his guys tearing him apart, throwing his body to mangy dogs, his spine suddenly like ice, his body jerking spastically, fighting to control himself but his arms jerked and spun, his legs trembling and folding, suddenly doubled over with nausea, trying to look around but unable to control his movements, crumbling to his knees not knowing how he got there, trying to crawl away but not knowing from what or why or where to go, cursing himself for being a Gauddamn fool and suddenly the cataract was clouding his vision and he didnt know who was sneaking up on him and he tried getting to his feet but his legs wouldnt support him and he was suffocated by the images when he tried to get away and his body was battered but he somehow kept moving, but now there was no place to run, no streets, no people, no place to hide, and he couldnt even raise his hands to defend himself, and a voice in his head kept screaming at him that he was a muthafuckin fool, dead fuckin meat on a roof top, and Raul was gonna be gettin his ass and throwin him over the side an hed be splattered on the street just like Maria and he tried to roll out of the way as he felt a club coming at his head and he kept rolling and crawling and trying to stand and run until he fell against the ledge and all he could see was the street below, far, far below and he tried to keep his balance but sweat stung his eyes and terror kept his body trembling and completely out of his control and he could see the street getting closer and closer and his body suddenly froze, rigid, and he screamed and screamed and screamed and went limp, rolling off the ledge onto the roof and once again stiffening, eyes jammed closed, aware only of the scream inside his head and his struggle to breathe as he waited for the impact ... eyes suddenly opening, his temples throbbing, pain stabbing his head, his body slowly curling into a fetal position, arms wrapped around his head, rolling over on his side, aware of the cold roof, the smell of old tar and ice, his breath bouncing back into his face, wanting to sleep, to burrow into the side of the roof edge out of the wind and cold and sleep, sleep ...

eventually rolling over and crawling to the corner and leaning his back against the edge as hard as possible, clutching his knees to his chin, fighting the nausea, dizzy with relief, and sat as quietly as possible, hearing the wind around him, crumbling into himself, his feelings, thinking of the wind heard and unfelt, then hearing his breathing, feeling it warming his knees, his face, allowing the sense of relief to bathe over him, eventually calming him until there was only his breathing that he heard and felt, unconsciously trying to cuddle deeper into the relief and breath and warmth, his body continuing to relax more and more, drifting in little bits and pieces deeper within the warmth and breath, feeling lighter like being in the whirlpool bath, his body seeming to go deeper within itself, his thoughts seeming to just drift away, his breathing easing, slowing, feeling warmer, safer, more and more floating free of himself, the darkness behind his eyes speckled with dots of light like stars in his own, personal sky, slowly becoming more and more a part of that sky, the stars, the light increasing but soft, very, very soft, so comforting, becoming more and more a part of the light, almost as if he was the light, and its comfort and peace, the comfort and peace gently flowing through him until there was only comfort and sitting there peaceful, less and less aware of Bobby, more and more aware of the peace, the beautiful lightness of the peace, no time, no roof, no body, only the lightness of peace, totally immersed and taken over by the lightness. . . .

then wanting to stay with it, not wanting it to leave, struggling to keep it, becoming more and more aware of his body, the air around him, the cold roof under him, forcing his eyes shut each time they tried to open, but in time his eyes did open, blinking against the darkness, and he felt his knees under his chin, his arms around his head . . . then slowly, very gradually lifting his head, lowering his arms, seeing his knees, the roof, the sky, closing his eyes for a moment, opening them again and leaning back and looking at the edge, knowing the street was below, the reason for him being there forcing itself on him, staring at the edge of the roof, his sight slowly concentrating more and more on the iced-edged rim of the small parapet, staring through the ice at the chipped bricks and bits of cement, the ragged and ripped edges, their ugliness at first fascinating then concentrating on the gaping holes, the cracks and tears becoming gargoyles and demons that seemed to move, huge mouths opening and spewing forth a vomit of curses that seared his brain and he slowly started crawling toward the edge feeling more demons behind him, knowing they had long handled axes ready to chop yet he continued to stare and crawl, now unaware of the ice under his hands and knees, the cold chilling his bones, until he was face to face with the demons and they told him to pull himself up, offering him a hand that was blackened and grotesque, and he clutched the edge of the roof as they spoke with fiery fury, LOOK, LOOK OVER THE EDGE, commanding him to pull himself up and lay on the edge of the roof and his hand went out, then the other, and he leaned his chest on the sharp edges of cuts and ice and looked over, then down at the garbage covered alley below into the ugly faces, mouths growing larger and larger until there were only blackened mouths screaming at him that he was worthless, a useless piece of shit as he continued to pull himself over the edge, balancing on his stomach ready to fall into the screaming mouths and then they became Marias head, thousands of them smashing on the ice, bits of blood frozen in air, reflecting the light of the stars like the tinsel on the Christmas tree and he could see all her mouths screaming in twisting silence and he stared, paralyzed, slowly becoming aware of the cold chilling his bones then suddenly thawing with the heat of rage he screamed into the tomb of an alley FUUUUCKKKKKKK, then fell back on the roof, gasping for air, rolling over and laying spreadeagled on his back looking up at the cataract sky, then slowly rolled over and sat up, back to the edge, leaning into the monsters, shutting them up, breathing deeper and deeper, slower and slower until he took one last deep breath and stood, looked around quickly, then walked to the door, opened and closed it carefully and quietly, then rapidly down the stairs to the basement, through the same alley, fully alert, eyes seeing, mind sensing every little shadow, feeling quiet, determined, he knew where he was going and what he had to do. It was all very clear. Raul would join Maria and the monsters, and the muthafucka would take forever to fall, hed make the sonofabitch watch those mouths twisting and dripping blood and have him begging him not to push him over the edge and hed laugh in the fuckin pricks face and watch him slide over the edge inch by inch, every onct in a while pulling him back jus a bit so he be thinkin he not going to be lettin him go, then hed push him some more, letim jus hang, jus hang so he can be lookin nowheres but down, down at the muthafuckin groun that be waitin to smash his haid like a melon and every time he squirm and beg and cry hed laugh jus a little bit louder and louder . . . yeah, he be laughin so loud fuckin Raul be pissin in his pants and then hed twist the muthafucka roun sos he be lookin right into Bobbys face and he grin the shit outta him and then he be lettinim go, *Adios* mutha fucka an he be watchin him fall, hopin he never do hit the bottom but jus keep fallin, scared hes gonna be hittin that muthafuckin cement the next second an he be afraid to blink his eyes and afraid to keep them open an he die a thousand times before he splat hisself on the dog shit that he be

the fury continuing to fill Bobby until he was almost blind, yet still knew where he was and where he was going, a knot of sickness forming in his gut, spreading slowly through his body, reaching up to his head, until he stopped at the edge of the roof across from Rauls apartment and stared at the people inside laughing and singing and drinking wine an he saw Raul pulling a new sweater over his head then prancing about the room like he was hot shit and Bobby stared, alert, swallowing down the sickness, his head pounding with adrenaline until he saw Raul putting on his jacket so he could go down to the streets and show his friends his new sweater and he was laughing and waving his hand, Yeah, Merry Christmas muthafucka, and Bobby put the plank he had stashed across the gap between the roofs, tested it, took a deep breath and crawled across to Rauls roof, then quietly down the stairs, and was waiting in the shadows, staring at the door, waiting for that first tiny sliver of light as it started to open. Bobby hugged the wall in the shadows away from Rauls line of vision when he would come through the door, unaware of breathing, unaware of taking the scarf from his neck and rapping the ends around his hands, not feeling the blood gorge through his body or the tension in his body, unaware of anything except the doorknob on Rauls door and the door jamb, all his senses focused, alert, and when he heard Rauls hand on the knob he dug deeper into the shadows and then there was the sliver of light, then a beam, then a shaft filled with loud voices, all laughing, laughing, and Raul was yelling back into the laughter, his face one huge, monstrous grin filling Bobbys body and mind with a sickening rage, yet he remained frozen until the door clicked shut and the instant Rauls hand slid off the knob Bobbys scarf was around his throat and Bobby yanked as hard as he could, wrapped a second turn around his throat, then dragged Raul to the staircase, not hearing the gurgling coming from Rauls mouth, avoiding his flailing arms and reaching hands, then slammed Rauls head against the staircase then quickly dragging him up the stairs to the roof, quietly closing the door, standing for a moment, feeling the throbbing in Rauls throat through the scarf, looking into his dazed, bulging eyes, looking as deeply as he could into the panic in those eyes, then dragging him to the edge of the roof and slamming his head into the side and letting Raul fall, gently, as he held his body suspended by the scarf, then releasing enough of the pressure as Raul lay on the ice to allow enough air into his lungs to keep him alive, he wasnt going to allow the son of a bitch to die that fast, no, the muthafucka goin to take some time, Bobbys own sweet time, jus like Maria had to take so long, so very, very long to die, and Bobby knelt over him, staring into his face, smiling, grinning, hearing the air fighting to get past Rauls throat as he gasped, spit and blood gurgling from his lips, Bobby staring, watching, grinning at the struggle until he could see Raul was reviving and knew who was grinning at him then tightened the scarf slightly and dragged him over the edge of the roof, forcing him to lay on the edge on his stomach and look down at the shit-covered ground, just as Bobby had done, locked one hand in the scarf and held Raul by the belt with the other, forcing Rauls head down in tiny little increments, rocking him back and forth, each time Raul going further and further over the edge until he could feel the silent screams in Rauls throat and head and body, then yanked him back and rolled him on his back on the edge of the roof, stamping hard on Rauls feet, keeping him clamped to the roof, silently grinning into Rauls face until he could feel his grin burning its way through Rauls flesh, through his bones, burning every part of his fucking brain, lowering his face until he was so close light could not pass between them, then jerked him over and suspended him over the edge again, his minds eye still filled with the look of panic, terror and pleading on Rauls face, yeah, plead, beg muthafucka, beg, you not even given Maria a chanct to beg, but you be beggin, dontchya, shoving him closer and closer to the point of no return, that point of delicate balance when all he would have to do is unwrap the scarf and Raul would slide nice and slow over the side, and Bobby looked down at the ground waiting for Raul and once again saw the huge monstrous mouths waiting, the hideous and grotesque black-ness screaming, the stench of their breath burning his nostril, and Bobby started staring, fixed on the mouths, unable to break away, feeling himself devoured by their now grinning faces as they gleefully awaited the offering Bobby was giving them and suddenly something seem to snap in Bobby, he could hear it ringing through his head, whining louder and louder and he stiffened, his hands locked on the scarf, his body vibrating, the screaming, laughing demon mouth stench cutting off his breath, Rauls face turning blue, his eyes looking as if they would pop from his head, Bobbys body still trembling with the whine in his head. . . .

then he suddenly yanked the scarf and Raul was on the roof, on his back, Bobby staring maniacally into Rauls face, Raul hanging limply, too weak to raise his hands to clutch at the scarf, air completely cut off, life sustained only by whatever air was left in his lungs, then Bobbys hands suddenly let go of the scarf and his body jerked back, unable to control his movements, powerless over his ac-tions, air starting to scream itself down Rauls shattered throat, Raul still paralyzed with fear as he looked at the expression on Bobbys face, his features so distorted he didnt recognize him, but as he started to reach up to the scarf Bobby suddenly fell on his knees and grabbed the scarf and yanked it tight and pulled Rauls face close to his and spoke quietly but with such fierceness it burned into Rauls heart, We be through muthafucka. Jus dont ever be gettin close to me, yo hear — twisting the scarf harder, endless screams ripping through Rauls body yet never leaving his mouth — yo hear what I be sayin???? It be over. . . .

Bobby suddenly jerked up and stood staring down at Raul, the crazed look on his face almost shattering Rauls bones. . .

then Bobby was gone, Raul continuing to stare at where Bobbys face had been, his mind and body filled and paralyzed by that demonic look until the cold air in his lungs and head revived him enough for him to roll over and get to his hands and knees and tremble spastically as the reality of what had happened slowly assaulted him.

Bobby was still unaware of what had happened, unaware of where he was, what he was doing, or even of who he was, moving totally and only on instinct as if he still had nothing to say, or do, about what was happening, and went back over the roof and down to the street, something inside of him screaming that he had to run . . . run . . . that he had to get away from wherever he was, unaware of turning corners, the people, the cars, only running as fast as possible, desperately trying to outrun the screaming in his head, until he suddenly collapsed and lay in the rubble of an empty lot just a short distance from Moishes cellar, laying on his back, his body twitching as he struggled to breathe, rolling over and curling in a fetal position still unaware of where he was, of what had happened, the icy ground under him, feeling only the screaming in his gut and lungs for air . . . until something within him suddenly fell apart and he rolled over on his back groaning as he became aware of his breathing, staring until he became aware of the cataract sky . . . who he was . . . then what had happened . . . and he started to cry as he heard his voice telling Raul its over . . . its over. . . .

*

Moishe sat in his chair feeling the pounding of the silent clock, the incessant dirge of seconds passing, telling himself he was not hearing a clock that makes no sound, that Bobby wasnt gone too long, he was just talking with his brother and friends, after all, it is Christmas Eve, it is not really such a long time and maybe hed get up and get some ice cream, he could always have more when Bobby got home, it doesnt really mean anything if he should have a bowl of ice cream alone, can having a bowl of ice cream mean he doesnt believe Bobbys alright, that he wont come home . . . of course hes coming home . . . home . . . yes this is his home suddenly Moishe crumbled over as panic wrenched his gut, an involuntary groan agonizing itself through him and he had to struggle to breathe as he clutched himself bewildered, confused, struggling to understand what was happening as he struggled to breathe, trying to force himself erect as he almost fell from his chair, pushing harder and harder against the force that was pulling him down until he was suddenly thrust against the back of the chair, his eyes bulging, clutching the arms of the chair, feeling himself moan as an all consuming terror stiffened his body and paralyzed his mind, a scream for mercy trying desperately to pass his lips, straining to get air in and words out, staring at the wall in front of him but seeing the train and the stares of death, hearing the wolves tearing frozen flesh from frozen bones, his knuckles white, hands blue from clutching the arms tighter and tighter, a band around his chest so tight his jaw fell as he gasped for air, his body twitching and jerking until a tomb-like plea came from beyond his being from the depths of hell. . . . NOOOOOOOOOO

and Moishe suddenly collapsed in his chair, hands clutching his head, moaning, Bobby Bobby. . . .

then shoved himself against the back of the chair and rocked back and forth, no no no . . . back and forth, no no no no . . . hanging locked in a limbo of torturous agony as not only the pain of the moment wrapped itself around him, but the misery of a lifetime tormented every cell and fiber of his being as image upon image assaulted him, images of Bobby laying dead in the streets, Karl-Heinz, Gertrude, the camp, the years, the years, over and over and over. . . .

Oh please, please, no no no no

until tears flooded from his eyes, his voice mute yet the pleading continuing to sob through him, as he sat in his chair, clutching the arms, tears streaming down his face, tears of desolation and devastation, large, enormous, wet tears trembling over the banks of a lifetime of sadness and sorrow, grievous, grieving tears of despair flooding his world, his universe, bathing his anguish so he could breathe the next breath of life when he had no will to do so, the horror of the past in the midst of the crushing weight binding him to his chair, for a moment without thought, without hope, simply sustained by the river of tears, surrendered to his weeping, one with each and every tear and the pain they absorbed, the silent clock no longer ticking . . . the world no longer binding him. Moishe was simply the weeping and the tears.

Bobby walked slowly through the no mans land, the cold stinging. He reached to pull his scarf tighter around his neck, but it wasnt there. He stopped. A sudden emptiness weakened his legs and he staggered and fell to his knees, but quickly jerked up and spun around, then zipped up his jacket tight against his chin and continued walking, shoulders slumped, chin halfway to his chest, the sudden emptiness now filled with a ferocity that sought release from his eyes and he started crying.

He slowly descended the steps to the cellar, then gathered some cardboard and newspapers and sat on them and leaned against the wall, the same wall he had been leaning against when Moishe discovered him. He raised his knees and leaned on them with his arms then rested his head and closed his eyes yet still the tears flowed from his eyes, feeling at first warm on his cheeks then getting colder and colder as they rolled down, feeling like ice as they hit his hands . . . then it seemed to get brighter and he opened his eyes and blinked a few times expecting to see a light, but saw only the impenetrable darkness of the cellar, staring for a moment at the darkness, then slowly closed his eyes and again the light was there, brighter this time yet it did not hurt his eyes and again when he opened them he saw only the darkness and he shook with fear, yet could not keep his eyes open, they seemed to just want to close and he tried to squeeze the light away but it continued getting brighter and softer, and when he opened his eyes the darkness was filled with the image of him walking away from Raul and the hideous, faces and mouths mocking him as he crossed the roof and even though no sound came from the mouths, he knew they were calling him a punk and chicken shit mutha fucka and even within himself Bobby had no reply, no defense, and he pushed his forehead harder against his arms, squeezing his eyes tighter until they pained, terrified the demons would be replaced by Marias face, the face he could not get free of, the face he knew would now be weeping because Bobby had abandoned her to hell because he was a chicken shit punk muthafucka and her tears would burn into his head and heart and he could smell them already and see the smoke and he clutched tighter and tighter at his knees to keep her face away yet knowing that it would suddenly be there and he would have to watch Maria fall and splat against the cement, over and over, that she would just keep dying because he did not let her stop hurting by killing Raul and his body stiffened, spasmed until he screamed a long, torturous scream yet only a deep agonizing groan came out of his clenched mouth. . . .

Bobby suddenly slammed his back and head against the wall over and over and over, forcing himself to reach down deep within to find the energy and will to fight through the pain and continue to pound and pound against the wall until he simply folded against his knees and pulled his hat down as hard as he could, then sat motionless until he found himself standing, swaying back and forth, then started walking through the darkness.

Moishe was still sitting in his chair when Bobby opened the door. He wanted to rush to Bobby, but his body would not move, nor could he speak, unable to do anything but stare and feel overwhelmed by the pain coming from Bobby, unable to be unaware of the tortured look on his face, making him look like a stranger yet he knew it was Bobby but unable to accept that he could have changed so much. For hours Moishe had sat in his chair waiting, hoping, praying that the door would open and Bobby would walk in, but now the sight of him was more terrifying than his absence. He wanted to know what had happened, but was more afraid of knowing. Bobby stopped for a second, but then started walking to his room, avoiding looking at Moishe, saying only, I lost your scarf.

Moishe stared at the empty space in front of him, then suddenly collapsed in his chair, folding into himself as if his bones had turned to jelly, grabbing his face with his hands as if he were trying to suffocate himself, as if he were trying to smother an enemy, his body convulsing as he was tormented with terror, as he had earlier in the evening, the pain of not knowing where Bobby was, the fear of what was happening, now seeming like a luxury as he clamped his hands tighter and tighter on his face trying to block out the image of Bobbys face, trying to deny the evidence of that image, desperately seeking some way not to believe that Bobby had done something that would destroy his life, trying desperately to believe his tears were relief and not panic, the tears burning into his hands and arms as they flowed from his eyes, poured from his heart and erupted from his soul, having no idea what was keeping him alive, how air was getting into his lungs, unable to will himself to breathe, all of his being a grieving mass of terror and agony, the absence of sound, even in his mind, so devestating it crushed and stabbed him until he felt a groan, a groan of blackness and despair twisting and grinding from some place so deep within him it seemed an eternity before it gagged and choked him and finally burst forth into his hands and his mind was momentarily shattered by memories, his nose seared with the stench, the rage and hatred, the endless hunger and cold, the burning, paralyzing cold, all the darkness of millions of hearts and minds and endless tormenting nights, always nights, the nights at sunrise, the nights at noon, nights, nights, the hollow, lifeless eyes O god those terrible living-death eyes, the blackened-hearts eyes, the breathing-dead eyes, eyes that stared with incomprehensible despair and burned their way into his brain whether his were opened or closed, awake or asleep, always the eyes. . . .

O god, not again. No . . . not again. I survived those years, and I survived this night. Enough. No more . . . no more. . . .

then faintly, ever so faintly there came the sound of the silent clock and Moishe was crushed by the unmoving hands.

Bobby sat on the edge of his bed wishing there were rats behind the wall he could torment, or smell the pissy diapers, or hear the screams from the streets and the buildings . . . punch a wall, get in someones face, something, anything tangible that would force him to move, to speak, to think, something, anything, to stop the images and feelings, the feelings he had no words for, the feelings that made him feel as if he were being butchered, the feelings that made him cringe and burn, that made his spine feel weak, the feelings that made him feel as if everyone knew something about him he didnt want them to know and they were all staring at him calling him a pussy, the feelings that made him think if he could just suddenly turn around he would see hundreds, thousands of eyes looking at him with disgust, eyes that would spit on him, but he was unable to move, unable to find the energy to suddenly snap his head around, the feelings taking all his energy, O shit, if only he could scratch the wall and hear those ugly muthafuckas squeal and scratch but all he could do was sit and be overwhelmed with feelings, feelings vague and undefined, feelings twisting and tormenting him until he heard a groan come from his mouth and he was suddenly on the floor, his head hanging back against the bed. . . .

Moishe was suddenly

rigid in his chair, the thump of Bobby sliding to the floor sounding thunderous in his ears, clutching the arms even tighter and shoving his head against the back of the chair as if he were trying to avoid a sharp blade swinging back and forth just an inch from his face. For an endless moment he had no heartbeat, no breath, his eyes wide, staring at the blade swinging back and forth in front of him, not getting closer, but keeping him frozen in his chair. . . .

time suspended for an eternity until the hands of the clock released him and his heart started beating and air fought its way through the fear clogging his throat. . . .

then he was standing in the doorway staring at Bobby sitting on the floor trembling, staring at nothing, Moishes mouth open but no words coming out though he could feel them struggling to be formed and released, Moishe leaning heavily against the doorjamb, unable to keep himself erect, feeling his strength slowly ebbing once again, feeling the tears still flowing down his cheeks, waiting, wondering, trembling. . . .

then Bobby

slowly turned his head. . . .

looked at Moishe and a great sense of relief started strengthening Moishe as he looked into Bobbys face . . . yes, it was Bobby, he was once again Bobby and even though Moishe could see the profound pain and despair in Bobbys eyes he still felt a slight surge of relief, it was Bobbys face, Bobby was back, back from wherever he had been, but the joy quickly disappeared as he was caught in Bobbys pain as he watched the tears trickling down his dark cheeks, seeming to glisten and shimmer in the light. . . .

They continued looking into each others eyes, Moishe more and more feeling the pain behind Bobbys eyes looking at him with despair and pleading, looking to him for something . . . anything to ease his torment. . . .

Moishe moved.

His legs, somehow, moved him to Bobby.

He sat beside him.

They continued looking at each other.

The pleading in Bobbys eyes tore at Moishes heart, yet the hands of the clock were moving in their own natural way, unnoticed. Moishe could feel the blood flowing through his body, his face relaxing, his expression softening, his heart murmuring simply, I love you Bobby.

Time passed. Yes, yes it moved. The pain still tore at Moishes heart, but time was passing, O dear, sweet god, time was passing.

Moishe remained as silent as the clock as he watched Bobby struggling with something unknown to both of them. Moishe could see the tremors in Bobbys cheeks and chin as he searched for words and the ability to speak them. Moishe could feel Bobbys struggle, his desperation, his sense of overwhelming hopelessness and it continued to bring tears to both their eyes, but thank god time was passing. . . .

Bobbys mouth opened and Moishe rejoiced in this small yet monumental victory, and then his words cut through Moishe tearing whatever was left within him to agonizing shreds and he folded to the floor – I fucked up Mush. . . . I fucked up bad . . . they stared at each other through their tears, Bobbys voice filled with anguish – I couldnt do it Mush. . . . I couldnt do it – still looking at Moishe pleadingly, tears flowing down his cheeks, sparkling in the light as they fell like little crystals onto his shirt and pants – I couldnt killim – his voice was soft, lyrical, his words sweet and soothing to Moishes ears – I hadim. . . . I hadim, jus like I plan . . . hadim hangin over the edge of that roof an he be so scart he look like he be dyin . . . but I couldnt do it. O Mush, I couldnt do it, now Maria dont never get to jus die but gotta be fallin over an over O Mush, what Im gonna do – even in his rejoicing Moishe knew how Bobby felt, how weakening it is to have the hate that was the foundation of your life be gone, to be without the violent fantasies that kept you alive when there was no reason to live, nothing to hope for other than to satisfy that hate, the hate that was the structure and reason for your existence and when it was gone you seemed to crumble into a bottomless pit

— An I be losin the scarf Mush, the muthafucka be gone O shit, what the fuck Im gonna do Mush . . . what the fuck Im gonna do???? and his body slowly slid along the edge of the bed until he was leaning against Moishe and Moishe held him and rocked him, silently, as Bobby sobbed, Moishes tears falling on the top of Bobbys head, Moishe bathed in a blessed relief and sense of such overwhelming gratitude he was partially blinded by his tears, all of his being rejoicing yet still aware of Bobbys unrelenting fear and agony, cradling Bobby in his arms, the image of Sols face so clear in his mind, a face smiling in a way he had never seen before . . . or since, and a quick prayer spontaneously filled his heart and he hoped that that smile was now on his face, hoping that his arms felt to Bobby as Sols had to him, bringing a sense of acceptance, under-standing and comfort that could never be defined as it flowed not only through his heart, but his mind. . . . Yes, his mind as if the tangible love that flowed from Sol into his heart not only lightened his body almost to a point of weightlessness, but brought a light that cleansed the darkness from the furthest and deepest parts of his mind, to the parts Moishe was unaware of, the parts so long forgotten, those tiny corners and recesses not only beyond memory, but were thousands, millions of years old. . . . Yes, those tortured parts that were born at the beginning of time. . . .

So they sat on the floor, time now meaningless . . . non-existent, the hands of the singing clock soothing them. . . .

In time they stirred . . . moved. . . .

each wet with their own and each others tears. . . .

then sat up and leaned against the bed and looked at each other, Moishe still seeing dancing angels in Bobbys tears, yet aware of the pain as Bobby tried to grin, looking like a child suffering with a toothache but not wanting to cry, Moishe suddenly filled, yet again, with memories of Karl-Heinz, Sol, Gertrude, the camps, yet all viewed through the joy of the moment, the glorious song of Bobbys words, I couldnt do it Mush. . . . I couldnt killim. . . .

Bobby looked at Moishe with so much torment and pleading in his eyes Moishe almost crumbled, I dont know what be happenin Mush — shaking his head in bewilderment — I jus dont know.

Moishe reached out and put his arms around Bobby and gently pulled him close, Is alright Bobby, is —

I hadim Mush. I had the muthafucka — Bobby extending his fists as if he had Raul by the throat — But I — he suddenly opened his hands and dropped them to his lap and shook his head, bewildered. . . .

Moishe remained silent, love, compassion and empathy flowing from him in almost tangible waves. . . .

Tears flowed from Bobbys eyes, looking like stars to Moishe, as he looked at Moishe, then told him what happened. . . . I be havin no idea I be sayin that. It jus be comin out my mouth. I never even be thinkin that — shaking his head, swallowed sobs trembling his voice — It jus come out my mouth but I didnt say it Mush — leaning more heavily against Moishe whose shirt was soaked with Bobbys tears — I dont really be sayin that but it come out my mouth, how can that be Mush — clinging desperately to Moishe — an I dont be wishin forim, not *really* wishin O Mush, what Im gonna do????

Moishe continued to hug Bobby, all of his being singing, Thank You. . . . Bobby, is beautiful what is happening. Ya, beautiful . . . no words to say how beautiful — Bobby still clinging to Moishe like a drowning man his rescuer — But so scary. Is an unknown feeling, ya? Is so new its like the world is falling apart . . . like . . . ya, like theres no place to stand, like nothing to lean against, no walls . . . like so sudden the ground is all soft an youre thinking, Im going to sink, it will swallow me up.

Bobby trembled for a moment, I dont be knowin whats happenin bro . . . but thats how I be feelin . . . but how can it be good Mush, I never feel so bad in my life . . . I hadim —

Moishes expression was as gentle and loving as his voice, Is simple Bobby . . . you didnt want to kill him.

Bobbys head jerked back, his eyes wide, bugged, What

the fuck you mean? I be wantin to kill that muthafucka so bad it be chewin me up . . . for how long? It be a long ass time I be afta that muthafucka, a long time Mush.

Moishe continued smiling and holding Bobby in his arms, No Bobby, in your heart youre not wanting to kill him. Youre thinking youre *supposed* to, but youre not really *wanting* to.

O Mush — shaking his head in disbelief — that be bull —

Bobby, youre not having to believe me . . . look what happened.

Bobby blinked at Moishe. . . .

Youre having him over the edge of the roof . . . hes able to do nothing . . . nothing and —

Thats just it Mush, I gotim just like I planned, I had him —

So . . . if youre really wanting to kill him hes already dead. Ya — Bobby looked at him wide-eyed — He cant stop you. Bobby — Moishe spoke slowly, gently, lovingly — if you truly wanted to kill him you would have. No one could stop you. Is obvious, ya? you did not want to kill him — Moishe could feel the softness of the smile on his face, the singing in his heart, Is alright Bobby. Is fine. What is happening is good. Ya, is very good.

Bobby stared at Moishe for a moment, then shrugged and shook his head. Moishe could see the heaviness in Bobbys eyes, could feel the tension and energy draining from him, So, maybe now you sleep and we talk more later, ya?

Yeah. Guess maybe you be right. I be feelin like I cant move this black ass nowheres right now.

So, is best you put it to bed, ya? grinning at Bobby, Moishe leaning on the bed as he got to his feet.

Bobby looked dazed, weak, as he stood, wobbling slightly, blinked his eyes a few times and shook his head, Damn.

Moishe smiled, So, tomorrow we talk. Sleep Bobby, sleep good, ya?

Yeah — nodding his head — I be feelin like I never be wakin up.

Ya, you sleep good.

Moishe wobbled slightly as he went to the kitchen, filled a bowl with ice cream and sat at the table. He watched a tear fall onto his ice cream, sparkle like a jewel, then disappear. A second one fell and he smiled, then chuckled at the idea of eating his own tears, O, how often have I done that, but there was no smiling then, no joy as now. How strange to feel so happy yet to have so many tears. With good news, a happy time, you laugh and cry, but when death is turned into life . . . there are no words, only tears . . . sweet water tears flowing like an offering quenching the thirsty hunger of the heart. . . . No . . . no, there are words . . . thank you. Yes, yes, thank You, thank You, thank You. O, so many more words struggle to come . . . they fill my heart, yet all I can say is, thank You . . . and . . . I love You, yet of what use are words to express whats in my heart? All my words are so feeble . . . so limited . . . so . . . so human yet they are all I have to try and tell You whats in my heart . . . my heart of hearts, and, perhaps, they are as sweet to Your ears as they are to mine. I am only me, one little, inconspicuous and powerless me, yet I am so much more with You so much more. . . . It is always You that lifts me from the darkness and anguish of my despair, that makes it possible for me to go so far beyond my human agony and limitations and put the shattered, painful pieces of me back together, and I am always so much more than I was before the darkness devoured me . . . yes, that too is true, *I* must do what is needed or nothing is done, but it is You that provides the power for me to reach beyond my ability and discover I can do what I believe I can not. O my Beloved, so often it seems I have doubted, cursed, and screamed at the darkness only to be transformed and I am so much more than me . . . like life, so fragile yet so strong! Yet I know all birth comes after a death and You are more powerless here than I am so I keep dying to give birth to You . . . and how wondrous to give birth to You . . . to You! Not hatred, not vengeance, not fear . . . not even love, but You. . . . True, it is my willingness to forgive, to love, but You are so beyond that, so much beyond my understanding, so much beyond what I call love. Just a word . . . a word . . . a feeble attempt to explain the unexplainable, but You take me to where there are no words, no limitations, only the exquisite awareness of Your

Presence and the infinite possibilities of life, and I feel, all through me, our hearts sing . . . sing as one heart, one song . . . and yes, we are all Your song . . . every one, all needed to make the song complete . . . me, Bobby, Klaus, all . . . all Your song, and how incredible to *hear* that song, to *hear* it sing through me and around me, in me . . . to just be the song O dear, dear, sweet Love I know someday I will never hear the song again . . . will only *BE* the song. But for now I just keep singing, waiting for that day . . . yes, the infinite possibilities that brought Bobby into my life, O Bobby, you have given me so much . . . so very, very much . . . the son I pined for all these years, a reason to live when I thought all purpose was gone and then you bring me your love O Bobby, someday you will *see* . . . yes, dear, sweet Bobby you will see that you *see* . . . you will see how well you love . . . you will see what you have done for this tired old man . . . Moishe still without any sense of time, or space, free of the weight of his body, his closed eyes seeing a light more brilliant yet soothing than open eyes have ever seen, aware of the exquisite essence of his being . . . filled with the bliss of the infinite oneness of this eternal moment . . . but gradually . . . gently . . . time and space began to intrude themselves and he started becoming aware of his body, Moishe resisting, his mind still with the experience as he became increasingly aware of his body, of Werner . . . of Moishe . . . of the physical world. . . . Yes, always I come back to the body no matter how much I want to leave it behind, to simply be the Light and the Song. Someday I will not return, but there is more work to be done. . . . Yes, there is yet more that needs doing. . . .

O, the body is so heavy . . . how do we move it. . . .

how do we survive it